HOMO SAPIENS
EUROPÆUS?

PETER LANG
New York • Washington, D.C./Baltimore • Bern
Frankfurt am Main • Berlin • Brussels • Vienna • Oxford

HOMO SAPIENS EUROPÆUS?

Creating the European Learning Citizen

Michael Kuhn • Ronald G. Sultana

EDITORS

PETER LANG
New York • Washington, D.C./Baltimore • Bern
Frankfurt am Main • Berlin • Brussels • Vienna • Oxford

Library of Congress Cataloging-in-Publication Data

Homo sapiens europæus: creating the European learning citizen /
edited by Michael Kuhn, Ronald G. Sultana.
p. cm.
Includes bibliographical references.
1. Education and state—European Union countries. 2. Educational sociology—
European Union countries. 3. Comparative education.
I. Kuhn, Michael. II. Sultana, Ronald G.
LC93.A2H63   379.4—dc22   2005029927
ISBN 0-8204-7600-5

Bibliographic information published by **Die Deutsche Bibliothek**.
Die Deutsche Bibliothek lists this publication in the "Deutsche
Nationalbibliografie'; detailed bibliographic data is available
on the Internet at http://dnb.ddb.de/.

"Towards the European Society—Challenges for Education and Training Policies
and Research arising from the European Integration and Enlargement"
has been funded by the European Commission,
DG Research, Framework Programme 5.

The paper in this book meets the guidelines for permanence and durability
of the Committee on Production Guidelines for Book Longevity
of the Council of Library Resources.

© 2006 Peter Lang Publishing, Inc., New York
29 Broadway, New York, NY 10006
www.peterlangusa.com

Printed in the United States of America

Table of Contents

THE EURONET PROJECT
Towards the European Society
Michael Kuhn   vii

CHAPTER 1
Introduction: Creating the European Learning Citizen—
Which Citizen for which Europe?
Michael Kuhn and Ronald G. Sultana   1

CHAPTER 2
The Case of the UK: *Homo Sapiens Europæus* vs *Homo
Quæstuosus Atlanticus*? European Learning Citizen or
Anglo-American Human Capitalist?
Roger Dale and Susan Robertson   21

CHAPTER 3
Danish Learning Traditions in the Context of the European Union
Palle Rasmussen   47

CHAPTER 4
Governance and the Learning Citizen: Tensions and Possibilities
in the Shift from National to Post-national Identities
John Field and Mark Murphy   69

CHAPTER 5
Knowledge in the Bazaar: Pro-active Citizenship in the
Learning Society
António M. Magalhães and Stephen R. Stoer   83

CHAPTER 6
The Modification of Learning through Cultural Traditions
and Societal Structures
Gabriele Laske   105

CHAPTER 7
National and European Policies for Lifelong Learning:
an Assessment of Developments within the Context of the
European Employment Strategy
Mark Stuart and Ian Greenwood   131

CHAPTER 8
The Main Actors in the National Action Plans on Employment
—Who can Bring Forward the Education and Training
Dimension of the NAPS?
Ewart Keep   149

CHAPTER 9
Lifelong Learning for Civic Employees and Employable Citizens?
Odd Bjørn Ure   167

CHAPTER 10
Making Citizens: From Belonging to Learning
Terri Seddon and Suzanne Mellor   189

CHAPTER 11
Models of Lifelong Learning and the Knowledge Economy/Society
in Europe: what Regional Patterns are Emerging?
Andy Green   221

CHAPTER 12
Manufacturing the 'European' in Education and Training
Anja Heikkinen   257

CHAPTER 13
The European Dimension in Teacher Training in France:
Squaring the Circle?
Dominique Ulma   277

CONTRIBUTORS   295

The EURONET Project

TOWARDS THE EUROPEAN SOCIETY

Challenges for education and training policies and research arising from the European integration and enlargement (EURONE&T)

Michael Kuhn

This volume is a result of research undertaken in the framework of the project "Towards the European Society: challenges for education and training policies and research arising from the European integration and enlargement" (EURONE&T). The thematic network was funded under the European Union's Fifth Framework Programme "Improving human research potential and the socio-economic knowledge base".

The Thematic network EURONE&T aimed at investigating the impact of the European integration and enlargement processes on learning related policies in the European Union (EU) new and old Member States and acceding countries. Given the new global context of EU policies the discourse about a Learning Society cannot be restricted to the discourse within Europe, but needs to be looked at as a topic of an *international* debate that goes beyond the European social science research community.

The term *learning related policies* has been chosen in order to include policy fields that relate to learning but that are not usually covered by a somewhat narrower concept of education and training policies. Different from mainstream discourses, which are mostly focused on economic, technological and institutional policy views on knowledge and learning, EURONE&T focused on *the central position of the learning citizen* while analysing learning related policies in the present context. Aspects considered by EURONE&T included a) political, cultural and historical features that influence the generation of the learning citizen, b) trends and developments towards EU integration, and c) challenges that result from the process of transition. These interrelated factors and their dynamic interplay constituted the general dimensions of the project and were addressed from different interdisciplinary perspectives by scholars from Europe and abroad.

The outcomes of the EURONET discourse include the following titles:

"The Learning Society in Europe and beyond"
Edited by Michael Kuhn and Ronald G. Sultana

"Homo Sapiens Europæus? Creating the European Learning Citizen"
Edited by Michael Kuhn and Ronald G. Sultana

"The Clash of Transitions. Towards the Learning Society"
Edited by Olga Strietska-Ilina

 "The European Learner—a new Global Player?"
Edited by Michael Kuhn

CHAPTER ONE

Introduction: Creating the European Learning Citizen—Which Citizen for which Europe?

MICHAEL KUHN AND RONALD G. SULTANA

Introduction

This volume is one of the outcomes of a European Union-funded thematic network—EURONE&T—which brought together scholars from Europe and beyond in order to critically reflect on the way the European Learning Space is being constructed. The network set out to investigate the implications of the European integration and enlargement processes on learning related policies[1] in the EU, including the new member states. As we will note in more details further on, education and training have historically been outside of—or at best marginal to—the policy remit of the European Commission, given that the key concerns of the EU have tended to focus more specifically around economic and political agendas. Learning moved much more to centre-stage in the post-Maastricht, and more so in the post-Lisbon era, when the EU aspired to make important strides forward in establishing itself as a 'knowledge-based society' in an attempt to turn the tide of global competition in its favour.

As many of the contributors to this volume note, this new policy focus on education, articulated as a response to the perceived threats of globalisation, produced specific effects at both member state and Community levels, promoting a particularly economistic and technocratic approach to learning. A key concern of EURONE&T was to understand the learning society more broadly and holistically, that is as a society where knowledge and continuous learning occupy a central position and affect *all* aspects of life: not just the economic, but the political and social as well. In contrast to mainstream discourses which tend to privilege economic, technological and institutional issues, EURONE&T set out to put the *learning citizen* at the centre of its work. This volume reflects this stand-point. It thus investigates the impact of the

European integration and enlargement processes on learning related policies, but it does so by foregrounding the manner in which such policies contribute— or *fail* to contribute—to creating and supporting the learning citizen.

The present collection of papers has to be seen within the context of the overall thematic project, discussing learning related policies from different perspectives by the four thematic EURONET domains guiding the interdisciplinary discourses among scholars from Europe and abroad.

Framework Domain

The Learning Society visions in Europe and beyond

Thematic Domain 1. Learning related policies in member states/regions between internationalised challenges and national systems.

Thematic Domain 2. Learning related policies and EU enlargement from the perspective of member states and candidate countries during transition to market economy in accession countries.

Thematic Domain 3. Learning related policies from the European perspective: European policies and research.[2]

This particular collection of papers addresses mainly the issue of the Domain 1 of the network. It therefore focuses on learning-related policies in member states and regions as these are being developed in response to the challenges of Europeanisation and globalisation. In their attempt to respond creatively to our invitation, the authors of these chapters have articulated a number of overlapping and inter-connected concerns in a way that, to our mind, rises to the challenge we set ourselves in the ambit of intellectual work. This is understood as a labour that necessitates '...freedom from the powers, criticism of received ideas, demolition of simplistic alternatives, [and] restitution of the complexity of problems' (Bourdieu, 1998, p.106). This introductory chapter sets out to provide a synthesis of the themes and concerns that emerge from the chapters, placing them squarely within the context of the lifelong learning (LLL) discourse that is increasingly gaining hegemonic status both within and across Member States.

But first a note about the title of the volume: *Homo Sapiens Europæus*— somewhat tongue-in-cheek, of course, but also purposefully reminiscent of another utopian endeavour to create the 'new man'—the *Homo Sovieticus* of the then 'second world'—who needed to be moulded in such a way as to further the social and economic fortunes of another version of a 'brave new world'.

For, as Heikkinen argues, there is little doubt that what we are seeing across Europe is the discursive 'manufacturing' of a new type of 'wo/man', and, we would add, a new—and restrictive—form of 'citizenship'. The key in this 'performative' endeavour is 'lifelong learning', on which, it seems, Europe is placing its bets in the hope of becoming 'the most competitive and dynamic knowledge-based society in the world.' We shall also argue that in the LLL discourse, the 'absent centre' is, ironically, the 'citizen', who, ultimately, is supposed to reap nothing but benefits from a lifelong investment in learning, where, in a latter-day version of a new social contract made to measure for inhabitants of a 'risk society', a 'new deal' is struck in what has aptly been dubbed the 'ruthless economy': learn or be damned.

Key themes

In considering the implications of the European integration and enlargement processes on learning related policies in the EU, and in the way such policies are mediated via national systems, traditions, cultures, and values, the contributors to this volume address five key overlapping themes, namely:

- the production of the lifelong learning discourse;
- the ideological *context* that shapes the LLL discourse;
- approaches to learning and to the Learning Society;
- the construction of the 'citizen' in relation to a Europe of learning;
- the EU, the Learning Society, and member states.

Some of the central insights that the authors generate in considering these inter-related themes are discussed below.

Producing the Lifelong Learning discourse

A major theme addressed by practically all the contributors to this volume is the production of lifelong learning discourse. This critical inquiry as to both *why* and *how* LLL has become so deeply inscribed in our world views and everyday discourse is in itself salutary, given the almost common sense—and hence hegemonic—quality that the very term—and its use/s—have attained. It is salutary to remember that the idea of 'lifelong learning' is far from new, and in Europe has been around for well over a century at least. Indeed, the notion of 'lifelong education' more broadly has a long history that is anchored in the world view of several civilisations and cultural traditions, including those that emerged in China, India, classical Greece, medieval Arabia, and renaissance

Europe (Lê Thành Khôi, 1995). What characterises contemporary discourse about LLL is that over the past few decades the notions of education 'from the cradle to the grave' has become mainstreamed and popularised (Gelpi, 1985), with technological, cultural and economic transformations driving the notion that learning is, or should be, an ubiquitous phenomenon.

The authors in this volume make a number of points regarding the production and intensification of discourse on LLL. First of all, several authors note the role of the European Commission in the development of the discourse. There is indeed little doubt that the Commission's *Memorandum on Lifelong Learning*, the consultation exercise in Member States, and the myriad follow-up activities—including meetings, reports, and EU-funded research—have served to intensify the discourse around LLL and the Learning Society—perhaps to an extent that was hardly imaginable a few decades ago. This does not mean that debates and reflections about LLL were not present in the member states prior to the *Memorandum*—rather, as Rasmussen notes, the EU policy texts draw on, combine, and filter educational discourses that are often present in national contexts, even if they may have different meanings and significance. But the Commission has done more than simply that. It has not simply and neutrally drawn on the different views on LLL that emerged through its consultation process. Rather, EU texts re-introduce the resultant discourses in the individual countries, leading to what can be called 'harmonising effects'. This process has, in the post-Lisbon phase, been reinforced by the Open Method of Coordination which, as Dale and Robertson note, ends up assigning to the EU far more of a policy role than it had previously been able to establish in the area of education and training.

Several authors in this volume point out, however, that despite the increasing visibility of LLL as a policy theme across and within the EU, what we have here is still a *discursive* construction, that is, a *gesturing* towards a set of social practices that have yet to be realised. Ure, for instance, notes that while there is a slow penetration of LLL in national education and training systems, the latter are not yet transformed into anything like a LLL *system*. There might very well be a national discourse on LLL, but in many countries across Europe it is not at all evident that there are practices, social actors and institutions that constitute *systemic* elements of LLL.

Another key issue raised by a number of contributors to this volume refers to the *reasons* underpinning the Commission's interest in promoting LLL. It is a well-established fact that initially, the definition of learning within Commission deliberations on LLL drew almost exclusively on a human capital approach, a perspective that was slightly modified due to the reactions during the consultation process, where more emphasis was placed not just on LLL as economically related to employability, but also to 'personal fulfilment', 'active citizenship', and 'social inclusion'. But, as Stuart and Greenwood aptly note, despite this seemingly genuine attempt to take into account the 'citizens' views', the fact remains that the European Employment Strategy (EES) is, in effect, the key trans-European policy vehicle with which to monitor the development and the implementation of LLL. The tight coupling between learning and employment means that the prospect for the implementation and monitoring of a more holistic LLL strategy is compromised.

Keep, writing in the same vein, also points out that the National Action Plans (NAPs) that have to be developed by the different member states in relation to the targets established by the EES are, necessarily, employment-oriented, and privilege an economistic focus that sees the value of LLL in terms of its potential contribution to employability and productivity. This, in turn, leads to reduced attention to the wider societal, cultural, and citizenship aspects of LLL associated with the development of the individual for life and leisure outside the workplace. Such concerns appear to be justified when one considers the recent Communication on the Lisbon Strategy by the President of the Commission, Barroso (COM(2005)24 on 2.2.05) where 'growth' and 'jobs' are placed centre stage, almost to the exclusion of anything else. Within this document, LLL is practically exclusively tied to workplace development, and knowledge and education in a 'renewed Lisbon strategy' are meant to be mobilised in order to 'give people the opportunity to climb the productivity ladder', besides guaranteeing that the EU's overall productivity grows at a faster pace (p.14).

Other authors note that this intensification of discourse around LLL leads to a number of assumptions that need to be problematised, not least because such assumptions feed the policy making process at both the nation state and Community level. Chief among these assumptions is the one that draws a direct link between investment in learning and economic growth. As Keep notes, there is a problem in seeing education and LLL as a key lever for change, and for addressing what ultimately are *economic* challenges. Thus, more and better LLL need not necessarily provide people with better paid and more interesting employment, if there is little real growth in job opportunities. Seeing LLL in this light raises major questions about the value of endlessly investing in education, leading not only to qualification inflation but also to chronic underemployment. It is useful to quote Livingstone at some length in this regard, given that he has carried out some of the more extensive, empirically-grounded work on LLL (Livingstone, 2003). Summarising this research, Livingstone (2004, pp.17-18) notes:

> '...there appear to have been only gradual changes in skill upgrading of the general job structure and incremental gains in the proportion of jobs predominantly involving the knowledge work of planning and design in the post-WWII period, while rates of completion of post-compulsory schooling and participation in further education

courses have grown exponentially. Employment-related informal learning remains even more extensive. Rates of underemployment—in terms of general unemployment, involuntary reduced employment and educational attainments exceeding job requirements—have also grown significantly during this period...Such evidence suggests that *we already live in a learning society in both formal and informal educational terms, but not yet in a knowledge-based economy.*' [our emphasis]

What we tend to end up with, suggest many of the chapters in this volume, is an overly optimistic and ultimately misguided belief that LLL will set most things right, for individual and society alike. Of course, this 'education gospel'—as Grubb and Lazerson (2004) have called it—is not new: throughout the history of industrialist capitalist societies, formal education has been touted as the solution of economic crises. What is surprising is the extent to which this 'mantra' keeps being intoned, despite the fact that human capital approaches have been definitively debunked (Livingstone, 1999). But then, perhaps it is not so surprising after all, given that 'to insist that more education and training are the only solution to economic problems, to the exclusion of any serious attempt to address economic reforms themselves—as many current politicians do—is merely to divert attention from the central problem, lack of decent jobs' (Livingstone, 2004, p.12).

Another related assumption underpinning the LLL discourse that is challenged by several contributors to this volume is the unproblematic connection between increased education and training on the one hand, and social inclusion and cohesion on the other. Rasmussen and others indeed point out the fact that the consumption of LLL is a *competitive* feat, which enables one citizen to get ahead of the other in the queue for employment and improved life chances: while education is often couched within a discourse that furthers social inclusion, the fact remains that education and training have become yet another strategy in a meritocratic struggle for survival in a competitive, Darwinian society, signalling 'positional battles' between an ever-increasing number of highly certified applicants for a small pool of 'good jobs'. Citizenship here is necessarily associated not with collective good, but with a competitive individualism where the devil takes the hindmost.

The ideological context that shapes the LLL discourse

Linked to many of the points made by the different authors in relation to the way the notion of LLL is being 'framed' discursively is the fact that the 'master discourse'—the actual 'frame'—is neo-liberalism. What we have referred to as a discursive intensification around LLL in Europe has been accompanied by a shift in the way the nature and purpose of education are articulated. Seddon and

Mellor capture well the significance of this shift, not only in relation to the EU, but also to other regions of the world, including their native Australia: 'Market reform insists that we learn, all the time, about everything, exhaustively and exhaustingly all through our lives. But it also insists on learning that is utilitarian in character and oriented to enhance productivity, narrowly conceived. It is learning framed largely by the market rather than by citizenship.' The critique here is not simply that the view on humans should be *widened* towards other social components, for this would mean that for the *homo economicus*, the economy *as it is* is fine. The critique is also a critique of this 'real existing' economy which apparently requires a specific type of a social creature—a person who lives to work, and not works to live.

Here again the exercise of our historical imagination becomes critical: it is therefore important to recall that initially, much of the discourse on lifelong education galvanised around the idea of education as an *emancipatory* practice that enhanced participatory citizenship in a democracy (Ranson, 1998; Jarvis, 2001; Borg & Mayo, 2002; Wain, 2004). Drawing on the writings of Dewey, Gramsci, and Freire among others, the adult education field produced a series of key texts that promoted the idea of education beyond schooling, culminating in the highly influential Unesco report by Faure and his colleagues in 1972, significantly entitled *Learning to Be*. Influenced by the deschooling movement, by radical critiques of the way education served the interests of capital and contributed to the reproduction of inequality, and by the left-leaning post-war climate, liberal humanist and even radical agendas were developed, alongside more utilitarian ones, with a view to ensuring that all citizens had access, throughout their life, to an education that was enabling and empowering socially, politically, and economically. A typical, summative definition outlining the philosophy of lifelong education and the politics of the LLL movement current at this time—one that we would be hard put to place in the present-day forum on LLL—is that articulated by Dave (1976, p.34):

'Lifelong education is a process of accomplishing personal, social and professional development throughout the life-span of individuals in order to enhance the quality of life of both individuals and their collectives. It is a comprehensive and unifying idea, which includes formal, non-formal and informal learning for *acquiring and enhancing enlightenment so as to attain the fullest possible development in different stages and domains of life. It is connected with both individual growth and social progress.* That is why ideas such as 'learning to be' and 'a learning society' or 'an educative society' are associated with this concept.' [cited in Wain, 2004, p.9—our emphasis]

Most of the contributors to this volume note that this emancipatory view of education has all but been silenced in the current preoccupations about European competitiveness in the global economy. The intensification of discourse has not succeeded in maintaining the equitable balance in agendas that underpinned earlier movements in favour of LLL: what seems to matter in the mainstream view of LLL is 'learning to *have*'. As has already been noted, while pressure arising from the consultation exercise led to the expansion of the Commission's Memorandum to take on citizenship issues, the actual evaluation of progress to LLL is based on the European Employment Strategy, and thus unabashedly vocationalist in orientation. All in all, progressive strands have been largely domesticated within the current construction of the 'official' lifelong learning discourse at European level. True, as Dale and Robertson note, learning within the context of the Lisbon declaration is framed by five distinct discourses—namely competition, the knowledge-based economy, sustainable growth, more and better jobs, and greater social cohesion. But these ultimately contradictory discourses are conditioned by—and fall within the shadow of—the imperative to regain and maintain competitiveness in the global market—an imperative that has taken on an even more resolute turn following the Kok Report (European Commission, 2004).

The human capital imperative is driven by a widely-held assumption and a deep-seated conviction that advanced societies can only thrive if they transform themselves into knowledge-based economies. In other words, survival in the face of global competition depends on the capacity of the individual—our new European *Homo Sapiens*—to remain open to learning, and to the perpetual re-fashioning and re-creation of the self in order to be of service to a greater cause, and to fulfil his/her duty towards two 'imagined communities' (Anderson, 1983)—not just the state, but Europe as well. In this scenario, 'learning is next to godliness', for it contributes towards the wealth-generation process, to the development of 'high ability' economies, and to ensuring that citizens do not become a burden to society by losing their economic use-value. It is the resolute self-investment in education and training, on the part of the European 'citizen', that will ensure that the ambitious aims of Europe—i.e. nothing less than becoming 'the most competitive and dynamic knowledge-based economy in the world by 2010'—are fulfilled.

Approaches to learning and to the Learning Society

This imperative to learn is, in a sense, species-specific. Indeed, many have pointed out that the distinctive characteristic of *Homo Sapiens* is the 'will to learn' (Bruner, 1966). However, never, historically, has learning been touted with such force, presented as nothing less than a moral obligation. Several of the chapters in this volume consider different aspects of 'learning': its nature, its meaning within specific national, cultural, and regional contexts, and its transformation within a knowledge-based economy. A key observation is that, for all the concern that there apparently is with education and training, much of the discursive density in the Europe-wide consideration of LLL is on Member State education *systems*, rather than on *processes* of education as such. And as Dale and Robertson note, the fact that an overwhelming theme is the issue of early drop-outs from formal education and training gives away the game: the concern, as has already been suggested earlier, is with ensuring the availability of adequately trained human capital, and not with learning *per se*.

Several contributors to this volume note that the reductionist and homogenising discourse on learning in the EU fails to recognise the fact that different countries have different conceptions and traditions of learning. A focus on process rather than on outcome, and a consideration of the cultural contexts in which flesh-and-blood citizens—rather than disembodied, atomic individuals (*vide* Heikkinen)—engage in learning, suggests that it is problematic to adopt a 'harmonised' view of LLL that is promoted at EU level. Rasmussen, for instance, notes how the Danish educational tradition promoted the social and personal dimensions of learning, besides the cognitive and instrumental ones. He attempts to rescue from his own country's past some of the features that are largely missing from the vocationalist approach to learning that has become hegemonic, including: the recognition of the rights of citizens to participate in education throughout their lives and the concomitant obligation of the state to support this; the commitment to open educational access to facilitate social equality; and the linking of public education systems to collective actors, such as labour market partners and social movements. This lies in stark contrast with the views on learning promoted by UNICE, one of the employers' fronts on a Europe-wide scale which, as Stuart and Greenwood note, not only unrelentingly stresses economic competitiveness and employability in its approach to LLL, but which has categorically rejected the ETUC's attempt to advocate LLL as an individual *right*.[3]

Laske also engages in historical excavation and comparative analysis in an attempt to retrieve notions of learning that seem to be increasingly silenced in the current debates on LLL. She thus makes reference to the VET tradition in Germany, where training was not a purely economic construct based on the division of labour, but encompassed the citizen both as a working and a social being. This lies in contrast with the narrow view of a *homo economicus* that is often found in Anglo-Saxon countries but which, according to Laske, has no equivalent in the German vocational education tradition.

Green, on his part, takes up this notion that learning is culturally determined and addresses the overarching question of whether we can identify different regional models of lifelong learning within Europe, deriving from longstanding historical affinities in cultures, political systems and socio-economic structures. He is concerned with analysing how far these models depend on certain regional socio-economic contexts, and whether they are constitutive of the different models of the Learning Economy/Society which have been posited in the literature. Most importantly, he concludes that the EU generally has much to learn from the Nordic 'model' or approach to LLL, given that it comes closer to the vision of a 'competitive and dynamic knowledge-based economy ... with more and better jobs and greater social cohesion' than any other region does. In other words, it is the Nordic states that seem to most closely approximate to a model of the knowledge society that combines high level of economic competitiveness with relative equality and high levels of social cohesion—a point that is also made by Keep.

A key aspect of LLL that is addressed by a number of authors in this volume concerns the fact that learning is being reconstructed and re-imagined within the context of a (largely 'mythical') knowledge-based economy. Heikkinen, for instance, notes how the management of learning by the 'Eurobusnocracy' has reduced knowledge to the accumulation of 'competences', a fragmented approach that obfuscates the relationship between 'knowing' and 'being', and between 'knowledge' and 'wisdom', while at the same time rendering the process more open to measurement in relation to perceived skills gaps. The 'management of learning' becomes increasingly important, so that all forms of knowledge and skills acquisition have to be identified, assessed and made visible and valued according to the needs and occupational standards set by employers. The role of the individual *qua* learner is to accumulate such competences, and to provide 'evidence of learning' in a sophisticated exercise of 'self-promotion' and 'self-marketing'.

In relation to this, Magalhães and Stoer note that the notion of LLL, particularly when couched in economistic terms, signals and vehicles the idea that education is now 'individualised', i.e. it is 'no longer a public good demanding social/collective responsibility, but rather a private commodity which leaves it up to the individual, condemned to struggle throughout life to remain attractive to the market of employability'. Stuart and Greenwood also note that one result of this individualisation of responsibility for education and training is a shift in the terrain of the debate from a focus on full employment, to the individual's characteristics that make him or her employable—such as flexibility, adaptability, and so on. Through the individualisation of responsibility for training, the individual ends up having only himself or herself to blame for his own unemployment.

At one level, such individualisation and the accompanying emphasis on the strategic consumption of educational and training services strongly suggest the need for mechanisms that facilitate equal access to learning resources. In other words, such changes require the development of a *system* of LLL to sustain learning, and the variety of learning initiatives that are said to have a lifelong and lifewide perspective. But the individualisation of learning (for employability purposes) in contrast to collective learning (to advance citizenship) also means that the investment in LLL is driven by the tempo of business cycles and of the unemployment rate. Ure is quick to point out that as a consequence, the vocationalisation of adult education leads to a policy focus on those who are employable—with deleterious repercussions for the rest and for the whole notion of equal access.

Some of the authors also note that the way learning is being conceptualised in mainstream discourse on the knowledge-based economy—exemplified, for instance, by the notions of a 'learning organization', or of 'communities of practice'—is weakening the boundaries between sites of learning, work, leisure, and communities. While such developments are often portrayed 'heroically' by those who work from within the human capital paradigm, many of the contributors to this volume are somewhat more sceptical and cautious. The multiplication of learning centres from which 'clients' buy services could encourage the dismantling of educational systems, and to any concern for equal access. Ure also is rightly worried that the individualisation of learning and the delegation of LLL to various learning environments of everyday life can lead to a situation where learning needs are defined not by teachers and educators, but by employers and leading organisations. A case in point would be the increasing emphasis on workplace as a site for learning. Work-based learning, Keep notes, challenges aspects of work organisation and job design, and promotes the upgrading of the workplace as a learning environment with roles for employers and trade unions. However, much of the rhetoric around work-based learning and the learning organization remains highly problematic given the dynamics of capitalism in the ruthless economy. As Ure points out, capital accumulation increasingly depends on maintaining market flexibility through short-term contracts. The emphasis on cost containment and flexible labour markets discourages long-term investment in human capital.

The learning citizen

As has been pointed out from the outset, one of the key goals of EURONE&T and of this volume is to make the 'learning citizen' the object of analysis, an especially important goal given the fact that the 'citizen' tends to disappear in the macro discourse around knowledge-based economies, both in terms of being grounded anthropologically (as flesh-and-blood beings), as well as socially and politically (as active members of a participatory democracy). In contrast, several of the authors in this volume are keen to focus on the historical and geographical constitution of humanness between nature and culture.

Reading about 'lifelong learners' in much of the mainstream literature on the learning society gives the impression that, as Heikkinen rightly notes, they 'have no bodies, sex, age, families, no social or ethnic characteristics.' When the complex 'messiness' of individual lives are referred to, it is largely in relation to the way that the low achievers, the unproductive, the poor and needy, the incompetent, the disengaged and dissident—all represent wasted investment and failure in the development of European human resources. But attention to the way individuals and groups make sense of the 'heroic myths' surrounding the LLL discourse can be very revealing.

Indeed, it has already been intimated that much of the LLL discourse is based on 'push' factors (i.e. the social, labour market and technological transformations that 'impel' citizens to remain constantly engaged in learning and training). But the question needs to be raised: why should this 'learning imperative' 'resonate' with the citizen? The standard rhetorical response would be that in the knowledge-based economy, where change and innovation are the order of the day, continued learning is the key to the management of insecurity and risk. But as Keep points out, and as we have made clear earlier on in this chapter, such a response does not stand up to the evidence, given that it is only a minority of workers that are actually employed in the knowledge-rich sector. As Grubb and Lazerson (2004, p.245) note in relation to the extreme claims made on behalf of the knowledge-based economy:

> '... the Knowledge Revolution has directly touched only a minority of jobs at this point, perhaps 1 to 5 percent of all nongovernmental workers... Some claims, such as the statement that college for all is 'just common sense,' are simply absurd when only 30 percent of job openings require any kind of postsecondary education.'[4]

And citizens know this. Those studies which, like Antikainen's (2005), take a life-history approach and try to connect with citizens as *subjects* rather than as objects of research, amply show that lifelong learning is far from becoming a reality in the life-courses of people.[5] This, of course, does not mean that there is a disengagement from learning, but that as by far the greater majority of workers feel that they are underemployed, they prefer to that invest in learning that is not necessarily work-related. Keep underlines this point when he shows how for many, the re-engagement with learning seems to most often start with learning experiences that are focussed on issues other than development for employment. This consideration is worth dwelling on a bit further, particularly in the light of the fact that we see Europe-wide a new phenomenon of disengagement from personal investment in building one's identity around work, signalled by the publication of two best-sellers, i.e. Corine Maier's *Bonjour Paresse* and Tom Hodgkinson's *How to be Idle*. Both authors advise that the route to well-being is to refuse to have one's energies absorbed by one's work, and to save oneself for 'real life' outside the workplace—a stark contrast to the admonitions of the policy-makers, in a case that might be termed 'the citizen strikes back'. The promise of 'salvation' in and through work might make sense from the perspective of the policy making and employing classes, but it cuts little ice with the citizen who knows that ultimately, despite the rhetoric, a few jobs may indeed be fulfilling, but the majority are not and never can be. To quote Terkel's (1974) classic study on work, too many people feel trapped in 'jobs that are too small for [their] spirits.'

Another aspect of the focus on the 'learning citizen' concerns the social and political dimension of citizenship, namely, that of being an active player in a participatory democracy, and the role of learning therein. The contributors to this volume are unanimous in noting that within the prevailing ideological context, the 'good citizen' is defined as one who is constantly engaged in learning/training to maintain 'use value'. They resist this notion, and find the coupling of 'learning' with 'citizenship' strategically useful in pointing out the social and civic dimensions of education and training. As Seddon and Mellor note, within a neo-liberal context, education has increasingly become considered to be a 'private good', and it only has value as long as it gives an individual social and economic advantage (Kuhn, 2005). Within such a perspective, learning is a commodity, with the individual being construed as an innovative entrepreneur, a 'can-do' achiever striving for individualistic and particularistic benefits. Seddon and Mellor, like other authors in this volume, articulate a different vision for the 'learning citizen', one for whom learning is a collective responsibility, and whose goal is collective and universalistic benefit—what the classics refer to as the 'virtuous life'—a doer of public good in collective decision-making arenas.

Many of the authors therefore argue for a different kind of education, one that equips citizens to act in ways which can enhance *both* the individual *and* society. Underlying this view is a concern that the Lisbon agenda severely constrains the possibilities for the development of the kind of citizenship learning not associated with economic citizenship. Thus, several authors wonder about the extent to which citizens are getting an education that provides them with the tools to interpret the complex realities around them. Indeed, Seddon and Mellor argue that schooling in neo-liberal times creates a narrow kind of citizenship that does not question market liberalism, with citizens not even aware of the right to challenge the dominant discourse, or that alternatives exist.

From a different though related perspective, some of the authors wonder about the extent to which the European integration project succeeds in helping citizens rise above their rootedness in nation-states, in order to exercise their citizenship rights on a European scale. Ulma considers the (largely limited) successes in the attempts to inculcate a European dimension among teachers in France, using mobility in order to promote 'Europe as a state of mind', and to facilitate 'the critical reflexivity that puts national conceptions into perspective, and [the] redefinition of value systems thanks to objectivization and dialogue', which, she hopes, 'opens up the education area in such a way as to have a significant influence on living together in Europe.' Field and Murphy, on their part, are somewhat less sanguine about the notion of European citizenship, and of the Habermasian notion of a learning society entailing Europeans making the 'abstract leap' from local to national to supra-national democratic consciousness. While education and training could make a contribution to the development of European citizenship and post-national identities, for Field and Murphy the prospects for a genuinely European civil society remain remote, largely due to the manner in which the EU project is being formed, with 'a loosening of ties binding elites to the masses.'

The EU, the Learning Society, and member states

A critical consideration of the project 'Europe'—and particularly of the 'learning Europe'—was very much at the heart of the concerns of the thematic network, and consequently of this volume. A key question we asked authors to consider is the way the EU has promoted a specific understanding of the Learning Society and of LLL, and how such an understanding has had an impact on the policy-making process in the member states.

Some of the authors raise issues about the nature of the EU in relation to the enterprise of learning, noting a contradiction between Europe being seen as a *shield* against globalisation and rampant neo-liberalism, while at the same time aspiring to be a dominant actor in global economic competition. Heikkinen makes much of this contradiction, arguing vehemently—from the point of view of a citizen from one of the more 'peripheral' of Europe's member states—that Europe's aspirations are reminiscent of war, pillage, and colonialism, serving to silence and cut out the non-European inside and outside the EU. What she sees, under the guise of global competition, is 'the struggle on ownership, control and exploitation of natural resources', which, historically, has 'always gone hand-in-hand with military, political, ideological and educational supremacy.'

Of course, Europe's (Lisbon) agenda is no different from that of the US or Japan—or even of some of the Member States individually. It is indeed about the struggle for domination of markets in a context of cut-throat global competition. Some of the authors still entertain the hope that, despite these similarities, the EU project is—or rather, *could* be—formulated within a context of the European Social Model. Magalhães and Stoer, for instance, consider a variety of possible metaphors for Europe, making a case for seeing the EU as a 'bazaar', a place where citizenship expresses itself through the community of general rules that do not violate the differences of citizens. They, like Field and Murphy, wonder if the EU can construct itself as a new type of entity, a political model that can reconfigure the feeling of national belonging, providing the basis for a reinvented form of citizenship. In doing so, they are echoing the sentiments expressed by Rifkin (2004), when he contrasts the EU with the USA, saying:

> "While the American Spirit is tiring and languishing in the past, a new European Dream is being born... [that dream] emphasizes community relationships over individual autonomy, cultural diversity over assimilation, quality of life over the accumulation of wealth, sustainable development over unlimited material growth, deep play over unrelenting toil, universal human rights and the rights of nature over property rights, and global cooperation over the unilateral exercise of power."

But ultimately, the overwhelming impression one gets from most of the authors is that this European Dream—of tempering the market economy by a strong social dimension that gives pride of place to the citizen—increasingly appears to be just that: a dream. The increasingly neo-liberal turn within the Commission, signalled by its President's recent communication, confirm the extent to which the commitment to market logic is deepening as panic sets in with the Lisbon targets fading away in the horizon.

The authors of the volume were asked to consider whether learning-related policies adopted at the EU level are having an impact on the member states. In other words, it is not only necessary to ask what shape the EU project is taking at supra-national level: it is equally important to ask whether that form is also shaping learning-related policies at the member state level. A consideration of this relationship between levels proved both challenging and complex, given that the European integration process includes both the development of supra-national structures and identities, and the preservation and development of regional and national cultural characteristics. This is especially true for education, with individual member states jealously guarding their autonomy in the field.

A point made by several contributors to the volume is that EU action in the field of education and training has intensified in the post-Maastricht, and especially post-Lisbon phase. While initially, EU intervention in education focused on the development of a so-called 'European dimension', with a view to promoting the *feeling* of being European, in response to charges that this new supranational entity was a politicians', not a citizens' Europe, increasingly this European dimension has come to be seen as a strategy to add value to the efforts of each member state's efforts to transform itself into a knowledge-based society. From the point of view of the Commission, trans-border EU efforts in education and training—through mobility, harmonisation of educational cycles, and equivalence structures in qualifications—are expected to generate a new dynamics where the whole would be larger than the parts, putting Europe firmly on track to attain the Lisbon targets.

Contributors to this volume refer to several ways in which the EU has, in Field and Murphy's words, asserted its 'creeping competence' in matters educational. Among these one can mention funding leads via EU programmes, muscular invitations to harmonise policy and practice (e.g. the Bologna, Copenhagen, and Maastricht processes), key officials becoming socialised into the trans-national culture of EU policy making, peer pressure tactics, and the incitation to the emulation of what is benchmarked as 'good practice' through the so-called 'open method of co-ordination' (OMC). Dale and Robertson, Field and Murphy, and other authors in this volume in fact conclude that developments post-Lisbon—and particularly the setting up of the Concrete Future Objectives, together with the establishment of a mechanism to co-ordinate the attainment of these objectives through the OMC—assign to the EU far more of a policy role in education than it has previously been able to establish. Through the OMC, member states may remain free to develop their own coherent and comprehensive strategies, and to design and manage their own systems, but the goal ultimately is that they broadly move in the same direction, on the basis of a shared normative basis for common action.

An even more structured influence on the LLL agenda in the member states could be attributed to the European Employment Strategy, given that in terms of policy convergence, the EES has played an important role in making LLL a political priority, generating debate, but also providing raw data for evaluating comparative progress towards pre-established goals. Four authors in this volume in fact focus on the impact of National Action Plans, providing comparative evidence to show that while in some of the Member States the NAPs are used as a reporting mechanism, in others they actually set the agenda for policy making. Because of their role in monitoring and auditing progress, NAPs, argues Keep, are a means of getting a Commission foot in the nation state's policy door.

Despite the undoubted influence of the Commission in setting member state educational agendas, several authors suggest that such influence is dependent on a number of factors. As the first, most explicit form of a 'networked state', the EU opens up possibilities for individual and group affirmation at different levels (i.e. local, regional, national, and global). As Stuart and Greenwood note, the Member State level still acts as an important filter for EU-wide discourse, so that the convergence of market-oriented policy levers that are pushing the agendas for training and LLL through outcomes at nation state level are not determined, as at this level they are mediated and shaped by historical, traditional and institutional structures. It clearly makes a difference to the extent of the impact of EU-level policy directions if, at member state level, LLL is managed centrally by the state or is decentralised and outsourced, if employers and the social partners play an important role in provision or if they do not, and if the balance between education and training fluctuates one way or the other—a point that is also made by Green. Furthermore, in some cases, EU policy directions may simply serve to crystallise trends *already present* in member states. Both Rasmussen and Heikkinen note, for instance, that the documents produced at EU level on LLL may not serve to develop and implement specific policies as much as they *reflect* and *legitimise* policies that have already been adopted.

The filtering of EU-level policy directions in education by the member states, note some of the authors, depends on the power they enjoy within the Commission—in this regard, Rasmussen points out to the relative weight of Germany or France compared to Denmark, for instance—not to mention the new member states, many of which seem to be happy to fall over themselves to accommodate Brussels—at least on paper—in order to be in the Commission's good books (*vide* various chapters in Strietska-Ilina, 2005). Dale and Robertson note that while no member state is against Lisbon in general, none, and certainly not the more powerful countries, are positively 'for' it as a guide to their own national policies in education—a fact which seems to certainly be true for the UK, a clear instance of a case where 'Lisbon has not really penetrated the thinking of the Ministry in relation to LLL.'

Overall, then, there is plenty of evidence of gaps between Community aspirations for LLL, and the realities of implementing such targets. Keep, for instance, points out that the benchmark of 35 hours dedicated annually to LLL is not very visible in most member states; that technological literacy targets have been ignored by the UK, where the LLL policy rhetoric is in sharp retreat and is being replaced by narrowly defined workforce development measures; and that the objective of setting national targets in LLL has not met with much success in most of the member states. This, however, should not blind us to the fact that the Lisbon agenda has made important inroads into the way education is defined narrowly in relation to employment and economic growth, and that the Commission has an increasing number of instruments in its arsenal to not only promote that agenda, but also to support the ruling elites in the member states in walking the same road.

Beyond a synthesis

This synthesis of some of the key themes and issues raised by this collection of chapters is necessarily partial in both meanings of the term: it is a selection from a much richer set of ideas, and one that resonates most closely with what is of concern to us. Readers will undoubtedly find much more to consider as they work through the different chapters, identifying other themes and arguments that they will, we are sure, find helpful in the challenge of thinking through the challenges posed by the notion of lifelong learning.

The over-riding impression one gets from most of the readings is that neo-liberalism and the concomitant reduction of education to its economic function have, as Heikkinen argues (but see also Kuhn, Tommasini & Simons, 2005), colonised and hijacked the LLL debate at both the EU and member state level, to such an extent that while educational institutions, workplaces and communities are increasingly acknowledged as learning contexts, they are largely considered within the frames of economic rationalist discourse, which is concerned about business outcomes, but which seems unconcerned about social and civic outcomes. Such a state of affairs should not blind us, however, to the spaces that remain, and which we must occupy if we are to make a difference. As Magalhães and Stoer note, 'it is at the site of the tension between the depoliticisation of education, resulting to a large extent from the effects of the current wave of neoliberalism, and its repoliticisation through the assumption of reclaimed citizenship that, in our view, the political agenda for education is being reconfigured.' The case for a 'reclaimed citizenship' is made by several authors in this volume, a task which requires both sophisticated analysis and political action. Field and Murphy, for instance, wonder about the extent to which the partial legal competence of the EU in education and training can be harnessed as a means of facilitating the construction of a post-national identity at the EU level. Magalhães and Stoer go on to argue that 'to see amongst the threats and opportunities that are arsing from emergent social dynamics only the 'invisible' hand, inevitably dirty, of neoliberalism may be a way of refusing renewed forms of political agency.'

If this volume contributes to this important task of redefining education from the perspective of a reclaimed citizenship, and of further galvanising the will to actively engage in promoting alternative, more emancipatory educational practices and democratic civic spaces, then our labour, and that of the authors, will have served its purpose.

Notes

1. The term 'learning related policies' signals that the focus includes a range of policy fields that relate to learning but that are not usually covered by the somewhat more narrow concept of 'education and training policies'. The project therefore adopted a wide interdisciplinary approach that looked beyond educational research to consider such fields as labour market and science and technology policy research. Such a broadened view seems particularly necessary with regard to the stated aim of developing the EU into a learning society and the fact that various policy fields are affected by—and need to contribute to—this development

by promoting innovation and learning in many fields The term 'policies' is understood to stretch from 'intentions' to concrete measures of implementation. 'Policies' are represented by laws, government programmes, constitutions, decrees, whereas 'measures' are actions that put these intentions into practice (in various areas, to various degrees). EURONE&T aimed to reflect and map 'learning related policies' in accord with this definition of the term.

2. The outcomes of the EURONE&T work feature in four volumes, all published by Peter Lang. Other than the present book, the publications include: *The Learning Society in Europe and Beyond* (edited by Michael Kuhn and Ronald G. Sultana); *The Clash of Transitions— Towards a Learning Society* (edited by Olga Striestka-Ilina); and *The European Learner— A new Global Player?* (edited by Michael Kuhn). Dr Michael Kuhn, the Director of the Forum for European Regional Research at the University of Bremen in Germany, was the overall co-ordinator of the network.

3. For a discussion of the role of organised employers as a lobby group that influences Commission thinking on education, see Sultana (2002). This paper focuses in particular on the European Round Table of Industrialists.

4. Livingstone (2004) draws on a number of sources to make similar points regarding Canada, where knowledge workers still made up less than 10 percent of the labour force in 1996. He also estimates that for the US labour force only about 20 percent of job openings will require a university degree in the early part of this century, compared with over a third of new entrants who have one, while the vast majority of new jobs will require only short-term training. Livingstone's conclusions are that in aggregate terms, formal educational qualifications in Canada and many other advanced industrial countries clearly exceed formal job entry requirements.

5. Antikainen focused on lifelong learning in Finland, in comparison to eleven other countries.

References

Anderson, B. (1983) *Imagined Communities*. London: Verso.

Antikainen, A. (2005) 'Is lifelong learning becoming a reality? The case of Finland from a comparative perspective.' In A. Antikainen (ed.) *Transforming a Learning Society: The Case of Finland*. Frankfurt: Peter Lang.

Borg, G. & Mayo, P. (2002) 'The EU Memorandum on lifelong learning. Diluted old wine in new bottles?' Paper presented at the 2002 BAICE Conference, *Lifelong Learning and the Building of Human and Social Capital*. University of Nottingham, 6-8 September 2002.

Bourdieu, P. (1998) *Contre-Feux*. Paris: Liber, Raisons d'Agir.

Bruner, J. (1966) *Toward a Theory of Instruction*. Massachusetts: Harvard University Press.

Dave, R.H. (1976) *Foundations of Lifelong Education*. Oxford Pergamon Press.

European Commission (2004) *Facing the Challenge: The Lisbon Strategy for Growth and Employment*. Report of the High Level Group chaired by Wim Kok (November). Brussels: Commission of European Communities.

European Commission (2005) 'Working together for growth and jobs: a new start to the Lisbon strategy.' Communication to the Spring European Council by President Barroso. Brussels: Commission of European Communities. 02.02.05: COM(2005)24.

Faure, E. *et al.* (1972) *Learning to Be*. Paris: Unesco.

Gelpi, E. (1985) *Lifelong Education and International Relations*. London: Croom Helm.

Grubb, W.N. & Lazerzon, M. (2004) *The Education Gospel: The Economic Power of Schooling*. Cambridge, Mass.: Harvard University Press.

Jarvis, P. (ed.)(2001) *The Age of Learning. Education and the Knowledge Society.* London: Kogan Page.

Kuhn, M. (2005) 'The learning economy – the theoretical domestication of knowledge and learning for global competition.' In M. Kuhn, M. Tomassini & R.-J. Simons (eds) *Towards a Knowledge Based Economy? - Knowledge and Learning in European Educational Research.* New York: Peter Lang.

Kuhn, M. (2005) *The European Learner—A new Global Player?* New York: Peter Lang. [forthcoming]

Kuhn, M. & Sultana, R.G. (2005) *The Learning Society in Europe and Beyond.* New York: Peter Lang. [forthcoming]

Lê Thành Khôi (1995) *Éducation et Civilisations: Sociétes d'Hier.* Paris: Unesco & Nathan.

Livingstone, D.W. (1999) 'Beyond human capital theory: the underemployment problem.' *International Journal of Contemporary Sociology,* Vol.36(2), pp.163–192.

Livingstone, D.W. (2003) *The Education-Jobs Gap: Underemployment or Economic Democracy.* Toronto: Garamong Press & Clinton Corners; NY: Percheron Press. [2nd revised edition]

Livingstone, D.W. (2004) 'The learning society: past, present and future views.' 2004 R.W.B. Jackson Lecture, OISE/UT, October 14.

Ranson, S. (ed.)(1998) *Inside the Learning Society.* London: Cassell.

Rifkin, J. (2004) *The European Dream: How Europe's Vision of the Future is Quietly Eclipsing the American Dream.* Jeremy P. Tarcher/Penguin.

Striestka-Ilina, O. (2005) *The Clash of Transitions—Towards a Learning Society.* New York: Peter Lang. [forthcoming]

Sultana, R.G. (2002) 'Quality education and training for tomorrow's Europe: a contrapuntal reading of European Commission documents.' In A. Nóvoa & M. Lawn (eds) *Fabricating Europe: The Formation of an Education Space.* Dordrecht: Kluwer.

Terkel, S. (1974) *Working.* Harmondsworth: Penguin.

Wain, K. (2004) *The Learning Society in a Postmodern World: The Education Crisis.* New York: Peter Lang.

CHAPTER TWO

The Case of the UK: *Homo Sapiens Europæus* vs *Homo Quæstuosus Atlanticus*? European Learning Citizen or Anglo-American Human Capitalist?

ROGER DALE AND SUSAN ROBERTSON

Introduction

The focus of this volume is on how the relationships between the EU and Member States (MS) are being played out in the fields of education, particularly in respect of how they might be involved in the creation of *Homo Sapiens Europæus*/European Learning Citizen. In this chapter, we shall address that question in terms of the relationships between the European Union and possibly the most Eurosceptic member state, the United Kingdom (UK).

In this chapter we will be arguing that the basis both for the shaping of the European Space of Education (ESE)[1] and characterisation of the European Learning Citizen (ELC) has been the declaration at the end of the Lisbon summit (2000). This declaration set the target of Europe becoming, by 2010, 'the most dynamic, competitive, knowledge-based economy in the world, with sustainable growth, more and better jobs and greater social cohesion'. This introduced three qualitative shifts of vital relevance to the topic of this chapter: in the nature and possibility of a European Space for Education; in conceptions of 'Europe'; and in the emphasis on the centrality of 'productive social policy' in the European Social Model. We shall be arguing in this chapter that these shifts have the potential collectively to provide a basis for a ELC, whose citizenship component is limited to a form of *economic* citizenship, and that the UK is much less likely to take up such possibilities for a range of structural reasons, centred around its attachment to Anglo-American forms of capitalism and social policy, as well as for historical, institutional and attitudinal reasons.

The chapter will proceed as follows. In the first part of the chapter we will discuss some of the ways that the objectives laid out at Lisbon, and the ways that these have been developed since Lisbon, have framed the development of a ESE. We will then turn to the implications of that framing for the development of a ELC. Following this we will focus on, and compare, European and UK understandings of the three eponymous elements of the European Learning Citizen construct. In the final part of the chapter we discuss some conclusions that might be drawn about the ways that the idea of the ELC might be taken in the UK.

The Lisbon Declaration and the development of a European Space for Education

While education has been a matter of continuing interest to the EU since its earliest days, there are five dimensions where it is possible to recognise qualitative shifts to the idea of an ESE arising from the Lisbon Declaration and its assumptions. They are not all of equal weight and importance, but they are all necessary elements of the gestalt. They are (i) the relationship between the European Community and its Member States; (ii) the procedures through which that relationship was to be played out; (iii) the instruments through which it was to be installed; (iv) the mechanisms through which it would be implemented; and (v) the substance of the relationship.

As is well known and widely acknowledged, in terms of the European treaties, education has always been recognised as a matter for national competence. In particular the Community has to respect fully the responsibility of the Member States for the content of teaching and the organisation of education systems and their cultural and linguistic diversity. It is fully subject to the principle of subsidiarity—that decision-making should be performed at the lowest possible effective administrative level. And while the relevant article (149) of the Treaty of Amsterdam did recognise that the Community might also contribute to the European dimension in education through promoting mobility, languages, institutional cooperation, and improving the quality of their education systems (in what might be called the functional and scalar division of competence between the Community and the MS) at which level authority over particular education-related responsibilities, decisions and actions should be located was straightforwardly based on the principle of subsidiarity. However, it is important to note the fundamental nature of the changes for EU involvement in education policy signalled by the Lisbon declaration.

The nub of our argument in this chapter is that, first, while respecting the functional and scalar division of *formal competences* represented in Article 149 and the principle of subsidiarity, Lisbon involved effectively a new understanding of subsidiarity in education and, second, that it led to the creation of a new European Space for Education based on a functional and scalar division of the labour of *educational governance*, that co-existed with subsidiarity without superseding it. In terms of the first, Lisbon, for instance, by both detailing a set of Concrete Future Objectives for Education Systems and specifying that they could only be met at the Community and not MS level, could be seen as either replacing subsidiarity with 'supersidiarity', or as interpreting the nature and seriousness of the Lisbon agenda to mean that the Community itself was the lowest possible effective administrative level. In terms of the second, Lisbon essentially both announces Europe as a space of educational governance that creates the conditions for, and asserts the necessity of, a functional and scalar division of the labour of educational governance that cross-cuts Article 149, and provides the crucial mechanism that makes this possible in the form of the Open Method of Coordination (OMC).

The Open Method of Coordination, which, as stated in the Bulletin on the Conclusions of the Portuguese Presidency, 'is designed to help the Member States to progressively develop their own policies', involves:

- Fixing guidelines for the Union combined with specific timetables for achieving the goals which they set in the short, medium and long terms;
- Establishing, where appropriate, quantitative and qualitative indicators and benchmarks against the best in the world and tailored to the needs of different Member States and sectors as a means of comparing best practice;
- Translating these European guidelines into national and regional policies by setting specific targets and adopting measures, taking into account national and regional differences;
- Periodic monitoring, evaluation and peer review as mutual learning processes. (European Presidency 2000, para 37)

The OMC has been subject to a great deal of academic debate (for a review focussing on its uses in education, see Dale, 2004). In essence it is based on a Commission led and brokered consensus between MS (and the social partners) around benchmarks, indicators, best practice and so cn. Though very much part of 'soft governance' rather than seeking to apply the Community method, or harmonisation, the OMC is expected to bring about a convergence of goals while retaining a diversity of practices—which is in itself an interesting statement both of the importance of the concept of governance, as the 'coordination of coordination', and of a functional and scalar division of that governance labour in the fields that are to be subject to trough the OMC.

This also entailed a change in the nature of the *instruments* to be employed by the Community. Whereas traditionally it had been limited to providing support and resource for curricular initiatives such as Comenius, or mobility measures such as Erasmus, post-Lisbon it was essentially to coordinate and promote *policies* for MS education systems in the form, for instance, of common benchmarks and indicators which would be backed up, not by fiscal or regulatory resources but, by monitoring and peer pressure.

These were key parts of the shift in the *mechanisms* through which the relationship as to be implemented. DiMaggio and Powell's (1983) comparison of three forms of what they call 'isomorphism', or why institutions tend to respond to new challenges in very similar ways, illustrate the point well here. They distinguish three such bases of legitimation of practices, mimetic, where legitimation is based on the imitation of existing practices, normative, where legitimation is based on adherence to a set of recognised principles, such as those absorbed through professional socialisation, or membership of epistemic communities, and coercive, where legitimation is based on doing what they are told. Traditionally, the EC has confined itself to mimetic mechanisms, whereby it supplied examples that it encouraged MS to take up, or imitate. Post-Lisbon, however, it seems clear that something rather more pro-active is required. Since coercion is ruled out by the unavailability of hard law in the education area, the Lisbon process, and especially the OMC, may be seen at one level as an effort to provide a shared normative basis for common action, to set up, or approximate, a particular form of epistemic community.

In terms of the substance of the Lisbon agenda there are two key points to be made, besides the obvious one that education is specifically assigned a major role in achieving the massive and ambitious set of targets contained in the Declaration. First, the Lisbon declaration presents a far from straightforward or homogeneous agenda for education; and second, notwithstanding the specification of Concrete Future Objectives of Education Systems, it also provides the occasion for fairly extensive discursive elaboration on the part of the EC.

In terms of the first of those points, we will suggest that the Lisbon declaration is not 'unitary'. Rather, it is made up of at least five distinct discourses, each with their own histories and trajectories, and separate implications for education, learning and citizenship. It is not clear whether these distinctions are recognized officially, or, if they are, whether one intention in forming the EES is to override their individual and *national* differences at the *regional* scale. The discourses are: *'Competitive'; 'Knowledge-based economy'; 'sustainable growth'; 'more and better jobs';* and *'greater social cohesion'*. It is very important both to recognize that these discourses are to a considerable degree *mutually contradictory* and to note that they are not all 'equal'. It is clear, for instance, that *'competitiveness'* is the *'master discourse'* (Radaelli, 2003; see also Rosamund, 2002; Dale, 2003).

What is of particular interest and significance in the context of this chapter is the assumption in the Lisbon objectives that 'social cohesion' can and should be promoted and achieved at the European level. It is this above all, that might be identified as a contradiction in the Lisbon agenda, for two reasons. First, there is a permanent tension, or contradiction, for education systems in that they are expected (usually by different groups within societies) both to advance the forces of change and to provide a basis for stability. Second, it has been traditionally assumed that 'social cohesion' is very much a national rather than a regional responsibility, something that is best ensured at a lower than European level. It is central to our argument that this double contradiction can only be resolved through a narrowing and reorienting of the idea of social cohesion. More specifically, it is through the recasting of social cohesion as both an element of and a result of 'productive social policy' that the contradiction is resolved. As we shall suggest below, this confines the idea of 'European citizenship' to economic citizenship, with the wider elements of citizenship effectively remaining at the national level.

We are now in a position to combine these different elements of the constitution of the ESE, and to consider their consequences for the development of a ELC. Thus, for instance, the dominance of the competitiveness agenda means that the redivision and rescaling of responsibility for the existing functions of national education systems takes place around an agenda that maximizes the likelihood that they will facilitate, and minimizes the likelihood that they will act as significant obstacles to, the development of the overall agenda of making Europe the most competitive economy in the world. Very broadly, we might suggest that those elements of national education systems more directly associated with the extended reproduction of the mode of production (e.g., the support of accumulation and the development of collective capacity [for instance in the area of ICT]) will move to the European level (increasingly the site and focus of extended reproduction), while those linked to the reproduction of national social formations will remain at the nation-state level. The reconfiguration of these relations is likely to be emergent, fragmentary, uneven and experienced differently in different MSs, regions and educational institutions. This partial and selective shift of scale to the European level may be seen as a key foundation stone in the construction of a EES.

The discursive elaboration of 'Lisbon' in the construction of the ESE

The key determining criterion for the development of the ESE has been increasing education's contribution to the achievement of greater economic competitiveness. This was elaborated most formally and fully in the Detailed Work Programme agreed by the Council in June 2002. This work programme was seen as a 'single comprehensive strategy (within the framework of the OMC) for education and training' (OJEC 2002, p.6). However, the method by which the strategy was to be implemented is as interesting and significant for our purposes as its content. In the model to be used in the follow-up of the quantitative indicators, each of the objectives of the programme is measured against four benchmarks; EU average, average of three best performing countries in EU, 'USA', and 'Japan'—which demonstrates dramatically how the competitiveness agenda permeates the whole of the strategy for education and training. Discussion of the content of the objectives is outside our remit here, except in the case of the objective most closely related to the ELC. This objective is entitled 'Supporting active citizenship, equal opportunities and social cohesion', and the benchmark for it is 'the proportion of the population aged 18-24 with only lower secondary education and not in education or training'. While it is important to acknowledge the major difficulties involved in drawing up a benchmark of active citizenship, its association with early school leaving does seem to confirm the sense of a dominant human capital agenda.

More recently, these aims have been pursued with an increasing sense of their importance to the achievement of the Lisbon goals, culminating in the joint report of the Council and Commission to the 2004 Spring Council meeting (CEC, 2004). While there is no space to go into this document in any detail, it is worthwhile alluding to what it has to say on matters around citizenship. It contains a section headed 'Consolidating the European dimension of education', where it states that 'Fifty years after its launch, the European project has still not succeeded in attracting the appropriate level of interest and the full support of the people of the Union…School has a fundamental role to play allowing everyone to be informed and understand the meaning of European integration' and it suggests that 'By 2010, all education systems should ensue that their pupils have by the end of their secondary education the knowledge and competences they need to prepare them for their role as a future citizen in Europe' (p.30).[2] This appears to hand 'Europe' at best an auxiliary role in enabling national education systems to provide the basis for future citizens *in* Europe, (rather than future *European citizens*, or even future citizens *of* Europe).

In terms of our overall argument so far, we have been suggesting that the ESE framed by the response to the Lisbon agenda is characterized by a functional and scalar division of labour that sees issues broadly associated with economic competitiveness—including the economic role of education— becoming a EU responsibility, and issues to do with social stability remaining MS responsibility. Crucial to this division of labour, however, is the designation of 'social policy' as *'productive* social policy'. Further to this, the main means by which this is to be achieved, the OMC, assigns to the EC far more of a 'policy' role than it has previously been able to establish. We have also been arguing that the overall significance of this framing of the ESE is that it provides an opportunity structure that would enable the development of a form of economic citizenship at a European level, but drastically curtail the possibility of constructing any broader form of ELC.

Discourses of 'Europe' in Lisbon

One highly significant and relevant feature of the Lisbon Declaration that has major consequences for the framing of the ELC is the 'heroic' nature of the claims advanced in the declaration about 'Europe' as an entity. The Lisbon Declaration boldly hailed 'Europe' as an economy, as an entity with the political-administrative capacity to achieve the targets, as being capable of, and responsible for, organising its MS to achieve the targets, as the beneficiary of the putative success of the strategy, as well as an education space. The detail of the strategy for education and training after Lisbon that we mentioned above also contains, in its comparisons with the USA and Japan, the identification of 'Others' against whom 'Europe' can identify itself. The identification of common, European level, problems is an important part of the discursive construction of Europe and a ESE, and the identification of common policies in response, extends that construction. As Ben Rosamund puts it, ''Europe' as a policy space suggests (a) an area with boundaries; (b) an area affected by external variables such as 'globalisation'; and (c) an area that should be subject to common regulatory practice' (2002, p.172). In terms of these three conditions, we have suggested above that the boundaries are not only spatial; that (as Rosamund also contends) globalisation as the external variables gives rise to the centrality of the competitiveness agenda; and that both the 'traditional Community method' and the OMC construct 'Europe' as subject to common regulatory practice, albeit that the intention of the OMC is that common policy goals can and should be met through a diversity of means.

All this goes well beyond Jens Henrik Haahr's (2004) felicitous identification of Europe as a 'community of fate', to a conception of Europe able to proclaim itself a community whose collective fate is in its own hands. There are few better examples of this than may be found in the process of construction of a European Space of Education, which, again as we have been suggesting above, assumes (a) that 'Europe' is an entity that has authority over these areas; (b) that it is able to act effectively in the absence of the existing 'Community method'; and (c) that in doing so can 'act on itself'.

Further, the OMC itself represents a similar assertion of Europe as a competent policy actor'. We can see this most clearly if we recognise that rather than its being 'introduced' at the Lisbon summit as a freshly-minted initiative, it would be more accurate to see what happened there as the ex post 'naming' of a series of similar existing processes, such as those introduced in the Amsterdam Treaty, the Monetary Union strategy and the Employment strategy (see Pochet, 2001, p.8). This 'naming' of the OMC is in itself a highly significant move; it gives a substance, authority and degree of legitimation to the process that its multiple predecessors individually could not aspire to. Indeed, Claudio Radaelli sees the OMC as eminently a 'legitimising discourse', 'that provides a community of policy makers with a common vocabulary and a legitimising project...with the result that practices that... a few years ago would have been simply labelled 'soft law', new policy instruments and benchmarking are now presented as 'applications' if not 'prototypes' of 'the' method' (2003, p.7). Moreover, with its emphasis on the importance of the participation of the 'social partners' in the processes of benchmarking, identification of best practice and so on, it promises some movement towards the reduction of the EU's democratic deficit, and the 'encitizening' of the people of Europe.

European and UK perceptions of discourses of 'European'

The first component of the ELC, 'European', is strongly tied to the heroic claims made, or implied, in the Lisbon Declaration and the follow-ups to it, for 'Europe' as an entity, or a community of fate, or a community able to determine its own fate. We have become used to the 'national differences' and the 'nation as the basis of citizenship' arguments in this area, but they are by no means the only arguments to be made here, nor necessarily the most important. In addition to the national uniqueness arguments (on which attitudinal forms of British Euroscepticism draw), the substance of the heroic claims contains at least three important potential fault lines, which may divide UK from 'continental' European assumptions.

The first is that the discourses of the Lisbon declaration are by no means exclusive to the EU. As we shall elaborate below, they are broadly shared, in their identification and to some extent in their purported solutions, by other supranational organisations, such as the OECD, which comes to very similar conclusions on some of the issues (see Jacobsson, 2004), and, as importantly, by the individual MS themselves, most of whom (at least before May 2004) were also members of the OECD. More than this, they are also shared by the identified major competitors, the United States and Japan. It is hard to discern anything about the Lisbon discourses that is uniquely European. However, it could be argued that it is their grouping together as a single project to be achieved by a single entity, Europe, that both distinguishes them from other similar programmes and adds something distinctively European. Indeed, such is the basis of some of the arguments about the European Social Model, constructed as 'productive social policy', and explicitly contrasted with American social policy, which we shall be examining in the next section. In this argument the apparent contradictions between the discourses are turned into sources of strength as they are resolved through European level productive social policy. It is also important to note that the EU is different from organisations such as the OECD in significant ways (Jacobsson, 2004); for instance, while the instruments it has available for bringing about adoption and implementation of policies by MS may be relatively few and relatively 'soft' (see Dale, 2004) in the social policy area, they are more powerful than those available to the OECD (though here it is important to recognise the power of peer pressure in the OECD, that comes mainly from the mechanism of peer review; see Pagani, 2002).

However, this is another significant area where the British and 'continental' positions have rather different bases. This difference might be summed up most succinctly by the argument that for Britain, 'globalisation', certainly in the form of neo-liberal Anglo-American capitalism (on which Jacobsson argues that the OECD draws more than the EU, certainly than its more 'social' Directorates), is a powerful stimulus and force for greater competition worldwide, while 'Europe', particularly when seen as connoting red tape and regulation, is a potential obstacle to its progress rather than a facilitator of it, but the opposite is the case for France, where globalisation is portrayed negatively and Europeanisation positively (see Hay and Rosamund, 2002), who also make very important points about the varying interpretations of globalisation and Europeanisation in different national settings). We might develop this point further by suggesting that for Britain, its relationship with Europe is an *instrumental* one, regarded as little different in kind from the OECD or WTO, while for France and at least the other original signatories of the Treaty of Rome, it also has a clear and important expressive dimension. We might almost go so far as to suggest that for the UK 'Europe' is as much an 'Other' against which it defines its own specificity, as an 'Us' to which it belongs. These different perspectives are likely to shape the respective interpretations and evaluations of the heroic claims.

The second basis for questioning the heroic claims is that while the conception of a 'national economy' has undoubtedly been rendered almost without meaning or substance over the past decades, this does not mean that it has somehow passed to a 'European' level that acts as a higher scale economy, mutatis mutandis. This is because the forces that undermined national economies were, not pre-formed or even potential supranational political economies, but multi-national corporations and international financial institutions, that are as inimical or indifferent to the development of 'Europe' as a competitive entity as they were to, say, Denmark or Ireland. Thus, the same arguments about the difficulty of maintaining national welfare states in the absence of national economies may apply equally at the European level. Here, however, it could be argued that Europe is more than a discourse. It has considerable substance, in the form above all of the euro, but also of the Growth and Stability Pact and Broad Economic Policy Guidelines (whose significance in the context of discussions such as this one may paradoxically be increased through their recent 'flouting' by the German and French governments). Once again, however, British commitment is clearly less than that of the members of the euro at least.

The third argument that might be seen to challenge the heroic claims made for 'Europe' is that competitiveness characterises inter-state relationships *within* the EU as well as those with the rest of the world. While the idea of Europe is given substance by being regarded as a (single) competitor with the US and Japan, at the same time, competition within the EU is increased, not diminished, by the existence of the single market. The consequences of this have been especially clearly expressed by Wolfgang Streeck. He argues that, 'International competition affects countries differently, and is differently received by different national institutions. This is one reason why the rethinking of solidarity that is under way in Europe takes its own course in each country, reinforcing the importance of national political arenas inside the European 'social model'…That renewed solidarity is *not* sought in a unified political community reflects as well as perpetuates the *pervasiveness of intensified competition*' (1999, p.4, emphasis in original). However, it might be argued that a common conception of at least economic citizenship could add a distinct and more 'human' dimension to the rules of the single market, and make them more effective as well as more palatable. Indeed, Streeck seems to suggest something like this when he goes on to suggest that

> 'While the political-institutional base of solidarity remains national, its *substance* is rapidly transforming under the pressure of intensified competition. In trying to adapt to the new economic circumstances, national communities seek to defend their solidarity, less through protection and redistribution than through *joint competitive and productive success*—through politics, not *against* markets, but *within* and *with* them, gradually replacing *protective* and *redistributive* with *competitive* and *productive* solidarity…and indeed reinforcement of national diversity would seem an important element of the sort of *competitive adjustment* into which European social policy has become enmeshed' (pp.6-7, emphases in original).

Thus it seems that not only contradictions between its key discourses, but competition between its member states are to be transformed into positive features of 'Europe' through the development of the European Social Model in the form of productive social policy. It is to this development that we now turn.

European and UK conceptions of (economic) citizenship

As we argued above, fundamental to the resolution of the apparent contradiction between competitiveness and social cohesion are (a) the reconstitution of social policy in the EU as productive social policy , as part of, rather than a drain on, economic policy (the Commission pointed out that its contribution to the preparation of the Lisbon Economic Council, 'Building an inclusive Europe', was 'based on the will to promote social policy as a productive factor' (EC, 2000, p.1), while as Anna Diamantopoulou, then European Commissioner for Employment and Social Affairs, put it in a speech in Warsaw, 'good social policy is good economic policy…We all gain from the fact that well-designed social policy is a productive factor in improving economic performance' (Diamantopoulou, 2001, pp.2,3) and (b) the characterization of the European Social Model (ESM) as an 'indissoluble link between economic performance and social progress' (Annex to Nice report).

Conceptions of economic citizenship have changed rapidly over the past two decades across the world and not just in the EU, or even in advanced countries. What is most clearly at issue in the present context is captured well by Kerstin Jacobsson, when she argues that 'The adaptation to a competitive and knowledge-based economy has altered the balance between social rights and individual responsibilities' (2004, p.60). It is this balance that lies at the core of what we might understand by economic citizenship, and in this part of the chapter we will discuss some pertinent differences of approach to that balance, or relationship. The first point to be made, of course, is that this relationship has been radically transformed from that which held in the era of the 'Keynesian Welfare State settlement', which was concerned with decommodification, redistribution and state protection against social risks. In the current neo-liberal era, all those things are changed, with the responsibilities implied in this list—including that for unemployment—passing from the state to the individual, and with states' responsibilities limited essentially to providing a competitive market- and business-friendly environment. What is involved, then, is not merely 'brute' 'cutting back of the *welfare state*, but the redesign of *social policy*, not the simple modification of existing parameters of social policy, but changes in the intent, the overall logic and the orientation' (Palier, 2004, p.12)

More broadly, we can distinguish four overlapping but not identical discourses that together frame the new relationships between social rights and individual responsibilities. However, our central argument will be that despite their apparent overall consistency, these discourses have given rise to a variety of different conceptions of economic citizenship, rather than a broadly common one, and that the differences are most apparent when we compare the EU and the UK. The discourses in question are those of 'productive social policy', supply-side policy, active labour market policy and 'employability'.

As we argued above, the apparent contradiction between the economic—competitiveness, knowledge-based economy—goals of the Lisbon declaration, and its intention that this shall happen alongside greater social cohesion can be resolved through the design and implementation of 'productive social policy', and this is at the heart of a newly conceived 'European Social Model'. Palier (2004) suggests that it was central to the EU's 'taking back' social policy and that it was elaborated particularly through the work of research networks that could be taken up by the successive presidencies. In this, he points particularly to the report prepared for the Portuguese presidency and later published as Esping-Andersen et al. (2002). The claim for productive social policy was first discussed at the 1997 Amsterdam conference on Social Policy as a Productive factor and taken up in European Social Policy Agenda endorsed by the Nice European Council. Thus,

> 'As a result we are beginning to see a much greater appreciation, at national and international level, of the wider, positive, contribution of employment and social policy to raising productive potential—investing in human resources, preventing market failure and minimising costly social failure. In the light of these analyses and debates, it is now easier to appreciate that the role of social policy is much wider than traditionally thought; that it is integral to the dynamic development of modern, open economies and societies; and that it brings cumulative benefits through time' (CEC, 2003a, p.1).

Associated with this has been a widespread shift from demand-side to supply-side policies in the social policy area, including education and employment. Rather than the criterion of the success of a policy being (the potentially redistributive one of) how many demands it meets and how well, for instance the adequacy of social benefits for the unemployed, or governmental stimulation of demand for labour (including through the creation of public sector jobs), for instance, the purpose of supply side policy is essentially to improve the operation of markets through interventions that remove barriers to the free play of markets, such as trade union reform, or promote investment in education and training, or shape incentives to labour market participation; a criterion for supply-side policies is how effectively they shape demand and allocate responsibility for meeting it through the supply and implementation of programmes and policies whose aims are determined in advance. The basis of social policy, that is to say, shifts from response to needs to the definition of, and allocation of responsibilities for meeting, those needs. This approach clearly dominates social policy today, particularly but not exclusively, employment policy. It is clearly highly influential in education policy, with the emphasis on improving the supply of appropriately qualified human capital (rather than assuming that the supply will adjust to the demand for it).

The idea of 'active labour market policy' suggests, in one sense, that the individual is to become active in her/his social protection, actively seeking work, for instance, in contrast to passively relying on unemployment benefits. As Palier points out, such a policy is based on an approach whose function 'was no longer to protect individuals from risk, but to change their behaviour' (ibid, p.13). More broadly, it suggests—in line with the supply-side orientation—an active rather than passive role for the state in labour market regulation and incentivisation. Active labour market policies (ALMPs) have a long history in Sweden, but their current popularity is as a part of the 'family' of approaches that we have been discussing. Like the other approaches they are aimed at improving the operation of labour markets, but what distinguishes them is their focus on unemployed people. They are intended to help people (back) into the labour market. They may employ a range of strategies, from job creation, vocational training to job placement and job searching. What varies across these schemes somewhat is the element of compulsion and sanction they carry.

The final discourse we need to consider is 'employability'. In a sense, it is implicit in all the previous three discourses. However, it does stand in its own right as the first of the four 'pillars' of the European Employment Strategy. As part of that strategy it is subject to a detailed system of monitoring and reporting coordinated by the Commission, and it is quite closely associated with education and vocational training. Employability has been defined as 'the capacity for people to be employed; it relates not only to the adequacy of their skills but also to incentives and opportunities offered to individuals to seek employment' (CEC 1997, quoted in Jacobsson, 2004, p.50). However, as Jacobsson points out, drawing on Serrano (2000), there are several senses in which employability may be invoked, and they are differently enrolled by different countries. Is it, for instance, primarily a matter of training, in which case it can be assisted through the provision of relevant skills? Or is it a matter of prevention, which might be remedied through the provision of appropriate social competencies and career guidance? Or is it a matter of activating the 'work shy' through appropriate incentives? The consequences of each of these versions will reflect in their different ways the point made by Wolfgang Streeck, that 'political commitment to 'employability' typically coincides with heavy pressures on educational institutions to improve their efficiency and adjust their output to market demands' (1999, p.4).

What we can infer from this very rapid tour of four discourses of social policy is that:

- as we pointed out above, they contain a large amount of overlap;
- they all have a clear European level reference;
- they all, to greater or lesser degrees, target individuals and ascribe responsibility to them;
- they may individually and collectively function, as Jacobsson (2004, p.53) argues, as means of socialising subjects into a particular ethos;
- they all carry aspects of economic citizenship.

It is important to note that as well as the different varieties of capitalism that shape different conceptions of 'productive social policy', there are differences in the discourses emanating from different sectors of political administrations. As Jacobsson points out, the message coming from the more 'economic' Directorates within the Commision tend to take a more rigidly neo-classical line which involves being rather more inclined to see unemployment as a personal responsibility, related to a conception of unemployment as voluntary and of its solutions as lying in removing regulatory disincentives to unemployment than those contained within the EES. The same also holds within the OECD, where, as Noaksson and Jacobsson report, while the OECD's approach to problems...brings together expertise from a number of directorates, the fact that the responsibility for reviewing and overseeing the national attempts to implement the [Jobs] strategy came to rest with the Economic Development and Review Committee under the economics directorate meant that the ultimate source of assessment was a neoclassical economics perspective' (2003, p.19). The same authors also make an important point about the different nature of the consensus making processes of the EU and OECD; 'While the OECD can rely on an expert—and often neo-classical economist—consensus, the EU has to moderate many other interests, including the two sides of industry and various national and political interests' (ibid, p.41). This means that while the EU consensus is likely to be more broadly based than the OECD's, it may also be less precise in its guidance.

Our argument about the relationship between UK and EU conceptions of economic citizenship revolves around the issue of whether UK policy is influenced more by US than by EU approaches. The differences between EU and US conceptions of social and especially employment policies, and their influence on UK policy have been the object of considerable discussion. The nature of these differences has been clearly stated by Annesley (2003): 'The American welfare state is an archetypal liberal welfare regime which relies on market mechanisms and provides residual and means-tested welfare intervention as a last resort. Entitlement rules are strict to discourage welfare dependency and welfare receipt is very often stigmatised...' (p.145),while 'At the heart of the EU's social policy is the conviction that social policy is not a counterweight to market integration or a correction of market forces, but the belief is rather that social cohesion promotes market efficiency.' And she goes on, tellingly in the context of this chapter, 'The Commission emphasises the 'investment' dimension of social welfare... it favours social policies which are conducive to growth (education and training and active labour market policies) over those which make no contribution to economic growth. For this reason, too, the EU has mostly been concerned with promoting social rights for workers rather than for citizens' (p.149).

We can distinguish two different views on the issue of comparative influence on UK social policy, that which sees the US as the dominant influence on UK, and the view that both US and EU are (separately) influential on UK social policy. The first position can be illustrated from the work of Anne Daguerre and Peter Taylor-Gooby (2004). Their argument is that US approaches to social policy are more influential on UK policies than European approaches, and they base this conclusion on analyses of membership of and collaboration between policy networks. They argue, using evidence drawn from interviews with senior British officials, that the network ties between UK and US are much stronger and more pervasive than those between UK and European networks. They advance a number of reasons for this, including: a shared neo-liberal model of capitalism; long-standing policy conversations based on this (and fostered especially in the Thatcher-Reagan era); membership of the same 'family of nations', with similar cultural values (and, we might add, a single common language); the greater 'goodness of fit' between US polices than EU policies with UK policies; and similar criteria of policy success—'What counted as success was the ability to reduce the welfare rolls on the one hand, and on the other to facilitate the return to paid employment of as many people as possible' (p.27). Thus, 'Despite the shift towards a skills-oriented strategy for a productive workforce, [British] governmental thinking tends to neglect European Union influence' (p.33).

The second position is clearly enunciated by Annesley (2003), who argues that 'Americanisation and Europeanisation are fundamentally, and mutually exclusive phenomena, both in terms of their content and process... Americanisation is a voluntary one-way transfer of ideology rhetoric and policy... that stresses the negative impact of welfare on social policy and economic performance... whereas Europeanisation is a two-way process of obligation (that)... clearly sees a positive role for welfare in the macroeconomy ' (pp.144, 153), but that the UK is influenced by both. Her argument is 'that UK social policy under New Labour continues to be Americanised, but at the same time is being increasingly Europeanised' (p.156). As one example of this, she refers to New Labour's social exclusion discourse, which she suggest is 'a mixture of European Social Integrationist discourse (that) places its central focus on paid work as a means of social inclusion' and American Moral Underclass Discourse that [quoting Ruth Levitas 1998, p.7] 'centres on the moral and behavioural delinquency of the excluded themselves'' (p.157). Two notable features of Annesley's paper are that on the one hand it does effectively draw attention to what might be seen as the 'unacknowledged Europeanisation' of UK social policy, for instance, through the activities of the European Court of Justice, but that, on the other, almost 'balancing' this emphasis, it makes scarcely any reference to the OMC; and though she does emphasise 'mutual obligation' as the basis of EU social policy formation, this is a coinage that does not effectively capture or equate to the processes of the OMC.

What conclusions can be drawn from these different accounts of influences on UK policy in the area of economic citizenship? First, most of the 'European' influence claimed is the result of the use of legal and regulatory mechanisms that it is clearly recognised, in and since the Lisbon declaration, are no longer valid or appropriate. Second, with the exception of legislation on gender equity, the ESM is itself increasingly, and it might be argued, effectively exclusively, based on the close relationship between citizenship, social inclusion and employment. And third, on either reading, UK social policy is at the very least at the furthest 'American' 'economic before social' end of the ESM.

In terms of our argument, while Lisbon may have provided an opportunity structure for a ELC confined to economic citizenship, that terrain seems likely to be occupied in the UK by an economic citizenship that is shaped at least as much by American as European influences.

European and UK conceptions of 'learning'

When we move now to consider the third element of the ELC troika, 'Learning', the first thing that strikes us on reading the literature, and especially the official documentation, around the 'Learning' component of the ELC, is that learning in the sense implied by 'the learning *citizen*', as a particular target, process and outcome of education systems, is not especially prominent. While there are copious references to 'learning' throughout the documents published by the various EU bodies, for instance, they are almost entirely confined to ideas of 'policy' learning, or education systems learning from each other. Indeed, it may be a reflection of the continuing significance of Article 149, but it is very noticeable that the focus of the discursive density that we spoke about above is MS *education systems*; the *processes* of education, and especially of learning, are scarcely, if ever, touched upon. In terms of the argument about the ESE and its consequences for the development of a ELC, then, we might say that in addition to the shaping imposed by the ESE, the terrain it circumscribes is inimical to the development of the kinds of learning processes that might be associated with such developments.

There are clearly important reasons for this bias. The first, as we have noted, is Article 149, but it is by no means the only one. A second is the explicit encouragement of 'common goals, multiple routes', which also entails a 'hands off' approach to national processes, curricula and so on. Moreover, the degree of self-denial in this ordinance is distinctly limited, given the major and fundamental differences between MS education systems and polices, that are embedded deeply in their structures and textures; to take only one relevant example, the relationships between educational qualifications and the labour market take multiple and incompatible forms (see e g, Maurice et al. (1986), Shavit and Muller (1998). And if all this is the case, what case is there for discussing a 'European' *Learning* Citizen'?

These serious obstacles do not preclude totally any European level attempts to shape 'learning' in the individual sense at MS levels, though they do mean that they have to take place outside the boundaries set by Article 149 and the formal encouragement of diversity, and patrolled by the depth and intensity of national structures and assumptions. Some considerable efforts have been made through 'add on' and 'transversal' initiatives sponsored by the EU directly to promote conceptions of European citizenship through education, but (a) these are not directly what is entailed in the idea of the ELC, and (b), there is little reason to assume that they will have a greater impact in the future than they have had in the past.

Notwithstanding these reservations, in this section, we consider briefly three such attempts at Community level to 'shape' the learning component of the ELC; though they are necessarily somewhat tangential to the work of the systems themselves, they do offer an indication of the possible parameters and purposes of the learning element of the ELC. The three initiatives we will discuss are lifelong learning, e-learning and the attempts to draw up lists of basic competencies. The possibilities of each of them to shape the ELC depend on their not infringing the set of obstacles outlined above; lifelong learning falls outside the compulsory sector (though as we shall see, it is allowed to impinge on the compulsory sector, since that is where, it is argued, the basis for effective lifelong learning is laid down); e-learning is equally 'new' to all systems, being essentially without national educational path dependencies; and competencies, which can be seen to 'cross-cut' curricula and thus offer little threat to national authority since they can in principle be accommodated to any national curriculum.

When we peruse the very ample literature on lifelong learning, it rapidly becomes clear that it is as fully implicated in the 'productive social policy' agenda as any of the other components we have been discussing. It is predicated on individual achievements aimed at securing or improving individuals' employability. The crucial importance of lifelong learning to the attainment of the Lisbon goals is promoted with great urgency. It is seen as central to improving the possibilities of labour force participation, which is in turn taken, again, as the basis or social inclusion/citizenship. But once again, we see this economic rationale receiving at least equal emphasis in the UK case, where it is linked to the theme of individual responsibility; in both these ways, the liberatory and collective potential of lifelong learning as perceived in earlier realisations such as recurrent education disappear under the neo-liberal waves. As Stedward puts it, 'it is around the issue of lifelong learning that we see [n the UK] the real interface of interest between the departments of industry and education', while 'much of the New Labour model of the 'learning society' is predicated on individual motivation' (2003, p.144).

The place of e-learning in the ESE is more than somewhat ambiguous, with several distinct strands leading in different directions and with different drivers (see Robertson and Dale, forthcoming). On the one hand, the use of ICT can be seen as a considerable boost to 'transversal' projects such as Comenius, with, for instance the development of the European Schoolnet. On the other hand, it is clearly seen in some documents as offering a substantial boost to the possibilities of lifelong learning in the sense outlined above and as crucial to the development of the Knowledge Economy. Discussions of the value of e-learning, and its potential contribution to a conception of European citizenship are at least as likely to be found in the area of the DG for the Information Society as they are in the publications emanating from DG12. Beyond this, one of the main areas of potential seen for e-learning, that of making possible a future of 'customised, 'just for me' educational provision represents in many ways the antithesis of education for citizenship. In the UK policies for e-learning and the use of ICT in education, we see not just a focus on UK competitiveness versus other countries in Europe as well as across the world, but an explicit emphasis on the provision of computer hardware and software as offering major opportunities for 'our' computer industry as well as 'our' children.[3]

Finally, in some European documents, competencies are coming to play a very prominent role. As one of the Lisbon follow-up documents puts it, 'Key competencies represent a package of knowledge, skills and attitudes which all individuals need for employment, inclusion, subsequent learning as well as personal fulfilment and development. These competencies should be acquired by the end of compulsory schooling. They are a prerequisite for participation in lifelong learning. Research demonstrates in fact that participation in lifelong learning is closely linked to successful participation in previous education' (CEC, 2003b, 15). Further, the competencies are sometimes quite directly associated with citizenship. Thus, the Foreword to a Eurydice Survey of Key Competencies states that '(Against the background of the detailed work programme on the future objectives of Education and training systems up to 2010) it was considered necessary to identify a *common European perception* of the definition and selection of *competencies* that all *citizens* should acquire' (Eurydice 2002, p.3, emphases added). The Eurydice report is based on a survey of all EU countries of 'whether and how the concept of 'key competence' was defined, how they were reflected in the curriculum, and assessed' (ibid).

However, the report does contain an element of agenda amplification when it moves to discuss developments at international level. In this section we are told that 'many countries reported that their approach to curricular design and their regard for key competencies have been influenced by developments at EU and international levels' (p.23). It alludes to the eight principal dimensions of key competencies published in the detailed work programme, before going on to point out that many other EU policy areas were concerned with identifying key competencies, and that 'As a result of the close relationship between education and training, and employment, action in the area of key compe-tencies is an integral part of both European cooperation in education and training and he Community employment programme' (p.24). Not much that is new or surprising here, then, in the light of the arguments we have been making in this section.

What we conclude from these discussions of the 'Learning' component of the ELC is essentially twofold. On the one hand, the terrain of the ESE shaped by Lisbon quite severely constrains the possibilities for the development of the kinds of 'citizenship learning' not associated with economic citizenship. On the other hand, the kinds of initiatives introduced within that confined terrain themselves appear to be at least as likely to reinforce the development of a conception of economic citizenship as to challenge or extend it in a more 'social', or 'civic' direction.

The UK response to Lisbon and the possibility of the ELC

We have concentrated so far on relatively indirect aspects of the UK response to Lisbon in terms of its implications for the ELC. In this final section, we will focus on some more direct responses on the part of the British government. The most direct response comes from the Minister of State for Lifelong Learning,

Further and Higher Education at the Department for Education and Skills (Alan Johnson), who told a House of Commons Select Committee 'scrutinising' the Commission interim report (CEC 2003d), 'the Government is fully committed to the priorities set by the Lisbon Council. It has already taken action to achieve them, including the new strategies for higher education, skills and training and changes to the curriculum for 14-19 year olds'.[4] Our focus here will be on the new proposals for the education of 14-19 year olds, since it is there that we may find the most direct association with the preparation of ELCs, and that least confined a priori to economic citizenship.

It is not possible here to go into those proposals in any depth, but nor, unfortunately, is it necessary to do so, since they have so little to say that has any bearing on the idea of the ELC at all—and that, of course, is in itself the most significant message of the proposals in this context. So, we will pick up just two of the more obvious features of the report in this context, before concluding with an assessment of what it may mean for the main arguments of this chapter.

First, despite the Minister's avowals, the word 'Lisbon' never appears in the text, nor is it easy to discern any connotations of it. There is no sense at all that there may be a European agenda that may have been taken into account. Indeed, it is interesting that following much speculation that what the report would recommend would be a form of 'British baccalaureate'[5] the report explicitly rejects the baccalaureate as a model for the diploma framework that it proposes. The clearest references to EU members in the text are to France and Germany as benchmarks on international indicators. And this also reminds us that, almost emblematically, the UK has to be excluded from any EU indicators that refer to 'upper secondary education' since there is an unresolved dispute between the UK and the EU over the status of the GCSE qualification, which the UK insists is at 'upper secondary' level, a claim that the EU rejects.

Second, while heretofore the UK has appeared in compilations of educational statistics in Member States as requiring *all* students to learn a foreign language up to the age of 16, the 14-19 report does nothing to take any distance from the slightly earlier decision to remove compulsory status from foreign languages in the 14-16 curriculum.[6] This response typifies the focus of the whole document. It is driven essentially by local UK concerns MORE (Contrast also helps us see more of nature of EU intervention).

While the UK response to Lisbon may appear to be extreme in its explicit neglect, it may not be so far from the mainstream, at least formally, as may appear from the comments we have just made. That is to say, we may infer from the differences between the 'Euro enthusiasm' of the Commission's draft contribution to the Report to the Spring Council and the rather more reserved position taken by the Ministers, with the Council's clear watering-down of the assertion of the need for action at a European level, that while no one is 'against' Lisbon in general, no one, and certainly not the more powerful countries, is positively 'for' it as a guide to their own national policies in education. This position may be especially strongly held in the UK—the example of the 'downgrading' of modern foreign languages in particular appears to be a display of indifference towards the demands and expectations of not just 'Lisbon' but 'Europe' and 'European citizenship'.

On the other hand, the 14-19 document does contain a number of 'silent coincidences' that do chime very well with some of the elements we have focussed on above. This is clearly the case with the economic assumptions of the document, but it is not confined to that. The knowledge, skills and attributes that the report seeks to encourage are to be achieved through three dimensions – *'the reflective and effective individual learner'* (e.g. skills such as problem solving, independent learning and the attribute of personal persistence); *'the social learner'* (e.g. interpersonal and teamwork skills and the ability to empathise) and *'the learner in society and the wider world'* (e.g. the development of active citizenship and international awareness)' (p.26). These reflect the objectives for education and training, as in the case of e-learning (ICT is one of three subjects suggested for the compulsory core of the proposed diploma, along with 'communications' and mathematical skills; 'ICT skills are central to many aspects of modern life. Their place must be assured within 14-19 programmes.' (p.25)). There are a number of equivalents to some of the Eurydice competences; they are not referred to by that label, but have clear affinities of content and purpose, such as 'acquir(ing) and demonstrate(ing) a range of research, planning, analytical, critical and presentational skills required in employment and higher education. develop(ing) a range of knowledge, skills and attributes, such as self-awareness, self-management, working with others, *international awareness* and personal and interpersonal skills; participat(ing) in wider activities based on personal interest, contribution to the community as active citizens, and experience of employment.' (p.7. Emphasis added). Once again, however, we should note that 'international awareness' has rather different connotations from the kinds of European citizenship sought by the EC; it connotes 'learning about Europe' rather than becoming a citizen of, or even in, Europe.

Finally, there is explicit recognition of the importance of education for citizenship. Though it is not a compulsory part of the National Curriculum, as we have seen the Tomlinson report recommended that it should be part of the core of the Diploma which it is proposing should be the basic framework of 14-19 education. However, when we examine what is involved and included in the national Curriculum for Citizenship, it becomes evident that (a) 'Europe' occupies a fairly small space in the subject and (b), that while it is clearly intended that it be taken seriously it is still very much in the 'learning about Europe' paradigm, in ways that might contribute to the Council's idea of learning to be a European Citizen rather than to the Commission's idea of a European citizen.[7]

Conclusion

We have attempted in this chapter to consider the UK's relationship to, and response to, the idea of the European Learning Citizen. We have sought to do so recognising the UK's tendency to 'resist' European initiatives but seeking to ground the argument at a more structural level than the trivia and banalities that sadly typify, and are called in to explain, the UK's Euroscepticism.

We therefore began at the European level and attempted to indicate how the construction of the European Space for Education in response to the Lisbon Declaration created that space as a terrain that was hospitable only to economic conceptions of citizenship. This was largely the result of the emphasis on education as a part of a social policy regime that was to be 'productive', that is, supportive of economic development rather than seeking to redistribute its benefits or to mitigate its worst effects, as in more traditional conceptions of social policy (in which conceptions of citizenship were consequently rather broader that the economic).

We then argued that in terms of each of the three components of the ELC, the UK demonstrated greater distance from the concept than other MS. In terms of 'Europe' it was likely to see globalisation as a more positive and Europe as a more negative challenge. In terms of citizenship, we argued that particularly as a result of its shared model of capitalism and continuing close relationship with the USA, including in matters of social policy, it was more inclined than other MS to the more 'neo-liberal' versions of productive social policy, with their correspondingly narrower and thinner conceptions of even economic citizenship. In terms of learning, while acknowledging the lip service paid to the Lisbon objectives, we pointed to an apparent total indifference to any idea of an ELC, exemplified in the decision to make the learning of foreign languages non-compulsory, at a time when the European dimension of education was being seen as requiring the learning of at least two other European languages.

Finally, we considered the UK agenda for citizenship education and found that while it did pay more than lip service to the importance of Europe, the tone and emphasis were on learning about Europe rather than learning to be European. We conclude that for a range of significant structural reasons, as well as for banal attitudinal reasons, the UK will continue to be a reluctant and slow adherent to the idea of European Learning Citizenship.

Notes

1. This form, rather than the more usual 'European Education Space' is adopted to avoid acronymic confusion with the European Employment Strategy (EES) to which reference will be made below, and which is awarded acronymic priority on the basis of the duration and status of its usage within the EU.

2. However, the draft of the joint report prepared by the *Commission* goes on to suggest that initiatives at national level may suffer from lack of coordination and effectiveness and to propose that 'The definition by 2005 of a Community reference regarding a profile of European knowledge and competences to be acquired by pupils should make it possible to support and facilitate national action in this area, both on the legislative front and in terms of the production of appropriate materials and instruments' (CEC 2003d, p.15). The apparent rejection of this claim to 'European competence' by the Council appears to reflect a lower level of enthusiasm for the European level among Ministers than within the Commission.

3. As Tony Blair put it in the final paragraph of his Foreword to the government's major policy statement about ICT and education (DfEE, 1997) 'this strategy [the National Grid for Learning] will be good for our children and our companies.'

4. House of Commons Select Committee on European Scrutiny Second Report, 'European Education and Training Objectives; Commission Communication Education and Training 2010.' (25064) 14358/03COM 003) 685. para 8.9

5. The Minister for School Standards, David Miliband, had been an early supporter of the idea of a British baccalaureate, and after the commissioning of the Tomlinson report was still explicitly referring to 'baccalaureate-style qualifications' as a possible model for 14-19 reform in England. See 'Excellence and Opportunity from 14-19'—Speech by David Miliband to AOC/NAHT/SHA Conference London 21 January 2003.

6. From 2002 students were permitted to 'disapply' from the requirement to take a modern foreign language at Key Stage 4 (end of compulsory schooling) under particular conditions; from 2003 they were allowed to 'disapply' under any conditions, and in 2004 Modern Foreign Languages will no longer be a compulsory subject and hence no 'disapplication' will be necessary. See Qualifications and Curriculum Authority 'Disapplication of the national curriculum subjects at KS4' http://www.qca.org.uk/14-19/11-16-schools/index_s3-4-disapplication.htm Downloaded 3/4/04

7. The best example we have found about how 'Europe' is taught under the category of citizenship is found in a 'model' unit for KS4 citizenship. The unit is one of twelve making up the scheme of work. See http://www.standards.dfes.gov.uk/schemes2/ks4citizenship/cit11/11q1?view=get

References

Annesley, C. (2003) 'Americanised and Europeanised: UK social policy since 1997.' *British Journal of Politics and International Relations*, Vol.5(2), pp.143-65

Commission of the European Communities (1997) 'Proposal for Guidelines for Member States Employment Policies.' COM (97)102

Commission of the European Communities (2003a) 'The Cost of non-social policies.' Memo to Conference on the Mid-term Review of the Social Policy Agenda. 19-20 March, Brussels. http://europa.eu.int/comm/employment_social/news/2003/jan/costofnonsocialpolicy_en.pdf

Commission of the European Communities (2003b) 'Implementation of the 'Education and Training 2010' programme.' Commission staff Working Document. SEC (2003) 1250

Commission of the European Communities (2003c) 'Investing wisely in education and training: an imperative for Europe' Communication from the Commission.' COM (2003) 779 [final].

Commission of the European Communities (2003d) 'Education and Training 2010': the success of the Lisbon Strategy hinges on urgent reforms.' Communication from the Commission COM (2003) 685 [final].

CEC (2004) 'Progress towards the Common Objectives in Education and Training: Indicators and Benchmarks'. Commission Staff Working Paper SEC (2004) 73.

Council of the European Union (2004) 'Education and Training 2010: the success of the Lisbon Strategy hinges on urgent reforms' 5648/04 EDUC 14.

Daguerre, A. & Taylor-Gooby, P. (2004) 'Neglecting Europe: explaining the predominance of American ideas in New Labour's welfare policies since 1997.' *Journal of European Social Policy*, Vol.14(1), pp.25-39.

Dale, R. (2003) 'The Lisbon Declaration, the reconceptualisation of governance and the reconfiguration of European Educational Space'. Paper presented to RAPPE seminar, *Governance, Regulation and Equity in European Education Systems*, Institute of Education, London University 20 March.

Dale, R. (2004) 'Forms of governance, governmentality and the EU's Open Method of Coordination.' In W. Larner & W. Walters (eds) *Global Governmentality*. London: Routledge.

Department for Education and Employment (1997) 'Connecting the Learning Society, National Grid for Learning: the Government's Consultation Paper.' London: Department for Education and Employment

Department for Education and Skills (2004) *14-19 Curriculum and Qualifications Reform. Interim Report of the Working Group on 14-19 Reform* ('The Tomlinson Report'). February.

DiMaggio, P. & Powell, W.W. (1983) 'The Iron Cage revisited: institutional isomorphism and collective rationality in organizational fields'. *American Sociological Review*, Vol.48(2), pp.147-160.

Eurydice Education Unit (2002) *Key Competencies: A Developing Concept in General Compulsory Education*. Brussels: Eurydice

Haahr, J. H. (2004) 'Open Coordination as advanced liberal government'. Special Issue on OMC, *Journal of European Public Policy*, Vol.11(2), pp.209-230.

Hay, C. & Rosamund, B. (2002) 'Globalization, European integration and the discursive construction of economic imperatives'. *Journal of European Public Policy*, Vol.9(2), pp. 147-168.

Jacobsson, K (2004) 'A European politics for employability: the political discourse on employability of the EU and the OECD.' In C. Garsten & K. Jacobsson (eds) *Learning to be Employable: New Agendas on Work, Responsibility and Learning in a Globalizing World*. London: Palgrave.

Levitas, R. (1998) *The Inclusive Society? Social Exclusion and New Labour*. Basingstoke: Macmillan

Maurice, M.; Sellier, F. & Silverstre, J-J. (1986) *The Social Foundations of Industrial Power*. Cambridge: MIT Press.

Noaksson, N. & Jacobsson, K. (2003) 'The Production of Ideas and Expert Knowledge in OECD: The OECD Jobs Strategy in contrast with the EU employment strategy.' *Score Report* 2003:7, Stockholm University.

Pagani, F. (2002) *Peer Pressure: A Tool for Co-operation and Change. An Analysis of an OECD Working Model*. Paris: OECD.

Palier, B. (2004) 'Social protection reforms in Europe: strategies for a new model.' Canadian

Policy Research Networks Social Architecture Papers: Research Report F/37 Family Network. January.

Pochet, P. (2002) 'From Subsidiarity to the Open Method of Coordination in Social Policy Issues'. *www.uni-bamberg.de/sowi/europastudien/dokumente/pochet.doc* 9/12/02.

Radaelli, C. (2003) 'The Open Method of Coordination—A New Governance Architecture for the European Union.' Research Report, Swedish Institute for European Policy Studies.

Robertson, S. & Dale, R. (forthcoming) 'ICT as medium, target, benchmark and outcome for Learning Europe/Schooling the Future.' In J-L. Arostegui (coord) *Globalazicion e Educacion*.

Rosamund, B. (2002) 'Imagining the european economy: 'competitiveness' and the social construction of 'Europe' as an Economic Space.' *New Political Economy* Vol.7(2), pp. 157-177.

Serrano Pascual, A. (2000) 'European strategies to fight youth unemployment: a comparative analysis and critical assessment.' In A. Serrano Pascual (ed.) *Tackling Youth Unemployment in Europe*. Brussels: ETUI, pp.17-28.

Shavit, Y. & Muller, W. (eds) (1998) *From School to Work: a Comparative Study of Educational Qualifications and Occupational Destinations*. Oxford: Oxford University Press.

Stedward, G. (2003) 'Education as industrial policy: New Labour's marriage of the social and the economic'. *Policy and Politics*, Vol.31(2), pp.139-52.

Streeck, W. (1999) 'Competitive Solidarity: Rethinking the 'European Social Model'.' Presidential Address, 11th Meeting on Socio-Economics, Society for the Advancement of Socio-Economics (SASE), June 8-11, Madison, Wisconsin.

CHAPTER THREE

Danish Learning Traditions in the Context of the European Union

PALLE RASMUSSEN

Introduction

The European Union is a paradoxical construct. Throughout its existence it has built on an uneasy mix of economic and political functions and strategies. Although it was conceived partly as a way of overcoming inter-nation tensions and securing peace, the emphasis was for many years on the economic collaboration and the benefits of market integration. Although governments and administrations of the member countries were involved more and more in collaboration and decision-making, much of this work was and is still regarded as a redistribution game, where individual countries and their trades and institutions try to get a little more than their 'own' share of the pooled resources. Even after it chose to call itself a 'union' instead of a 'market', the EU has continued to be held together and legitimated mainly by the medium of money.

But this is changing. For the last decade the EU has definitely been moving towards a stronger political identity, closer coordination in all policy areas and a higher level of cultural commonality. There are many reasons for this, and I will not try to analyse them here. The break-up of the Soviet Union and the uneasiness in many European countries about a political world order dominated by the USA are certainly important factors, but so are processes of social and cultural modernisation that manifest themselves in most European countries. Where the present developments of the EU will lead is by no means certain; conflicts between the major players surface from time to time, and the ambitious project of expansion may loose its support among the old members. But the present trend is that EU legislation and discourse influences and interacts increasingly with day-to-day decisions and debates in the member states. This is quite evident in the area of education.

National systems, policies and practices of education are shaped by many factors; but they often have a distinctive character reflecting the specific pattern of cultural elements in the individual nation. For instance English education reflects a specific kind of liberalism while French education reflects a specific kind of republicanism (Osborn et al., 2003). When the EU tries to develop and implement union-wide educational strategies, these become a forum for interaction between different concepts of education. The EU policy texts draw on, combine and filter educational discourses that have different meanings and standings in the individual nations; and in turn the EU policies re-introduce the resultant discourses in the different national educational contexts.

The topic of this paper is the interaction of EU strategies with the national educational context in Denmark. I shall focus especially on the area of adult education and learning. Following the introduction I sketch out the roots and development of the Danish EU membership. In the following two sections I present some main characteristics of adult education traditions in Denmark and their evolution in a modernising society. This society is increasingly influenced by the EU, and in the two following sections I turn to EU policies on lifelong learning and their implications for citizenship. I then return to Danish adult education, outline the most recent reform and discuss its relationship to EU policy. Finally I summarise the impact of EU learning discourse on Danish adult education traditions and discuss the prospects of these traditions.

Denmark and the Union

Denmark became a member of the EC in 1972 and has participated in the evolution of this organisation towards the EU (Branner and Kelstrup, 2000). The decision to join the 'common market' was a major new step in Danish politics. In the first half of the 20th Century Denmark had pursued political neutrality and economic independence. The country stayed neutral during the First World War and tried to do the same during the thirties, when Europe was clearly moving towards war. However, Denmark was occupied by Germany, and although the occupation was less oppressive than in many other countries, it demonstrated to many the futility of political neutrality. Two alternatives seemed to present themselves in the post-war years. One possibility was strengthening the links between the Nordic countries, which shared many historical and cultural roots, and whose languages (except for Finnish) were closely related. A Nordic Union was actually proposed and seriously debated (Nordic Council 2003). The other possibility was to join a Western military alliance in the form of NATO and engage in social and economic collaboration with the countries of Western Europe. In the end, the Nordic countries chose different paths. Denmark joined NATO along with Norway, while Sweden and Finland opted for neutrality and self-reliance. Nordic collaboration came to focus on cultural and educational issues, and significant initiatives were in fact developed; but without the economic and political dimension the perspectives were limited.

As the prospect of Nordic collaboration lost credibility, it became more inviting for Denmark to join the emerging European Economic Community, formalised in the Treaty of Rome in 1957. This came to be supported by the major political parties, but there was widespread popular opposition both in the liberal and the social democratic camps. Denmark actually applied for membership in 1961 together with the UK, but this was blocked by French opposition. After renewed negotiations both countries were admitted in 1973. In Denmark the decision to join the EC was confirmed by a referendum. Both voting patterns and public debate showed that the positive motives were mainly based on expectations of economic gains (not least for agriculture, because of the generous subsidies for farming), while there was still widespread opposition to closer political and cultural cooperation.

This pattern has manifested itself again and again during the last three decades (cf. Togeby et al., 2002). Initiatives to strengthen the political side of European cooperation have met persistent popular opposition in Denmark, which was made evident when the Maastrict treaty of 1992 was rejected (narrowly) in a referendum. The opposition has also influenced official Danish policy towards the EU, which has emphasised strong national control of participation in EU negotiations and policies. Over time Denmark has also been one of the strongest opponents to extending European collaboration into new areas like education. Denmark also declined the use of the Euro as currency. Support for the EU is mainly found around the middle of the political spectrum, while opposition is strong on the anti-capitalist left and the nationalist right. Support is strongest in the well-educated segments of the population. And support is much stronger among members of parliament than among the voters (Flockhart, 2003).

While political attitudes have changed only slowly, integration in the EU has proceeded on the administrative level. The processes of implementing a rising number of EU agreements and standards in national legislation as well as the negotiation of new EU policies mean that at rising number of administrators in all Danish ministries are in continuous contact with EU administrators. The processes of applying for and administrating different types of EU funding mean that a wide range of public institutions also interact with the EU (cf. Halkier, 1998). This is clearly the case in education and research, where many types of funding are available through direct application to the EU. An explicit aim of the educational programmes is to promote contact and mutual understanding between partners across borders; but they also promote interaction with the EU administrative apparatus.

In sum, it can be said that the Danish elites generally support the EU and the initiatives to strengthen it (Hedetoft, 2000). Much of the political debate on EU membership during the last decade (since the Maastrict referendum) can be seen as a process where the elites try in different ways to convince the citizens that EU membership is a simple necessity. In current debates proponents of the EU often argue that the Danish economy (the basis of welfare policies) is far too vulnerable without European cooperation, and that the EU provides protection against the ills of globalisation and US dominance. Opponents continue to see the EU as a threat to national independence and identity, and also as a wasteful bureaucracy.

Concepts of learning in Danish culture

In the controversies surrounding Danish EU membership education has often been an important theme. This reflects the fact that educational ideas and values, especially related to adult education, have been an important aspect of Danish culture and identity. During the late nineteenth and early twentieth century a tradition of popular adult education was developed both in theory and practice. The main example of this is the educational model of the folk high schools, proposed by Nikolaj Grundtvig from around 1830 and taken further by Christen Kold. The folk high schools comprised an educational initiative from below, rooted in one particular class, the farmers. The educational model was formulated in a situation where the farmers increasingly became manifest and self-conscious as the central group of population who ensured the economic and social basis of society by means of their work and their ability to organise production (Olesen and Rasmussen, 1996).

The educational philosophy of the folk high schools contained a unique combination of elements (Grundtvig, 1976; Warren 1987). While the high schools were to enhance young people's commitment to and competence in developing agriculture, the teaching mainly consisted in general and cultural subjects such as history, Nordic mythology, literature and biblical history. Although the schools were to be independent of the state, to a high degree the purpose was to boost national culture and consciousness. Christianity was part of the ideological basis but in a more open and joyous version than mainstream Protestantism. Grundtvig was highly critical of the established academic educational tradition which, in his opinion, was characterised by written learning with no roots in the lives, culture and tradition of ordinary Danes (at the time Latin still played an important role in the school system and German was widely used in public administration). Teaching was to be based on 'the living word', i.e. oral narration and discussion. It was to take place in the native tongue and to be based on Danish culture and literature. There were not to be any examinations and the students were to live-in at the schools so that they shared not only learning but also everyday life and its practical activities.

The folk high school idea achieved great impact and became a kind of social movement with Christian Kold as the central figure. The impact was not only due to the close links with the class of farmers, but also due to a widespread sense of national purpose following defeat in a war against Prussia in 1864. The theory and practice of the folk high schools also had strong influence on Danish educational tradition, not only in the area of adult education but also, for example, in basic school education and teacher training. This was an educational ideal that was anti-elitist and liberal, that emphasised oral presentation and dialogue, and that linked education to national and local rather than international culture.

This educational ideal also influenced the liberal evening school, which was institutionalised in a unique way in the nineteen forties. A scheme was adopted which allowed and supported teaching by voluntary associations linked to different ideologies and movements. The basic idea was that when a number of people assemble with a teacher and a programme or a subject, they are entitled to support from public funds. All the main political parties have had their own educational associations offering evening courses in both practical subjects (like housekeeping), general subjects (like languages) and ideological issues. In continuation of the folk high school these evening schools had no sharp distinction between cultural and vocational rationality. The existence of this tradition also meant that when adult education was made part of welfare and labour market policies it retained a strong humanistic dimension.

There are, however, also other notions of adult learning in Danish education (cf. OECD 2001; Olesen and Rasmussen, 1976). One strong current has been connected to vocational training. This was developed early in the twentieth century and institutionalised during the nineteen fifties through an Act on the training of semi-skilled workers. In the beginning its objective was only to contribute to the migration of labour that was both part of, and a prerequisite for, industrialisation. The training programmes were the responsibility of the Ministry of Labour Affairs, and the partners of the labour market—trade unions and employers' associations—were strongly represented in the management of both the schools and the training programmes. The labour market training system reflected the strong element of corporatism in Danish industrial relations. It gave influence to the trade unions and it provided standardised qualifications seen as important for workers' mobility and self-esteem. But the basic pedagogical idea in this vocationally oriented education system is mimetic: to imitate and to adapt the participants to the present labour market and to the qualitative character of working life. This, of course, does contain an element of workers' culture to the extent that workers' culture is reproduced in work, but the political and cultural sides of the education are subordinated a functional objective.

These concepts of learning have contributed to shaping the educational policies and institutions of the Danish version of the welfare state. As a result policies and institutions have often

- Promoted the social and personal dimensions of learning as well as the cognitive and instrumental;
- Recognized the right of citizens to participate in education throughout the life course, and the obligation of the state to support this;
- Perceived participation in education as a contribution to social equality, and attempted to provide free education for all;
- Linked public education systems with collective actors outside the systems, like labour market partners or social movements.

It should be noted, however, that the educational ideas presented here do not constitute a coherent educational tradition; rather they constitute an educational mainstream with internal tensions. There is a strong collective element, both in relation to social partnership in labour relations; but there is also an emphasis on individual freedom vis-à-vis state authority. There is a progressive emphasis on the social and personal dimensions of learning, but also an instrumentalist notion of education as a resource that can be appropriated and exploited. These tensions have become more visible as Danish education has confronted the conditions of modernisation and internationalisation.

Modernization, learning and the citizen

Embedded in policies and practises, the ideas of learning connected with the folk high school and vocational training have led a long life and still have considerable vitality. But since they were introduced, the social and cultural foundation of education has changed profoundly. Like other societies of Western Europe, Danish society and the everyday life of citizens has been transformed through the long-term processes of modernisation.

From the turn of the nineteenth century and for considerable time thereafter, the dominant trend in Danish society could be described as a process of evolution from an agricultural to an industrial society. Up to the sixties, the process of modernisation mainly took the form of extensive industrialisation accompanied by continued geographical and social movement of population from farming to the towns and cities and to urban occupations. Industrialisation was partly based on natural resources (like the cement industry), partly on products from agriculture and fishing, and partly on special skills and innovatory contexts (like medical equipment). Industry developed both in the main towns, but also in other areas due to the availability of raw materials and labour. Denmark changed from a mainly agricultural society, but industry never came to dominate in the same way. At least from the sixties, industry and service trades co-existed, with growth in the service sector picking up speed.

The same happened in other countries, and social scientists tried to express the new prevailing trend through such concepts as 'the post-industrial society' and 'the service society'. Recently the term 'knowledge society' has found widespread use (Rasmussen, 2004)—a term that points to the increasing importance of knowledge, learning, and qualifications. The development and dissemination of new information and communication technologies contributes to this trend by enabling an extensive rationalisation of management, supervision, and information dissemination in the private sector and in all other areas of society. Businesses, public authorities, and people in general have access to far more information than previously; but people are also required to process information on a continual basis, and this creates new social disparities that weaken and displace the class-based forms of living that had been the political and cultural basis for the traditional Danish forms of adult education.

For lifelong learning in Denmark the two most important consequences of modernisation have been (1) the institutionalisation of adult education and (2) changes in the educational motivation of adult citizens.

Institutionalisation means that a system of adult education is developed. The concept of systems differentiation captures some of the logic of this. In discussing the causes for the differentiation of education as an autonomous system, Luhmann (2002) argues that the interaction in learning and teaching settings need a system to frame them. Educational interaction demands that some decisions are made outside the setting itself, otherwise interaction will be too unstable and there will be nothing to check an inherently growing demand for educational interaction. This is a very fundamental point, and it should be supplemented with arguments at other levels, like the drive towards internal coordination of public polities. As a result of such forces, Danish educational authorities have since the eighties invested considerable political and administrative effort creating an adult education system that can coordinate the various adult education programmes and connect adult education to rest of the educational system. Gradually administrative standardization has been introduced and attempts have been made to clarify the premises for public spending on adult education. The recently introduced system of continuing adult education, which I shall discuss further below, is a clear example of this ongoing institutionalisation.

A driving force behind institutionalisation has been a strong growth in educational activities in response to increased demands for adult education in the adult population. These demands are an expression of changes in educational motivation (Rasmussen, 1996; Illeris, 2003). The two main strands of Danish adult education have traditionally drawn on two different types of motivation. Liberal adult education (like the evening school) has addressed people's needs for productive activities, knowledge and personal development. Continuing vocational education (like the labour market training centres) has met people's job-related needs for better qualifications and skills. Nowadays, however, the predominant form of educational motivation found in the adult population no longer confines itself to one of these two categories. Modern educational motivation is individualised. The point of gaining an education is to change a person's situation and opportunities primarily by acquiring qualifications of use in the labour market. This kind of educational motivation connects personal development with career strategies, and accepts the necessity of acquiring through individual study outside working hours.

The emergence of this new type of motivation is linked to changes brought about by modernisation. Ziehe (1991) argues that the everyday knowledge of modern individuals is characterised by both cognitive inclusion (as traditional boundaries are eroded) and cognitive exclusion (because traditional reference points for envisaging life courses and occupational identities are less readily available). People have access to a multitude of everyday realities, and the spectrum of knowledge, signs and experiences has been greatly expanded compared to earlier generations. For this reason it is more difficult for individuals to develop coherent and stable identities. People are receptive to the many different themes being offered in public communication. Cultural events, environmental risks, ethical issues are among the themes that attract attention and feed the individual's reflection on his or her life perspectives (cf. Beck et al., 1994).

For this kind of individual reflection education and learning is also an attractive theme, which offers both a choice between different occupational identities, a vision of individual competence and a promise of a career. Modern discourses on lifelong learning reflect in many ways this blend of value-oriented and instrumental motives in individuals.

Under the conditions of modernisation Danish educational traditions face serious challenges as the social basis and the cultural significance of learning undergo rapid change. Danish traditions in adult learning have been closely connected to different types of collective actors and identities, for instance in local rural communities, in social movements and in labour market organisations. Today such collective actors have a less prominent role, and new types of identity and solidarity are emerging in modern societies. A trivial but nevertheless telling example is the fact that the folk high school tradition strongly emphasised the Danish language as an expression of popular experience and national identity, while modern young Danes embrace American culture and enthusiastically speak English whenever they have the opportunity. This does not mean that educational traditions and their cultural roots are now irrelevant and should be abandoned. The social and personal aspects of learning, the right to adult education and educational equality are still important values, but they need to be reinterpreted and reaffirmed. As argued by Habermas (inter alia, 1995), open and democratic communication with inclusion of all relevant partners offers a potential way to undertake this.

Lifelong learning EU-style

The European Union also takes an interest in the development of lifelong learning systems and the mobilisation of learners. However, this is a recent development. For most of its existence the EU did not interfere much at all with educational policies. This issue was clearly not covered by the EC treaties, and many member states—including Denmark—were strongly opposed to any attempt at cross-national coordination of policies. There were some cautious initiatives during the seventies (notably the idea of a 'European dimension' in the school curriculum), but the main educational impact of the EU was in two areas not directly related to educational structures or curricula: EU-funded exchange and development schemes in education and mutual recognition of educational qualifications. The EU-funded programmes in higher and vocational education undoubtedly increased the professional and cultural opportunities of students and teachers; but they also helped promote the EU as a beneficial agent in education and underlined the need for cross-national structures and procedures. The initiatives towards mutual recognition of qualification were argued for by referring to the right of graduates to seek employment anywhere in the common market of the EU. They were launched as practical measures, expressly not aimed at harmonising educational structures. It is interesting to note that in recent years the same kind of argument has in fact been expanded to include educational structures: the Bologna agreements stipulate that bachelor degrees are a precondition for studying at the master level, and that bachelor degrees demand no less than three years of study.

Since the middle of the nineties the EU has increasingly tried to develop common educational policies. This is a logical development given the movement towards a more politically defined union, which also means that EU bodies (especially the Commission) has a more valid legal basis for initiatives in education. Also members of the professional staff of the EU are now in a position to play a more active role in policymaking, a role for which they have undoubtedly been socialised by working in the international environment of the EU headquarters.

An explicit basis for educational cooperation within the EU was first introduced in the Maastrict Treaty (1993). Today EU policies in this area rest mainly on two articles in the Nice Treaty (2002), these being article 149 (on education and youth) and article 150 (on vocational education). At the Lisbon meeting in 2000, the EU heads of state set up two general aims to be realized within ten years. The EU should be developed into the most competitive and dynamic knowledge-based economy in the world, and growth should be sustainable, creating new and better jobs and social cohesion. In order to realize these aims the heads of state called for ambitious reforms, among them a programme of modernising the educational systems. This led a work programme entitled 'Education and Training 2010', which fixed three strategic objectives:

- Increasing the quality and effectiveness of education and training systems in the European Union
- Facilitating the access of all to the education and training systems
- Opening up education and training systems to the wider world

Through the realisation of these objectives European education and training systems are to contribute to the success of the Lisbon strategy (cf. Council of the European Union and Commission of the European Union, 2004). The work is based on the 'open method coordination', which briefly stated means that action at the EU level focuses on definition of common objectives and standards, and on the development of indicators and data that make it possible to assess the educational systems and results of the member countries. The question of adjusting policies and practices in order to meet the common objectives is in principle left to the member countries, but they can cooperate on the development of policy tools.

Promotion of lifelong learning is a key element in EU educational policy (Council of European Union, 2002). It is significant that in the presentation of the three strategic objectives cited above, the EU Ministers of Education added that 'in particular the high priority given to learning at all stages of life will imply a demand for adequate resources' (Council of European Union, 2001).

The theme of lifelong learning had been developed alongside the general development of EU educational policy. In the November 2000 the European Commission published a memorandum on lifelong learning and invited comments from the member states. A year later, following the consultation, the Commission brought out a document entitled 'Making a European area of lifelong learning a reality'. In the summer of 2002 the European Council also adopted a resolution on lifelong learning, in which general objectives were stated, contributions from different branches of the EU apparatus were acknowledged and the division of labour between the EU and the member states was laid out. A survey of national initiatives to implement lifelong learning in the EU member states (Cedefop and Eurydice, 2001) showed that many initiatives taken in different European countries were largely in agreement with the principles laid out in the EU memorandum on lifelong learning. But on the other hand, 'largely' means that the initiatives do not precisely follow or refer to the EU recommendations—which would indeed be difficult, as these recommendations are not very precise or specific. It remains to be seen whether the ongoing process of developing and benchmarking common objectives will change this.

There is good reason to be sceptical about the open method of coordination. Some of its elements (the idea of clear objectives and benchmarking) reflect a rationalistic approach that has often been seen to fail in evaluation research. But the policy documents that are produced in the process, as well as the networks of administrators and experts involved, may in themselves be important results. The growing pile of EU documents on lifelong learning contains a number of characteristic features. Some of the points emphasised in the documents are:

- linking lifelong learning to the needs of the knowledge-based economy and society;
- emphasizing the necessity of new basic skills (like IT skills, foreign languages and social skills) to live and work in the knowledge society;
- securing access to learning throughout the life course;
- recognition of adults' non-formal learning and qualifications;
- the use of ICT in lifelong learning;
- the role of lifelong learning in the strengthening of citizenship, democracy and intercultural understanding.

The main effect of all this work may not be to develop and implement specific policies, but rather to summarise trends already visible in the developed Western societies and to legitimise these trends in the EU and its member states. This also means connecting lifelong learning to the idea of European citizenship.

Learning and European citizenship

The promotion of citizenship is an important element in the policy of lifelong learning being developed by the EU. 'Active citizenship' is generally listed as one of the good things that education and learning will bring about, others being social cohesion, personal and professional fulfilment, adaptability and employability (Council of European Union, 2002). This raises an important question: if lifelong learning, as developed and mediated by the EU, is used to 'activate' citizenship, how will it then influence the character of citizenship?

The concept of citizenship has traditionally been closely linked to national culture and identity. When asked whether a multinational citizenship was possible, Raymond Aron stated that the idea was a contradiction in terms; multinational entities would never be able to take over the sense of identity and responsibility that connect citizens with their nations (quoted in Wind, 2002). However, citizenship is (as Aron acknowledged) not only a question of identity, culture and moral obligation; it is also a question of rights. In both respects the social foundations of citizenship in Western Europe are today less connected to nation-states. The individualisation of modern life and the international dissemination of information and entertainment by the media lessen the distinctive character of national cultures, while the growth of individual rights based on international institutions makes individual citizens less dependent on nation-states.

The EU has played an important role in the development of international law. Since its creation, the European Court of Law has consistently maintained that rights defined in EU treaties (and accompanying legislation) apply directly to individual citizens in the member states, and that the member states are not allowed to modify or suspend these rights. In fact the European Court has often supported individual citizens against perceived unfair treatment by their nations. Originally these rights were mostly connected to the mobility of workers in the single market, but they have gradually been extended to most citizens. New aspects have also been included, like the right to equal treatment regardless of gender or ethnic origin. So as regards individual rights, EU citizenship, although limited in scope, does in fact exist (Wind, 2004). While this no doubt contributes to the erosion of national identity (Hedetoft and Hjort, 2002), its 'positive' effect is probably a reinforcement of individualism rather than the development of a European identity.

The question of European identity troubles many EU politicians, and sources for such an identity are often debated. One obvious way of improving the popular identification with the EU is to improve the interaction with individual citizens through rights, democratic influence and services. Steps in this direction have been taken, for instance in the creation of a directly elected parliament and the idea of a European constitution; but given the fundamentally bureaucratic character of the EU institutions as well as the reluctance of member states to give up their formal powers, this is a long and difficult path.

Another way of fostering EU identity is the creation and mediation of discourse in which certain qualities are ascribed to Europe or the EU. One example of this is concept of the EU as a shield against the ills of globalisation, which has been significant in recent Danish debates on the EU and which has also been encountered in other member states. This is a discourse which creates identity through defining a threatening other (the wider world, globalisation) and a beneficial collective self (Europe, the EU) to which the individual can ally himself or herself. In his analyses of policymaking in the OECD, Marcussen (2002, 2003) recounts the emergence of the discourse of globalisation in the nineties, and argues that it was originally launched in the United States as part of an attempt to divert attention from domestic problems of economic policy, and since 'exported' to international organisations. To be sure the idea of strengthening the EU to counter globalisation seems contradictory, as the EU does in fact strive to become a dominant actor in global economic competition. The point here, however, is not whether the EU does in fact alleviate or spur globalisation, but that at the cultural level this discourse attempts to install EU identity in citizens.

This kind of 'cultural struggle' is also evident in EU policy documents and debates on lifelong learning. I have mentioned some main themes in these documents above; but it should be added that they are generally characterised by a harmonising discourse. The concept of learning is wide, and includes formal, non-formal and informal learning; the potential conflicts between these forms of learning are not addressed, however, but rather glossed over through the idea of recognizing non-formal learning. The potential contribution of education and learning to social cohesion is emphasised, but virtually no reference is made to the forces undermining social cohesion, of which the struggle of social groups to secure life chances through education is surely one. The role of ICT is celebrated, but the impact of ICT on the distribution of learning opportunities is not questioned.

In spite of the harmonising trend, EU discourse should not be interpreted as a coherent system of ideas. It draws on and blends ideas and traditions from the national cultures of different member states; but the member states still exist as actors, and in many cases the interpretation of a given concept will at least partly be determined by the balance of power between member states. Take a concept like 'learning'. A recent study of schools and learners in three European societies (Osborn et al., 2003) has highlighted some of the national differences in the meanings and practises attached to this concept. While schooling in Denmark has historically emphasised the social context of learning in the form of local democratic communities and social partnerships, schooling in France has been based on a republican ideal emphasising values like universalism, rationalism and utilitarianism. While the social dimension of learning has generally been recognised in Danish education, the cognitive dimension of learning has dominated strongly in French education. It stands to reason that the power differential between member states like Denmark and France will influence the interpretation of 'learning' in EU agencies.

Through the EU policy documents on education and learning, a specific aspect is added to the idea of a European citizenship. A European citizen is pictured as a learner, not through being a student, but through being actively engaged in learning in professional contexts as well as in other areas and aspects of life. He or she moves effortlessly between informal, non-formal and formal learning and is an enthusiastic ICT user. The citizen participates in tightly-knit communities and is active in shaping individual life as well as communities and society at large. But if one looks closer, taking the perspective of the majority of Europeans, the picture of the learning citizen is distorted. The meaning of 'learning' changes from context to context and slips between the fingers like sand. Risk, conflict and impoverishment appear in communities and in individual lives.

A European citizenship containing not only individual rights, but also a significant element of collective identity is not around the corner. Still, steps are being taken to construct it. Genuinely democratic communication and influence would be a possibility but seems unlikely given the bureaucratic and elitist character of the EU. The attempts to install learning as an aspect of citizenship creates a cultural model which will not serve to include the majority of Europeans in active learning because it takes little account of the reality of learning and education in present-day European societies.

Adult education reform in Denmark

The method of open coordination pursued in EU policy-making presupposes that member states themselves govern and develop their systems and institutions of education and learning, but that they are guided by general goals and benchmarks fixed at the EU level. This raises the question of how and to what extent EU policies are present in member state educational policy. As an example of this I shall now discuss a recent comprehensive reform of adult education in Denmark and the process leading to it.

In recent years adult education has become a noticeable issue in Danish politics. This reflects the growing importance of education and qualifications in all parts of society, and also concern about the gap between well-educated youth and the older generations. In the second half of the nineties the Danish government (led by the Social Democrats) placed a reform of adult education high on the political agenda. Much preparatory work was done, but the reform proved to have complex and conflicting aims. One aim was to expand 'second chance' opportunities in general; another was to focus the adult education system more on the provision of vocational qualifications, and yet another was to check the rising costs. A reform was finally passed by parliament in the summer of 2000 (Minister of Education, 2000). It introduced a number of changes in funding and benefits, but the most important element was the creation of a new system of vocational adult education for all levels of education (Rasmussen, 2004).

The new system builds partly on a previously established system of open education, which had created the legal and financial basis for offering existing study programmes (more or less subdivided in modules) to adults on a part-time basis. In open education students pay some of the costs of study, but most of the funding is covered by the state, and courses take place outside normal working hours. The year 2000 Act upholds these principles, but creates a system of educational levels and degrees which are parallel to, but different from the ordinary system of vocational and higher education. Several reasons were given for this:

Government assessed that participation in vocational adult education, although rising, was still too limited to meet the new demands for skills and competencies. In particular, the university sector was criticised for lack of initiative in the areas of adult education and in-service training for graduates. The new system is to be an incentive for the expansion of vocational adult education.

Government also argued that many existing degrees, especially at the university level, were not very relevant to professional work in business or in public organisation. The new system allows for the creation of programmes and degrees which are not bound by existing divisions between scientific disciplines, which try to combine theory and practise, and which are better suited to recognize and accredit mature students' professional experience.

The act on continuing adult education comprises a framework for study programmes and degrees at three levels:

- Continuing adult education level (which is parallel to secondary vocational education);
- Diploma level (which is parallel to the bachelor or profession bachelor level in the ordinary system);
- Master level (which is parallel to the *candidatus* level in the ordinary system).

A certain amount of previous relevant work experience is required to enter study at a given level. The study time is smaller than in the corresponding full-time programmes because part of the competence is supposed to be provided by work experience. For instance, a master study programme normally has one year of study time (which amounts to a duration of two years on half-time basis), while entrance requires two years of previous relevant work experience and a degree at diploma or bachelor level.

The three levels are linked to the existing educational institutions. The general principle is that programmes at the first level are the responsibility of secondary vocational schools, programmes at the diploma level are the responsibility of institutions of medium-cycle higher education, and programmes at the master level are the responsibility of universities.

What is the relation of this Danish reform to EU policy on lifelong learning? The new Danish system was developed during the same years that the EU bodies were preparing the Lisbon strategy and the new initiatives in education that had been authorised from the Maastrict Treaty onwards. Many of the elements of the new system are clearly in accordance with EU recommendations, as given in, for instance, the 2000 Memorandum on Lifelong Learning. For this reason it would be logical to expect references to EU legislation as part of the legitimation of the reform. On the other hand the pronounced Danish 'euroscepticism', not least in cultural and educational matters, could mean that explicit references to EU recommendations would lead to political complications.

In fact neither the Act on continuing education and training, as adopted by parliament, nor the massive reports that provided the background, nor the debate in parliament, made reference to EU policies. In motivating the reform government argued that the new system was necessary in order to meet the demands of the knowledge society, but the Lisbon strategy was not mentioned. The main preparatory report had a section on international aspects of adult education, but this was a comparison of adult education programmes, activities and funding in four European nations (Ministry of Education et al., 1999). While the results were interesting, the conclusions were cautious and did not suggest any kind of European coordination. The only 'European' element is a reference to the European Credit Transfer System (ECTS). At the time this system was already in use in many parts of the Danish educational system, and as part of the reform is was also to be used in the new types of adult education.

So in the political process surrounding this reform EU discourse was almost completely absent. Afterwards, the relationship to EU policies has been commented on. In the Danish response to the Committee memorandum on lifelong learning, given together by the three ministers of education, work, and social affairs, it is argued 'With the new reform of adult education and continuing training, which came into effect on 1 January 2001, the framework has been created for offering all adults relevant further and continuing education and training (…) and new possibilities have been created for having knowledge and experience from other—also non-formal—learning settings credited as part of an education programme, which will give the participants formally recognized vocational competences. (…) With the reform of adult education, Denmark is now already living up to the conclusions of the European Council in Lisbon in March 2000 when it comes to ensuring the framework for lifelong learning' (Minister of Education et al., 2001).

Impacts of the learning discourse

The new national framework for continuing education and training embodies many of the principles that the EU promotes in its policy documents on lifelong learning. As indicated above there was little explicit EU influence in the debates and processes leading up to the reform, but close affinity with EU policy has been proclaimed afterwards. And it is to be expected that this affinity will persist and become more explicit in future Danish debates and initiatives in the area of lifelong learning.

There are several reasons to expect this. In general Danish attitudes towards EU involvement in matters of education and culture are becoming more positive. This is partly because the political elite, among socialists as well as liberals and conservatives, have increasingly propagated the benefits of EU membership, but also because many institutions and organisations have over the years been awarded grants from EU programmes or participated in EU-funded networks. As indicated above, EU activity in the area of educational policy and not least adult education has risen steeply during the last decade, and especially after the Lisbon agreements. This means that an increasing number of national officials are involved in this activity, and are being socialized into the trans-national culture of EU policy-making. The open method of coordination represents a type of trans-national policy that the Danish elites can legitimize both to themselves and to broader segments of the population; because EU principles only influence national educational policy indirectly, through benchmarks, they stand a chance of not being rejected as an authoritarian imposition.

How then will EU discourses impact on the concepts of learning that have been present in Danish national culture and informed Danish educational practices? This is a difficult question, and my answers will have to be provisional and to some degree speculative. I see three types of impact.

The first and probably most important type is a strengthening of the nexus between individualism and vocationalism. As mentioned above, a work-related instrumental perspective on education and learning has been an important element in Danish adult education, especially in the area of labour market training. But this vocational perspective has had a strong link to cultures of collectivity. Together with the state, the organised social partners have been the main actors in shaping and maintaining the labour market training system, both as regards curriculum and funding arrangements. Courses have generally been seen as a way of improving worker skills to meet the demands of companies, not as steps in individual career ladders. On the other hand many non-vocational adult education courses have mainly been tailored to individual leisure needs. But the new systems and discourses of lifelong learning connect individualism and vocationalism. Courses and learning contexts are seen   more and more as possible contributions to the individual accumulation of competencies, tied into an individual careers strategy. This must be seen against the background of a slow drift in many parts of the labour market away from collective bargaining towards individual employment contracts. As regards the participants in lifelong learning there is also a change of focus, from the skilled and unskilled workers towards the fairly well-educated employees.

A second type of impact is a weakening of the social and personal dimensions of learning. In the mainstream of Danish educational traditions, these dimensions have been seen as no less important than the cognitive dimension. That the impact of EU policies and discourses will contribute to changing this balance is not immediately apparent. After all, the EU policy documents on lifelong learning and related issues do give considerable attention to personal growth and social competencies. But the documents must be interpreted in the context of the dominant national traditions that they draw on, as well as the institutional arrangements they promote. Among the national traditions, especially French and German education emphasizes cognitive learning and academic skills, and this surely leaves it mark on EU recommendations and evaluation criteria. In the institutional arrangements academic institutions still have a dominant position. It should be noted, for example, that in EU discourse the recognition of informal learning becomes a question of transforming this learning into academic credentials.

A third type of impact is a (further) weakening of universalistic welfare principles in educational provision. Most actors in Danish educational policy have traditionally been concerned with keeping education a free and accessible good. The threat to this has of course been raising educational expenditure, and both socialist and liberal or conservative governments have over the years struggled to maintain a balance in this matter. Since the eighties, however, a more aggressive neo-liberalism has manifested itself, promoting the view of education and learning as individual investment. According to this view private individuals should bear at least part of the costs of education as an investment in their own educational capital, which will grant them income after graduation. The new system of continuing education and training, which I have discussed above, partly reflects this philosophy. EU policies generally serve to strengthen this trend, being influenced by member states that do not have a tradition of universalistic welfare provision.

These three types of change do not manifest themselves as a dramatic shift in values. They are rather a gradual and pragmatic adjustment to EU policies and discourses, which are only discretely present in the national political contest, but which are nevertheless perceived as powerful.

It should be emphasized again that the policies pursued and the arguments put forward by the EU and its agencies are not the only and not even the main force behind these changes. The EU reproduces and crystallizes social trends like a growing individualization in work and other areas of everyday life and a growth in the role of markets and quasi-markets; but these social trends themselves also have direct impact in the field of lifelong learning.

Conclusion

What then are the prospects for Danish traditions of adult education and learning in the EU context? In some ways they are promising. Several of the ideas about learning presented in EU documents on lifelong learning, such as the recognition of personal and social dimensions of learning, the recognition of informal and non-formal learning and the right to learning throughout the life course, clearly have resonance in the Danish tradition of adult learning. The implication of this is not only that EU policies could help consolidate lifelong learning in the Danish context, but also that traditions originating in Denmark could inspire other EU states in the interpretation and implementation of lifelong learning policies. The adoption of the name 'Grundtvig' for one of the Socrates sub-programmes may be regarded as a recognition of this inspiration.

However, I have argued that EU policies also contribute to changing Danish traditions in lifelong learning, and that this change is not beneficial. Individualistic types of vocationalism, cognitive and utilitarian concepts of learning and neo-liberal concepts of educational provision are growing and becoming steadily stronger. This is evident in the new system of adult education. A main reason for this change is that social and cultural modernisation has been changing the individual motivation and the social context for learning. EU policies reinforce the trend through the involvement of national actors in the process of 'open coordination' in educational policy and through the potential construction of a model of citizenship that includes a right to lifelong learning but invalidates this right through a discourse obscuring the real conditions of learning.

The alternative to the EU versions of lifelong learning and citizenship is not a return to well-known Danish educational traditions. As I have indicated above, these traditions must be re-interpreted in order to preserve and develop their potential under the conditions of modern society.

References

Branner, H. & Kelstrup, M. (eds) (2000) *Denmark's Policy Towards Europe after 1945.* Odense: Odense University Press.

Beukel, E. (2001) 'Educational policy: institutionalization and multi-level governance.' In S.S. Andersen & K.A. Eliassen (eds) *Making Policy in Europe.* London: Sage Publications. [2nd edition]

Cedefop & Eurydice (2001) *National Actions to Implement Lifelong Learning in Europe.* Brussels and Thessaloniki: Cedefop & Eurydice.

Council of the European Union (2001) *The Concrete Future Objectives of Education and Training Systems.* Brussels: European Union.

Council of the European Union (2002) 'Council Resolution of 27 June 2002 on Lifelong Learning.' Brussels: Official Journal of European Communities.

Council of the European Union & Commission of the European Union (2004) *Education and Training 2010. The Success of the Lisbon Strategy hinges on Urgent Reforms.* Joint Interim Report. Brussels: European Union.

Flockhart, T. (2003) 'Critical junctures and social identity theory: explaining the gap between Danish mass and elite attitudes to Europeanization.' European Studies Occasional Paper no. 37/2003. Aalborg University: European Research Unit.

Beck, U.; Giddens, A. & Lash, S. (1994) *Reflexive Modernization. Politics, Tradition and Aesthetics in the Modern Social Order.* Cambridge: Polity Press.

Grundtvig, N.F.S (1976) *N.F.S. Grundtvig, Selected Writings.* [Translated and edited by Johannes Knudsen]. Philadelphia: Fortress Press

Habermas, J. (1995) 'Was bedeutet 'Aufarbeitung der Vergangenheit' heute?' In J. Habermas, *Die Normalität einer Berliner Republik.* Frankfurt am Main: Suhrkamp.

Halkier, H. (1998) 'Danish regions and the Europeanization of regional policy'. European Studies Series of Occasional Papers, no. 27. Aalborg University: European Research Unit.

Hedetoft, U. (2000) 'The interplay between mass and elite attitudes to European integration in Denmark.' In H. Branner & M. Kelstrup (eds) *Denmark's Policy Towards Europe after 1945.* Odense: Odense University Press.

Hedetoft, U. & Hjort, M. (eds)(2002) *The Postnational Self.* Public World Series, No. 10. Minneapolis: University of Minnesota Press.

Illeris, K. (2003a) 'st10/om_inst10/Personale/VIP/ki/in_english/publications/experien.pdf/" Adult education as experienced by the learners.' *International Journal of Lifelong Education,* Vol.22(1), pp. 13-23.

Luhmann, N. (2002) *Das Erziehungssystem der Gesellschaft.* Frankfurt am Main: Suhrkamp.

Marcussen, M. (2002) *OECD og Idéspillet - Game Over?* Aarhus: Aarhus University Press.

Marcussen, M. (2003) 'The OECD as ideational artist, arbitrator and authority.' In Bob Reinalda & Bertjan Verbeek (eds) *Decision-Making Within International Organizations*, London: Routledge.

Minister of Education (2000) *Forslag til lov om Erhvervsrettet Grunduddannelse og Videregående uddannelse (videreuddannelsessystemet) for Voksne*. Copenhagen: Ministry of Education.

Minister of Education et al. (2001) *General Comments of the Danish Ministers responsible for the Consultation to the National Consultation on the European Commission's Memorandum on Lifelong Learning*: 29. June 2001. Copenhagen: Ministry of Education.

Ministry of Education et al. (1999) *Mål og Midler I offentligt Finansieret voksen- og Efteruddannelse*. Copenhagen: Ministry of Finance.

Nordic Council (2003) *The Nordic Agenda*. Copenhagen: Nordic Council.

Olesen, H.S. & Rasmussen, P. (eds) (1996) *Theoretical Issues in Adult Education. Danish Research and Experiences*. Frederiksberg: Roskilde University Press.

OECD (2001). *Thematic Review of Adult Learning: Denmark. Background Report*. Paris: OECD Publications.

Osborn, M. et al. (2003) *A World of Difference. Comparing Learners Across Europe*. Maidenhead: Open University Press.

Rasmussen, P. (1996) 'Adult education, gender and social change.' In H.S. Olesen & P. Rasmussen, (eds) *Theoretical Issues in Adult Education. Danish Research and Experiences*. Frederiksberg: Roskilde University Press.

Rasmussen, P. (2004) 'Ready for the knowledge society? Reforming adult and vocational education in Denmark.' Paper for NERA 2004 Conference. Aalborg University: Department of Education and Learning.

Togeby, L. et al. (2003) *Magt og Demokrati I Danmark. Hovedresultater af Magtudredningen*. Aarhus: Aarhus University Press.

Warren, C. (1987) *Grundtvig's Philosophy of Lifelong Education Through the Living Word*. University College of Cape Breton Press.

Wind, M. (2002) 'Det europæiske medborgerskab.' In T. Pedersen (ed.) *Europa for Folket*. Aarhus: Aarhus University Press.

Wind. M. (2004) 'Post-national citizenship. The EU as a 'Rights Generator'.' Paper under review. Copenhagen: Department of Political Science.

Ziehe, T. (1991) *Zeitvergleiche. Jugend in kulturellen Modernisierungen*. Weinheim/ München: Juventa.

CHAPTER FOUR

Governance and the Learning Citizen: Tensions and Possibilities in the Shift from National to Post-national Identities

JOHN FIELD AND MARK MURPHY

Introduction

The movement towards a European civil society has been on the policy agenda for some time. At one level, it can be said to have at least been implied in the original Treaty of Rome, with its stated desire to facilitate a political as well as an economic Union. The idea acquired added momentum during the employment crisis of the 1970s, as is witnessed by the rapidly growing significance of the European Social Fund and the 'Document on European Identity' approved by the foreign ministers of the European Community in 1973. As an explicit element in policy discourse, however, the linked ideas of a European civil society and a European citizenship really came to the fore in the period between the Single European Act and the completion of the Single Market in 1992. Significantly, this period also saw dramatic steps in the Europeanization of policies for education and training, a process in which ideas of a shared civic identity played an important role (Field, 1998).

While talk of European identity, culture and citizenship is a relatively recent phenomenon, it nevertheless reflects a logical development in the movement towards European integration. It shares with the integration project as a whole a deep underlying tension between the desire to benefit from a steep increase in the economies of scale, and the corresponding opportunities that this presents at the social and cultural level, and the constitutional obligation (and desire) to maintain national sovereignty as a keystone of the Union. In the orthodox doctrines of the European political class, this is presented as a positive conception of the emerging 'European society' as a society where citizens will have 'the feeling of belonging to the European Union' while at the same time being 'rooted in regional traditions and cultures'. This statement also reflects the formal EU position on European citizenship, one that is concerned in practical terms with the difficult compromises and shifting alliances involved in carefully negotiating subsidiarity and the myriad sensitivities revolving around national traditions, cultures and notions of citizenship. It has been increasingly accompanied by reforms of governance that are designed to bring the EU closer to its citizens, as well as new approaches to social partnership that seek to engage the Union's decision making structures with the representatives of non-governmental actors and civic movements alongside the more conventional players (governments, employers' associations and trade unions).

Yet in recent years, this vision of a shared European citizenship and civil society has been confronted by new populist movements that express considerable scepticism over the claims of the European political elite, and often articulate hostility towards large parts of the European project. Surveying a range of evidence from surveys conducted between the 1970s and the late 1990s, Martin Kohli asserts that 'Europe is indeed an elite project, especially so in the less developed countries' (Kohli, 2000, p.113). The losers of internationalisation—according to Kohli, people in rural areas, those with the lowest income levels and above all those with the weakest educational qualifications—are empirically far less likely to identify positively with the Europeanising project.

While a whole host of issues rear their heads in debates over EU citizenship, what concerns this paper is the significance of education and training in any future shift to at least a partial identification by individual citizens with the notion of a European civil society. We particularly seek to understand the process of constructing a European identity within the context of the developing lifelong learning agenda within Europe, which is itself one example of the process of deepening the Union and to some extent is also bound up with enlargement. Given the bleakness of institutional governance without a corresponding demos, can the partial legal competence of the EU in education and training potentially be harnessed as a means of facilitating the construction of a post-national citizen identity at the EU level? The following brief discussion highlights some of the initial tensions and possibilities inherent in the combination of EU governance, learning and citizen identification.

Civil society and European integration

When reviewing what is written about European civil society, it becomes apparent that the crucial issue is not so much civil society per se, as what civil society can do to fill some form of gap in the process of European integration.

The model of civil society at work in this approach is the model associated with the rise of the modern nation state. There can be little doubt that in the nineteenth and twentieth centuries, it was within the framework of the nation state that individuals learned abstract solidarity, coming to think of themselves as members not only of known, bounded and primordial groupings such as the village or neighbourhood, but of what Benedict Anderson has named as 'imagined communities'—that is, to feel themselves connected to others with whom they have no interpersonal or familial connection (Anderson, 1982). Of course, this process could also involve a remorseless eradication of local and regional traditions, including the deliberate destruction of linguistic and cultural patterns that were at odds with the official dominant definitions of the nation, as well as the invention of 'national traditions' covering such diverse areas as costumes, cuisine and official holidays (Hobsbawm and Ranger, 1983). However, the 'imagined community' of the nation state also generated high levels of solidarity among citizens, and facilitated their mobilization and capacity for mutual co-operation. In today's sociological language, it promoted 'bridging social capital' among people who were not even aware of one another's existence.

In this analysis, a disjuncture exists at the heart of European integration, one that threatens to fragment and divide the 'integrative image of a cohesive EU' (Rumford, 2003, p.37). The EU is being forced to play catch up—while political and economic integration at the post-national level have occurred to a greater or less extent, *social* integration, as Rumford puts it (2003, p.25) 'remains largely underdeveloped'. Ideas of a social Europe, or a citizen's Europe, were widespread at the level of rhetoric during the period of Jacques Delors' presidency of the European Commission, and to some extent Delors was able to push forward an embryonic set of measures designed to mobilize the citizenry on behalf of the European project. The debate around Giscard d'Estang's model European constitution turned partly on the question of how to mobilize citizens on behalf of what was widely perceived as a project belonging solely to Europe's political class.

This emphasis on civil society in the European context results from its perceived role in creating and sustaining a viable trans-national 'public sphere'. The term 'public sphere', perceived as a crucial component of liberal democracies, denotes an 'organising principle for the legitimacy of political order' (Kohler, 1998, p. 236). It comprises an unstructured area for discussion and will-formation (Chevigny, 2000, p. 313), the function of which is to 'articulate and aggregate social demands' (Kohler, 1998, p.236). To some extent, such a European-level public sphere already exists, with the development of structures of representation via networks, policy communities and organised groups working at a trans-national level. Crucially, what is deemed not yet to exist is 'a stage where a nascent civic identity at the grass roots meets the institutionalisation of European civic competence' (Chryssochoou, 2002, p. 766). This public space, supported by civil society, is viewed by many to be, while not a panacea, a major player in countering any so-called democratic deficit (Warleigh, 2001, p.620; Meadowcroft, 2002, p.182).

Given the haste with which the EU has championed the efficacy of civil society, it is not difficult to take some basic pot shots at some of the assumptions underlying this attraction to civil society as provider of a trans-national social 'glue', upon which European forms of solidarity, citizenship and identity are to be constructed. One starting point would be to take umbrage with the use of an old concept like civil society in attempting to fill in gaps in new political orders—an argument put forward by Ashenden (1999, p.143), who agues that civil society is a concept based on a 'juridical account of power relations', an account that is incapable of assessing modern state relations. Nevertheless, if the importance of civil society in the framework of what is still formally liberal democracies is to be taken seriously, a more troublesome blind spot is the apparent belief that the development of a European civil society will not only strengthen the integration process, but also conform to the basic principles of liberal democracy.

As Rumford (2003, pp.36-7) puts it, 'why should European civil society organisations ... work for rather than in opposition to integration?' This is the potential scenario raised by what Chambers and Kopstein (2001) refer to as 'bad' civil society, in which the views of participants do not necessarily coincide with the liberal democratic theory within which so much talk of civil society is embedded. And unfortunately, historical precedents can be found for such apparently counter-intuitive developments. When Femia (2001, p.146) asks whether or not a pluralistic civil society can 'happily embrace movements, aspirations, struggles, desires and oppositions that are openly hostile to liberal values', Chambers (2002, p.101) can answer in the affirmative, by referring to the organised civil societies and publics in the Weimar Republic and Mussolini's pre-war Italy.

These criticisms should add a note of caution to any over-zealous championing of civil society in the context of post-national Europe. Further, we may join Kohli in asking whether a European civic identity is really necessary (Kohli, 2000, pp.118-20)? In so far as the EU remains essentially a highly integrated free trade area, underpinned by common regulatory frameworks and involving only a limited degree of social solidarity, there is little need to mobilize European citizens. Things might be different if the EU were to ask its citizens (usually male) to give their lives on its behalf, or to take a significant role in taxation and social distribution, but even then a modern citizenry may well take a reflexive and conditional view of how far its loyalties may be taken, whether by the nation state or by a new and supranational body. This is compounded by the limited extent of democratic engagement by citizens with European policy making. The opportunity structures governing civic participation are stunted and narrow, and seem systematically designed to exclude citizens from democratic involvement in most of the European institutions; for their part, most citizens appear to view the single democratic institution—the European Parliament—as an irrelevance, and either do not vote in elections or vote for parties that are against the European project. Finally, a surprising number of Europe's citizens appear to be entirely happy with the absence of democratic opportunities. According to the Eurobarometer Survey in 2001, 40% of respondents across Europe with either very or fairly satisfied with 'the way democracy works in the European Union'. Admittedly, the level of satisfaction varied enormously by country; while 60% of Danes and 57% of Swedes were dissatisfied, levels of satisfaction reached 59% in Spain, 58% in Ireland and 52% in Portugal (Commission of the European Communities 2001, p.13). Given the economic impact of EU membership on the last three nations, it might be concluded that democratic satisfaction is more a product of consumer affluence rather than civic engagement. At any rate, there is little to suggest that the European political class has much to fear from the disaffection of its citizens.

Nevertheless, proponents of further European integration are still left with a conundrum, one that strikes at the core of European democracy. In order for European forms of legality to be perceived as *legitimate*, the fit between what Burgess (2002, p.468) refers to as 'pure legality' and 'cultural identity' must be made stronger. The tension between the hard and soft law of Europe must be allowed to work itself out, as EU institutions can 'neither assure their legitimacy by mirroring the cultural norms of European reality, nor by abstracting themselves from it' (Burgess, 2002, p.471). This lack of an adequate fit between the legal 'facts and cultural 'norms' of European integration, provides the rationale for the championing of a European civil society, a development that, on the surface, appears to provide the most appropriate channel for negotiations between the ideal and the real of European democracy.

Citizenship and European identity

As Preub (1998, p.144) points out, however, in order to open up the 'symbolic space' necessary for the development of a civil society beyond the boundaries of nation states, it is necessary to generate a specifically European notion of *citizenship*—a development that, according to Preub, could be regarded as a step towards a 'new kind of politics'. Obviously, any talk of a European citizenry or citizenship is guaranteed to provoke debate at the national level, but it has also warranted the attention of the academic community, with 'enormous' energies being devoted to the topic (Closa, 2001, p.180). Much of this energy has taken the form of scepticism regarding the prospects of European citizenship. According to Lehning (1998, p.348), for instance, the concept of European citizenship is a 'mirage', with no European equivalent to the kinds of nationally shared cultural and historical myths to be found (See also Streeck, 1995, p.414; Prentoulis, 2001, p.199; Schmalz-Burns, 2001, p.565). There is no doubt that 'the nation' has remained a 'captivating idea', maintaining an 'astonishing allure and grip on our collective psyches' (Weiler, 1997, p.497). Unsurprisingly then, citizenship constitutes one of the 'battle crises' in conflicts over boundary construction in the context of European enlargement (Giesen and Eder, 2001, p.3).

At the same time, however, without the development of some form of European citizenship, of a Europe-wide demos, the prospects for a democracy specifically within the boundaries of the EU, look more bleak than ever. A lack of 'citizen identification with Europe' would certainly put the brakes on achieving a 'European society' (Streeck, 1995, p.414). It could also be argued that using the statist argument against the notion of developing a post-national form of citizenship is itself a bit redundant, considering the fact that 'traditional notions of democracy are losing their normative appeal' (Chyssochoou, 2002, p.759). It could just as easily be argued that the EU is in a viable position to transcend 'issues of market integration' and also touch upon 'sensitive issues of state authority' (Chyssochoou, 2002, p.757). Is it not the case that, potentially, what some commentators see as a deterrent to the development of EU legitimacy—the disjuncture between national forms of identity and post-national forms of legality—could in fact be a fertile ground for the development of some form of European solidarity? The legitimacy of the EU may be in a so-called crisis, but this crisis can at the same time be seen as taking the form of a creative and dynamic tension between the real and the ideal, a point which Eurosceptics have conveniently ignored. As Burgess (2002, p.471) puts it, the 'legitimacy of any legal institutions, and the EU in particular, depends on the tension between the ideal form of law and the empirical terrain on which it is to have validity'.

While the sceptics do make a legitimate point regarding the current lack of citizenship identification with the EU, it does not negate the possibility of such an identification occurring in the future. The connection between democracy, and hence citizenry, and the nation-state, is 'not normatively compulsory but rather empirical' (Decker, 2002, p.263). While citizenship has tended to revolve around issues of national identity, this does not indicate a 'natural' state of affairs, but is rather a historical development that can potentially be shaped by political actions. It is, as Habermas argues (1998, p.318), not 'completely without plausibility' that a 'compulsive cosmopolitan solidarization' can develop in the civil societies and public spheres of post-national entities like the EU. In reference to the historical transition from feudal to national entities in the European context, Habermas asks,

'If this form of collective identity was due to a highly abstractive leap from the local and dynastic to nation and then to democratic consciousness, why shouldn't this learning process be able to continue?' (Habermas, 2001, p.103)

In considering how citizens might 'learn' (or construct) a 'post-national identity', it is instructive to consider a little further how 'national identities' in Europe were constructed. The experience of nation building in western and central Europe can certainly be regarded as one in which people acquired a new sense of themselves as belonging to a wider community of interest, whose boundaries coincided with those of the nation state.

Essentially, this process of nation building in the modern sense reached a peak between the early eighteenth century and the settlement that followed the Armistice in 1918. During this process, Europe's citizens learned what it might mean to be British or Polish or French; national identity acquired a new significance as an integrating mechanism. It was also an integrating mechanism which united the new middle class and much of the working class, and which might be seen as contributing to the social settlement of the mid twentieth century. In this context, we should note Marshall's classical formulation of citizenship, which he presented as a series of lectures in the late 1940s. For Marshall, social entitlements constituted the third dimension of citizenship, along with juridical and political citizenship, both of which had been achieved in the past. As a sociologist, Marshall was concerned with the foundations of social order; a broadening of social citizenship, he argued, was required under conditions of mass democracy and juridical equality precisely in order to maintain and legitimate the economic inequalities required to underpin capitalist recovery and growth (Marshall, 1950). And it was one which was typically active, engaging large parts of the population and not only the elites of the political class. It is therefore tempting to consider whether there are potential similarities with the notion of 'post-national identity'.

Our initial hypothesis is that while there are indeed some potential similarities, these may be limited and not necessarily positive. First, it is important to recall that nationhood is of course a social construct: as Ernest Gellner joked, nations do not have navels; they are made, not born. And in the construction of one dominant unifying identity, of course, the sources of other minority identities were suppressed, more or less as a matter of deliberate intent. The examples are legion, and include linguistic displacement (with the downgrading and dismissal—and occasionally proscription—of merely local dialects and languages) and the standardisation of linguistic forms, as well as the imposition of national educational systems or the dissemination of a national press. They might also include what some historians have referred to as 'the invention of tradition': the eighteenth century was particularly rich in the forgery of cultural icons, while the nineteenth century was rich in the codification of authenticity (Hobsbawm and Ranger, 1983). Yet such a pathway is closed to the institutions of the EU, as well as to the wider European political elite more generally. Rather, the sources of post-national identity might be discovered in the widespread embrace of global cultural phenomena such as pop music, fast food, the cinema and mass sport, or in the (re)creation of 'identity politics' based on cultural belonging. The relationship between such consumption-based identities and identity politics on the one hand, and post-national state formations (such as the EU) on the other, is not close.

Lifelong learning and a European demos

It is noteworthy that Habermas talks about 'learning process' as it reflects to some degree the radical republican tradition of political citizenship, which placed emphasis on what Von Meyme has called 'civil religion' (2001, p.81)— a religion that did not yet exist but had to created by *education*.... Habermas' use of the term 'learning process' also points to a gap: the formal education and training system has rarely been viewed, either by policy makers or academics, as a key actor in the creation of a European citizenship. Yet proposals for a European area for education and research played a central part in the Commission's thinking during the period when the Single Market was under completion. Education in particular was treated not solely as a form of vocational training (although this provided the legal basis for the Commission's claim to competence), but as a means of fostering a wider European identity among young people. The 1992 Treaty redefined the basis on which European policies were developed for education, with important consequences for the ways in which education, identity and citizenship are intertwined. Yet Habermas is surely right to downplay the role of formal education and training, hinting as he does at the significance of other fields of communication and interaction in creating sites for learning, formal and informal. While the European Commission and a number of member states acknowledge the importance of learning as a lifelong and lifewide process, it is clear that this broad (even loose) and open (arguably fuzzy) concept is not readily open to direct steering by the established policy community (Field, 2000).

Lifelong learning policy poses remarkably wide challenges to policy makers. First, policy on lifelong learning must typically be delivered through a process that is complex and sometimes opaque. It characteristically involves more than one government department, posing a considerable problem of coordination. Typically, it will involve ministries with responsibilities for social affairs, employment, research, industry and education, each of which has its own timetable, internal administrative divisions, organisational culture, and policy agenda (we might add the finance ministry to this list as well). As policy moves out from the point of conception to the point of delivery, so the problems of coordination multiply (Field, 2000). Many of the organisations involved are not themselves a direct part of the State, but are private actors with differing relationships with the State, ranging from private employers to semi-state agencies such as labour offices, research institutes and deregulated training suppliers. At the point of delivery itself, there is a complex interaction between workers who either mediate with the public or directly supply the service ('street-level bureaucrats') and their clients (learners, unemployed people, companies). In these circumstances, it is possible for actors to refuse central coordination altogether, or to follow strategies of visible compliance while in fact pursuing their own separate interests.

Second, though, lifelong learning is a fuzzy concept. This is not simply, as so often suggested, merely a matter of its loose definition (though the fact that it is potentially all-encompassing does mean that policy makers must decide where and how to focus their efforts). Much more problematic is the focus on learning and knowledge acquisition, which turns attention to the behaviour and attitudes of those who learn and acquire new competences—that is, to individuals and networks of non-governmental actors. It also calls attention to the application of new skills and knowledge, since it is only through application that the alleged benefits can be secured. Yet this in turn depends on the behaviour, attitudes and capacities of third parties who may have only an indirect involvement at best in the learning and knowledge transfer that has gone on. For example, for workers to apply their new skills effectively, they must be placed in a context where those skills are utilised to a relatively high level. Boreham has pointed out that this may involve organisational changes that are beyond the capacity not only of the workers who have acquired the skills, but also of their line managers (Boreham, 2002). More awkward still for the policy maker, many of the issues experienced at this level are 'soft' cultural and social ones which are not readily tackled in terms of the hard indicators traditionally used in classical economics (as is illustrated in the recent recognition of the importance of trust based networks to business innovation). Some member states have explicitly called for 'culture change' in order to promote lifelong learning and innovation, but this is far from being a straightforward means of securing the goals intended. Indeed, it is obvious that actors may in practice apply their skills in ways that run contrary to the original goals intended. While governments have experimented with loose-fit incentive measures to stimulate and channel demand, these have often proven difficult to control effectively (the extreme example being the UK government's attempts at introducing Individual Learning Accounts).

The European institutions have nevertheless sought to develop a range of measures that enable a greater degree of focussed attention on lifelong learning and knowledge transfer. As we might expect, these share many of the features of governance that have characterised policy development more broadly within the EU. There has been considerable incremental use of what neo-Weberians have termed 'creeping competence' (Pollack, 1994), followed in turn by a redefinition of the policy competences belonging to the European institutions and the member states. A variety of policy actors has been involved, each of which has sought to pursue its own interests while repositioning itself as a player on the European level. A number of the non-governmental actors have been both parties to policy dialogue within the framework established by the institutions and lobbyists outside those institutions. And there are clearly different interests at work within the Commission itself, with individual actors forming strategic and tactical alliances with others to promote their own preferred policy solutions. We can also see some of the common problems and challenges that are typical of policy issues such as lifelong learning and knowledge transfer. For example, they cut across a number of departmental boundaries: thus, this is a field which spans the core functions of at least three Directorates General (DG-5, DG-12 and DG-22), and touches on the interests of several others. And the difficulties of coordination, definition (scope) and agency mean that policy accomplishment is an extremely uncertain and complex process. Finally, differing components of the policy system may act in ways which are outwith the agreed parameters of the EU's institutions. An obvious example is the achievement of the Bologna agreement, which was reached by education ministers from a range of European countries, some within the EU and some not, on issues judged to be of common interest.

We may illustrate this general analysis by reference to the European Commission's plans for the new generation of Community education and training programmes after 2006 (Commission of the European Communities, 2004). The plan is presented as centering on 'a new Integrated Programme for mobility and co-operation in lifelong learning', and justified as helping to achieve the target set by the Lisbon European Council of 2000, 'of making Europe the most competitive knowledge-based economy in the world by 2010, while nonetheless strengthening social cohesion' (Commission of the European Communities, 2004, p.2). Under the open system of co-ordination, the Commission proposes to proceed by developing frameworks for transnational comparison, alongside an expansion of the existing programmes to promote individual student movement within the EU's borders and partnerships between providers from different member states. Within the new Integrated Programme, however, the bulk of attention and resources are focussed on the comparatively well established areas of European activity. These include the ERASMUS programme of student mobility, a programme that is clearly limited in its impact to the existing and future European elites; and the LEONARDO programme of partnerships purportedly designed to promote the exchange of expertise between training providers. Mobility schemes for adult learners under the GRUNDVIG programme are set at a modest level (with a target mobility level of well under one-seventh of that under ERASMUS); this scheme also remains far smaller than the parallel COMENIUS programme for schools. In short, the new 'integrated Lifelong Learning Programme' is designed to concentrate on the front end of the education system, with the bulk of resources being dedicated to supporting the Europeanization of the future administrators, managers and professionals. Its effects must therefore be to widen further the cultural division between the winners of internationalization and the losers, and thereby further erode the bases of social solidarity, in a manner that is at odds with the proclaimed ambition of fostering a civic Europe.

Conclusion

In studying the emerging policies of the EU institutions, then, complexity and ambiguity are essential starting points. This is even more the case when the analysis is placed within the context of changing conceptions of national and supranational identity. According to Shaw (1999, p.586), the current challenge for the EU is that of 'capturing the essence of post-nationalism, and combining it with understanding the process of building a new kind of polity which is based in the existing diversity of the member states.' As briefly explored in this paper, any attempts at capturing the essence of post-nationalism, while also building a new kind of polity, run into a range of difficulties and complexities, at both a cultural level and also at the level of institutional governance and bureaucracy.

It would seem at this stage, that the tensions far outweigh the possibilities in the shift from national to post-national identities. Given that, according to Wallace (1999, p.520), this lack of a shared identity in the post-sovereign order, combined with a loosening of the ties binding elites to the masses within nation-states, constitutes the weakest dimension of European governance, this is not surprising. This is the case, before the discussion even moves onto the level of EU jurisprudence. Certainly the role of law as a lever of post-national governance can never be discounted, but it needs to be acknowledged that a European identity will never arise merely through legal fiat (Cronin and De Grieff, 1998, p.xxiii). Indeed, many of the influences that appear to shape the shifting and ambivalent identities of contemporary Europeans may lie outwith the reach of the State. While the role of education and training in facilitating the development of the learning citizen must be taken into account, it is important that their significance should be set against the working out of factors that are more influenced by market forces (such as fashion trends) and changing values (such as individualisation). The prospects for a genuinely European civil society therefore remain, in our judgement, remote.

References

Anderson, B. (1982) *Imagined Communities*. London: Verso.

Ashenden, S (1999) 'Questions of criticism: Habermas and Foucault on civil society and resistance.' In S. Ashenden & D. Owen (eds) *Foucault Contra Habermas: Recasting the Dialogue Between Genealogy and Critical Theory*. London: Sage.

Boreham, N. (2002) 'Introduction.' In N. Boreham, R. Samurçay & M. Fischer (eds), *Work Process Knowledge*. London: Routledge.

Burgess, P. (2002) 'What's so European about the European Union? Legitimacy between institution and identity.' *European Journal of Social Theory*, Vol.5(4), pp.467-81.

Chambers, S. (2002) 'A critical theory of civil society.' In S. Chambers and W. Kymlicka (eds) *Alternative Conceptions of Civil Society*. Princeton, NJ: Princeton University Press.

Chambers, S. & Kopstein, J. (2001) 'Bad civil society.' *Political Theory*, Vol.29(6), pp.837-65.

Chevigny, P. (2000) 'Law and politics in *Between Facts and Norms.*' In L. Edwin Hahn (ed.) *Perspectives on Habermas*. Chicago, Illinois: Open Court.

Chryssochoou, D. (2002) 'Civic competence and the challenge to EU policy-building.' *Journal of European Public Policy*, Vol. 9(5), pp.756-73.

Closa, C. (2001) 'Requirements of a European public sphere: civil society, self, and the institutionalisation of citizenship.' In K. Eder & B. Giesen (eds) *European Citizenship Between National Legacies and Post-National Projects*. Oxford: Oxford University Press.

Commission of the European Communities (2001) *How Europeans See Themselves*. Luxembourg: Office for Official Publications of the European Communities

Commission of the European Communities (2004) *The New Generation of Community Education and Training Programmes after 2006*. Communication from the Commission, Brussels: CEC.

Cronin, C. & De Grieff, M. (1998) 'Editors' introduction.' In J. Habermas (1998), *The Inclusion of the Other: Studies in Political Theory*. Cambridge, MA: MIT Press.

Decker, F. (2002) 'Governance beyond the nation-state: reflections on the democratic deficit of the European Union.' *Journal of European Public Policy*, Vol.9(2), pp.256-272.

Deflem, M. (ed.) (1996) *Habermas, Modernity and Law*. London: Sage.

Femia, J. (2001) 'Civil society and the Marxist tradition.' In S. Kaviraj & S. Khilnani (eds) *Civil Society: History and Possibilities*. Cambridge: Cambridge University Press.

Field, J. (1998) *European Dimensions: Education, Training and the European Union*. London: Jessica Kingsley.

Field, J. (2000) *Lifelong Learning and the New Educational Order*. Stoke-on-Trent: Trentham Books.

Giesen, B. & Eder, K. (2001) 'Introduction: European citizenship: an avenue for the social integration of Europe.' In In K. Eder & B. Giesen (eds) *European Citizenship between National Legacies and Post-national Projects*. Oxford: Oxford University Press.

Habermas, J. (1995) 'Remarks on Dieter Grimm's – does Europe need a constitution.' *European Law Journal*, Vol.3(1), pp.303-307.

Habermas, J. (1996) *Between Facts and Norms: Contributions to a Discourse Theory of Law and Democracy*. Cambridge: Policy Press.

Habermas, J. (1998) 'The European nation-state: on the past and future of sovereignty and citizenship.' In *The Inclusion of the Other: Studies in Political Theory*. Cambridge, MA: MIT Press.

Habermas, J. (1999) 'The European nation-state and the pressures of globalisation.' *New Left Review*, No.235, pp.46-59.

Habermas, J. (2001) *The Post-national Constellation: Political Essays*. Cambridge, UK: Polity Press.

Hobsbawm, E. & Ranger, T. (eds) (1983) *The Invention of Tradition*. Cambridge: Cambridge University Press.

Kohli, M. (2000) 'The battlegrounds of European identity.' *European Societies*, Vol.2(2), pp.113-37.

Kohler, M. (1998) 'From the national to the cosmopolitan public sphere.' In D. Archibugi, D. Held & M. Kohler (eds) *Re-imagining Political Community: Studies in Cosmopolitan Democracy*. Cambridge: Polity Press.

Lehning, P. (1998) 'European citizenship: between facts and norms.' *Constellations*, Vol.4(3), pp.346-367.

Marshall, T.H. (1950) *Citizenship and Social Class and other essays*. Cambridge: Cambridge University Press.

Meadowcroft, J. (2002) 'The European democratic deficit, the market and the public space: a classical liberal critique.' *Innovation: the European Journal of Social Science Research*, Vol.15(3), pp.181-92.

Pollack, M. (1994) 'Creeping competence: the expanding agenda of the European Community.' *Journal of Public Policy*, Vol.14(2), pp.95-145.

Prentoulis, N. (2001) 'On the technology of collective identity: normative reconstructions of the concept of EU citizenship.' *European Law Journal*, Vol. 7(2), pp.196-218.

Preub, U. (1998) 'Citizenship in the European Union: a paradigm for transnational democracy?' In D. Archibugi, D. Held & M. Kohler (eds) *Re-imagining Political Community: Studies in Cosmopolitan Democracy*. Cambridge: Polity Press.

Rumford, C. (2003) 'European civil society or transnational social space? Conceptions of society in discourses of EU citizenship, governance and the democratic deficit: an emerging agenda.' *European Journal of Social Theory* Vol.6(1), pp.25-43.

Shaw, J. (1999) 'Postnational constitutionalism in the European Union.' *Journal of European Public Policy*, Vol. 6(4), pp.579-97.

Streeck, W. (1995) 'From market building to state building? Reflections on the political economy of European social policy.' In S. Leibfried & P. Pierson (eds), *European Social Policy: Between Fragmentation and Integration*. Washington, D.C.: The Brookings Institution.

Von Meyme, K. (2001) 'Citizenship and the European Union.' In K. Eder & B. Giesen (eds) *European Citizenship between National Legacies and Post-national Projects*. Oxford: Oxford University Press.

Wallace, W. (1999) 'The sharing of sovereignty: the European paradox.' *Political Studies*, Vol.7(3), pp.503-521.

Warleigh, A. (2001) 'Europeanising civil society: NGOs as agents of political socialisation.' *Journal of Common Market Studies*, Vol.39(4), pp.619-39.

Weiler, J. (1997) 'To be a European citizen—Eros and civilization.' *Journal of European Public Policy*, Vol.4(4), pp.495-519.

CHAPTER FIVE

Knowledge in the Bazaar: Pro-active Citizenship in the Learning Society

António M. Magalhães and Stephen R. Stoer

Introduction

This chapter aims at identifying relationships between the transformations underway within capitalism itself, within the state and with regard to the nature and role of knowledge in present social contexts (characterised by social analysts such as Beck, Giddens, and Harvey as risk societies and as societies in which appears a reconfigured economic determination in the 'first instance') and their impact on the reconfiguration of the mandates addressed to education, and to education systems, at the beginning of the new century. The chapter is divided into two main parts.

The first part has as its aim precisely the analysis of the transformations and respective relations of capitalism, the state and the exercise of citizenship in present contexts. The increasingly visible presence of examples of pro-active citizens who claim their difference with regard to an institution such as the school constitutes that which we might designate as a process of the repoliticisation of education where citizens refuse to see themselves as the passive objects of action by the state (which appears more and more to speak in the name of the market). Indeed, a tension appears to develop between a process of the individualisation of citizens, by way of which they are made responsible for everything including, above all, their own failure, and a process of individual and institutional reflexivity (in Beck's terms [1992] 'individuation') enacted by the pro-active citizen who claims her own difference, in which citizens redefine themselves, not only on the basis of the homogenising logic of the market but, also, on the basis of heterogeneity. We aim here to develop further an assumption of a previous work (Magalhães and Stoer, 2003) according to which not only the concept of citizenship is re-appropriated by individuals and groups in a process of reclaiming sovereignty, but also this process of reclaiming is carried out not on the basis of that which people hold in common, but, rather on that which differentiates them, namely identity.

In the second part, and on the basis of these new claims for citizenship, we centre the discussion on their expression, namely in the field of education. As this field is increasingly framed by entities and energies at the supranational level, it is on this basis that we analyse the impact of the change in the nature and function of knowledge in present societies. In taking up again the question of the repoliticisation of education and of the role of knowledge within education, we attempt to relate the exercise of reclaimed sovereignty with the political models on the basis of which Europe is being thought as a new political entity. In a recent work (Stoer and Magalhães, 2003), we have argued that it is the metaphor of 'Europe as a bazaar' that, among other metaphors such as 'the flag', 'issues or themes', or 'network', best captures a European construction process capable of promoting unity within diversity. The bazaar as a political metaphor for European construction incorporates and mediates the flag, issues/themes and the network without destroying these latter in some overarching synthesis and without losing its own specificity, that is, the fact that it is founded on the enunciation of what we term below 'difference is us'. Within the bazaar, knowledge, in an epoch of globalisation, has taken on a new role as central element in the production process. As a result, it can be argued that knowledge as formation of the individual is moving from the school as an institution to 'society', both to society as a network and to society as a site of local sociabilities. There are important implications here for the design of the so-called (in various official EU documents) 'learning society'.

Finally, this chapter will take this discussion further in its attempt to better understand a process of reconfiguration that offers new definitions not only of 'Europe', but also of 'learning' and of 'citizen'. We refer to this process in relation to the school as the consequence of its very repoliticisation, that is, a school as a context where citizenship is not only 'prepared for' but, rather, where it exercises its claims.

The repoliticisation of education

Schooling, as it derived from the social project of modernity, is intrinsically political. In this project, it is the state's responsibility to promote and implement the education of individuals and their transformation, via schooling, into citizens (Magalhães, 2003; Magalhães and Stoer, 2003a). It is the state's responsibility because the state emanates from the nation (see below), while the school, in turn, is the privileged pedagogic mechanism for accomplishing this task, because it was designed as the ideal form for the socialisation of citizens, that is, for removing them from the influence of the family and of tradition (Parsons, 1959; Touraine, 1997). Thus, originally, the school is the place, *par excellence*, for the politicisation of education, in the sense that it defines the individual on the basis of his place in the *polis* (city). Durkheim (1984) defined education as the action of one generation on another, but this definition does not appear to sufficiently emphasise the function of schooling in the transformation of individual identities into national political identities, that is, into citizens. Citizenship, such as it is conceived by the modern social contract, delocalises and universalises individuals as an integral part of the state. By way of the modern social contract, the legitimacy of the sovereignty of the state resides precisely in the fact that it originates in the sovereignty that individuals and groups give up to the state (see Magalhães and Stoer, *ibid.*). The political character of education resides also in the fact that education is a vehicle for national culture. It is up to the state to assure that educational institutions, especially the universities, produce, preserve and diffuse national culture. The state is the state of national culture.

When capitalism becomes intertwined with the development of this sociocultural project, the political character of education becomes even more apparent. In addition to producing 'good citizens', the school is also expected to produce 'good workers'. Thus the function of economic regulation is joined to the project of modernity embodied in the state making this latter a capitalist state (cf. Dale, 1989). As a result of this process, the state deepens its political character by recognising that its legitimacy goes beyond the sphere of the modern social contract. In other words, the state has a legitimacy of regulation that is inevitably committed to the good functioning of the capitalist economy. As stated by the more sophisticated Marxists, the state guarantees, in the last instance, that the accumulation process can take place in the most legitimate way possible. The liberal state, in this sense, is that state that arises both 'above' production relations and as an instance of the promotion and legitimation of their conditions of existence (cf. Lenhardt and Offe, 1984).

The political project of the working class, in general, also made itself felt in schooling during this period (second half of the 19th century in most of Europe and beginning of the 20th in Portugal, for example). As the British historian Richard Johnson (1981) has demonstrated, this project, at least initially, had as its objective the development of an alternative schooling to that provided by the capitalist state. This alternative schooling was to be based on the notion that it was possible to produce a form of schooling—based on 'really relevant knowledge'—that would lead to the emancipation of the working class. Examples of this project can be found in the pedagogic projects inspired by, among others, Freinet, or, in the Portuguese case, by Adolfo Lima (cf. Candeias, 1994). One can see in the tension between 'bourgeois schooling' and the schooling 'demanded by the working class' that the political character of schooling not only broadens but also becomes more vertical. The non-neutral nature of the education process shows itself in all its splendour. It is as if a part of society, the working class, sought an alternative form of schooling as a way of gaining access to full citizenship. The public character of schooling reveals in this way its seminal political contradiction: it proclaims the universality of citizenship while in fact only allowing some citizens full access. Those citizens without full access to citizenship include not only the working class but also, for example, women.

It is the welfare state that, after the two world wars, tries to manage this political contradiction between the universal character of citizenship and what one might term the partial character of schooling. This management was carried out, on the one hand, by broadening the principle of equality of opportunity in education and, on the other, by promoting a range of pedagogies that extended from pedagogies oriented towards professional formation, with the aim of direct insertion into the labour market, to the pedagogies of compensatory education, while along the way active pedagogies were also consecrated, for example in the modern school movement. One of the most important effects of this management was the strengthening of the position of what Bernstein (1996) terms the 'new middle class' with regard to schooling. In other words, this 'new' class, to all intents and purposes, appropriated schooling for itself as a means for guaranteeing a safe passage to the places of social 'distinction' (Bourdieu, 1986). Indeed, this class of reproducers, to a large extent the liberal professions and upper echelons of public functionaries, hegemonised not only education systems but also their ideology. This positioning of the middle class further deepened the political character of the public school to the extent that its universality arose as conditioned by the social strategies of this class. To prove that his is so appears to be the action of critical pedagogy that aimed at deepening this political aspect through the construction of immediate, pre-figurative, alternatives, under the banner of the imperative of transforming equality of opportunities of access into equality of opportunities of success.

This pedagogic action inspired by the political mandate of the new middle class is linked, simultaneously as a cause and an effect, to the growing individualisation of citizenship, of the project of schooling and of other social and cultural projects. This phenomenon has been subject to two kinds of interpretation that only through ignorance or bad faith can not be distinguished. Bauman (2001) talks of an 'individualised society' distinguishing, in the wake of Beck (1992), between 'individuation' and 'individualisation', the former being the desired product of the project of modernity, in the sense that it aimed at enabling individuals to take charge of themselves, and the latter being a kind of condemnation of individuals to nothing more than they are, that is, individuals. In this case, it is suspected that it is the invisible hand of neoliberalism that is configuring our societies as aggregates of individuals who are fragilised as citizens. Sennett (1998) goes even further, arguing that individualisation not only articulates the logic of organised capitalism but also corrupts the very character of individuals. It is in these latter senses that individualisation may become a form of depoliticisation, in the first place, of citizenship ('I cease to be a citizen in order to become an individual abandoned to his own luck and his own competencies') and, in the second place, of work ('my salaried relationship depends only on me and on the vicissitudes of the market').

In the case of individuation, the predominant logic appears to be that one emphasised by Giddens in his different works on social and individual reflexivity (1990; 1994). That is, on the basis of these processes the capacity of individuals to manage their lives and their options in a consistent and pro-active way may be developed. In the case of citizenship, it arises, in this perspective, as 'demanded' or 'reclaimed', that is, the modern social contract is reconfigured on the basis of the taking on by social actors and groups of the projects and the very objectives that are central to the legitimacy of a 're-appropriated' sovereignty. In the case of work, this capacity arises as one of the structural spaces (Santos, 1995) where personal and social identity is formed without this meaning that this space is privileged with regard to the other spaces of social determination (for example, the domestic space, the community space, the space of the market, and so on).

With regard to schooling, these two interpretations also clash and, in the first case, individualisation, one can argue that what is at stake is a process of depoliticisation. In fact, education, on leaving the public sphere of the state to become the individual's 'problem', appears, or at least appears in political discourses, as deposed of its dimension of collective responsibility. From public service and citizens' rights, it is transformed into a commodity to be transactioned in the form of services. It is as if education has become the individual's responsibility who, in this way, is condemned to acquire and manage in the market context the competencies that he/she needs to become employable throughout working life.

In the second case, individuation, schooling and education arise as a process in which individual and group choice play a central role. In another work (Stoer and Magalhães, 2003a), we spoke, in this regard, of schooling that is 'demanded or reclaimed', meaning by this that schooling takes on increasingly a framework where individuals manage their options rather than letting themselves be directed by education systems. To the extent that individuals and groups demand for themselves this centrality, where schooling is scripted by individuals (rather than they being scripted by the school system), we can say that we are dealing with the phenomenon of the repoliticisation of education. Groups such as the gypsies, or groups that claim *home schooling* (cf. Apple, 2000), appear to show that the universal project of schooling is being reconfigured through the narratives of the different actors involved. It is as if each individual goes to the school in order to get that which is perceived by the individual as relevant to his/her needs and/or interests (in the case of the gypsies referred to above, some research shows that that which they look for in the school is nothing more than observing the rules necessary to be recognised as beneficiary by the state). The case of the *Escola da Ponte*, in the north of Portugal, is also an example of this phenomenon, given that the parents of the school demand that their sons and daughters acquire 'a different form of state schooling'.[1]

The reconfiguration of the state implies that it not become vulnerable with respect to the, increasingly less invisible, hand of the market. That is the state can, as Carnoy (2002) suggests, take on new forms of action that include, for example, the strengthening of communities based on identity that in themselves constitute an important base for that which we have denominated 'demanded, or reclaimed, citizenship' (Stoer and Magalhães, ibid.). Differently to what one might expect, the reconfigured state can be an agent for the promotion of this form of citizenship. Thus, the repoliticisation of schooling appears to arise in a reverse direction to that of schooling as part of modernity, that is, it develops 'bottom-up', from citizens upwards to the state, as part of the exercise of reclaimed citizenship.

It is at the site of the tension between the depoliticisation of education, resulting to a large extent from the effects of the current wave of neoliberalism, and its repoliticisation through the assumption of reclaimed citizenship that, in our view, the political agenda for education is being reconfigured. This process of reconfiguration demands both sophisticated analysis and political action, for to see amongst the threats and opportunities that are arising from emergent social dynamics only the 'invisible' hand, inevitably dirty, of neoliberalism may be a way of refusing renewed forms of political agency.

Reflexive citizenship and 'difference is us'

It is at the juncture of the tension between the process of the individualisation of citizens, process by way of which they are made responsible for almost everything, including their own successes and failures, and the process of individual and personal reflexivity, identified with the dynamic of pro-active citizenship that is itself based on a claim for difference, that individuals and groups are increasingly redefined. The potential to give reasons for personal and group choices arises as clearly political and even the logic of the market, traditionally homogenising, appears to be susceptible to be, in some way, reflexively 'agencied'. In stating this, we are not thinking only of contra-hegemonic practices such as, for example, those of 'fair trade shops', which, in the form of networks of production, distribution and consumption, aim at reordering the market in order to, by way of consumption, not benefit parasitically-based production and/or distribution in the form of, for example, child labour, or wage differences based on gender, or ethnicity. Our argument is that the global marketplace, to the extent that it is reconfigured (above all on the basis of demand, that is, on the basis of consumption) reflects reflexive logics that it would be simplistic to characterise as a mere re-adaptation of the old market under new conditions.

This challenge to the homogenising logic of the market does not make the capitalist order less capitalist. What it does is to make the field of political action more nuanced and possible to be agencied. Stated in another way, the political action which emanates from the assumption of individuation, as an affirmation of individual and collective difference, does not appear to circumscribe itself only to forms of political organisation—trade unions, political parties, international organisations, and so on—that functioned on the basis of a citizenship attributed by the state. According to this logic, citizenship was a quality to which one had, at least formally, immediate access, through the state, as a consequence of being born in a given national territory. In accord with the logic that appears to be emerging, citizenship arises as something reclaimed, above all on the basis of the affirmation of identity by people and groups. And if this new configuration of citizenship appears to promote a strong repoliticisation of citizenship, making present, for example, in the public sphere that which for a long time was located in the private sphere, new forms of action and of organisation of citizens arise as necessary and as yet to be invented.

These forms of reflexive citizenship are being reflected, as has already been suggested, in the relationship that individuals and groups maintain with school systems. The logic of a national education provided by an all-embracing public network is clashing with other rationalities that expect to find in educational institutions ways of affirming local identity, of expressing ethnic specificities, of, in the case of the new middle class, promoting new strategies of the preservation of their already traditional fields of social mobility, above all those provided by higher education. In this clash, it appears to be this latter rationality, that of the middle class, that is setting the agenda in education and is defining the mandate that is addressed to the education system (see Magalhães and Stoer, 2003b).

In this mandate, which in another work we have tried to identify more fully (Magalhães and Stoer, 2003a), the role of knowledge in the formation of individuals arises, in an increasingly incisive way, in the form of 'competencies'. The coincidence between this process and the process of current European construction appears to be central, for it is above all at the Lisbon Summit (2000) that the relationship between knowledge and formation is presented as constituting the privileged strategy by way of which nation-Europe will affirm itself in the, now global, concert of the large economic blocs.

Europe as a bazaar and the reconfiguration of knowledge in the network society

If, as we argued above, education is becoming repoliticised by way of an education process that is itself polarised between individualisation and individuation, it appears crucial to relate the resulting tension with the European context that arises either as a framework for the elaboration of policies or as its very content. Still, European construction does not correspond to a unified project nor to a single intention, that is, when speaking of Europe there exist diverse Europes within our heads. This plurality of Europes can be identified through the metaphors that give it body in political discourses. Indeed, over time Europe has been conceived as a metaphor, for example in Greek mythology, and has been thought politically by way of metaphors (see below). It may even be possible to say that Europe has existed above all through metaphors and that, in a certain sense, Europe itself was created by these very metaphors.

The flag

The most well known of these metaphors is the 'flag'. Nation-states, whose origins go back to the Middle Ages, fully assumed this form of organisation mainly from the 18th century onwards. In many ways one can say that they are imagined political entities (Anderson, 1983), not because they invented nations, but because they translated nationality into this form of political organisation. The flag is the symbolic translation of the unity that the nation-state aims to construct on the basis of territory, language, religion, culture, etc. Its agglutinating strength with regard to national entities appears to survive even the anti-colonialist movements whose founding acts also were marked by the creation of a flag, of an education system and of an army stretching across national territory and becoming practically synonymous with this territory. The metaphor of the flag conserves in this way the founding moment of the nation as configured by the state. Up to now, the history of Europe has been the history of European nation-states, with nuances that extend from states in search of a nation (the case of Spain) to nations in search of a state (Ulster, for example). It has also been the history of the conflict between nation-states, in the name of territory, of religion, of markets. Indeed, the Europe captured by the metaphor of the flag is a Europe of bloody historical conflict (Coulby, 1997). From the 12th century, blood has flowed in the name of God, of motherland, of markets, but it is with the modern age that the flag has become most important as inspiration for political action. Societies organised by the state have become internally homogenised and externally have created societies of nations whose *raison d'être* has ranged from conflict to the creation of the United Nations.

The nation-states, under the banner of the flag, have created education systems as a privileged means of educating individuals 'belonging' to their sphere of regulation. As one has already suggested, to be born in a given territory, although constituting the formal reason on the basis of which citizenship is attributed, has not been sufficient, particularly after the consolidation of the link of capitalism to national societies to guarantee full access to citizenship. In fact, capitalism requires that the individual who is born in national territory be integrated into the wage relation. Only in this way is the individual fully recognised by the state as a subject with rights and duties. It is at this moment that knowledge and culture are configured on the basis of the national level. Modern universities were conceived as centres for the production, conservation and diffusion of knowledge in order to consolidate the national project, both in economic and in cultural terms. Both the Humboldtian university and the Napoleonic university emphasised, at the same time that they celebrated the universal character of knowledge, the national level. The education systems created within the scope of the consolidation of the nation-state are the disseminating mechanism of this knowledge and of this national character and, as such, are part of the tension between the universality of the former and the particularity of the latter.

The role of knowledge in this sociocultural paradigm of modernity reflects this tension between the formation of the universal subject and the national citizen. When combined with capitalism, this paradigm imposes on knowledge a third dimension that is made up of both the scientific input into the productive process and the scientific organisation of this latter. In the period of organised capitalism, or fordism, the work process includes both aspects of this third dimension, but the productive process in itself does not centre itself on knowledge. Rather this process is centred on work, in the transformation of raw materials and in the organisation of the work process. Knowledge arises as dependent upon work and not as the core of the work process.

Thus, knowledge and citizenship under the banner of the flag appear to converge in the functional task of creating good citizens and good workers, implicated in the strengthening and the prosperity of the nation-state. The projects of industrial growth are intertwined, during fordism, with the projects of national growth and affirmation. In general terms, education takes on a triple mandate: to make knowledge circulate in order to develop the individual, to prepare the worker and to educate the citizen.

The Europe that is thought on the basis of the metaphor of the flag is the Europe that we have inherited. It arises as a temptation, as what we have termed in other works as the temptation of the past, to think Europe on the basis of the model of the nation-state, such as we know it. Should Europe be a mega-nation that encompasses all others and, in some sense, regionalises them, asks Anne-Marie Thiesse (1999)? Or should it be a construction of a new type? In fact, it seems that neither the symbol that is the flag with stars, nor the common currency, nor even the promise of a European Constitution are by themselves capable of providing a political model that can reconfigure the feeling of national belonging, providing the basis for a reinvented form of citizenship.

Themes/issues

Thus it becomes necessary to look for other metaphors of Europe. Kaldor (1995) speaks of the Europe of themes, or issues: the environment, the Euro, social justice, etc. These themes would be the political basis on which Europe could (and should) configure itself. Thus, the common currency, the free circulation of people and goods, human rights, and so on, could constitute themselves as the vehicles of aggregation and the motors of common action. Still, given that the Europe of nation-states is an undeniable reality and given that the themes/issues are, in a manner of speaking, global and cosmopolitan in nature, it is possible to argue that if the Europe of issues/themes adds to the Europe of the flag a universal dimension that it did not possess, it does not respond clearly to the questions posed by the need for the national affirmation of identities. That is, one continues to kill and to die for the flag.

If, as Giddens suggests, we live in a markedly sociological, reflexive, society, in the sense that personal and institutional practices are permanently configured by the knowledge that we construct about them, it is also true that this reflexivity extends to the affirmation of more particularistic identities, often local, that more cosmopolitan and universal-oriented rationalities ignore at their own peril. These particularisms, which are not reducible to nationalisms, integrate us into important constellations of conflict: for example, the defence of the national economy and the defence of the environment, identity affirmation on the basis of given life styles and the defence of cultural traditions. Thus, the metaphor of the flag appears to provide something which the themes/issues do not provide, i.e., an intense sense of belonging. Although the thematic causes (women's rights, the environment, sexual identities) may provide important scope for identity formation and for strong militancy, it appears that nationality continues to awaken strong feelings of defence and attack.

Knowledge with regard to this metaphor, arises, in the first place, as a kind of political literacy, in the sense that it should serve the reflexive projects of individuals and groups. In the second place, knowledge arises as a crucial factor in the productive process due to its increasingly evident global/local dimension. With regard to the first aspect, we have already referred, in the first part of this work, to the tension between individualisation and individuation. It is here that this tension becomes particularly evident. At the same time that knowledge makes possible the reflexivity of individuals and groups and their capacity for agency, the productive process, referred to as a second aspect of the metaphor, articulates this same reflexivity. The productive processes are not only undergoing globalisation, they also demand a new kind of worker, such as the one identified by Stephen Ball on the basis of interviews with leaders of industry in England (1990; see also Guile, 2002). Communication competencies, innovation and co-operation are presented simultaneously as indicators of the well-being of individuals and as important factors of the productive process.

Thus, knowledge appears as an instrument of individuals and groups for the carrying out of their own projects and as an increasingly important factor in production. The distance between individuation and individualisation is subtle, it not being easy to identify whether these concepts correspond, or not, to other concepts clearly inscribed in capitalist modernity, such as alienation and anomie. Citizenship, in the same way, arises recombined between concerns for reflexivity and for new sociabilities. For example, the concern with the defence of the environment has implications at the level of daily occurrences, both in terms of the locality and in global terms, such that risk and confidence, as Giddens would say, are permanently present in both action and decision-making. It is as if, using another expression of Giddens (1990), the harnessing of the 'juggernaut' (which is known to be ungovernable) must constantly serve as the aim of the efforts of citizens, who through their very citizenry try to keep it minimally on the right track. To be a citizen, in this sense, is to contribute as actively as possible to the governance of risk societies.

A Europe configured by this metaphor of themes/issues seems to attribute to knowledge the cosmopolitan task of reconfiguring national citizenship on the basis of the causes and choices of individuals and groups. On the other hand, the competencies demanded of schooling, at the same time that they develop the individual as a reflexive actor, place the individual on the labour market reconfigured by flexible, 'casino', in the words of Harvey (1989), capitalism. Thus, if the themes/issues have at their base the assumption of a citizenship founded on cosmopolitan political literacy, they also expose individuals and groups to the non-regulated, or, at a minimum, difficult-to-regulate, global fluxes of capital.

The network

The metaphor of the network has prevailed at the level of the different discourses on social relations and on modes of communication and the diffusion of knowledge. The network arises as a keyword with regard to social organisation— the network society—to the circulation of information and knowledge—the world-wide web—and even at the local and individual levels—territorial and interpersonal networks. The network as a web of relations has become institutionalised as reality, that is, its virtual dimension shapes our daily lives. If the flag has been strongly embodied by, and through, national identities, it appears that the cultural practices of groups and individuals are also being shaped by this emerging metaphor, without it being yet possible to know, with precision, the consequences for identity construction and sociabilities.

With regard to political organisation, this metaphor can also be the starting point for rethinking Europe as a political construction. Carnoy and Castells refer to the concept of network state, which is defined as being

> '(...) made up of shared institutions, and enacted by bargaining and interactive iteration all along the chain of decision-making: national governments, co-national governments, supra-national bodies, international institutions, governments of nationalities, regional governments, local governments and NGOs (...). (...) This new state functions as a network, in which all nodes interact and are equally necessary for the performance of the state's functions. It is a state whose efficiency is defined in terms of its capacity to create and sustain networks—global, regional and local networks—and through these networks, to promote economic growth and develop new forms of social integration' (Carnoy, 2001, p.31).

This conception of network state arises at the same time as the presentation of a desirable model of state organisation and as something that already exists, namely the European Union. According to Castells (2001, p.121),

> '(...) there is one European state. It is not made up of the European Commission. The European Commission is a bureaucracy which many people hate and mistrust, and it clearly has no power. The power is in the European Council of Ministers, chiefs of Government of all countries meeting every three months, making decisions to be decided by the European Commission. It works (...) as a network state. It is the only explicit network state so far. The others are implicit.'

Therefore, between the desirable model and what is actually going on, the network state arises as an interesting political metaphor to be taken up. On the one hand, it contains an implicit language and a grammar that at the same time that they appear standardised and somewhat rigid also seem to be susceptible to being agencied. On the other hand, the network is a web of relationships that goes beyond the technique of informational processes and the diffusion of information. The network, in this latter sense, contains privileged, and potentially hegemonic, actors; it is not a transparent place since it is both epistemologically and politically marked (see, for example the case of Microsoft and the predominance of English as a language of informational traffic). These two aspects made the network a site of political agency and therefore far from being definitively marked by a top-down logic given that, as the citations above from Carnoy and Castells suggest, they provide, in their interstices, important possibilities for individual and group affirmation at different levels, local, regional, national and global. Networks are not, therefore, idle political places. Citing once again Castells:

'(…) networks constitute the new morphology of our societies, and the diffusion of network logic substantially modifies the operation and outcomes in processes of production, experience, power and culture. While the networking form of social organisation has existed in other times and places, the new informational technology paradigm provides the material base for its pervasive expansion throughout the entire social structure. Furthermore, I would argue that this networking logic induces a social determination of a higher level than that of specific social interests expressed through the networks: the power of flows takes precedence over the flows of power. (...) Networks are open structures, able to expand without limits, integrating new nodes as long as they are able to communicate within the network, namely as long as they share the same communication codes (for example, values for performance goals). A network-based social structure is a highly dynamic, open system susceptible to innovating without upsetting its balance' (Castells, 1996, pp.469-70).

As a metaphor for the reorganisation of Europe, the network arises not only founded on flows of power but also as founded on flows of information and knowledge. These flows are no longer produced, or controlled, by national institutions in charge of the production and diffusion of this same information and knowledge, namely, the institutions of the educational system. Effectively, information and knowledge, as essential functions of educational institutions are being placed outside the school system, as Carnoy has emphasised when he says that the function of selection by schools has to be relativised, with the production and diffusion of knowledge and competencies, on the contrary, being given emphasis. He says, further, that the state will have to transform a whole school bureaucracy and that if this transformation does not occur the very legitimation of the state will be at risk, as well as the capacity for the state to sustain economic development in a global environment (Carnoy 2001, p.32).

The reason for the urgency of this reconfiguration is that, at the same time that the nation-state—the metaphor of the flag—see its legitimacy with regard to the power of the media, regional territorialisations (NAFTA, ASEAN, etc.), local demands and even the redistribution of judicial power (for example, via supranational tribunals, such as the IPT and the European Court of Justice) diluted, information and knowledge have transformed themselves into central factors of production, making economic development dependent upon them, as we stated above. Thus, the political literacy, necessary for the exercise of citizenship, within the scope of the political metaphor of the network, becomes more complex in relation to the two other metaphors. The knowledge of the first metaphor, of the flag, was seen as a factor of the development of the individual, of the education of the citizen and the preparation of the worker. In the second metaphor, themes/issues, knowledge was framed as a form of political participation, par excellence, in cosmopolitan discussions and debates. In the metaphor of the network, political literacy needs to be developed at two different levels: at a first level, the citizen must possess the competencies (digital literacy) that will permit him/her to integrate the network as a flow of information and knowledge in order to have a place in the labour market, itself undergoing a process of reconfiguration; at a second level, it needs to take on an important degree of reflexivity (political literacy) in order to localise itself, as an identity, in a context where the very exercise of citizenship is an object of demand. These two forms of literacy are not opposed, as one might believe on the basis of those diagnoses that see the present development of western societies as a kind of imprisonment of the individual itself. As Castells has referred, there exist two forms of exclusion with regard to the network: the first relates to access, or lack of access, to the network, while the second develops on the basis of the quality of the individual as user of the network, that is, it is crucial to know if one is dealing with a mere passive user or with an actively intervening user.

The political model based on this metaphor, although it is open and promotes the agency of social actors, is still clearly marked by a logic that, as we stated above, is predominantly top-down. What is at stake here is not only a question of digital literacy, or illiteracy, but, rather, the conditioning of citizenship itself by this literacy. To be digitally illiterate means to be, therefore, doubly excluded, firstly as a user of the universal grammar of computers and, secondly, as a citizen who wishes to claim citizenship on the basis of his/her own difference or identity.

The bazaar

It is at this point when difference becomes a central ingredient of citizenship that a fourth and last metaphor for thinking Europe and citizenship comes to the forefront. For a long time, and presently with considerable frequency, the exercise of citizenship was directly related to questions of equality, above all equality based on redistribution. One is not attempting to deny here that class determination is important (see, further, Stoer and Magalhães, 2002), but, rather, to emphasise that that which is delimited by flexible capitalism is the amplitude of the reflexivity and the agency of individuals and groups. As Beck states (1992), all sociologists that have worked with the question of social class know that reflexivity, as the capacity to choose, is a learned capacity that depends on specific social and family origins, that is, the effect of class gives rise to that which he terms a new inequality, the inequality of the way one deals with insecurity and reflexivity (ibid., p.98). If knowledge as a central factor of production is that which is susceptible to be translated into bytes, present forms of citizenship are profoundly marked by the individual and group identities of citizens. To be a woman, of a given ethnic group, to take on a given life style or sexual identity, are increasingly factors that influence the exercise of citizenship. This appears to be contradictory with the universal character and more or less homogeneity of bytified information that circulates around the globe. Thus, it is not only important to be part of the network, in the sense of possessing digital literacy; it is also crucial to be sensitive to the fact that to be part of the social network is to be increasingly a part of it on the basis of the affirmation of one's difference and ensuing demand for rights and duties. It is in this sense that the metaphor of the bazaar appears to us to be important to consider.

In a well-know debate between the philosopher Richard Rorty and the anthropologist Clifford Geertz (see Stoer and Magalhães, 2001) on the organisation of modern western societies, the latter proposes the metaphor of the 'Kuwaiti bazaar' in order to account for the simultaneous tendency for the fragmentation and aggregation of these societies. Geertz speaks concretely of how in an epoch of globalisation local communities increasingly resemble an enormous collage, that is, in each one of its localities, the world seems increasingly to be more 'a Kuwaiti bazaar that an exclusive English club' (ibid., p.47). This latter represents the incommensurability of local/cultural differences: the 'portugueseness' of the Portuguese, the 'englishness' of the English, the arabic character of the Arabs, and so on.

The idea of the 'bazaar of Kuwait', as being able to structure a new conception of present societies, and of new sociabilities, needs a bit more development in order to understand what is at stake with this metaphor. Thus:

1. The bazaar is not a grand narrative that can structure some sort of new political utopia. Instead, it has a pragmatic value in the sense that it is proposed by Europeans in order to rethink the European context and European construction;

2. The bazaar is a regulated public space (political, social, cultural…) that is itself subject to regulation;
3. The state, if reconfigured as a network state, can be an important agent of the distribution of social justice and the diffusion of the recognition of difference, as well as an important instrument of the implementation of redistributive justice;
4. The sovereignty that 'differences' claim from the state does not correspond to the dissolution of the state as an agent of justice (above all redistributive), but relates to the legitimacy of differences to regulate their own lives (for example, 'I pay my taxes – duty - but I want to education my children—right—exactly as I see fit');
5. In the bazaar, one does not discuss the legitimacy of differences but, rather, negotiates forms and rules of conviviality, on the basis of the idea that 'we can live together' (*'Pourrons-nous vivres ensemble?'*, Touraine, 1998);
6. This negotiation is not a phase to be passed through, but is, rather, a permanent state; democracy is no longer a 'stage' of development, it is an end it itself (i.e., without end).

What is at stake in this political definition of the bazaar is the fact that it raises the question of power, emphasising that differences affirm themselves within the scope of an 'ideological battlefield' (Wallerstein, 1990), that is, dialectically confronting issues of discrimination, racism or exclusion with those derived from inequality in the distribution of wealth and vice-versa. The bazaar, as an orienting political metaphor, through the agency that it presupposes for social actors, although integrating on the basis of the top-down logic of the network, manages to relativise this logic by placing emphasis on the bottom-up logic of reclaimed, or demanded, citizenship. In this sense, the bazaar as a political metaphor appears to include the good points of the other metaphors we have referred to. From the first, the flag, it includes the recognition that the question of national identity cannot be ignored but must, rather, be integrated with difference. From the second, it integrates cosmopolitanism and the universal concern with that which refers to all human beings. From the third, it assumes that the network, on the basis of which information and knowledge flows, is the scope of the agency of social actors, of informational grammar and of the logic of flexible capitalism. With regard to this latter, it is fundamental to stress that it does not necessarily coincide with what is termed neoliberalism, whether as a regime for the accumulation of capital, or as a mode of social regulation. As we have already stated, flexible capitalism also implies the action of individuals and groups that may reconfigure it both as an ideology (for example the setting up of research grants on the environment by large oil companies) and as a practice (the case of the already cited example of 'just trade').

The bazaar as a political unit depends to a large extent on the reflexivity of citizens, considered both as individuals and in collective terms. As a group of negotiated rules for conviviality, the bazaar is the other side of that which Rorty calls 'exclusive private clubs'. That is, the bazaar is the place where citizenship expresses itself through the community of general rules that do not violate the differences of citizens. It is as differences that citizens congregate in this political space, differently from that which occurred with the exercise of citizenship in modern contexts, where citizens came together in public spaces and times on the basis of what they had in common, i.e., religion, language, territory, and so on.

Knowledge, information and the competencies that operationalise them thus arise as the basic ingredients of present citizenry. At the same time that the production of knowledge, of information and of competencies tends to distance itself from the school as a privileged locale, society, as a whole, and particularly European society, tends to become a society founded on the circulation of knowledge and information. The idea of the learning society, more than a simple journalistic platitude, arises here to underline the reflexive potential that at the same time is at our disposal and that can become a threat to the exercise of our very reflexivity. Both being aware of the potentialities and risks of knowledge and combining this knowledge with identity affirmation founded on differences appear to show that the demand for citizenship does not rest solely on the formal recognition of rights and duties but that it rests, above all, on the effective agency of these latter, not on the basis of the national homogeneity of individuals but, rather, on the basis on their identity choices.

Concluding remarks

In another work (2003a), we have already argued, and here we would wish to underline this argument, that the school was developed by the modern nation-state as the privileged way of educating citizens, of disseminating knowledge and of preparing workers for the labour market. This was a time when citizenship was configured essentially on the basis of state (legal) and national (attributed citizenship) homogeneity and not on the basis of local and individual differences. On the other hand, and also as we have already argued, there arises, articulated with the globalisation process, a strong tendency for 'glocalisation', in which the state becomes dilacerated, in terms of its exercise of sovereignty, between supranational demands and claims and the demands and claims originating in the locality. New sociabilities of a cosmopolitan flavour and/or of strong local origin appear to be complexifying and, up to a certain point, parting company with an attributed citizenship of the first political model founded on homogeneity. For example, the concern with the environment appears to be becoming less of a political concern, less part of a wider political programme, in order to become increasingly an identity, that is, a political project in itself, that implies new sociabilities. These new sociabilities appear to imply a reclaimed (pro-active) citizenship and, in this sense, they are profoundly political.

In conclusion, our argument is that the school is being reconfigured. In the first place, it is being reconfigured as the place that it occupies in the life trajectories of citizens. In the second place, it is being reconfigured as the place where knowledge is recontextualised as a mode of the education of individuals and citizens. In the third place, it is being reconfigured as an institution that, from being markedly national becomes also markedly local and global. The consolidation of the learning society appears to be at the base of this triple reconfiguration of the school, in the sense that the school has ceased to be, par excellence, the centre for the organisation and circulation of knowledge. As evidence for this reconfiguration of the school, we can point to, in the wake of Bernstein (1996) and Lash (in Beck, Giddens and Lash, 1994), the reconfiguration of the mandate addressed to the education system by the 'new' new middle class. We have recently begun to analyse this process in Portugal (Magalhães and Stoer, 2002) and it is currently the object of study of a research project on the claim for academic excellence in the context of the consolidation of mass schooling in Portugal.

In fact, the school increasingly arises in the life trajectories of individuals as something that is susceptible to being guided by individuals themselves. Above all for the middle class, this management has arisen as the most evident way for students and families to integrate their educational choices in strategies with the mark of this class. There are also indications, identified in research that has been carried out (see, for example, Cortesão and Stoer, 1995), that even the families and youth of less favoured social strata have also developed strategies that place the school on their own personal and family scripts (see also note on the *Escola da Ponte*). One is not saying that the schooling promoted by the state has ceased to be a clear and important factor in the dissemination of knowledge and competencies (for example, compulsory schooling has not only become more consolidated, it has also increased). Rather, one is saying that schooling is being reclaimed by individuals on the basis of needs that are perceived as being their own.

In the second place, the reconfiguration of the school is linked to the reconfiguration of the very knowledge of the present contexts of flexible and informational capitalism. This occurs in two ways: (i) through the reconfiguration of the nature of knowledge as information and (ii) through the reconfiguration of the educational role of knowledge (cf. Stoer and Magalhães, 2003c). In the first sense, knowledge that is assumed to be relevant in present contexts is susceptible to being translated into machine-language and circulated under this form. This means that the knowledge that flows in electronic and virtual circuits is a knowledge/information translated in accord with the criteria of performativity, where the aim is to achieve maximum output on the basis of minimum input. In fact, one is not dealing with knowledge in the sense that modernity attributed to the concept, but, rather, as what we have referred to as a bytified knowledge/information. In the second sense, the educational character of knowledge is recomposed as that which we have denominated *throughput* (ibid.), that is, as a form of knowledge that goes through the individual, providing the individual with instrumental competencies, but without educating, or forming, the individual (in the sense of *Bildung*).

Finally, and in the third place, the school is being reconfigured by its move from a markedly national institution to an institution more 'glocal' in character, meaning that it is becoming an institution that situates itself between the network society and the new sociabilities to which we have referred. To be part of the network state means to be located, simultaneously, in the network society and to be involved in the new forms of sociabiltiy. Just like the network society, just like citizenship in the scope of the network state, and in the context of the new sociabilities, the school arises as a composite of opportunities and threats different from those of the school of modernity. In the context of the learning society, social exclusion through schooling needs to be simultaneously relativised (as we said above in the wake of Carnoy, the education system can transform itself from a system of selection into a system of knowledge and competencies production) and confronted head on. By neglecting it, many risk remaining outside the network.

Note

1. The *Escola da Ponte* in northern Portugal has become known for its pro-active stance with regard to both the elaboration and the implementation of education policy. With regard to the former, this state school has managed through the development of its own educational project, and through resistance to many aspects of official education policy, to elaborate its own policy, including a regime of self-government by the school's pupils (policy is based on pupil's demands), the promotion of co-operative learning and a strongly-based inclusive school practice (*all* pupils are considered pupils with special educational needs). With regard to the latter, the *Escola da Ponte* has developed over the years a strong relationship with the surrounding community to the extent that many parents, often from lower social strata, have become spokespersons for the school's policy. What is interesting here is the way these parents have developed an identity based on the educational project of the school that enables them to reclaim the school on the basis of this identity (cf. Stoer and Silva, 2005).

References

Anderson, B. (1983) *Imagined Communities*. London: Verso.

Apple, M. (2000) 'Away with all teachers: the cultural politics of home schooling.' *International Studies in Sociology of Education*, Vol.10(1), pp.61-80.

Bauman, Z. (2001) *The Individualized Society*. Cambridge: Polity Press.

Beck, U. (1992) *The Risk Society: Towards a New Modernity*. London: Sage.

Beck, U.; Giddens, A. & Lash, S. (1994) *Reflexive Modernisation*. Cambridge: Polity Press.

Bernstein, B. (1996) *Pedagogy Symbolic Control and Identity*. London: Taylor & Francis.

Bourdieu, P. (1986) *Distinction*. London: Routledge & Kegan Paul.

Candeias, A. (1994) *Educar de outra forma: A Escola Oficina Nº 1 de Lisboa, 1905-1930*. Lisbon: Instituto de Inovação Educacional.

Cortesão, L. & Stoer, S.R. (1995) *Projectos, Percursos, Sinergias no Campo da Educação Inter/ Multicultural: Relatório Final*. Lisbon: Calouste Gulbenkian Foundation/Junta Nacional de Investigação Científica.

Coulby, D. (1997) 'Intercultural education in the United States of America and Europe: some parallels and convergences in research and policy.' *European Journal of Intercultural Studies*, Vol.8(1), pp.97-104.

Dale, R. (1989) *The State and Education Policy*. Milton Keynes: Open University Press.

Durkheim, É. (1984) *Sociologia, Educação e Moral*, Porto: Rés Editora.

Giddens, A. (1990) *The Consequences of Modernity*. Cambridge: Polity Press.

Giddens, A. (1994) *Modernidade e Identidade Pessoal*. Lisbon: Celta Editora.

Guile, D. (2002) 'Skill and work experience in the European knowledge economy.' *Journal of Education and Work*, Vol.15(3), pp.251-276.

Harvey, D. (1989) *The Condition of Post-Modernity: An Inquiry into Origins of Cultural Change*. Oxford: Basil Blackwell.

Johnson, R. (1981) *'Education and Development' Course E353, Unit 1*, Milton Keynes, The Open University.

Kaldor, M. (1995) 'European institutions, nation-states and nationalism.' In D. Archibugi & D. Held (eds) *Cosmopolitan Democracy*. Cambridge: Polity Press.

Lenhardt, G. & Offe, C. (1984) 'Teoria do Estado e Política Social.' In C. Offe (ed.) *Problemas Estruturais do Estado Capitalista*. Rio de Janeiro: Tempo Brasileiro.

Magalhães, A.M. (2003) 'As transformações do mercado de trabalho e as novas identidades individuais e colectivas.' In J.A. Correia & M. Matos (eds) *Violência e Violências da e na Escola*. Oporto: Edições Afrontamento/CIIE.

Magalhães, A.M. & Stoer, S.R. (2002a) *A Escola para Todos e a Excelência Académica*. Oporto: Profedições.

Magalhães, A.M. & Stoer, S.R. (2002b) 'A nova classe média e a reconfiguração do mandato endereçado ao sistema educativo.' *Educação, Sociedade & Culturas*, Vol.18, pp.25-40.

Maghalhães, A.M. & Stoer, S.R. (2003a) 'Performance, citizenship and the knowledge society: a new mandate for European education policy.' *Globalisation, Societies and Education*, Vol.1(1), pp.41-66.

Magalhães, A.M. & Stoer, S.R. (2003b) 'Education, knowledge and the network society.' Paper given at the Nicosia Conference of the European Thematic Network GENIE, July.

Parsons, T. (1959) 'The school class as a social system.' *Harvard Educational Review*, Vol.29(4), pp.297-318.

Santos, B.S. (1995) *Toward a New Common Sense*. New York: Routledge.

Sennett, R. (1998) *The Corrosion of Character. The Personal Consequences of Work in New Capitalism*. New York: W. W. Norton Press.

Stoer, S.R. & Magalhães, A.M. (2001) 'A incomensurabilidade da diferença e o anti-anti-etnocentrismo.' In D. Rodrigues (ed.) *Educação e Diferença*. Oporto: Porto Editora.

Stoer, S.R. & Magalhães, A.M. (2003a) 'A reconfiguração do contrato social moderno: novas cidadanias e educação.' In D. Rodrigues (ed.) *Perspectivas Sobre a Inclusão: da Educação à Sociedade*. Oporto: Porto Editora.

Stoer, S.R. & Magalhães, A.M. (2003b) 'Europe as a bazaar: a contribution to the analysis of the reconfiguration of nation-states and new forms of 'living together.' Paper given at the Midterm Confererence of the Sociology of Education Research Committee of the ISA, Lisbon, September.

Stoer, S.R. & Silva, P. (2005) *Escola-Família, Uma Relação em Processo de Reconfiguração*. Porto: Porto Editora (in press).

Thiesse, A.-M. (1999) *La Création des Identités Nationales*. Paris: Éditions du Seuil.

Touraine, A. (1997) *Pourrons-nous Vivre Ensemble? Égaux et Differents*. Paris: Fayard.

Wallerstein, I. (1990) 'Culture as the ideological battleground of the modern world system.' In Mike Featherstone (ed.) *Global Culture*. London: Sage.

CHAPTER SIX

The Modification of Learning through Cultural Traditions and Societal Structures

GABRIELE LASKE

Introduction

During the last decade work and learning have become strongly coupled. Never in recorded history has the need for continuous learning taken on such an economic slant. One could phrase this new paradigm as: 'Without continuous learning one will lose one's capability to work'. It no longer seems to be merely a lack of physical capacity or the lack of certain talents that limits one to remain employed: what excludes one from the labour market is lack of, or the refusal to undertake, continuous learning. The Anglo-Saxon and West European worlds nowadays are especially ruled by the economic conviction and ideology underpinning this paradigm. The latter's dubious nature shall not be discussed here. Rather, this paper will emphasise the fact that the discussion on learning is, amongst others, characterised by the implicit assumption that everybody has a mutual understanding of what learning is. For example, when strategies about workforce development with respect to learning are discussed during a meeting of European researchers or international managers, the aspect that learning is culturally determined is hardly ever taken into consideration.

The present volume, '*Homo Sapiens Europœus*—Creating the European Learning Citizen', focuses on two essential concepts: citizens and learning. The meaning of both concepts/terms is highly subjective, and depends on the social and cultural context in which they are used or discussed. For instance, there is much American literature available that stresses the importance of the school in the development of active citizenship. Yet, the very idea of citizenship in the US is a result of the specific cultural and historical development of this country. As Labaree (2000, p.28) notes:

'The urge to preserve individual liberty is a key to understanding American society, and it is what defines distinctive approach to politics, economics, and education. 'Don't tell me what to do' has long been our national slogan. By it we have meant in particular that government should keep off our backs—especially government that is far removed from our local community. All you need to do is to remember that this nation was born of an uprising against a colonial government that tried to impose modest taxes on it from afar.'

The coupling of the idea of citizenship and education is very unique to the American culture and value system. In Asian cultures like China or Japan, a concept that relates education and citizenship does not exist. Also the European concept of citizen is still very vague compared to the strong sense of citizenship that exists in the United States. In this sense Marks (2003) raises the question: 'Could it therefore not be the case, that the idea of citizenship in fact being witnessed is the Americanisation of the globe (and by definition Europe)?' But this chapter will not stress the origin and connotation of citizenship and its correlation to learning or education. Rather, its main concern will be the cultural determination of learning and education. Thus, whilst Marks concludes his discussion of the Americanisation of the globe by asserting that '...comparative accounts of education and education systems are becoming increasingly redundant since we are all becoming more and more alike' (2003), this chapter makes the case for quite the opposite perspective.

Besides work, learning is the activity by which the socialisation process of citizens takes place. Yet socialisation through learning occurs from early childhood, while socialisation through work takes place at a later age. In most cultures learning and work were, and still are, deeply related. One cannot work without having learned to work. But as work is embedded in a specific set of values and norms of a given culture (the source where work ethics stem from), so also is learning, knowledge, and expertise. Each culture and society has developed its specific ways of learning and teaching. Learning to work means to have access to a certain body of knowledge (including practical knowledge) and while putting it into practice, one learns to work in meaningful ways. However, what one understands as meaningful is also culturally determined. The way we learn is part of the process of socialisation and we learn in accordance with what our culture considers as learning. These ways and forms of learning have been developed through history. They are defined by specific values and norms concerning learning and teaching, which differ from society to society and culture to culture.

Culture determines—amongst other things—the value systems and norms that guide the individual's actions and attitudes. Structures regulate the different aspects and functions of society. They set the frame for how, at a macro-level, national education system, and at a micro-level, training activities of companies and single institutions, manifest themselves.

Given the quite diverse historical and philosophical roots of education in the countries that make up the European Union, the way learning is understood cannot be expected to be the same. Of course, one may question the need for a common concept of learning, or whether different forms and approaches towards learning may not be an advantage after all. Whatever the case, it is clear that a great sensitivity as well as adequate research instruments are needed in order to identify the meaning and practice of learning in different European cultures—a process that must necessarily underpin the common effort towards the creation of a learning European society.

This chapter addresses the cultural and structural dimensions of learning, and the interdependency of the micro- and macro-level of education or vocational education systems. It is based on the findings of the project 'The Construction of Learning Cultures as a Process of Micro-Macro-Interdependency between Educational Traditions and Learning Cultures,' funded by the German Ministry of Education and Research. The study addressed learning for work in production settings. Because the countries of comparison—USA, Germany and Japan—have very different approaches to educating their workforce, it was necessary to include the general education systems of Japan and the US in this analysis, while for Germany the emphasis was placed upon its vocational education system. A key finding of this study is that the globalisation of learning has in fact not yet taken place. The instruments and approach applied may serve as an example of how to address the need for grasping cultural dimensions that are essential for education and training of the workforce, and help to determine the structural manifestations of a society's educational policy and institutions at the macro- and micro-level.

Theoretical assumptions and framework for cultural dimensions of learning

Important elements contributing to the theoretical formulation of the instrument for comparison of culturally determined learning processes can be found in Giddens' theory of societal structuration (1992). One of these elements concerns the notion of 'practical consciousness.' Giddens understands actors' reflections as the basis for practical consciousness and as a precondition for meaningful, continuous action, of which learning and work constitute a significant part. The meaningful direction of action can only occur through reflection. The reflexivity of past and even more of future actions leads to direction and to goals of action. Thus, two major dimensions are already accounted for in the task of analysing and comparing different cultural approaches of learning: the actor, and the aim (i.e. the direction of actions).

The instrument that has been developed in order to analyse and understand different culturally determined manifestations of learning incorporates five dimensions that are considered as generally applicable essential constituents of learning processes. The dimensions and their theoretical justification have been covered in detail elsewhere (see Laske, 2000). Here only the five dimensions that determine the culture of learning and their variables on the micro- and macro-level of society are mentioned:

1. *Aims and goals*, inherent in learning processes and education, determine current learning traditions and politics. In relation to the micro-level are education and training practices in companies and schools, where individuals need to be taken into account. Depending on the level of analysis, one can identify aims by interrogating historical developments and conflicts, values and traditions, as well as social, political, economic phenomena. In relation to the macro-level of education, one has to take into account the ways in which individual intentions, aims and objectives mould education and learning processes and systems.

2. In society, *actors* are those who pursue aims and goals. Therefore it is important to ask who the main actors are when it comes to inspiring, shaping, negotiating and influencing the constitution, reproduction and preservation of these goals and learning processes. Depending on the specific combination and constitution of education at the macro-level in different nations and cultures, main actors at the macro-level can, for instance, be politicians, political parties, trade unions, churches and employer associations. At the micro-level, the actors are those who learn and teach (i.e. students, trainees, teachers), as well as personal managers in charge of mediating learning processes in companies, and the like.

3. Aims and goals need to be communicated between actors, in order for them to be implemented in specific societal contexts and institutions. However, the *context* in which such communication happens, as well as *the way* in which such communication takes place, differs between cultures. Different cultural contexts have developed diverse ways of transmitting, exchanging, and negotiating knowledge. The mediation of the goals established for education is the result of a communicative process between actors, and it is this very process that determines the specific manner by means of which what society values as knowledge is decided upon, as well as the ways in which this knowledge will be transmitted and learned. Such communication processes are evident at the macro-level, such as when there are political negotiations regarding education and training, where

decisions are reached as to what should be taught, and how and by whom it should be learned.

4. Communication is the medium that also conveys the *content* of learning, i.e. what is considered to be worth learning. Learning and educational processes deal with content—i.e. the subjects to be learned—and this is another essential dimension that determines the culture of learning. Different cultures have a different understanding of knowledge, how to convey such knowledge, and which knowledge is important and worthy of being transmitted. One might find very different understandings, characteristics and emphasis of knowledge in different societies and cultures. At the macro-level, such cultural differences can be made manifest through, for instance, political decisions regarding educational standards, through the promulgation of a formal curriculum, and through setting benchmarks of what should be achieved in schools at different grade levels.

5. Finally, the fifth dimension that determines learning addresses *institutions and organisations* that host and organise learning and education, for educational processes are influenced and moulded by those institutions and organisations. At the micro-level schools, colleges, and educational establishments that offer workshops, lectures, on-the-job training, and so on mould teaching and learning in specific ways, through the manner in which they organise and institutionalise educational processes. Examples of macro-level institutions and organisations that influence the development of specific cultures of learning are ministries of education, teacher unions, teacher training institutions, and so on.

The dimensions presented above are dynamically connected to each other, and continuously produce and reproduce learning cultures in a mutually interdependent manner. However, as these dimensions have been presented above, they are somewhat too abstract and general in nature to be helpful in carrying out cultural analysis and comparison. For the latter to be facilitated, the dimensions need to be more specifically and concretely applied to social phenomena. In the case of the present study, this was done by defining those variables at the macro- and micro-level where these dimensions were most prominently visible.

At this stage only macro-level variables will be considered, given that they are then taken up in the analysis of the historical development of education and learning in Germany, Japan and the USA. Table 1 below provides an overview of the whole range of both micro- and macro-level variables specifically addressing those factors that are important for the processes of learning to work, and that have been set out as an instrument of analysis.

Homo Sapiens Europæus?

TABLE 1: Variables at the macro-and micro-level of education and learning processes

Variables at the macro-level

At the macro-level, variables that are relevant for the education and training sectors are historical roots, and value systems. Value systems arise out of historical contexts and dynamics, and themselves give rise to particular tendencies and orientations in relation to the form and functions that education develop in a particular social context. By focusing on how historically-embedded processes lead to specific ways in socially constructing education and training, one can get a better understanding of the dynamics and mechanisms that regulate a given learning culture (cf. manifestations of the dimension aim/goal).

Another macro-level variable is educational politics and the processes by means of which particular orientations towards education and training are decided upon. In what follows, examples are provided in order to show how learning has been shaped in three different cultures. These different country contexts serve to demonstrate how educational politics, and negotiation about the goals and orientations towards learning, leads to articulating the nature of learning in specific ways. In other words, educational politics acts upon the communication of goals and orientations in respect to learning, with Germany, Japan and the USA serving as good examples to show how the analytic approach referred to earlier can be applied.

The findings presented below do not encompass the whole range of variables that culturally determine education at the macro-level. Nor do they address the ways in which education and learning are shaped at the micro-level in different cultures. What the following analytic account does do is to focus on two macro-level variables, namely *historical roots and value system* and *education politics and their negotiation processes*, in order to argue that when learning processes are considered from within an international and comparative discourse, the cultural determination of learning and teaching needs to be taken into account.

Germany

Germany still has a relatively clear profile of initial vocational training that applies throughout its federal states. This training path was, and still is considered an alternative to an academic career, though not with the same social status and prestige. The craft trade education during the high Middle Ages can be regarded as the strongest historical root of the dual vocational training system. Norms, conditional framework and implementation of the latter guaranteed the reproduction of the guild and were geared entirely to the socialization of the apprentices in the 'spirit' of the guild. To understand the German concept of profession and its specific implication on how a person learns to work, it is useful to look back to the roots where the concept of 'profession' stems from.

The craft trades, also called guilds, came into being in the medieval city all over Europe. The terms 'guild' and 'craft trades' were used synonymously during the Middle Ages. The old craft trades were experienced as a much more extensive social entity than can be ascribed to a branch of industry or sector today. As a stratum of society, a craft trade i.e. a profession, had all social functions more or less intensely integrated into it. The guild offered its members a political, economic, cultural and to a certain extent also a military and religious environment. The profession identified the individual as a member of the guild. The membership and unity of the guild were defined via the profession. The guild, in turn, clarified the relationship of its members to the city, state, authorities and church, which provided the individual with a secure social position in which his economic and social tasks were clearly defined (Kurtz, 1997).

The existence and performance of craft work and trade with its products was guaranteed by the guild, and it was only possible within this framework. The economic efficiency of a business was of secondary importance. Professional respectability, which was lived and represented in the craftsman's establishments, had priority in every respect. The guild secured the existence of the production shops in which its morals and view of respectability were lived and personified (Kurtz, 1997). However, it was not the moral code of a guild alone that guaranteed the corporations' unity and ability to act. Intellectual property and, as one would say today, specialized know-how and professional qualifications, were also passed on, maintained and kept as property of the corporation. That meant this know-how was not accessible to the environment outside the guild.

The master's household was the workshop, and the master's family was a community of people working and living together. It encompassed an economic community and a group of persons living together that included the master and his natural family as well as all those working in the craftsman's establishment, apprentices, journeymen, maids, servants, and so on. Since there was no separation between profession, workshop and the master's family, there was no delimitation between lifestyle, profession and workshop in the individual way that apprentices and journeymen saw their role in life. Identity was experienced through being part of and practicing a profession or craft trade, including the perception of all related corporate responsibilities.

The education of the apprentice in the master's household was unstructured and carried out without didactic, methodological principles. It took place as part of a non-systematically prepared 'environment-based education'. In addition to the socialization of the apprentice in a lifestyle and respectability suitable to the profession, the apprentice acquired craft trade qualifications by watching the master and his expertise at work and being instructed by him. The training in the craft trade from the point of view of the master consisted of acting as an example and providing instruction, while for the apprentice it involved copying the values, norms and work methods set as an example and which were to be internalized. The knowledge and values handed down in the guild were acquired and passed on by means of this process. It must be emphasized here that it was less the manual skills or economic efficiency that constituted the goal of the training to become master than the criteria already laid down for selection of the apprentice, such as suitability or otherwise to be a member of the guild, Christian or not Christian, and, most importantly, whether the individual was respectable or not. Finally the achieved training goal—acquisition of the master craftsman's certificate by successfully passing the master craftsman examination—was confirmed through certified verification on the part of the guild.

While the craftsman's training in the Middle Ages was predominantly of a socializing nature and hardly had any 'rational' character, it nevertheless retained its validity for nearly 6 centuries through the way it was uniquely and holistically embedded in medieval society. Although the beginnings date back to the 12th century, guilds and master's households did not start losing their influence until the 18th century.

At the beginning of the modern era a differentiation took place in certain segments of society. To a certain extent, subsystems with societal functions—such as the legal system, the economic system and the education system—formed out of the previously predominantly holistic organization of the professions and social strata. The development and unfolding of liberal capitalistic modes of production were fostered according to the economic interests of the absolutist state, which favoured the rising bourgeoisie (Pätzold, 1982). This led to a gradual dissolution of the corporative associations of persons, as those represented by guilds. As a result, the moral code of the craft trades also changed. Respectability, as the previously dominant guiding principle, was subordinated to the economic criterion of solvency. The social and moral bases of the apprenticeship in the craft trades were increasingly called into question. Guild and master's household therefore lost more and more of their social importance in the 18th century. The altered production conditions finally led to the disintegration of the master craftsman's trades.

For the training of apprentices this meant that moral socialization was no longer the focus, but rather became subordinate to economic considerations and constraints. This already marks the beginning of a new interpretation of vocational education from a socialization process based on professional life to more work-related training, or formulated another way, a transformation took place from education in the respectability of the guild to the principle of bourgeois occupational efficiency. Training was increasingly provided for a profession that encompassed a more extensive spectrum of occupational activities, as a result of which the unity of profession and craftsman's establishment was gradually eroded. The principle of performance as a social institution developed and established itself.

A major consequence of this was that craftsman's establishment and profession were no longer viewed as one entity. The profession became the structural environment of the workshop. Finally, the guilds lost their autonomy with the introduction of independent commercial enterprises and the freedom to establish a business in the 19th century.

If the medieval craft trade or guild system and its form of training, as it has been outlined above, can be designated as a general European approach, national differentiation began with the modern age and the establishment of the absolute state. In the two industrialized nations that were initially the most important, England and France, the corporative associations were dissolved, while in central Europe, less under the influence of industrialization, the trade system was less affected. In France, for example, the organization of the guilds and all related bodies were prohibited from the time of the Revolution in 1789. The consequence was that it was no longer possible to bring about a revival of vocational forms of learning and training (Greinert, 1998). For this reason, new models of vocational training developed in France, such as the *Ecoles d'Arts et Métiers*, so-called production schools which were based on traditional craft trade forms of learning, but which pursued a new approach to vocational training through a combination of practical training phases and theoretical instruction that ran parallel to each other.

On account of specific political constellations a revival of the apprenticeship system took place in Germany. Around 1875 there was no structured apprenticeship system in Germany any more. The legislators in Prussia felt called upon—not least of all due to expertise and negotiations of the Society for Social Policy (*Verein für Sozialpolitik*)—to intervene in the development of apprentice training via the state. The Industrial Code of the northern German confederation meant that apprentice training was extensively left to the discretion of the enterprises. One of the consequences of this was that the quality of the training deteriorated. In small enterprises, abuse of apprentices was common. However, more and more apprentices also broke off their apprenticeships whenever they chose. Exploitation and use of corporal punishment on apprentices was increasingly the order of the day. The apprenticeship period lasted longer and longer, and enterprises began demanding an apprenticeship premium. As a result, there were increasing calls for legislators to introduce measures to counteract the decline of apprentice training.

The renewed institutionalization of the craft trade corporation had both a traditional and a modern aspect. The corporations were traditional in the sense that here again protectionist prerogatives were established for guild members. They were modern by virtue of the fact that they no longer enclosed the craftsman's establishments in protectionism, and maintenance of their existence was decided through assertion on the market in the face of economic competition (Harney and Zymek, 1994). An attempt was also made by the public sector to influence apprentice training by requiring apprentices to attend so-called further training schools. The roots of the development and establishment of a second place of learning in addition to that of the enterprise are thought to date back in the 16th century. From the 1870s at the latest there is documented proof of the first vocational training schools. Initial efforts at legal establishment of a second place of learning in addition to company training had already been made through the Industrial Code of the northern German confederation in 1869. The reasons for the institutionalization of a second place of learning for industrially oriented training, which was pushed forward in the 1870s, can be attributed to different interests. One of these interest groups emphasized the training aspect, which was primarily promoted by means of the industrial support of the southern states, such as Baden and Württemberg. Another line of argumentation that dominated in Prussia was more of a societal and social policy concern. The intention here was to use the further training schools as targeted policy for labour force development, and in this way to contribute to building a bulwark against the spreading of social democracy. In the case of this interest group, the schools were consequently conceived more as an instrument of state integration and in terms of legitimation strategies (Kurtz, 1997, p.27). Nevertheless, different, sometimes conflicting political currents were active in supporting this approach. Both conservative and liberally oriented interest groups in the government and church made efforts to offset a 'socialization deficit' in the craft trade, industrial lower class. The religious and industrial Sunday schools grew out of such interests, though they failed to generate any major social or qualification-related impact. Their lack of a legal foundation was a crucial issue here. In principle, the further training schools were initially a sort of 'non-independent continuation' of the elementary schools whose instruction was provided by the elementary school teachers and took place in the schoolrooms. Around 1900 the idea of giving the further training schools a role in the occupational and working world became more relevant politically. The political implementation of these schools, which were to take the place of the Sunday schools, was definitely regarded as a liberal experiment. The successive development of a second place of learning in addition to the company took place at the same time. Additional importance was attached to the vocational school when attempts were made through the development of a second place of learning to regain the civic trust of young persons through civic education. During the Third Reich vocational training was taken over in a totalitarian manner by the National Socialist ideology and its social interests.

One can regard the development of vocational training in Germany as a 'by-product of the small business policy of the empire' (Greinert, 1998, p.40), and this applies to an even greater degree to the development of the vocational school. Its precursors, the Sunday and further training schools, were not only supposed to have a certain qualification content, but also a socializing influence on young workers. It is important in this context to keep in mind that the concept of profession/trade was functionalized by the state via the medium of the vocational school such that a 'civic binding and quietization' of young workers took place (Stratmann, 1994, p.43). The profession became the 'didactic centre' of the new type of school (Kurtz, p.28), which is clearly reflected even today in the designation 'vocational school'. Vocational training was implemented both in the Weimar Republic (to regain civic trust) and during the Third Reich (as National Socialist indoctrination). After the Second World War vocational training retained its socializing nature, which was linked, inter alia, to the 'peculiar national cultural nature of the profession' in Germany.

Vocational training is aimed on the one hand at work-related qualification—it is in fact this principle that dominates in company training—and at civic and/or political education on the other. The vocational school is supposed to fulfil this mission as well as provide qualified training. Through vocational training the trainee experiences socialization both in terms of the future work-related activities of the profession and due to the fact that it entails a civic socialization that had definitely taken on ideologically dubious features in historical retrospect, or was misused ideologically. At this juncture it must be pointed out that vocational training in Germany, and thus the concept of profession, is not a purely economic construct or structure based on division of labour, but encompasses the citizen both as a working and as a social being. The narrow view of a *homo economicus* frequently found in Anglo-Saxon countries has no equivalent in German vocational tradition. In Germany the profession retained both an economic and social significance, though to a varying extent, that applied to all levels of education.

Japan

Since the 19th century the history of the Japanese education system has been marked by conflicts over power and authority in matters of general policy. This struggle originated in Japan's opening to the West and continues today. In particular, the expanding influence of western thinking was the cause of tensions and conflict, and has left its mark on the training offered within Japanese enterprises, even though the latter have undergone many changes over the years. What follows is a historical account of the educational system as well as of the reforms in that sector. The account reveals patterns that contradict the western perception of Japan as a very homogeneous nation, but which at the same time pave the way to an improved understanding of the present form of the Japanese educational system.

After a 250-year period of Shogun rule—a 'military' regime of the Samurai under the leadership of the Shogun and his Tokugawa clan, also known as the Edo period—Japan was forced to open its ports to the western world in 1853. Leadership of the government lay in the hands of intellectuals and politicians who were open to western thought and wanted to create a modern Japanese state in line with western models. One of the reasons for the change in power was the influence of western philosophy, particularly that of the Enlightenment, which had penetrated Japan and which had made a deep impression on progressive and leading Japanese intellectuals. Whereas the philosophy and views of Confucianism constituted the widely uncontested spiritual and moral basis of the nation during the Edo period, entirely new ideas from the West now infiltrated the state, civilization and education in Japan, leading to a critical reflection on the world and on life in society based on the natural sciences. The ideological foundation of Confucianism was vehemently attacked. Advocates of the new Enlightenment wanted to reduce the reach of the Japanese state as much as possible, defining its central task in relation to the protection of the rights of citizens, on the basis of equality and justice.

The early critical reflections in the Meiji period on ideas concerning civilisation and Enlightenment were based on the realisation that the 'spirit' of western civilisation had to be successfully assimilated in order to resist western imperialism. One of the radical demands in this context was the call to completely abandon Japan's historical identity (Sakamoto, 1996). Fukuzawa Yukichi, a leading, initially progressive mentor and philosopher advocating Enlightenment, argued against the conservative trend, which had adopted the slogan of 'Western Technology—Japanese spirit'. In contrast, he argued that Japan should not merely borrow the artefacts and products of the West, but also its view of civilisation, and in this way succeed in remaining independent of western expansion. He examined the works of western philosophers of the Enlightenment, in which all non-Europeans were barbarians and thus inferior to Europeans. The tautology on which this idea was based was: civilisation can be equated with Europe, and accordingly Asia is uncivilised. This ideology, by the way, is not part of a long vanished past. Noble (1984) refers to Norbert Wiener, the father of cybernetics, who sharply criticised the complicity of science in the dropping of the atom bomb on Hiroshima in the following manner: 'Wiener did not think that the use of the bomb on Japan, on Orientals, was without significance.' 'I was acquainted with more than one of these popes and cardinals of applied science, and I knew very well how they underrated aliens of all sorts, particularly those not of the European race.' (p.73)

For Fukuzawa Yukichi civilisation necessarily meant westernisation. Therefore, it was not possible to adopt solely the western artefacts of technology and industry while retaining one's own cultural and traditional identity. On the contrary, it was necessary to adopt and internalise the spirit of western Enlightenment and civilisation. Japan should no longer define itself on the basis of its past and traditions. A national Japanese identity could only be the result of future developments, for the sake of which one had to break with past traditions. Behind the rejection of the past and the opening to western thought, in turn, stood the motive of defying western imperialism. Thus, the basic intention was not total westernisation, but the instrument of opening and civilising Japan was to be used to retain the country's own independence (Sakomoto, 1996).

A group that was committed to the human rights movement was of the conviction that national well-being depended on the extent to which the successful development of a modern school and education system could be implemented. This was supposed to guarantee a new form of learning on the basis of equal educational opportunities for all citizens. For them education and training seemed to be a guarantee leading to the emergence of a new era that promised a world of enlightenment, prosperity and wisdom. The leaders of the Meiji revolution who advocated the body of thought of the Enlightenment recognised that the necessary process of national transformation into a modern state had to be based on education and training accessible to the entire population, no matter whether in the city or the country. A distinction that emerged in the following years between education (training) and science or learning was not initially perceptible during the Meiji restoration. The types of schools and education favoured by these politicians were primarily imports from the progressive European countries. Nevertheless, the Meiji revolution did not mark the starting point of an education system in Japan. Such a system was built and had to build on existing structures and institutions.

A quite well-developed education system already existed in Japan during the Tokugawa regime. Temple schools were responsible for the education of the population at large, and they were oriented to the respective educational needs of the region. The rising generation of Samurai received training in administrative and military skills at elite schools. These elite schools were organized by authorities of the Tokugawa regime and aimed at preparing the pupils for their future leading role in the state. For the Meiji government, therefore, it was expedient to fall back on these existing, well-functioning institutions when setting up a new education system. At the same time this meant that the conflict in Japanese society would inevitably extend to the school field. The collision of western thought and all its implications, with a 250-year heritage of feudal rule based on Confucianism, was bound to lead to profound ideological and social tensions.

On the basis of the tension between a traditional philosophy of life, with social values incorporated into it, and western influence, a current spearheaded by intellectuals and politicians soon emerged. These propagated the already-mentioned view that only the technological dimensions and know-how from the West should be applied to Japanese life, while holding fast to Japanese traditions. Typical slogans that this party adopted included: 'Japanese spirit—Western skills!' and 'Eastern morality—Western technology!' The counter current saw an ambiguity in this approach, and refused to accept such a formulation. They were convinced that western technology could only be mastered and made useful for a modern Japan if one also opened oneself to western thought and western science without reservation. Furthermore, they took the stance that this was only possible if equal and comprehensive educational opportunities were given to the entire population. Followers of both currents viewed themselves and their position as committed to the body of thought of the European Enlightenment. The conservative advocates of an enlightenment from the top found a powerful ideological and structural support in Japan's traditional imperial institutions, by means of which the emancipatory movement could be dominated.

As a result of a political predominance of the conservative approach, the public schools responsible for the general education of the population were essentially given the task of ensuring strict moral education. Horio (1989) cites in this context a passage from an essay by Ito Hirobumi, one of the conservative advocates of that period:

> 'The major task facing us today is inculcating within the entire populace the spirit of loyalty, devotion, and heroism (*chuyu gikyo*) that was formerly associated with the samurai class, and making these values their values. Thus we must teach the common people (*heimin*) to work and study hard for the sake of their neighbourhoods and villages, and to never waver in matters that would lead to the destruction of their families. Moreover, they must develop a peaceful and obedient character, show respect for the law, and demonstrate an understanding of our noble moral ideals and highly refined national sentiments.' (p.44)

In the course of political dominance of the conservative forces, the Confucian philosophy of life underwent a renaissance. While there was previously a trend towards totally denying Japan's historical heritage and seeking and perceiving the truth and future solely in western thought, a new self-assurance with respect to a Japanese cultural identity emerged. The national Japanese 'spirit' and its view of moral life were reinstated. Although the degenerated forms of Confucianism that dominated towards the end of the Tokugawa rule were criticised, the return to the true spiritual roots of Confucianism was viewed as the best way of integrating 'practical learning' into daily Japanese life. The term 'practical learning' was coined to describe the absorption and implementation of this new western knowledge. The European sciences were perceived as the gateway to the real, material world and severe criticism was levelled at Confucianism, which was claimed to confuse science and learning with discussions on poetry and prose, classical Chinese literature or detailed analyses of fables and stories with a moral. In this respect the advocates of the Enlightenment of both factions were in agreement. In spite of its close association with the use and handling of western technologies, the concept of 'practical learning' stemmed from Confucian thought. Horio (1989, p.41) points out that a central idea had already formed among conservatives around 1880, one '… in which the pursuit of 'practical learning' (*jitsugaku*) was already being identified with and largely restricted to technological concerns or to problems having an immediately practical focus.'

The teachings of Confucius became the moral-ethical basis for 'practical learning', which in plain language means that they became the initial basis for the acquisition of western technologies and industrial skills. This ideology provided the leadership elite with an extremely effective tool for controlling Japan's path into the modern age. The framework for the constitution of the Japanese education system was established through the proclamation of the 'Principle of education legislation through imperial decree' in 1889-1890. In this decree a strict distinction was made between science and learning on the one hand, and education or training on the other. Science and learning remained the exclusive domain of the Japanese elite. The general school system was regarded as a necessity for the education of the people. Learning and training in Japan, from the primary school to attendance of university and including scientific research, was controlled by the state from then on and served as an instrument for enforcing state interests. Although the new education system was formally open to all citizens, it had a polarising structure that was induced by the separation of science and education. As Horio (1989, p.49) notes, 'In this sense the Meiji educational system enabled the Imperial State to trap the Japanese people in a state of intellectual and emotional adolescence.' In the ultra-nationalist spirit that prevailed, it was easy to indoctrinate the general population into an acceptance of militarism, and into the conviction that Japan had the right to colonise other Asian countries.

At the end of the Second World War, when Japan was occupied by US troops, a radical reform of those social values that had put their stamp on the education system during the period of the empire was called for. Focus was placed on establishing a kind of basic legislation that would create a stable legal foundation guaranteeing the population a free education system. The democratic approach toward educational reform almost immediately gave rise to heated opposition, with the conservatives charging those in favour of the reform with conspiracy, while the progressive wing, including the newly established teachers' union Nikkoyoso, sympathising with the approach of the occupying power.

At this point it is important to emphasise that the lines of conflict over educational policy and educational reform as described for the Meiji period have remained largely the same right to the present time. However, this profound split cannot be accounted for simply with reference to the implementation of a foreign education system in Japanese society. A diverse struggle on the part of extremely different forces in society was and still is an integral part of this conflict-ridden process—even if the conflict is not treated openly in the same manner as it would be in western societies. Regarding it solely in terms of an opposition between two camps would be tantamount to failing to recognise the multi-faceted aspects of the respective positions. Within this framework, however, reference can only be made to basic tendencies. Japan's ongoing financial crisis after the economic boom of the 1980s and early 1990s, together with the resulting recession, also left their mark on the Japanese education system. What will emerge from this is difficult to predict. However, the previous statements have shown that education in Japanese society has a crucial significance and all major social transformation processes always have an effect on the design of the education system as well.

In the western world Japan became famous for having successfully completed two great transformation processes in its modern history. In both cases, the education system played a central role. The Meiji period, with its constitution of general education for the entire population and the establishment of a meritocracy, provided Japan with an educated labour force capable of learning, as well as with a highly educated, talented elite at a time when the Japanese leadership elite had to—and wanted to—exploit human resources in the most optimal manner possible, so that Japan could attain the level of development of the western world (the 'catching-up' period). After the Second World War the educational reform initiated by the occupying power, the USA, created an education system based more on equality and democracy. However, this new education system basically integrated a meritocratic mechanism more effectively than in the pre-war period, again at a time when Japan needed an educated labour force to manage the reconstruction of the post-war years.

In both transformations Confucianism also played a key role. During the Edo period the teachings of Confucius had been designated as the state philosophy, 'and until the Second World War learning Confucian rules of conduct by heart was one of the compulsory exercises for all primary school pupils' (Moritz, 1992, p.137). Japan's radical industrialisation was supported by Confucian ethics with their moral norms and virtues. They included the precept that state authority cannot be questioned. Thus, even Confucius was never asked by his students why morality was of such crucial importance for a society (Moritz, 1992, p.147). This way of thinking contrasted sharply with the critical approach of the Enlightenment, which attempted to question all phenomena, theories and goals.

When Japan was forced to open itself to western influence, this became a traumatic humiliation for a culture with a history that stretched back more than a thousand years. This culture had absorbed philosophical currents, such as the teachings of Confucius from China, or those of Buddha from India, and transformed them to meet its own needs. During the Edo period Japanese culture was characterised by a cultivation and ritualization of its traditional forms of life. The identity-promoting feeling of self-esteem inherent in the Japanese way of life was based on Japanese ethics, highly differentiated social norms and a strict moral code. When western thought on civilisation and enlightenment penetrated Japan, it taught at the same time that all peoples of non-European origin were enveloped by the darkness of barbarism. In their critical examination of the western theory of enlightenment Japanese intellectuals, who looked back on an old culture, learned that they had to view themselves as barbarians, which was tantamount to a degrading negation of their culture and historical roots by the West. This led those who had, over 120 years, stuck fast to the idea of maintaining Japan's traditional culture, to reject western influence with its assumptions of superiority. These forces of resistance, while acknowledging that western thought and artefacts could not be ignored, endeavoured to restrict their impact by selectively making use of technological and scientific achievements, while insisting on the preservation of Japanese values, ethics and morals. The forces and values that finally asserted themselves were those that were able to utilise Confucianism as an instrument and bulwark against western influence and as a catalyst for Japan's path into the modern age. The result was the development of a meritocratic system of education and society.

After World War II, the formerly explosive ideas of the Enlightenment were now integrated within Japanese society in the shape of a commitment towards democracy and individualism. When such terms as Japanese ethics and Confucian morals and virtues were mentioned in the above statements, this was done in connection with the debate over what significance the Confucian philosophy of life has as a determining variable for the Japanese education system.

It is important that, in conclusion, some of the Confucian values and virtues that are of central importance for the Japanese education and working world are briefly outlined.

Thus, when hiring new employees, Japanese enterprises still tend to select suitable candidates according to non-occupational qualities. The evaluation of their 'character' is decisive for this selection. An important quality of 'character' is education. According to the Confucian educational ideal, education aims at the unity of virtue and knowledge. This virtue or morality encompasses humanity, justness, seemliness, wisdom and trust. Confucian virtues can also be described as the striving for harmony and agreement, a humanistic attitude of mind and a sense of responsibility for other people. For this reason, acquisition of educational qualifications is regarded as a kind of proof of a person's ability to learn in Japan, not only with respect to specific qualifications, but also the development of personal, interpersonal and social abilities (Yamazaki, 1987, p.571).

Shintoism, Japan's original religion, already taught that work—and thus all occupational activities—are carried out 'on behalf of the gods'. A similar interpretation of the sacredness of work can be found in Buddhism because it is service for other people and for the nation. In this regard, Yamazaki (1987, pp.572-573) gives the example of Shosan Suzuki (1579-1655), a Zen monk during the Edo period, who 'not only preached to the Samurai, but also to farmers, craftsmen and merchants, that complete involvement in secular working life is equivalent to following the path of Buddha.' Today, the 'ideal' Japanese employee is still a person who has good general knowledge, is ready to fit in and to subordinate himself/herself, and to demonstrate that s/he is disciplined and flexible. In addition, such a person can stand stress, is loyal to the company, strives for harmony and is a good member of the group (Grein, 1994).

These qualities are so prized that Yamazaki (1987, p.575) notes that a problem arises, given that

> 'particularly in the case of in-house vocational training, there is a risk, in pedagogical terms, of forcing each individual employee merely to display loyalty and selfless dedication to the company and thus to disregard his individuality, to shape him into a first-class 'soldier' of the company. In addition, improvement of school vocational training at school and overcoming the regrettable concomitants of the 'school career society' are urgent tasks of the Japanese educational reform.'

Even though the last quote was written a decade and a half ago, it still remains very topical.

USA

Besides the democratic development of society, a unique feature of early American civilisation was widespread access to education. The first townships, with an economy based on farming and trade, had already introduced compulsory education by the 17th century. Individual work and effort, innovative craftsmanship, as well as a social and economic capacity of adjustment were essential for survival and for the foundation of the new communities. Hand-in-hand grew a strong commitment to providing neighbourly help, and a sense of solidarity. Although the general access to education, as well as reliance on such qualities as resourcefulness, neighbourly support in the struggle for survival, and celebration of democratic principles, were subject to modification over a period of three hundred years, they have nevertheless provided a basis for the US-American value system. Another essential tradition underpinning the US-American sense of identity also dates back to the time when the pioneering and democratic spirit of the early townships prevailed (Tocqueville, 1988; Dewey, 1965). I am here referring to the tight link, if not equation, between political power and the economy.

However, even in these early times, the constitution of the USA considerably restricted the emancipatory goals that had been formulated in the 'Declaration of Independence'. An alliance was forged between a rather formal democratic policy and an increasingly expanding, complex, and integrative economy. Consumption and an expanding labour market began to overshadow political ideals like equality, participation and the sovereignty of the people. Such developments might very well be at the root of the problematic US-American relation between economy and democracy, a relation that is still marked by tensions that are at the heart of the US-American society and education system nexus.

As already mentioned, during the time of the first settlements, general education was considered to be compulsory and a civil duty. With the beginning of industrialisation and an increase of capital accumulation the nature of education as a right no longer prevailed. Violent unrest, strikes and rebellions had to be resorted to on the part of workers and citizens in order to force concessions from economic interests regarding better wages, improved work place security, and educational access for one and all. It is important to point out that such concessions were not granted thanks to socially-minded, enlightened insights. They were the result of an understanding that production only could run smoothly when the needs of the workforce were met. It is against this historical, social and economic backdrop that the US-American education system, as we know it today, has developed.

The early settlement period was driven by the belief that education and schools are the guarantee of the democratic ideal for the society that was being constructed. The expectation was that schools prepare future citizens to support US-American democracy, and to be active and participative members in it. It was this aim that underpinned the development of the general education system. In these early times, founders of public schools still considered the democratic ideals of the young American republic endangered and needing consolidation. The existence and prosperity of the young states was considered to be dependent on having citizens with strong, democratic values.

Additionally, schools were considered to be a democratic force, counter-balancing the increasingly influential, self-centred orientation of the capitalist economy and its bourgeoisie.

As a result of such perceptions, the political goal for education was to educate the citizen with a strong democratic sense that could be maintained during—and indeed manifest itself through—economic activity. Another guiding principle was the equal right to education, regardless of class and race (Labaree, 1997). Soon, however, educational institutions became differentiated. Such differentiation between social groups could be seen in the number of years spent at school, in graduation rates at different levels of the educational sector, in curricular diets and standards, and in the status associated with these variable programmes of study. In addition, the education system was confronted with an increasing number of students while undergoing a process of strong diversification. In 1870 only 2 percent of the 17 year old High school students were graduates, while by 1950 the percentage had risen to 59 (Valverde, 1994).

At the end of the 19th century a political current surfaced, promoting a different educational aim. An alliance made up of interests from the economic sector, and from labour and educational institutions tried to link education more firmly with labour market needs. This group was convinced that US-American education would become insignificant if one could not manage to model education towards serving the current and future needs of the labour market. According to this movement, educational subjects should no longer favour traditional academic curricula but should instead emphasise skills and knowledge related to occupations and the working life. Secondary education and community colleges in particular began offering vocational classes, with the aim of providing employers and entrepreneurs with a continuous supply of adequately trained young employees. Maintaining the democratic principle of undifferentiated education was increasingly viewed as impractical and economically inefficient. The rather abstract ideal of educating democratic citizens who can sustain a democratic society was confronted with the economic aim of making education meet the needs of the labour market.

Within this 'vocational turn', education is closely linked to the perceived needs of the current and future economy. It became to be seen as investment in human capital, and investment from which all society would benefit if smart decisions were made. This trend, however, failed to totally prevail due to the counter-discourse that arose, fed by those who remained faithful to the US tradition that saw a strong relationship between education and democratisation. There are thus those who consider that today's high school and college graduates in the US are inadequately prepared to enter into the labour market, and that the curriculum is too liberal.

Despite the fact that there is a strong divide between the two educational orientations outlined above, i.e. those who stress the role of education in the formation of an educated citizenry, and those in favour of highlighting the economic and vocational role of education, both have one thing in common. Both, in fact, consider education as a public good. A third, contrasting trend has appeared during the past half century, one that treats education as a private good. According to the latter perspective, it is the benefit that education brings to the individual, in terms of social and economic advantage, that is paramount. In this scenario, the previous stress on associating education with public responsibility has little if any meaning. The emphasis is instead laid on improving an individual's advantages on the market via education, a position that inherently fosters educational stratification and differentiation. As Labaree (2000, pp.52-53) points out, one of the results of such an orientation is that

> '..... the value of a house in any community depends in part on the marketability of the local school system and [this is] why wealthy suburban communities aggressively defend the high status of their school systems by resisting any efforts to reduce the striking differences between systems... Parents are willing to spend as much as $30,000 a year to send their children to an Ivy League School, where the reputation rewards are potentially the greatest.'

In the list of values, democracy and equality are placed last, if they feature at all. In the struggle for marketability, cultural capital becomes transformed into economic capital (Bourdieu, 1986). 'The value of education from this point of view is not intrinsic but extrinsic, because the primary aim is to exchange one's education for something more substantial—namely a job, which will provide the holder with a comfortable standard of living, financial security, social power and cultural prestige' (Labaree, 2000, p.55).

Though all three mainstreams favour very different values and educational aims, each represents one aspect of the US-American value system, a system in which all three are embedded and from which they arise. They are more or less internalised by each American citizen, and also act as guiding principles for the education and training programmes of companies. The social class one belongs to or has managed to be part of will predominantly determine which aspect of the American value system one favours. Academics like lawyers, scientists, also managers, will mainly believe in the mechanism that education has provided them with, in order to have the advantage of social mobility. They claim their right to individual happiness, prosperity and social power, in relation to the deeply held American conviction that each citizen's social condition is a result of his or her own efforts and talents. Indeed, as Berliner and Biddle (1997, p.152) note, 'Americans tend to assume that most social outcomes are generated by the characteristic of individuals—rather than, say, by unfair laws, structural forces in society, industrial greed, accidents, or divine intervention.' The implication of this assumption is, of course, that if a person finds him/herself in an unfavourable social condition, the fault or responsibility lies with the individual. Another assumption that is widely held by Americans concerns the responsibility of schools to qualify students for success in the working life. Here, the belief is that if they do not succeed, such failure is due to poor schooling. This is precisely why American parents from the middle and upper classes make every endeavour to send their children to noted schools.

Another side of the picture is that the US Constitution promotes equality as an important feature of society. The specific US-American meaning of equality places an emphasis on the notion of 'equality of opportunities', i.e. equal opportunities to *compete*. This belief has been the driving force that led to the various radical reforms in the US education system. The Land Grant Colleges or Community Colleges owe their existence to the conviction that education should contribute to equality, in the sense defined above. As such, American youth should, for instance, have the opportunity to access an academic career, even if they are growing up in remote, rural regions.

Of course, the fact is that the majority of American people work in such sectors as production, accounting, service industries, and so on, and not in the academic field. For them, to be a citizen of the democratic America is also of central importance. Today, it is management that largely determines which aspects of the US-American system guide education and training programme. Despite all that, most Americans still hold dear the values that were first promoting by the founding members of the first settlements in New England. Among those values we find belief in the capacity of social and economic adjustment, trust in innovation, and a strong sense for neighbourly support and solidarity. Such values and democratic impulses are however in contrast to the strong connection that there is between political and economic power.

Conclusion

The analysis of the two macro-level variables that have a prominent impact on how learning and education develop, and how they are manifest in different cultures or societies, demonstrate how much the philosophical and historical roots of learning and education, as well as the political framework and intentions, differ in the three countries considered. In each culture the meaning and purpose given to education and learning serve very different aims and consequently lead to different functions and manifestations in the respective societal contexts. While in Germany the education and training system, developed for the majority of youth, serves the purpose to socialise a young person to become a loyal and work-oriented member of society, the aims of education in the USA have privileged quite different agendas. As has been noted above, one aim for the US system is to educate the democratic citizen; another important if perhaps less prominent goal is to provide an educated workforce that responds to the needs of the labour market. Furthermore, the contemporary focus is on how education serves the individual's personal interests regarding social mobility and the access to social and economic advantages. We have described yet another tradition in Japan, where education is valued inasmuch as it develops a person's character, so that s/he becomes a cooperative and dedicated member to a group or company. The fact that basic aims for education differ also has an impact on the way learning takes place in the diverse societal contexts. In relation to this, an analysis that considers micro-level variables would be necessary in order to show the different ways in which teaching and learning are shaped.

It is not only the aims and practices in education that differ across countries: due to the way education systems have been socially constructed in different contexts, they also end up having different meanings and significations in different societies. If we consider the concepts of a 'learning society' and the 'learning citizen', a number of aspects related to learning and that they are socio-culturally determined can be highlighted.

Thus, given that, as has already been noted, learning takes on different forms in different societies and cultures, the 'learning citizen' in a given context becomes socialized into ways of learning according to the values and orientations that the specific social cultural environment s/he inhabits provides. In the examples given earlier, the medieval apprentice learned by watching and imitating the master, and by following and applying his advice. But more importantly, he learnt how to be a respectable member of the supportive social community—the guild—that he would eventually belong to. In contrast, a young, achievement-oriented US-American of today, hailing from the middle or upper class, and educated in one of the Ivy League colleges, may have received the message that attending such an institution as well as earning the right credentials will give him or her access to a network of peers and job opportunities, leading to a successful, well-paid career, and a prominent position in US society. The value system transmitted by learning, as a social practice embedded in a particular environment, to a large extent determines one's position and the way one is inclined to play one's part in society.

Education and learning are major determinants of the positions one achieves in society. But they are more than that. Through learning and education the individual comes to an understanding of the value s/he has in and for society. Differentiated ways in providing education also define one's position in the social structure. The socio-cultural determination of learning is never neutral but always implicitly carries with it the principles by means of which a particular society works. By participating in education and learning, the individual is socialised into a particular understanding of what his/her duties are, which responsibilities s/he has, what right and wrong behaviour are, and so on. Given the extent to which learning is culturally determined, and also the extent to which it is a powerful socializing tool, it is not surprising that throughout history it has been abused by totalitarian regimes, keen to have their sway over people's minds.

Increasingly, the danger nowadays seems to come from a strong economic bias in understanding what education is/should be about, so that the discourse around the 'learning society' elides a consideration of some central aspects related to education, including the way learning citizen relate to their social environment, and the values that learning transmits in a learning society. In focusing on the benefits and disadvantages that accrue to society and to the individual by particular forms of education and learning, one must never bracket a consideration of how such forms have an impact on democracy, and the extent to which they give rise to political or economic abuse.

References

Alisch, L.-M.; Baumert, J. & Beck, K. (eds) (1990) *Professionswissen und Professionalisierung.* Braunschweig

Berliner, D.C. & Biddle, B.J. (1997) *The Manufactured crisis: Myths, Fraud and the Attack on America's Public Schools.* White Plains, NY: Longman.

Blankertz, H. (1969) *Bildung im Zeitalter der großen Industrie. Pädagogik, Schule und Berufsbildung im 19. Jahrhundert.* Hannover: Schrödel.

Bourdieu, P. (1986) 'The forms of capital.' In J.G. Richardson (ed.) *Handbook of Theory and Research for the Sociology of Education.* Greenwood Publishers: New York.

Dewey, J. (1954) *The Public and its Problem.* Athens Press: Ohio.

Dewey, J. (1965) *Erziehung und Demokratie. Eine Einleitung in die Philosophische Pädagogik.* Taschenbuch-Ausgabe, Weinheim: Beltz.

Eswein, M. (1997) 'Rolle des Berufsbildungssystems in der apanischen gesellschaft.' In H.-H. Krüger & J. H. Olbertz (eds) *Bildung zwischen Staat und Markt.* Opladen, Leske + Buderich

Friedeburg, L.V. (1992) *Bildungsreform in Deutschland. Geschichte und gesellschaftlicher Widerspruch.* Franfurt/M. Suhrkamp

Giddens, A. (1992) *Die Konstruktion der Gesellschaft. Grundzüge einer Theorie der Strukturierung.* Frankfurt: Main.

Grein, M. (1994) 'Das japanische Bildungswesen und sein Einfluß auf die japanische Arbeitswelt.' In M. Grein (ed.) *Japan und China im Visier.* Mainz, Liber-Verlag

Greinert, W.-D. (1998) *'Das deutsche System' der Berufsausbildung. Tradition, Organisation, Funktion.* 3. Überarb. Auflage. Baden-Baden

Harney, K. & Storz, P. (1994) 'Strukturwandel beruflicher Bildung.' In D.K. Müller (ed.) *Pädagogik, Erziehungswissenschaft, Bildung.* Köln, Weimar, Wien. p 353-381.

Harney, K. & Zymek, B. (1994) 'Allgemeinbildung und Berufsbildung. Zwei konkurrierende Konzepte der Systembildung in der deutschen Bildungsgeschichte und ihre aktuelle Krise.' *Zeitschrift für Pädagogik*, Vol. 40, pp.405-422.

Hedenigg, S. (1997) 'Biomacht und Disziplinarmacht. Zur Verstaatlichung pädagogischer Interventionen in der Tokugawa- und Meiji-Zeit.' In H.-H. Krüger and J.H. Olbertz (eds) *Bildung zwischen Staat und Markt*. Opladen, Leske + Buderich

Horio, T. (1989) *Educational Thought and Ideology in Modern Japan. State Authority and Intellectual Freedom*. Tokyo, University of Tokyo Press

Imai, Y. (1997) 'Auf der Suche nach der vermißten Öffentlichkeit—Diskussionen in der japanischen Pädagogik der Nachkriegszeit.' In H.-H. Krüger & J.H. Olbertz (eds) *Bildung zwischen Staat und Markt*. Opladen: Leske & Buderich.

Kelly, E. A. (1995) *Education, Democracy & Public Knowledge*. San Francisco: Oxford Press.

Kurtz, T. (1997) *Professionalisierung im Kontext sozialer System: der Beruf des deutschen Gewerbelehrers*. Opladen, Westdeutscher Verlag

Labaree, D.F. (1997) 'Public goods, private goods: the American struggle over educational goals.' *American Educational Research Journal*, Vol. 34(1), pp. 39-81.

Labaree, D.F. (2000) 'Resisting educational standards.' *Kappan Professional Journal*, Vol.82(1), pp.28-33. [online article]

Laske, G. (2000) 'Metamorphosen beruflicher Bildung und betrieblicher Quali-fizierung.' In *Zeitschrift für Berufs- und Wirtschaftspädagogik*, Franz Steiner Verlag, Stuttgart

Manning, S. (1990) 'Tradition und Zukunft beruflicher Bildung in Japan.' *Forschung der sozialistischen* Berufsbildung, Vol. 6, pp.274-280.

Marks, A. (2003) 'The 'Learning Society': A literature review.' A working paper, Institute of Education, Stirling University, England.

Moritz, E.F. (1992) 'Konfuzius—Japan—Technik. Ein alter Hut neu aufgesetzt. In *Wissenschaftliches Jahrbuch 1991. Deutschen Museums*. Vol. 7 München. R. Oldenbourg

Münch, J. (1989) *Berufsbildung und Bildung in den USA. Bedingungen, Strukturen, Entwicklungen und Probleme*. Berlin. Eugen Schmidt Verlag

National Commission on Excellence in Education (1983) *A Nation at Risk: The Imperative for Educational Reform*. Washington DC: US Department of Education.

Noble, D.F. (1986) *Forces of Production. A Social History of Industrial Automation*. New York: Oxford Press.

Pätzold, G. (1983) *Quellen und Dokumente zur Geschichte des Berufsbildungsgesetzes 1875-1981*. Vol. 5 Köln, Wien. K. Böhlau

Putnam, A.R. (1998) 'Entwicklung und Organisation der beruflichen Bildung und des Faches Technik im staatlichen Bildungssystem der USA.' *Zeitschrift für Berufs- und Wirtschaftspädagogik*, Vol. 94(2), pp.302-320.

Sakamoto, R. (1996) 'Japan, hybridity and the creation of colonialist discourse.' *Theory, Culture & Society*, Vol. 13(3), pp.113-128.

Schoppa, L.J. (1992) *Education Reform in Japan*. London: Routledge.

Stratmann, K. (1994) 'Die historische Entwicklung der Gewerbelehrerbildung.' *Die berufsbildende Schule*, Vol. 46, pp.40-51.

Tocqueville de, A. (1988) *Democracy in America*. Translated by George Lawrence, New York, Harper Collins

Valverde, G.A. (1994) 'United States: System of Education.' In T. Husén & T.N.Postlethwaite (eds) *The International Encyclopedia of Education*. Oxfdord, Pergamon Press

Yamazaki, T. (1987) 'Der anthropologische Hintergrund der beruflichen Bildung in Japan nach dem Zweiten Weltkrieg.' *Pädagogische Rundschau*, Vol. 41, pp.569-576.

Zinn, H. (1995) *A People's History of the United States, 1492—Present*. New York: Perennial.

CHAPTER SEVEN

National and European Policies for Lifelong Learning: an Assessment of Developments within the Context of the European Employment Strategy

MARK STUART AND IAN GREENWOOD

*'[M]ember States must develop and implement coherent and comprehensive strategies for lifelong learning; and it requires concerted action initiated at **European level...**'*
—EC 2001a: 8. Com (2001) 678 final *[emphasis in original]*

Introduction

It is uncontroversial to note that *employability* and *lifelong learning* now constitute key areas for development and debate within national and European policy circles. Significant points of commonality can be traced across national states and within the broader community and, at a rhetorical level at least, it appears that the 'hymn sheet' is relatively well established. For example, the 'building blocks' for coherent and comprehensive lifelong learning strategies and the 'priorities for action' identified by the European Commission (2001a) in its Communication document *Making a European Area of Lifelong learning a Reality* all resonate with key policy pronouncements, and in some areas practice, at the level of the national state. This is not to say, however, that it is possible to delineate a common European model or system coherence in the area of lifelong learning and employability in national practice. At the level of the nation state the 'hymn sheet' will be interpreted and shaped by historical legacies of education and training, the nature of industrialisation and the broader institutional make-up of the political economy (see, for example,

Ashton and Green, 1996; Crouch et al., 1999). The experiences of the 'learning citizen' will, as a result, vary across Europe.

Against this backdrop, this chapter examines recent developments in lifelong learning discourse and practice at the European and national levels. The chapter is split into three broad sections. The first section examines the recent EU review of lifelong learning (European Commission, 2000, 2001a), the debate that took place over defining lifelong learning and the proposed monitoring process for advancing the lifelong learning agenda (which follows the Open Method of Co-ordination). Building on this, the second section considers explicitly, with reference to the European reporting mechanism, the extent to which comprehensive and co-ordinated systems of lifelong learning are developing at the national and European levels. The third section focuses on the points of tension between the rhetoric and practice of lifelong. It pays specific attention to the level of engagement by the social partners with regard to lifelong learning. In the final section we draw out some of the potential tensions that may exist with regard to the furtherance of employability and lifelong learning within the European model.

Making a European area of Lifelong Learning

The consultation process

The European Commission (EC) staff working paper, *A Memorandum on Lifelong Learning* (EC 2000), was presented for consultation in November 2000. The response was significant. Respondents included all governments within the European Union (EU), peak social partner organisations, civil society groups and relevant organisations (such as CEDEFOP) and over 12,000 citizens. The Memorandum was structured around six *key messages* that formed the basis of the consultation process. The messages were (numerical order in the original):

1. *New basic skills for all*—the objective of which was to 'guarantee universal and continuing access to learning for gaining and renewing the skills needed for sustained participation in the knowledge society' (page 10).
2. *More investment in human resources*—'visibly raise levels of investment in human resources in order to place priority on Europe's most important asset – its people' (page 12).
3. *Innovation in teaching and learning*—'develop effective teaching and learning methods and contexts for the continuum of lifelong and lifewide learning' (page 13).

4. *Valuing* learning—'significantly improve the ways in which learning participation and outcomes are understood and appreciated, particularly non-formal and informal' (page 15).
5. *Rethinking guidance and* counselling—'ensure that everyone can easily access good quality information and advice about learning opportunities throughout Europe and throughout their lives' (page 16).
6. *Bringing learning closer to home*—'provide lifelong learning opportunities as close to learners as possible, in their own communities and supported through ICT-based facilities wherever appropriate' (page 18).

The Lisbon and Feira European Councils of 2000 and the Stockholm Council of 2001 provided the political context for the Memorandum. Driving the political outlook was, and is, the analysis that globalisation, knowledge based societies, new technologies and demographic trends are presenting the EU with new challenges. Competitive advantage, so the argument runs, is predicated upon the development of human capital; 'knowledge and competences are therefore also a powerful engine for growth' (EC, 2001a, p.6). Within this context, lifelong learning is categorised as a central component of the strategy to make Europe the most competitive and dynamic knowledge-based society in the world (by 2010). The European Employment Strategy was identified as a key vehicle through which, for the time at the European level, coherent and comprehensive strategies for lifelong learning could be developed, measured and monitored.

The response to the consultation exercise was presented in the Commission document, *Communication from the Commission: Making a European Area of Lifelong Learning a reality* (EC, 2001a). Within this document, the direction of the EU towards a knowledge-based society, in response to economic and social change, was seen as axiomatic. Economic uncertainty, however, renders the traditional institutions and policies of education and training problematic and calls for a 'radical new approach to education and training ...and renewed emphasis and importance of lifelong learning' (ibid, p.3).

Like the Memorandum, the Communication was structured around a number of themes. Six building blocks endeavour to aid member states to engage with *comprehensive* and *coherent* strategies for lifelong learning. These blocks dovetail with the criteria used in the Joint Employment Report 2001 (EC 2001b) for assessing, and quantifying, the coherence and comprehensiveness of Member States' lifelong learning policies. They were developed in response to the consultation exercise, Member States' Employment and Social Inclusion National Action Plans and other inputs. Incorporated into the formulation of the building blocks are the objectives of active citizenship, personal fulfilment, employability and social inclusion, in conjunction with the conception of lifelong learning developed in the Communication (ibid, p.10). Following on from the building blocks are 'priorities for action' (ibid, p.10). The priorities relate to the building blocks and are in essence the six key messages of the Memorandum modified by the consultation process. Table 1 shows how the building blocks and priorities for action come together in terms of the implementation of comprehensive and coherent strategies. The first three priorities relate to the European dimension of lifelong learning, the second three invite national, regional and local action.

TABLE 1: *The building blocks and priorities of action for coherent and comprehensive lifelong learning strategies*

Building Blocks Priorities for Action	Coherence			Comprehensiveness		
	Partnership working	Creating a learning culture	Striving for excellence	Insight into demand for learning	Facilitating access to learning opportunities	Adequate resourcing
EUROPEAN						
Valuing learning		X	X		X	
Information, guidance and counselling	X	X			X	
Investing time and money in learning			X		X	X
NATIONAL REGIONAL AND LOCAL						
Bringing together learners and learning opportunities	X	X		X		
Basic Skills		X		X	X	
Innovative Pedagogy			X	X		

The thematic 'priorities for action' are accompanied by a series of calls from the Commission for key stakeholders and Member States to develop and adopt specific types of initiatives. Thus, in terms of raising investment levels, Member States are exhorted to 'set national targets to raise overall investment levels in human resources, in line with the Lisbon European Council conclusions and the Employment Guidelines' (EC, 2001a, p.17). In line with the overarching emphasis on partnership working, the social partners are accorded a key role and are challenged to develop a series of frameworks and collective agreements around various aspects of lifelong learning (Wallis and Stuart, 2004). Thus, for example,

> '[T]he social partners are invited to negotiate and implement agreements at all appropriate levels to modernise the organisation of work, with a view to increasing investment in lifelong learning and to providing more time for learning…they should work towards the recognition of all learning activities, including non-formal and informal learning, and integrate this into all aspects of human resource policies and practices at the enterprise level' (EC, 2001a, p.20).

This can be seen to 'fit' within the broader European 'social model' and the increasing promotion (by the Commission) of European social dialogue over issues such as learning and training (Haworth and Winterton, 2004). However, given the diversity of social partnership arrangements across Members States and the nascent state of sectoral agreements and social dialogue at the European level (Kollewe and Kuhlmann, 2002; Leisink, 2002), this represents a significant challenge, a point we shall return to later.

Defining Lifelong Learning

The definition of lifelong learning presented in the Memorandum was taken from the European Employment Strategy (EES):

> 'all the purposeful learning activity, undertaken on an ongoing basis with the aim of improving knowledge, skills and competence' (EC, 2000a, p.3).

A consensus was to emerge throughout the Consultation exercise that this original definition was too skewed towards a labour market conceptualisation, giving little attention to the broader non-work, social and community related conceptions of learning (see, for example, the CEDEFOP review of reports). In other words, the objective of lifelong learning should not just be economically related to employability, but to 'personal fulfilment, active citizenship' and 'social inclusion' (EC, 2001a, p.9). In response, the Communication cast a far more broad-ranging definition of lifelong learning:

'all learning activity undertaken throughout life, with the aim of improving knowledge, skills and competences within a personal, civic, social and/or employment-related perspective' (EC, 2001a, p.9).

This definition relates not just to the formal mechanisms of learning, but also the more informal and non-formal aspects of learning; which the Commission is particularly keen to promote. It is worth noting, however, that whilst the definition of lifelong learning was broadened in the Communication document, the actual evaluation of national strategies and progress with regard to lifelong learning are to be framed by the EES.

Towards a European Area of Lifelong Learning—how does the national influence the European and vice versa?

The stated objective of the Communication is, to 'contribute(s) to the establishment of a European area of lifelong learning' (EC, 2001a, p.3). The notion of an area of lifelong learning involves the maximisation of both the knowledge and mobility of individuals in order to enhance the tolerance, democracy and prosperity of the EU. Lifelong learning provides the framework within which education, training, social inclusion, research policy and employment are fused. However, the Communication is clear that new processes or legislative harmonisation will *not* be involved in the creation of a European area of lifelong learning. Instead, a more efficient use of existing mechanisms and resources is promoted—i.e. more efficient co-ordination and benchmarking of national practice in order to develop 'synergy between Member States' policy in the field of lifelong learning' (EC, 2001a, p.26). Thus, as the Communication notes, whilst the EU has a role to play in:

'....supporting and stimulating the implementation of lifelong learning across the Community. At the same time, policy interventions need to be adapted to local and national circumstances...[M]ember states remain free therefore to develop their own coherent and comprehensive strategies, and to design and manage their own systems, while *broadly moving in the same direction*' (EC, 2001a, p.25, emphasis added).

This is in line with the principle of subsidiarity, involving as it does, transnational, national, regional and local agencies, including the social partners, interacting in a decentralised fashion and using 'variable' forms of partnership (Lisbon European Council, conclusions, para 38). This approach to policy formation has been termed the 'open method of co-ordination' (OMC) (see Goetschy, 2003).

The expression or rather *modus operandi* of the OMC acquired coinage at the 2000 Lisbon Council. The process of OMC involves a flexible, multi-actor, decentralised, non-compulsory regulatory process that circumvents the requirement for decision-making based upon binding legislation. Implicit in the OMC is a process of establishing and comparing (benchmarking) best practice followed by an attempt to guide national policy in the direction of targets based upon such best practice. A system of calibration and evaluation then assesses national efforts to attain transnational goals. Recommendations for progress and improvement might then be issued. The process of the EES is probably the best-formed example of this process. On an annual basis National Employment Guidelines are translated into National Action Plans (NAPs), which are then assessed by the Commission and the Council (see Keep, this volume). This analysis results in a Joint Employment Report (JER) that feeds into Employment Guidelines for the following year. OMC opens up for deliberation new areas of policy formation—including those in the field of lifelong learning. This might be of considerable importance where for example highly conflictual policy fields or the requirements of unanimous voting would rule progress out and, indeed, this concern and problem was behind its evolution. Critics of the process of OMC argue that an approach based on *non-compulsion* may equate to non-compliance, and that OMC might undermine the ability or desire of the EU to engage in hard legislation or to extend the remit of particular social issues from unanimous to qualified majority voting (Goetschy, 2003).

The social partners, and particularly trade unions, view OMC as a generally positive development. Such an outlook is arguably predicated upon different strategic requirements. The response of employers to both the consultation on lifelong learning and the future of the EES indicate a strong desire to avoid any process, legislative or otherwise, that involves compulsion and constraint. Unions, understanding this deterrent to bargaining, see the OMC as a vehicle for the evolution of consultation and dialogue into negotiation and policy formation (see Greenwood and Stuart, 2002, 2003a). However in this field, the principle of subsidiarity remains supreme and its emphasis on decentralisation raises not only potential barriers to policy formation but also a key role for partnership forms of activity (in terms of building coherent systems). This is the case for the propagation of lifelong learning. The irony here, as noted, is that the original definition of lifelong learning was taken from the EES and in response to consultation widened beyond an EES, essentially employment-based notion, to include individual and civic dimensions. However, the EES is the key (only meaningful) trans-European policy vehicle with which to monitor and progress the development and implementation of lifelong learning. What then is the ultimate prospect for the monitoring and implementation of this more holistic lifelong learning and for 'binding' policy? What role can the social partners play in this process? And how does it impact (if at all) on the putative learning citizen?

The coherence and comprehensiveness of Lifelong Learning developments at the nation state level within the European context

Lifelong Learning policy at the national level: a short note on coherence and difference

Attempts to categorise the vocational, education and training systems of European nation states are relatively common, be they in terms of market-based versus educational models or neo-liberal versus corporatist (Ashton and Green, 1996; Crouch et al., 1999). Such categorisations are useful in showing the extent to which there are different national starting points with regard to lifelong learning policies and also the extent to which such policies may be shaped by a degree of 'path dependency' (Hyman, 2002, p.168). Yet, such categorisations can also be problematic, to the extent that they often obscure points of similarity across nation states as well as, more significantly, points of difference (such as in sectors of employment) within nation states. Accordingly, such taxonomies may often overstate the degree of coherence *within* 'national systems' of lifelong learning (Heyes, 2002, p.164). In our research, we examined recent developments in seven European countries (Finland, Germany, Netherlands, Norway, Spain, Sweden, and the UK).[1] Clear vocational, educational and training legacies were visible, in terms of the degree of high (Norway) or low centralised stakeholder (UK) involvement or the extent to which lifelong learning issues are incorporated into social pacts and sectoral agreements (Germany, Netherlands, and Spain). Nonetheless, for the purposes of this chapter, two developments are worth noting. First, even where lifelong learning had been incorporated in, and promoted through, agreements between the social partners, issues around implementation were common (Randle et al., 2004). We will return to the possible reason for this later. Second, it is equally clear that policy debate (loosely defined) has taken place in each country around the lifelong learning agenda and significant numbers of initiatives have been launched with the purpose of raising, and supporting, levels of individual demand for learning. Whether these initiatives can be classified as 'comprehensive' or 'coherent', or are influenced by the broader European agenda for lifelong learning, and to that extent are reflective of convergence, is, of course, a matter of debate. To consider this it is necessary to return to a more detailed examination of the monitoring and reporting process of the European Employment Strategy.

The NAPs, Joint Employment Reports and 'travel' towards coherent and comprehensive Lifelong Learning strategies

The most prominent mechanism for assessing and monitoring national developments in the area of lifelong learning is the Luxembourg Process of the EES. As noted, this process revolves around an annual round of National Action Plans (NAPs), which are then assessed by the Commission and Council, consolidated in a Joint Employment Report and fed-back through National Employment Guidelines. The influence of this process on policy formation and practice at the national level varies enormously. In Spain, for example, the NAP has been used to guide the changing legal framework around vocational qualifications and the changing nature of labour market skills (Laso and Estrada, 2002). Likewise, in the Netherlands the government published a National Action Plan report for lifelong learning and employability in January 1998, with a vision of lifelong learning articulated predominantly in terms of employability with a strong emphasis on enhancing competitiveness (Stevens et al., 2002). In contrast, in the UK, the NAP is treated primarily as a reporting exercise and has little impact on the broader process of public policy formation or engagement over lifelong learning issues with the social partners. Again, the level of involvement in the NAP by the social partners tends to vary from country from country, from significant in countries like Finland and Sweden to negligible in a country like the UK. And overall, they tend to be 'more involved in the elaboration of NAPs' than implementation (Goetschy, 2003, p.291). Despite this, it is possible to argue that the consolidation of the NAPs in the Joint Employment Report at least allows an ongoing assessment of the degree to which National States are putting in place coherent and comprehensive strategies for lifelong learning, as well as an explicit, and formal, avenue for engagement (in the area of adult education and learning) by the social partners.

Table 2 draws selectively from the Draft Joint Employment Report for 2002 and presents the progress of our country cases. With the exception of Spain, and to a lesser extent Germany and the UK, all seem to have developed an 'adequate' level of comprehensiveness in lifelong learning strategies. None are deemed to be 'inadequate'. There also seems to be a high degree of strategic coherence for most other countries, with Spain and Germany lagging behind slightly again. Whilst the Norwegian position outside of the EU means that it does not have a NAP and is therefore not assessed as part of the Luxembourg process, we conclude that it would rank high across both measures of coherence and comprehensiveness, like its Scandinavian neighbours Sweden and Finland.

Looking across the table it is clear that the areas most pronounced in terms of 'partial' progress include: the focus on disadvantaged groups; overall levels of investment and funding; and cross cutting aspects. At the more general level of all Member States, the Draft JER (2002b, p.24) concludes that:

> '*all have now laid the groundwork for comprehensive strategies* covering the whole spectrum of learning – from compulsory education to workplace training, and steps towards better recognition and validation of non formal learning. Incremental

Homo Sapiens Europæus?

TABLE 2: The building blocks and priorities of action for coherent and comprehensive lifelong learning strategies

CHARACTERISTICS	Finland	Germany	Netherlands	Spain	Sweden	UK	Norway
COMPREHENSIVENESS OF STRATEGIES							
Compulsory education	A	A	A	P	A	A	A
Format adult education/training	A	A	A	P	A	A	A
Workplace/other non-formal/recognised prior learning	A	A	A	P	A	A	A
Focus on disadvantaged groups	A	P	P	P	A	P	A
Overhall investment/ funding schemes	A	P	A	P	A	P	A
COHERENCE OF STRATEGY							
System development (policy needs, planning, targets, implementation, monitoring)	A	P	A	A	A	P+	A
Partnership working (social partners, public authorities, learning providers, civil society)	A	A	A	P	A	A	A
Cross-cutting aspects (advice/guidance services, education/ training mobility)	A	P	P	P	A	A	A

Notes:

A   Adequate. 'Adequate' denotes that a particular criterion is given appropriate priority within both the Nation State's strategy and concrete actions.

P   Partial. 'Partial' indicates that some attention is given to the criterion in both the strategy or actions *or* that it is given appropriate priority in one or the other.

I   Insufficient. 'Insufficient' refers to when the particular criterion is absent from both the strategy and the actions or is given some attention in one or the other.

Letters in **bold and grey cells** indicate changes on the previous year. + indicates improvements compared to the previous year.

Source: Taken from '*Communication from the Commission to the Council: Draft Joint Employment Report 2002* (COM (2002) 621 Final). Revised to include comparable Norwegian position.

progress on improving the coherence of lifelong learning strategies is also visible, although moving at a slower pace since it requires more far reaching reforms of systems and practices' (emphasis in original).

It is noted, however, that *'lifelong learning is still far from a reality for all'* (ibid, pp. 23/34), that figures reveal a widening gap in participation levels between the better and lesser educated and the young and the old and that Member States are still not developing targets in the area of human capital investments. Many of these concerns were also picked up by the Impact Evaluation of the EES focusing on lifelong learning (EC, 2002b).[2] Whilst noting various areas of progress and a general trend of levels of attainment and participation, the Impact Evaluation presents fairly depressing reading in terms of the development of coherent and comprehensive strategies. The report's key findings suggest that:

- There is little evaluation (at the national level) of the broad impact of lifelong learning policies and measures;
- The national evaluation reports focus heavily on policy formation with little data on effectiveness or impact;
- Whilst there has been an upward trend in the participation of the adult population in education and training across all age groups, particularly for females, overall rates are still low and inequalities in take-up remain;
- The national evaluation reports do not explicitly address what makes one lifelong learning programme more effective than another;
- Although the problem seems to be substantial, there is a lack of comparable data on the issue of literacy;
- An inability to foresee or predict future demand for skills is in part responsible for skill shortages and mismatching;
- The objective of setting national targets in the field of lifelong learning has not been successful;
- There is 'little evidence of increased appreciation of the importance of lifelong learning and its links to the labour market amongst individuals or firms' (p.16).

Nonetheless, in terms of policy convergence, the report notes that, 'the EES has undoubtedly played a role in making lifelong learning a top political priority' (EC, 2002b, p.5). Noting that the development of reforms at the national level has largely been shaped by the different starting points of the Member States, the Impact Evaluation notes that the 'Guidelines can be said to have promoted a common paradigm of lifelong learning and a convergence can be seen in terms of the scope and coverage of Member States education and training systems' (EC, 2002b, p.6). As we noted above, it is clear from the national cases that all countries have had a debate of sorts around the broad concepts, principles and building blocks of lifelong learning. In some cases, such as Finland and the Netherlands, this has involved specific committees dedicated to debating lifelong learning which to some extent mirror the consultative process on the Memorandum for lifelong learning. In all cases, the *rationale* for a restructuring of education and training structures and a 'new' focus on lifelong learning are underpinned by a common set of assumptions and perceived threats around the need to attain or retain competitiveness, or deliver more efficient labour markers in the face of globalisation and the knowledge economy (a key point, which we return to in the final section). At the level of rhetoric, at least, there is some degree of convergence.

There is also communality in the various concerns and critiques that are advanced at the national level around the degree of progress in implementing coherent and comprehensive lifelong learning strategies. In all cases, inequalities are identified in the levels of participation across generational, educational and regional indicators. Raising investment levels in SMEs is identified as a particular problem in all cases. At a more practical level, however, difference is more apparent as countries develop and implement their agenda's for lifelong learning within the framework of divergent traditions of policy formation. This relates to how the various issues are understood, for example around basic skills problems, as much as to how they tackled – eg. with strong social partner involvement or not.

In summary, then, the Luxembourg process can be said to have had an impact at the level of the nation state, generating some debate around lifelong learning (however minimal in some cases) and providing the raw data for evaluating comparative progress. Just how revealing the auditing of progress against targets presented in the JERs actually is, is debatable. Numerous points could be made here. Firstly, what does 'adequate' and 'partial' actually mean in measurement terms and is 'adequate' (implying as it does a basic level of achievement) an appropriate benchmark. Secondly, given the wide interpretation that can be placed on the various thematic elements of comprehensiveness and strategy coherence at the national level what does this mean for robust comparative analysis? Thirdly, and perhaps most important, what light does such a technocratic exercise actually shed on the complex politics of implementing lifelong learning and the relevance of the agenda to peoples' working and non-working lives within Member States. It is common amongst policy makers to assume that lifelong learning and employability are non-adversarial issues that all stakeholders are to keen to advance, yet evidence suggests something different: extolling the virtues of lifelong learning is one thing, putting it into practice is another. This can apply not only to obvious differences of interest between the state, employers and trade unions, but also between industry confederations and affiliates. These differences can be seen to exist as much in strong social partnership countries, like Norway, as weak ones like the UK.

Potential tensions from within: the social partners and Lifelong Learning

The role of the social partners in advancing the agenda of lifelong learning is prominent in the Communication document and also the EES. The EU strongly advocates the strengthening of social dialogue and sectoral agreements at the European level, particularly in the area of lifelong learning and employability. In this regard, a debate has started around the development by the social partners of 'frameworks of actions for the lifelong development of competencies and qualifications (CEDEFOP, 2002—see also the conference papers 23-24 September 2002 on this theme), following an important landmark joint declaration on 28 February 2002 by the ETUC, UNICE and CEEP. The declaration represents a general statement on advancing competence development and qualifications throughout the working life of an employee. This is deemed dependant on the implementation of four key priorities: the 'identification and anticipation of competencies and qualification needs; recognition and validation of competencies and qualification; information, support and guidance; and resources'. The social partners have committed themselves to advancing the declaration through promoting the framework at a national level, with an annual assessment of national actions against the four priorities. Just how successful this framework is likely to be in terms of developing national practice is an empirical question, and as ever enacting such frameworks in a meaningful way on the ground remain far from straightforward. Moreover, as Odd Bjørn notes (this volume) any assessment of its impact will have to take account of the fact that such European level declarations tend in themselves to be 'watered down'. In some cases it may already broadly correspond to national and sectoral practice (or development), such as in Norway or Spain, whilst in those countries without strong sectoral forms of social dialogue and co-ordination it will probably have little impact. The joint declaration also needs to be placed in an historical context, in terms of social partner dialogue over VET and lifelong learning at the European level.

The responses of the social partners to the *Memorandum on Lifelong Learning* consultation exercise revealed deep-seated points of contention (see, for example, UNICE, 2001 and ETUC, 2001). Two points are worth noting. Firstly, whilst the ETUC rejected the employment-related view of lifelong learning, UNICE stressed the centrality of lifelong learning to the promotion of economic competitiveness and employability, since 'only if training offers correspond to companies' needs will employability and competitiveness be enhanced (UNICE, 2001, p.1). Secondly, whilst the ETUC advocated that lifelong learning should be an individual right, UNICE rejected this categorically. These standpoints were indicative of a longstanding difference in opinion over the advancement of VET. Following a disagreement over progress in access to VET, the social partners did not have meaningful discussions over lifelong learning for most of the 1990s. Against this backdrop, the recent joint declaration at least represents some progress. Nonetheless, the tensions that are revealed over the broad ranging definition of lifelong learning and individual rights in this regard, against a more work and performance based conceptualisation are important and raise intriguing questions over the potential challenges for a meaningful European Area for Lifelong Learning. We conclude the chapter with a consideration of some of these broader questions and concerns.

Lifelong Learning or employability? The limitations of the European Employment Strategy and the constraining influence of European economic policy

In this concluding section, we briefly situate our discussion on the development of coherent and comprehensiveness lifelong learning strategies within a more critical context. We note what we see as some of the fundamental points of tension and contradiction within the lifelong learning debate: the way in which lifelong learning is often conflated with employability, a problem that is inscribed within the tenets of the EES; the nature of employability; the broader assumptions that underpin the call for increased investments in lifelong learning; and finally, the broader constraining influence of the European Monetary Union project.

The Memorandum on lifelong learning and the consultation exercise on its contents have provided a significant input to the EU debate on lifelong learning. The Communication offers a definition of lifelong learning based on the four objectives of personal fulfilment, active citizenship, social inclusion, employability and adaptability. The key question, and a highly problematic one, is to what extent is this *broad* definition of lifelong learning being assessed and its progress monitored? In the realm of European policy development, lifelong learning is to be codified and assessed by the EES. This presents a conundrum. Although the EES is a multi-faceted policy vehicle, its essential nature is one of job creation (EC, 1999); but job creation based upon enhanced employability, flexibility, adaptability and modernisation.

In this context, UNICE—the European business federation—is clear that lifelong learning empowers individuals with regards to their employability. The key attributes of employability are considered to be adaptability, flexibility and an ability to respond to the needs of companies (UNICE, 2000). If individuals do not posses such attributes then presumably they are unemployable. This being the case, the ability of policy to address the issue of social inclusion, and the broader social and civic orientated dimensions of lifelong learning outlined in the Communication document, must be brought into question.

Lefresne (1999) argues that in the context of current levels of EU unemployment, the rhetoric of employability is not about the possession of, or potential to possess, a job. What is occurring is an attempt to change the terrain of debate; whereby notions of full employment are replaced by considerations of the individual characteristics of the unemployed, an inadequate level of human capital and hence employability. In short, individuals are responsible for their own unemployability. This might be considered a somewhat bleak outlook but evidence from national developments and the response of the business community to the Memorandum on Lifelong Learning indicates a clear move towards an individualisation of responsibility for employment and training. Thus, in their evaluation of education and training within the EU, Demeulemeester and Rochat (2001) strongly question the ability of European level policy making to succeed in the development of a unified European perspective in this field. They argue that barriers to success will include the politically heterogeneous nature of the EU and, perhaps somewhat more fundamentally, the reality of profit maximising firms, particularly those of a multi-national nature, deciding for themselves their best route to profit. In the regard, any assumption that the knowledge economy (whatever that means) is the only route to competitive success cannot be taken for granted.

Furthermore, although the EES can be understood as a relatively progressive policy vehicle, it is caged within the strictures of monetary union and the requirements of the European Central Bank, Stability and Growth Pact and the limitations of the OMC. The broader economic project of the EU should not therefore be neglected. Within the field of employment and within the institutions of the EES statements of policy at both national and pan-European level are suffused with the rhetoric of economism, flexibility and individualism. Correspondingly, the policy agenda of the EU has illuminated the concepts of lifelong learning and employability in a precise way. Both are embedded in the need for individual responsibility and the necessity for flexibility through the workings of the labour market and within work.

The EU monetary strategy within which EU social policy—including that of the EES—is constrained, is a lucid force for convergence in the field of economics. In the same way, but through a less binding mechanism, the EES acts to direct and co-ordinate employment policy and dimensions such as lifelong learning that are contained within its remit. What is apparent is the variability, not only of policy-making superstructures but also, as Goetschy (2003) notes, the variation in employment policies that underpin strategies for learning. For example, the reduction of the working week, targeted training, part-time work and policies designed to increase employment flexibility. However, evidence at the level of the nation state is equally clear that a convergence of market-oriented policy levers pushing the agendas for training and lifelong learning is taking place. Learning is seen a vector towards increased flexibility, mobility and personal responsibility. In other words, at a rhetorical level, but also as a concomitant of this through various policy frameworks such as the EES, there is strong convergent push for the tenets of neo-liberalism (Greenwood and Stuart, 2003b). This does not mean that outcomes are determined, however, as at the level of the nation state historical, traditional and institutional structures, and most significantly social agency, can shape a variety of economic, employment and learning trajectories. Yet, clearly this will be an area of future struggle, most notably as economic imperatives continue to impinge on the so called continental model of social partnership. The role of the social partners will be central to the ultimate destination of the lifelong learning agenda. All the countries considered in this paper to a greater or lesser extent have lifelong learning policies in place. However, policies for lifelong learning alone will be insufficient to drive the agenda forward. All too often lifelong learning is presented as a panacea: yet policies for learning, in isolation, are often unlikely to make a difference, as the uptake and demand for learning is often predicated on a host of broader institutional, structural and societal concerns. Tackling these broader concerns—such as the nature and type of employment and work organisation and so on—means, of course, challenging the broader conceptualisation of the EES, employability and the economic rhetoric currently so pervasive within the EU.

Acknowledgements

The work for this chapter was funded by the EU Framework 5 grant HPSE-CT2001-00049.

Notes

1. See Greenwood and Stuart (2002, for the UK); Kevætsalo (2002, for Finland); Laso and Estrada (2002, for Spain); Nyen and Skule (2002, for Norway); Randle and Svensson (2002, for Sweden); Stevens et al. (2002, for the Netherlands); Trappmann and Kruse (2002, for Germany).

2. The impact evaluation is based upon national evaluation reports (of the EES) and also the Joint Employment Reports with other supporting data. The national evaluation reports covers 12 member states as Denmark, Holland and Ireland did not cover the theme of lifelong learning in the impact exercise. Also the exercise does not reflect data in the 2002 NAPs and in essence reflects 2000 data.

References

Ashton, D. & Green, F. (1996) *Education Training and the Global Economy.* Cheltenham: Edward Elgar.

CEDEFOP (nd) *Memorandum on Lifelong Learning – Consultation: A Review of Member State and EEA Country Reports.* Thessaloniki: CEDEFOP

Crouch, C.; Finegold, D. & Sako, M. (1999) *Are Skills the Answer? The Political Economy of Skill Creation in Advanced Industrial Societies.* Oxford: Oxford University Press.

Demeulemeester, J. & Rochat, D. (2001) 'The European policy regarding education and training: a critical assessment.' *SKOPE Research Paper No. 21.* Warwick: Oxford and Warwick Universities

European Commission (1999) *The European Employment Strategy: Investing in People.* Luxembourg: Office for Official Publications of the EC.

European Commission (2000) *A Memorandum for Lifelong Learning.* Commission Staff Working Paper, SEC(2000) 1832, Brussels.

European Commission (2001a) *Making a European Area of Lifelong Learning a Reality.* Communication, COM(2001) 678 [final].

European Commission (2001b) *Joint Employment Report 2001*, COM (2001) 438 [final].

European Commission (2002a) 'Impact Evaluation of the EES—Background paper—lifelong learning.' EMCO/24/060602/EN_REV 1, Brussels: EC.

European Commission (2002b) *Draft Joint Employment Report 2002.* COM(2002) 621 [final].

Goetschy, J. (2003) 'The European Employment Strategy and the open method of coordination: lessons and perspectives.' *Transfer,* Vol.9(2), pp.281-301

Greenwood, I. & Stuart, M. (2002) *Contextualising the Learning Agenda in the UK: Historical Legacies, Contemporary Policies.* Learnpartner report prepared for European Commission DG Research.

Greenwood, I. & Stuart, M. (2003a) 'Employability or lifelong flexibility: unpicking the contradictions of the European Employment Strategy.' In C.H. Jorgensen & N. Warring (eds) *Adult Education and the Labour Market VII: Volume A.* Roskilde: Roskilde University Press.

Greenwood, I. & Stuart, M. (2003b) 'We are all neo-liberals now—or are we?' Presented at *International Trade Unionism in a Network Society Workshop: What's new about the 'New Labour Internationalism'?* Leeds Metropolitan University, Leeds, May 2-3.

Haworth, N. & Winterton, J. (2004) 'HRD policies and the supra state: A comparative analysis of EU and APEC experience.' Paper presented at the *Fifth International Conference on HRD Research and Practice Across Europe*, University Forum of HRD, University of Limerick, Limerick, 27-28 May.

Heyes, J. (2002) 'Re-examining national models of skill formation: A comment on comparative VET research.' In R. Cooney & M. Stuart (eds) *Proceedings of the First International Conference on Training, Employability and Employment*. Melbourne: Monash University.

Kollewe, K. & Kulmann, R. (2003) 'Creating a more dynamic European social dialogue by strengthening the sectoral dimension.' *Transfer*, Vol.9(2), pp.265-280.

Kevaetsalo (2002) *Contextualising the Learning Agenda in Finland: Historical Legacies, Contemporary Policies*. Learnpartner report prepared for European Commission DG Research.

Laso, R. & Estrada, B. (2002) *Contextualising the Learning Agenda in Spain: Historical Legacies, Contemporary Policies*. Learnpartner report prepared for European Commission DG Research.

Lefresne, F. (1999) 'Employability at the heart of the European Employment Strategy.' *Transfer*, Vol.5(4), pp.460-480.

Leisink, P. (2002) 'The European sectoral social dialogue and the graphical industry.' *European Journal of Industrial Relations*, Vol.8(1), pp.101-117

Nyen, T. & Skule, S. (2002) *Contextualising the Learning Agenda in Norway: Historical Legacies, Contemporary Policies*. Learnpartner report prepared for European Commission DG Research.

Randle, H. & Svensson, L. (2002) *Contextualising the Learning Agenda in Sweden: Historical Legacies, Contemporary Policies. A System for Education, adapted to the Idea of Lifelong Learning, a Possibility or a Vision?* Learnpartner report prepared for European Commission DG Research.

Skule, S.; Stuart, M. & Nyen, T. (2002) 'Training and development in Norway.' *International Journal of Training and Development*, Vol.6(4), pp.263-276.

Stevens, B.; Leisink, P. & Spaninks, L. (2002) *Contextualising the Learning Agenda in the Netherlands: Historical Legacies, Contemporary Policies—Employability and Lifelong Learning: Institutional Actors' Policies and Workplace Practice*. Learnpartner report prepared for European Commission DG Research.

Svensson, L. (2002) 'Lifelong learning—a rhetoric concept or a reality?' Presented at *The First International Conference on Training, Employability and Employment*, Monash University and Leeds University Business School, Monash University Centre, King's College London, 11-12 July.

Trappmann, V. & Kruse, W. (2002) *Contextualising the Learning Agenda in Finland: Historical Legacies, Contemporary Policies*. Learnpartner report prepared for European Commission DG Research.

UNICE (2000) *For Education and Training Policies which Foster Competitiveness and Employment: UNICE's Seven Priorities*. Brussels: UNICE.

UNICE (2001) *Commission Memorandum of Lifelong Learning UNICE Position Paper*. Ref S/ 10.3 13/2002/ UNICE position LLL final. Brussels: UNICE.

Wallis, E. & Stuart, M. (2004) 'Partnership-based approaches to learning in the context of restructuring: case studies from the European steel and metal sectors.' *Career Development International*, Vol.9(1), pp.45-57.

CHAPTER EIGHT

The Main Actors in the National Action Plans on Employment—Who can Bring Forward the Education and Training Dimension of the NAPS?

EWART KEEP

Introduction

The European Employment Strategy (ESS), agreed at the Luxembourg Summit in 1997, aims to improve the Union's record on combating unemployment. Besides committing the Commission to produce an annual employment package for submission to the European Council, the Strategy also required member states to develop a National Action Plan (NAP) for Employment as a means of monitoring progress towards targets laid down in the ESS.[1] From the outset the guidelines set for the NAPs have asked member states, working in conjunction with the social partners, to develop policies on lifelong learning.

This chapter draws on an overview of lifelong learning (LLL) activity and its linkages to the National Action Plans (NAPs) for Employment in a sample of five EU states—England, the Netherlands, Finland, Sweden, and Italy. England rather than the UK was chosen as the unit for analysis here because although responsibility for the NAP and other employment issues remains a UK government responsibility, education and training is a now devolved issue, i.e. it is the responsibility of the four national administrations in England, Wales, Scotland and Northern Ireland. The overall aim of the chapter is to examine the tensions between the idealised model for the NAPs and their actual design and implementation, the different national structures for developing the LLL elements of the NAPs, and the interactions between the different actors who shape the plans within these systems. It also identifies a number of issues facing the future evolution of LLL activity within the context of the NAPs.

By way of introduction, a number of issues that will emerge in what follows need to be highlighted. The first is that many debates concerning European policy founder because people make the assumption that as the same word or phrase is being used by all participants a commonly agreed concept is being discussed. This is often not the case. As van de Kamp and Hake (2002, p.13) note:

> 'Despite the strong degree of interest in lifelong learning expressed by politicians, employers, trade unions and the educational community, it is still not evident that there is any universal agreement on what the term 'lifelong learning' actually refers to…'

Thus, when an English policy maker refers to lifelong learning, what they have in mind may be very different from what a Finn or a Swede would think the concept pertained to. To paraphrase Churchill, in many areas of its work, the EU is a group of nations divided by a common terminology. This chapter stresses the need to guard against assumptions of commonality of meaning, and to underline just how varied are the national paradigms currently being attached to the concept of LLL.

A second theme of much of what follows is the way in which LLL is a site of contestation (sometimes overt, more usually covert) between divergent visions of what LLL is for and what a national LLL strategy could or should be concerned with. Some approaches are very narrow and utilitarian, and view LLL as little more than workforce development writ large. Others are much broader, and afford greater priority to non-economic elements (such as cultural and citizenship issues). Insofar as the NAPs act as a focus for discussion about LLL and employment, they provide a forum in which these tensions may become manifest.

The third theme is the issue of who should be driving LLL strategies, particularly as they relate to employment issues. Again, it will become apparent that the relative weight accorded to different actors varies enormously from nation to nation.

Another aspect of the context set by the NAPs that deserves note is that the NAPs are primarily about employment and employability. As such, they tend to concentrate attention on those aspects of LLL that have as their main focus employment and work, and, as a consequence, on those preparing to enter or those already in the labour market. Thus, if LLL is a cradle to grave concept, the NAPs are only concerned with that portion of the population who will become or already are of working age. This facet of LLL may be in tension with other, wider aspects of what LLL might be about, and this may be of concern to some of the actors involved in the process of formulating the NAPs in some EU states.

A final point is that European policy on LLL, as on a number of other fronts, is handicapped by the lack of direct policy competence of the EU. The Commission can exhort and 'co-ordinate', and seek to demand information and reporting on targets agreed at ministerial level in inter-governmental meetings, but it has no direct levers to control or directly fund (outside a limited number of cases such as the European Social Fund and Leonardo da Vinci programmes) LLL activity in the member states (Field, 1997). The NAPs, along with other devices such as the EC's Memorandum on LLL, are a means of getting a Commission foot in the nation state's policy door.

An overview of the issues across five EU states

If we examine the development and implementation of the NAPs and their relationship with LLL activity in the UK, the Netherlands, Finland, Sweden and Italy, a number of commonalities and disjunctures emerge. These are outlined below.

Common issues and problems

In all these countries the national systems of LLL are battling with a set of similar issues:

- Increasing regional (and urban/rural) disparities in employment growth (see, for example, Richini (2002) for details of how the issue plays out in Italy; and Nyyssola and Hamalainen (2001) for Finland). Heavy geographic concentrations of the incidence of social exclusion and unemployment, often in outlying areas of the countries, are placing LLL and employability policies under strain. Correcting for the effects of divergent regional economic trends through LLL provision is proving difficult.
- The re-integration of excluded and marginalised groups, particularly ethnic minorities and older workers, back into the labour market. This is an important issue as countries try to improve their general levels of labour force participation, improve social inclusion, and battle the problems of an aging workforce.
- Tensions between EU aspirations and targets for LLL and national priorities (see below for further details).
- Increasing emphasis on a narrow reading of LLL as workforce development for employability (see below).
- Building closer links between initial education and learning throughout life (see van de Kamp and Hake (2002) for details of Dutch attempts to close the gap between initial VET and LLL).

- Developing the accreditation of prior learning (APL).
- The use of ICT and other new modes of delivery to encourage LLL (for details of the Swedish experience, see Bostrum et al. (2001); and Boudard (2000).
- Encouraging more firms to become learning organizations.
- Funding expanded ambitions from sources other than the public purse.
- Providing basic skills to adult workers.

In the space available more detailed review of these is confined to two issues that bear heavily on the main themes of this chapter.

Lifelong learning or workforce development? One of the dangers inherent in the NAPs is that they focus attention on one aspect of LLL—that relating to employability—thereby tending to prioritize those forms of LL that relate to economic activity and employment. It is possible to detect a general tendency in policy rhetorics surrounding LLL in Europe to place increasing stress on the economic aspects/impacts of LLL (employability and productivity), and a reduction in attention to the wider societal, cultural, citizenship aspects of LLL associated with development of the individual for life and leisure outside the workplace. This narrows the focus of LLL experiences that are seen as relevant to policy goals and centers attention on those of working age. The impetus behind this trend varies between countries, but appears to be weakest in Scandinavia, where strong traditions of wider LLL are in place (Nyyssola and Hamalainen, 2001) and to have gone furthest in the Netherlands (van de Kamp and Hake, 2002), and in England (Coffield, 1999), where LLL as a policy rhetoric is in sharp retreat and is increasingly being replaced by narrowly defined workforce development measures.

This development has important implications for the role that is then allotted to community and voluntary groups within LLL policies. If LLL increasingly becomes tied to purely economic ends and has as its central focus workforce development, it is likely that, in the long run, the role of community and voluntary groups in LLL will decline.

Besides the rather depressing utilitarian outcomes liable to be generated by so narrow a conception of LLL, it is possible that this type of emphasis will make it harder to engage with those lacking formal education qualifications working in lower skilled jobs. There is a considerable wealth of evidence, not least that collected by the UK Economic and Social Research Council's Learning Society Programme, that indicates that for many, re-engagement with learning is best started with learning experiences that are focused on issues other than development for employment (Coffield, 2000a, b).

Finally, as Brown (2003) underlines, the more that waged employment and the ability to achieve it (employability) are promoted as the sole or main source of individual wellbeing and value within society, and the more that employability is tied to policies of expanding education and qualifications in what is sometimes a zero-sum game for employment, the greater the danger that people's views of education shrink to an instrumental one. Education becomes a search for positional advantage achieved via the acquisition of qualifications. Thus learning is no longer inquisitive (for its own sake), but acquisitive (learning only what is necessary to pass examinations, in order to achieve qualifications, in order to improve the chances of obtaining employment). Some societies have already 'progressed' quite a long way down this path—in England, a student can expect to have undergone around 105 formal examinations before reaching the age of 18 (Brown, 2003, p.162). Love of learning for its own sake, or learning to achieve wider forms of self-actualisation and expression gradually become marginalised or smothered.

EU aspirations versus national priorities. Across all the countries studied there were implicit tensions between national LLL agendas and targets and EU goals. An example is the suggestion by the Commission (EC, 2001, p.18) that, '35 hours of learning per year for every employee might be an attainable benchmark'. Another is that, 'Member States should consider extending the right to compulsory education so that it covers free access to basic skills for all citizens, regardless of age' (EC, 2001, p.23). A third proposal was that, 'the social partners are invited to conclude agreements on the promotion of access to learning opportunities, in particular for workers with low levels of skill and older workers, to meet the objective of giving every worker the opportunity to achieve information society literacy by 2003' (EC, 2001, p.23).

The gap between EC aspiration and national reality is often large. For example, the 35 hour per year 'benchmark' remains invisible in the policy discourse in many countries, and national governments and their LLL systems made fairly limited progress on delivering the information technology literacy target (EC, 2002). Indeed throughout the UK this target was completely ignored by government.

This disparity between what can be agreed to at EU level and what actually gets delivered within national LLL systems indicates the problem of translating the European Employment Strategy (EES) into concrete reality. Signing declarations at EU meetings of ministers is painless, allocating the budgetary resources to deliver these objectives, or confronting employers with demanding benchmarks and then moving them towards these, requires a somewhat different level of investment of political capital—one that is often not forthcoming. Moreover, the Commission admits that, 'despite repeated calls…occasionally backed up by specific recommendations, less than half of the Member States responded to the invitation to set national targets to increase participation and raise investment (in LL)…..it must be concluded therefore that *the objective of setting national targets in the field of lifelong learning has met with relatively little success* (emphasis as in original)' (EC, 2002, p.7).

More generally, although European Commission statements emphasise the need for cooperation and coordination at European level, their own evaluations of the European Employment Strategy (EC, 2002) make it clear that the goal of a concerted approach is proving very difficult to achieve. Even arriving at a reporting structure that would allow meaningful evaluations of member states efforts is regarded as problematic (EC, 2002, p.3).

Areas of diverging policy and practice

Alongside the points of common concern, it is also clear that there are substantial areas of divergence across the five national systems, not least in terms of the importance afforded the to the NAPs, the role of the state in the management of LLL activity, the role of employers in providing LLL, the balance between education and training in delivering LLL, and the degree to which LLL was coming to be defined in a very narrow sense, so that it was little more than another way of thinking about workforce development.

The varying impact of NAPS on national LLL strategies. The impact of the NAPs on national LLL strategies varies enormously. In some EU states (for example, the UK) it is, 'seen by the government and social partners largely in terms of meeting the UK's reporting requirements under the European employment strategy', and 'does not have a high profile in terms of domestic political debate or media coverage' (Hall, 2002, p.4). Social partner involvement in setting the NAP is very limited and its impact on policy formation or implementation somewhere between minimal and nil. In other states, for example Finland, the NAP plainly plays a very different role, and is used by the state and social partners as a planning/audit mechanism at a strategic level of policy formation (Finnish Ministry of Labour, 2002).

Diverging conceptions of common concepts. There remain important philo-sophical divides between states in respect of how they generally conceive of many aspects of VET. One example would be basic skills. England has developed and maintained (by mainland European standards) an extremely narrow conception of the focus of vocational training—one which has almost no place for any element of wider general educational study within it (Green, 1998). Our approach to basic skills is similarly narrow in conception—the ability to read, write and use numbers. Wider EU definitions of basic skills (EC, 2001, p.22) that encompass items such as IT, foreign languages, technology, culture, entrepreneurship and social skills are liable to fall on stony ground in the English context, not least because even the very limited diet of learning to be found in our existing vision of basic skills is still proving too demanding for many English employers (Fuller and Unwin, 2003).

The roles of the different actors. It is clear that the scale and salience of the role attached to the various actors continues to vary very greatly. The prime examples here would be those of the national state, as opposed to elected local or municipal government, and the importance attached to employers and trade unions.

As ever in EU discussions, England (and the wider UK) is the 'odd man out'. Whereas in the other countries studied the devolution of responsibility for LLL to regional and local government (often working with the social partners) had been a strong strand in national policy, in England VET policies generally, and LLL specifically, tend to remain very much in the hands of the central state and its agencies. The role of elected local bodies is tiny. Central government and its agencies are the primary (often sole) architects and 'movers' of many aspects of LLL system. This tendency is reinforced by the almost total absence of any form of tripartite decision making structures within the VET system, and the lack of any real notions of social partnership (as it would be understood elsewhere in Europe) (see Keep, 2002).

The results are highly centralised policies and programmes, and a general lack of democratic accountability for decisions about LLL. In the absence of general collective bargaining over skills or well-structured social partnership arrangements, the role of trade unions is small. As there is no legal compulsion on employers to train (except largely in relation to health and safety at work issues), firms direct their training at meeting narrowly defined business goals and play only a very limited role in LLL. The main employers' confederation— the Confederation of British Industry (CBI)—has stated that if sections of the workforce are missing out on learning opportunities this is because there is no rational business case for more or better training for them, and that the solution is for the state to step in and fund remedial measures (CBI, 2000 and 2002). This is precisely what the state has done—it is now piloting a state-funded entitlement to adult workforce development (the Employer Training Pilots).

More generally, what emerges within the case study countries is the degree to which the roles of the actors are determined by the policy structures and political systems within which they operate. Actors working within the Dutch 'Polder Model' (van de Kamp and Hake, 2002; Cheallaigh et al., 2002) have open to them opportunities that their English counterparts can barely imagine.

These institutional structures reflect fundamentally different conceptions of policy formation. Thus the Swedish regional growth agreements, which provide regional fora for social partnership, are founded on the belief, 'that the greatest knowledge on the criteria and suitable measures for local and regional growth and employment is found among those most closely involved' (Bostrum et al., 2001, p.22). In England, the general rule is that central government and its agencies know best.

The policy structures also provide a power-base, and a means of exerting leverage and traction over policy which allow actors such as trade unions to have a greater impact than might otherwise be expected. Societies with dense and relatively rich networks of interaction between the different parties are potentially able to reduce free-riding and opting out, and develop coalitions of interest that can deliver wider social goals (Finnish Ministry of Labour, 2002; Bostrum et al., 2001).

States with traditionally much 'thinner' networking infrastructures are faced with major problems. Without strong systems of norms and expectations enshrined in legislation, and powerful collective bargaining and tripartite concertation, the likely outcome is a situation where employers can opt out and trade unions and other actors have limited impact. The UK provides a clear indication of these problems. In a largely voluntary training system, with very weak, patchy and disaggregated collective bargaining arrangements, where sectoral agreements are almost unknown, the vast bulk of private sector service workplaces are non-unionised, where the overwhelming majority of those collective agreements that do exist do not cover skills or training issues, and where formalised mechanisms for social dialogue are lacking, what can be expected from employers on LLL tends to be very limited. Within the vacuum that is then created, the only means of making progress is for the state to step in and take charge. Thus the kind of collective labour agreements that have produced sectoral training funds—as found in some sectors in the Netherlands (Brandsma, 2002), and Finland (Rensujeff and Nyyssola, 1999), and interprofessional joint funds in Italy (Richini, 2002)—are extremely difficult to replicate in England.

Co-determination in the workplace is also important. As Italian commentators underline (Chirone, 2000, 2001), issues to do with training within the enterprise are normally dependent upon higher order decisions about product market strategy, investment, technology, innovation and so on. If workers and their representatives have no direct input into these first order strategic decisions, their influence over how the skill needs that result might best be met may turn out to have limited impact on the overall outcomes that result.

As underlined above, another key dimension is whether the system is centralised or de-centralised. In Finland, Italy, Sweden and the Netherlands, de-centralisation is an important element and one that has generally been increasing in the last decade or so. In England, the opposite is the case. A more local focus plainly allows a range of local actors (particularly voluntary and community groups) to have greater influence on and role in the delivery of LLL.

Thus in trying to answer who can bring forward the LLL element of the NAPs—or indeed who can advance LLL policies more generally—one of the prime determining factors is the prevailing national system of decision making on LLL—how it is structured, who it encompasses and what social, political and legal norms buttress its operation. The systems architecture materially influences who is in a position to do what.

The future

Many of the most important issues raised by looking at LLL policies and their relationship with the NAPs in England, the Netherlands, Italy, Finland and Sweden concern future trends and issues. It is apparent from the national cases that the evolution of LLL policies is in transition, and that a number of significant challenges now face the national policy communities, as well as the EU collectively in seeking to answer the question, 'who can bring forward the education and training element of the NAPs?' A small number of the most important of these issues are reviewed below.

Over-reliance on economic developments to drive progress?

There is a tendency within EU policy discourses on skills to assume that current developments—namely globalisation, the impact of ICT, and structural shifts in the pattern of occupations—are propelling us all inexorably towards a high skills vision (Keep and Mayhew, 2001). There is some evidence to suggest that the impact of these developments varies between economies and regions (Hepworth and Spencer, 2002) and that the outcomes that they produce are mediated by a range of existing societal characteristics and choices. Data from the USA—the leading exemplar of the knowledge driven economy—does not suggest an explosion in the proportion of highly skilled jobs, nor of significant upskilling being demanded for those in lower skilled occupations (see Brown, 2001; and Hecker, 2001). Many academics now dispute some of the more optimistic labour market projects which downplay the growth in low skilled employment (see Thompson, Warhurst and Callaghan, 2001; Lloyd and Payne, 2002), and question whether a 'high skills for all' scenario is realistic (Regini, 1995). Although the Lisbon accord drives a policy rhetoric about becoming 'the leading knowledge driven economy in the world', the reality for the foreseeable future for many European employees is most unlikely to be one where they find themselves as knowledge workers.

This raises major questions about the value of endlessly expanding education and the dangers of positional battles over the good jobs among an increasingly over-large population of those qualified to undertake such work (Brown, 2003). It also suggests that we need to think far harder and more realistically about what is on offer (in terms of working conditions, pay and learning opportunities) to that significant proportion of the population who in the foreseeable future will not become knowledge workers. In countries with more solidaristic wage systems and higher levels of redistribution such questions may be less acute than they are in countries such as the England.

Future trends in the take-up of LLL

One of the chief assumptions in many of the national policy debates on LLL is that the underlying trend is upwards, i.e. that levels of LLL are increasing, that this is the natural order of things, and that policy can build upon a growing desire by an increasing proportion of the population to engage in learning throughout life. Recent data from the UK suggests that this may not be universally true. The National Institute of Adult Continuing Education (NIACE) runs an annual survey on adult participation in LLL. The surveys for both 2002 and 2003 indicate a general downward trend in the take-up of LLL among the adult population. In 2003, the overall rate among of engagement in any form of LLL (either current or over the preceding three years) among the adult population fell to 39 per cent. Figures for those who had engaged in learning in the last three years fell from 29 per cent in 2001, to 23 per cent in 2002, and just 20 per cent of the sample in 2003 (NIACE, 2003). Figures from the 2004 survey show the slow decline continuing, with fewer adults engaged in learning than was the case in 1997 (Kingston, 2004).

Elsewhere in Europe there are signs that policy makers are faced with residual groups of non-learners among the adult population who are proving hard to reach and motivate. These are often made up of those whose initial education and training was limited, older workers, and migrant workers and immigrants. It may well be that existing LLL policies have addressed the easier to engage sections of the population, leaving further progress to be made among the harder to reach segments of the population (Field, 2001). If this is the case, significant further progress may be harder to achieve and the issue of which actors might be responsible for addressing these groups is problematic. In this regard, experience in the UK has shown that trade unions have an important role to play in selling the benefits of learning to disadvantaged sections of the adult workforce (see Rainbird, Munro and Holly, 2004).

Funding LLL—the uncertain future of the ESF

Another source of future uncertainty concerns the European Social Fund (ESF). It is noticeable across all states studied that important elements of LLL provision—often that targeted at the most vulnerable within the labour market—is currently being funded (either in whole or in part) via the European Social Fund. With the arrival of the new succession states from the Baltic and Eastern Europe, current patterns of ESF disbursement to the older member states will undergo a fundamental change. A large proportion of the ESF is liable to flow into the new states, with concomitant reductions in what is available for older members. Such reductions could have very significant impacts on LLL provision, particularly in countries such as Italy (Richini, 2002, p.22), where a large proportion of VET and LLL is financed by ESF monies.

Thus, while the new additions to the EU family are very welcome and may well inject new thinking into debates about LLL, their arrival does mean that some of the other member states need to start planning for changing patterns of ESF distribution and developing alternative sources of funding. It is unclear to what extent member states have started this process, or begun to explore where new sources of funding might come from in a world where competing demands for finite resources are growing. For example, both employers and trade unions are also faced with calls to increase investment in pension funds.

Convergence or continuing divergence?

In their thinking about driving forward the LLL agenda, the Commission suggests that, 'the key challenge, therefore, is to ensure that member States remain free to develop their own coherent and comprehensive strategies, and to design and manage their own systems while moving broadly in the same direction' (EC, 2001, p.25). The foregoing suggests that achieving a broad commonality of direction is extremely difficult, if only because the starting points of individual states are so different and because some states (such as the UK) appear determined to follow a very different trajectory from others. Also, as suggested above, divergent trajectories may, at least in part, be a direct result of very different distributions of power among the various actors and of widely varying social, legal and political approaches to fashioning and supporting decision making structures on LLL.

As a result, a desire to arrive at a common policy or even at some foundation platform of levels of common provision across the EU may mean the adoption of a 'convoy principle' whereby progress and/or ambition is limited by the willingness of the slowest moving members to progress. Common baseline standards of LLL provision across the entire EU continue to look very problematic.

The future roles of the different actors

Given the foregoing it will be apparent that a range of choices about what should be learned and to what ultimate end that learning might be directed, will tend to have a very significant impact on who promotes the learning. Those countries that are better able (for reasons of political, cultural and historical legacy) to preserve a wider focus on the benefits of LLL beyond economic success or employability are liable to develop very different patterns of activity by the actors involved from countries where learning simply becomes another branch of workforce development or re-training for the unemployed.

It is also striking that those countries (for example, Finland and Sweden) that appear to have made the greatest progress on developing and sustaining relatively high levels of LLL are those that are characterised by systems of political accountability and policy formation that stress the construction of broad consensus and the use of social partnership, and which have tended to devolve responsibility downward to local level (Finnish Ministry of Labour, 2002; Nyyssola and Hamalainen, 2001; Bostrum et al., 2001). Although the state takes the lead, it does not dominate policy formation and it appears to act in partnership with other stakeholders. This suggests that the configuration of an appropriate systems architecture for VET and LLL is a key determinant in ensuring that the different actors are given the political space to operate to maximum effect. It also suggests that in countries where the political culture is tending to promote ever greater centralisation of decision making and an ever-larger role for the state (as leader, architect, funder and manager of LLL), progress may be more difficult.

It is also apparent that arrangements for collective bargaining and social partnership, coupled with legislative underpinning for certain forms of training activity, have a critical effect on the roles that can and will be adopted by employers and trade unions. For trade unions to play a major proactive role, it would seem important that they are afforded leverage through collective bargaining and/or social partnership systems. On the latter point, it is not merely the process of social partnership that is important, but also the institutional leverage that is afforded by full participation in various forms of tripartite or bi-lateral bodies that are helping to plan, deliver and fund LLL. To put it another way, as Giddens has argued (1984, 1993), structure is important because it provides both resources and rules by which parties can interact. If structures are absent, or are only open to a very limited number of players, the potential for those excluded to impact on LLL design and delivery is diminished.

Without recourse to reasonably powerful opportunities to exert influence over both public policy and the investment decisions of employers, the remaining role for trade unions tends to become one of outreach to its own membership in promoting the virtues of engaging in LLL. While this internal role is important (and can be seen across a number of countries, such as Finland, Sweden and England), on its own it constitutes a fairly narrow and limited agenda, particularly in societies where the coverage of union membership is patchy.

The need for realism on what LLL can deliver

One of the problems with policy discourses on LLL in the countries covered in this chapter is the tendency to heap ever-growing expectations on what learning can, on its own, be expected to achieve. As Grubb and Lazerson (forthcoming) and Brown (2003) argue, this reflects, at least in part, a belief that, in an increasingly globalised economy, the ability of nation states (or even groups thereof—such as the EU) to intervene to change patterns of economic development and income and life chance distributions is waning. The market, so the argument goes, will no longer tolerate economically inefficient re-distribution via taxation or other forms of state intervention. The only forms of intervention that can now be tolerated are those that equip individuals to operate and compete more effectively in the marketplace. Thus education is seen as one of the few ideologically-neutral forms of intervention still available to governments.

Within Europe, the UK may be seen as the prime exemplar of this type of reasoning in action. Indeed, it is precisely such thinking that stands at the heart of New Labour's 'third way'. As a result, a growing list of social and economic problems is now seen as best being tackled via education.

While there is obvious sense in viewing education as an important lever for change, the problem comes when it is increasing perceived to be the only lever (see Lafer, 2002; Grubb and Lazerson, forthcoming, for the results in the USA). More, and even better, LLL will not, of itself, necessarily provide people with better healthcare or housing, or even better paid and more interesting employment if the supply of qualified applicants outstrips the growth in such job opportunities. The danger with such overloading of expectations is that LLL and other forms of learning ultimately disappoint by being unable to fulfil the promises that have been loaded upon them.

A wider agenda—LLL and what else makes the difference?

These problems lead us to the issue of how LLL might be combined with other forms of policy intervention to improve life chances and economic performance. One instance is the issue of work organisation and job design. It is already the case that in some member states, particularly in Northern Europe and Scandinavia, there is a tradition of linking LLL issues with a concern to develop innovative forms of work organisation and job design. Such a concern makes good sense. In terms of vocational LLL, the workplace is, or should be, the major site for this take place, usually through informal learning on the job.

One way to boost the amount of learning that takes place is to try to upgrade the workplace as a learning environment. Moreover, if we want new skills to be put to good use, it may also be necessary to change the way work is organised and jobs designed in order that enhanced skills can be deployed to maximum effect (on both these points, see Skule and Reichborn, 2002; contributors to Nyhan et al., 2003; and Gerber and Lankshear, 2000). This means that in those countries that have not yet developed a strong policy focus on these issues, LLL policies will increasingly need to be combined with efforts to help leverage change in workplace configuration. As Keep and Payne (2003) underline, this is not an easy route to follow, but the added value of such a focus is that it helps shift attention away from the external education and training system and back towards employment as a site for learning and onto the roles of employers and trade unions.

Conclusion

Although LLL debates appear to be vigorous, with a wide range of policy interventions and rising levels of (usually state) expenditure, much of this thinking and activity may be, at least partially, misdirected. For example, much more thought and attention needs to be directed at what LLL can offer to those who will not become knowledge workers, and what the impact of the non-economic benefits of LLL might be. There are also problems around the narrow focus on employability that surrounds much LLL activity.

Perhaps the main issue flagged up in this chapter is the weakness of the NAPs as a European-wide co-ordinating and integrating mechanism. The Director of the EU's vocational education and training research arm (CEDEFOP) recently suggested that 'implementing lifelong learning is the paperclip that holds everything together—it lies at the heart of an integrated and co-ordinated approach to meeting the Lisbon goals' (CEDEFOP, 2004, p.9). The analogy may be a better one than its author imagines, as paperclips are a relatively weak and uncertain means of joining together sheets of paper. The individual pieces can very easily slip out. Staples are far more effective. The problem is that the EU lacks policy staples, and can only engage in weak forms of co-ordination in the area of education, training and LLL. The NAPs provide a common reporting mechanism, not a real means of policy co-ordination. Individual states have their own goals, targets and visions of what LLL policies might deliver, and tend to prioritise these over the goals of the Commission. In addition, there are substantial differences between states on LLL policy and practice, and on how responsibility for the funding and management of LLL is apportioned between the national actors. Thus, the NAPs and wider LLL policies face a number of challenges that may widen rather than narrow the divergence between national policy regimes.

Note

1. For more details regarding the drawing up of National Action Plans, see Stuart and Greenwood, this volume.

References

Alasoini, T. & Halme, P. (eds) (1999) *Learning Organisations, Learning Society*. Finland: Ministry of Labour.

Bostrom, A. K.; Boudard, E. & Siminou, P. (2001) *Lifelong Learning in Sweden*. Cedefop Panorama Series, Luxembourg: Office for Official Publications of the European Communities.

Brandsma, J. (2002) 'New forms of learning in labour organisations.' In M.N. Cheallaigh, C. Doets, B. Hake & A. Westerhuis (eds) *Lifelong learning in the Netherlands*. Cedefop Panorama Series 21, Luxembourg: Office for Official Publications of the European Communities.

Brown, P. (2003) 'The opportunity trap: education and employment in a global economy.' *European Educational Research Journal*, Vol.2(1) pp.142-180.

CEDEFOP (2002) *Panorama—Consultation process on the European Commission's Memorandum on Lifelong Learning—Analysis of National Reports*. Luxembourg: Office of Official Publications of the European Communities.

CEDEFOP (2004) *Getting to Work on Life Long Learning—Policy, Practice and Partnership*. (Summary conference report). Luxembourg: Office for Official Publications of the European Communities.

Cheallaigh, M. N.; Doets, C.; Hake, B. & Westerhuis, A. (eds)(2002) *Lifelong learning in the Netherlands*. Cedefop Panorama Series 21, Luxembourg: Office for Official Publications of the European Communities.

Chirone 2000 (2001) *Progetto Flessibilita*. (Rapporto finale). Rome: Chirone 2000.

Confederation of British Industry (2000) *Fact not Fiction—UK Training Performance*. London: CBI.

Confederation of British Industry (2002) *Tackling Low Skills: Finding the Right Approach*. London: CBI.

Coffield, F. (1999) *Breaking the Consensus: Lifelong Learning as Social Control*. Newcastle: University of Newcastle (Department of Education).

Coffield, F. (ed.)(2000a) *The Necessity of Informal Learning*. Bristol: The Policy Press.

Coffield, F. (ed.) (2000b) *Differing Visions of a Learning Society.* Bristol: The Policy Press.

European Commission (2001) *Making a European Area of Lifelong Learning a Reality.* Brussels: EC, Directorate General for Education and Culture (COM (2001) 678 (final).

European Commission (2002) *Impact Evaluation of the EES—Background paper—Lifelong Learning.* EMCO/24/060602/EN_REV 1, Brussels: EC.

Field, J. (1997) 'The EU and the Learning Society—contested sovereignty in an age of globalisation.' In F. Coffield (ed.) *A National Strategy for Lifelong Learning.* Newcastle: University of Newcastle.

Field, J. (2001) 'Lifelong learning and social inclusion: engaging the hard to reach.' In F. Coffield (ed.) 'What progress are we making with Lifelong Learning—the evidence from research.' Newcastle: University of Newcastle (Department of Education).

Finnish Ministry of Labour (2002) *Finland's National Action Plan for Employment.* Helsinki: Ministry of Labour.

Fuller, A. & Unwin, L. (2003) 'Creating a 'modern apprenticeship': a critique of the UK's multi-sector, social inclusion approach.' *Journal of Education and Work*, Vol.16(1), pp.5-25.

Gerber, R. & Lankshear, C. (eds)(2000) *Training for a Smart Workforce.* London: Routledge.

Giddens, A. (1984) *The Constitution of Society.* Cambridge: Polity Press.

Giddens, A. (1993) *New Rules of Sociological Method.* Cambridge: Polity Press.

Green, A. (1998) 'Core skills, key skills and general culture: in search of the common foundation in vocational education.' *Evaluation and Research in Education*, Vol.12(1), pp.23-43.

Grubb, W.N. & Lazerzon, M. (2004) *The Education Gospel: The Economic Power of Schooling.* Cambridge, Mass.: Harvard University Press.

Hall, M. (2002) 'Social Partner Involvement in the 2002 NAP', European Industrial Relations Observatory on-line, http://www.eiro.eurofound.eu.int/2002/06/Feature/UK0206101F.ht

Hecker, D. (2001) 'Occupational employment projections to 2010.' *Monthly Labor Review*, Vol.124(11), pp.57-84.

Hepworth, M. & Spencer, G. (2002) *A Regional Perspective on the Knowledge Economy in Great Britain.* London: Department of Trade and Industry.

Keep, E. (2002) 'The English VET policy debate—fragile technologies or opening the black box, two competing visions of where we go next.' *Journal of Education and Work*, Vol.15(4), pp.457-479.

Keep, E. & Mayhew, K. (2001) 'Globalisation, models of competitive advantage and skills.' SKOPE Research Paper No. 22, Coventry: University of Warwick (SKOPE).

Kingston, P. (2004) 'Adults learning less under Labour', *The Guardian*, 18 May.

Lafer, G. (2002) *The Jobs Training Charade.* Ithica: Cornell University Press.

National Institute of Adult Continuing Education (2003) *A Sharp Reverse—NIACE survey on Adult Participation.* Leicester: NIACE.

Nyhan, B.; Kelleher, M.; Cressey, P. & Poell, R. (eds)(2003) *Facing up to the Learning Organisation Challenge—Selected European writings.* Volume II, Cedefop Reference Series 41-II, Luxembourg: Office of the Official Publications of the European Communities.

Nyyssola, K., & Hamalainen, K. (2001) *Lifelong Learning in Finland.* Cedefop Panorama Series, Luxembourg: Office for Official Publications of the European Communities.

Payne, J. & Keep, E. (2003) 'Re-visiting the Nordic approaches to work organization and job re-design: lessons for UK skills policy.' *Policy Studies*, Vol.24(4), pp.205-225.

Rainbird, H.; Munro, A. & Holly, L. (2004) 'The employment relationship and workplace learning.' In H. Rainbird, A. Fuller & A. Munro (eds) *Workplace Learning in Context.* London: Routledge.

Richini, P. (2002) *Lifelong learning in Italy.* Cedefop Panorama Series 43, Luxembourg: Office for Official Publications of the European Communities.

Skule, S. & Reichborn, A. N. (2002) *Learning-Conducive Work*. Cedefop Panorama Series 30, Luxembourg: Office for Official Publications of the European Community.

van de Kamp, M. & Hake, B. (2002) 'Lifelong Learning policies in the Netherlands: an analysis of policy narratives, instruments and measures.' In M.N. Cheallaigh, C. Doets, B. Hake & A. Westerhuis (eds) *Lifelong Learning in the Netherlands*. Cedefop Panorama Series 21, Luxembourg: Office for Official Publications of the European Communities.

CHAPTER NINE

Lifelong Learning for Civic Employees and Employable Citizens?

ODD BJØRN URE

Introduction

How is learning being shaped for young people exposed to shorter front-end education and more regularised further and continuing education? How should learning for employees in their late 50's and early 60's be organised, with a view to having them employed for more years so that the pension systems are not suffocated? Is the only scope of training arrangements for unemployed to have them integrated in the market economy or could they also be trained for new challenges that the non-market economy ('économie sociale') and a growing number of (upmarket?) non-governmental organisations are dealing with? All these questions—extracted from the public debate in Europe—touch upon the citizenship as well as the employability dimension of lifelong learning (LLL). According to a Memorandum on Lifelong learning from the European Commission, LLL encompasses 'all purposeful learning activity, whether formal or informal, undertaken on an ongoing basis with the aim of improving knowledge, skills and competences' (EC, 2000).

Education has often been exposed to the contrasting demands of economic utility (the employability dimension) on the one hand, and societal utility (the citizenship dimension) on the other. Similarly, LLL is serving a double purpose: it provides training for ongoing as well as future changes in the labour market *and* it is meant to contribute to the socialisation of the citizens. Fratczak-Rudnicka and Torney-Purta (2001) point out that the very notion of 'knowledge' includes fundamental concepts of democracy and democratic institutions as well as concepts of citizenship.

The aim of this article is to discuss the possible impact of national and European measures for lifelong learning on European citizens as individuals in relation to the two dimensions employability and citizenship. This impact is elucidated by means of the notions *individual* and *collective learning*. In view of the national variations in the field of education and training and due to the dependence of the European LLL discourse on national practices, this discussion has to start at national level. For that purpose we will use Nordic countries (in particular Norway) and Spain as 'cases'. We assume that there is a slow penetration of LLL in national education and training systems. These systems are not yet transformed into anything like a *LLL system* although there is a national discourse on LLL.

The structure of the article is as follows: after a discussion of key notions behind the thematic field of LLL, we pinpoint what is needed in a framework for analysing the main underlying dimensions. Then we present a summary of observations from the Nordic countries and Spain with a view to identifying some national influences on the LLL discourse at the level of the European Union. Afterwards we focus on policy-making with regard to the citizenship and employability dimensions of LLL. In the following section we scrutinise some initiatives close to the citizenship dimension. In a section leading up to the conclusive part of the article, we discuss the chances of sustaining the citizenship dimension in an era of increased individualisation of learning.[1]

Key notions behind 'lifelong learning'

The intuitive meaning behind an 'employable' person is one that is suited or qualified for jobs in the labour market. The International Labour Organisation (2003, p29) suggests a broader definition touching upon a few aspects related to citizenship:

> 'Individuals are most employable when they have broad-based education and training, basic and portable high-level skills, including teamwork, problem-solving, ICT and communication and language skills, learning-to-learn skills and competences to protect themselves and their colleagues against occupational hazards and diseases'.

For this article, the ILO definition implies that the two dimensions of LLL are not mutually exclusive. Throughout the article 'employability' will refer to a person's inclusion in (or exclusion from) the labour market. A standard dictionary explanation of 'citizenship' is 'the quality of an individual's response to membership in a community' (Merriam-Webster dictionary). For our purpose the notion surpasses communities linked to the work sphere by also reflecting membership in the society as a whole.

It is a common view that EU Member states have distinct, national education and training systems, and several theories have been proposed to account for them. One general framework for a comparative analysis of national systems can be found in Ashton et al. (2000). Their project is to go further than a mere comparison of existing features of demand or provision of education and training by including the relations and the relative strengths of labour unions, employers and the State. Based on a study of changing historical relations between these actors, they propose a framework of 'national systems of skill formation'. Ashton et al.'s framework seems to be particularly apt for analyses at a global level, while the scope of this article is confined to Europe and we do not attempt to grasp global forces influencing on LLL at national, regional and local level.

Turning to the thematic field of LLL, a debate on LLL has been going on at national level, partly sparked off by the European Commission Memorandum on LLL (EC, 2000). Given that this debate has many similarities and that references are often made to the same issues, it appears that we are faced with a LLL *discourse*. However, this does not necessarily mean that policy objectives for lifelong provision of learning and the discourse on LLL reflect the existence of distinct and clearly defined LLL *systems*. In some countries, it can even be questioned whether there are practices, social actors and institutions that constitute *systemic elements* of LLL. On the other hand, the presence of a pervasive LLL discourse is beyond doubt. This point will be further developed during the discussion of our central hypothesis, which relates to the importance of supportive *systemic LLL elements* if learning practices close to the citizens are to prevail.

In order to capture the meaning behind LLL, there is a need for an analytical framework which can integrate the systemic elements mentioned above and, on the other hand, the learning which citizens actually undergo. Some building blocks for the development of this framework can be found in Heikkinen and Laiho (2000, p.259f) who propose three learning models that also are instructive outside a Finnish context. We will use their categorisation when trying to understand LLL in a citizenship perspective:

> '*Folk (or popular) education* is education for citizenship (with its changing connotations), consisting of initial folk education in folk schools (later comprehensive schools) and of liberal adult education or folk enlightenment. The basic pedagogical idea in folk education has been the promotion of participation in the life of the family (households), community and nation state (...) participation also included various forms of work and occupations. Later, education was increasingly transformed into initial or basic general education and adult education for civilised leisure time activities.

> '*Encyclopaedic education* in gymnasia (grammar schools) and universities. The guiding pedagogical principle has been to promote participation in bodies and the production of knowledge which is organised into disciplinary structures and practices (...) until recently, (it) has also included a certain kind of 'citizenship'...

'*Vocational education* ... (has)... distinctive pedagogical ideas ... (and) has come to focus on participation in the world of work. This is in the context of an occupationally structured society with specialised skills, technical expertise and trade (livelihood), which constitute people's occupational identities'.

It should be noted that vocational education in the theoretical framework offered by Heikkinen and Laiho differs from pure labour market considerations. Vocational education is closer to the 'practical culture of knowledge' which is opposed to an 'academic culture of knowledge' concentrating on formal qualifications and certification (Tøsse, 1996). The academic culture has had a strong say in defining rules for the translation of informal and non-formal competences into formal certificates (cf. Heikkinen and Laiho, 2000, p.273). 'Practical culture of knowledge' and 'vocational education' are two notions that valorise the self-identity of vocational practices. A similar approach for understanding popular education in a Nordic context is to define it to be the education of people as a social, political and cultural category (Korsgaard, 2002).

Our comparison of Nordic countries and Spain tries to couple the four notions employability/citizenship and collective/individual learning. We also lean on the categorisation of learning models discussed above. Employability can be associated with collective aspects, e.g. in the sense of 'learning at the workplace or for the workplace', but individual aspects are also involved in the sense that the employee embodies skills and competences. Citizenship is by itself a collective project but behind there is an individual citizen who is learning in many contexts, formal, informal and non-formal (Bjørnavold, 2000). As we will demonstrate in the next section devoted to national observations, validation of informal and non-formal experiences from the third sector has been inscribed in a citizenship perspective and is therefore central to our discussion.

Observations from Spain and Nordic countries

Differences in how national labour markets function can illustrate some characteristics of the employability dimension. Equally, learning activities aiming for social participation and cohesion (citizenship) differ substantially between European countries. There is a widespread phenomenon in contemporary policy making on LLL to explain such variations by putting together countries in geographical clusters. Hence, northern and southern European countries are often subsumed into distinct clusters and correspondingly analysed.

A hypothesis for our comparison is that in spite of obvious differences between Norway and Spain (and other Nordic countries), there are certain similarities in the way the labour market structures the employability dimension of LLL. We will also illustrate that the citizenship dimension of LLL is in both countries related to efforts to enlarge access to training for low skilled learners. This dimension is also related to the dissemination of learning models linked to 'popular education'.

In Spain education and training structures are often replicated at a regional level; this also applies for the social dialogue on training. Competencies in the field of education and training are devolved to the Autonomous Communities. Observers of the Spanish system (such as, for instanced, OECD, 2002) claim that there is a separation of education and training due to a split into three sub-systems of vocational training ('regulated' i.e. initial vocational training, 'continuing' training for the employed and 'occupational' training for unemployed). In particular, such divisions hamper mobility within the training system and the recognition of non-formal learning (cf. Laso and Estrada, n.d.). In addition, some observers refer to a 'dispersion', explained by very unequal training practices at a firm level (Bonal, 2001). However, the central government has introduced measures to integrate the three existing subsystems of training (regulated, occupational and continuing). One step in this direction is efforts to set up a national system for qualifications and vocational training based on a National catalogue of vocational qualifications (Ure and Teige, 2003). All in all, there are reasons to define these unfastened structures as forming part of a Spanish education and training system. This system increasingly copes with challenges linked to a LLL agenda but there is no overarching LLL reform in Spain. Present attempts to overhaul vocational training in Spain are done with reference to processes sparked off at European level.

From the late 1980's Spanish governments introduced reforms aiming to make labour markets more 'flexible'. Thus, the share of short-term contracts rose from 22.3% in 1988 to 37.2% in 1993. Recently, this trend has been reversed but as late as in 2001 the number of short-term contracts still represented 31%. The same year the EU average of short-term contracts amounted to 13.4% (EC, 2002). There is a strong relation between access to training and the length of labour contracts. Hence, in Spanish enterprises where a substantial part of the workers are on temporary contracts, participation in training is lower than in enterprises offering more stable contractual conditions (Fundación Tripartite, 2003, p.159).

To some extent, the overarching tendency in Spanish labour market policies and employer strategies has been cost containment and flexible labour markets (Martínez and Stuart, 2003), thus discouraging long-term investment in human capital. In the worst case scenario, the work force is considered as a fluctuating mass, which can be hired from the subcontractor who offers the lowest wage level. The transformation of work organisations into an array of subcontracting entities could strengthen specific labour market segments in Spain. This would concern 'low pay and low skill' segments. Such efforts to deviate the economy into a 'low skill route' seem to hamper the possibility of transforming collective learning for citizenship into something tangible for the individual learner.

Comparable statistics demonstrate that the sectors and branches with the lowest score in training investments are construction, agricultural activities as well as health and social services (Fundación Tripartita, 2003). Also in Norway, building and construction and the agricultural sector score low, while public health and social services are extensive users of training (Ministry of Education and Research, 2003). The latter can be explained by lower public investments in health and social services in Spain but, in general, the Norwegian public sector is a high consumer of training. However, Spain and Norway are almost equal when it comes to the weight of financial and management services and non-manufacturing industries in provision of training (EC, DG EAC, 2003, p. 22f).

Compared with Spain the Norwegian education system is less decentralised and until recently the Ministry of Education has had a close eye on its cohesion. This has historic reasons dating back to the process of nation building, which continued into the 20th century. During the 'project of nation building', general education and the 'unitary school' (i.e. equal access to education for everybody in the same schools) had the highest priority. To the contrary, (initial) vocational education had a low priority (Michelsen and Høst, 2002; Sakslind, 1998, p.53). Still today, the Norwegian training system (composed of vocational education and training) is more loosely coupled than the education system.

Over the last 30 years, the Norwegian education and training system has gone through numerous reforms and counter-reforms. One development line is that:

> 'Initial VET (vocational and educational training) has been reconstructed and supplied with a considerable curriculum of general subjects, and adult education has been broadened from its original humanistic conception to include the economic arena. High priority has been given to the development of a consistent educational system adequate for the task of lifelong learning' (Michelsen and Høst, 2002, p.95.)

One of the main instigators of a Norwegian LLL reform, the major trade union LO, regarded it as a response to worries about unemployment and high labour costs (Skule, Stuart and Nyen, 2002). During the period from 1960 to the late 1980's the unemployment rate oscillated between 1.7-2.5% but rose to 9% in 1993. By the early 1990's LO expressed strong concern that low-skilled employees in manufacturing industries were threatened by unemployment. Also, some branches of the labour union were unsatisfied with the amount of continuing training offered by the employers. In this situation the labour union reached agreement with the employers on exchange of more continuing and further training for employees against lower pay rise. Simultaneously, a political process started with the elaboration of a Green paper and later a White paper, leading up to the Competence reform of 1999 (Ure and Teige 2003).

To a larger extent than in Spain, Norwegian employers accept that they cannot compete internationally by offering low-cost products and services. Framework agreements concluded with labour unions impose them to pay for training of employees that is in the interest of the firm. The fact that such agreements contain recommendations for annual stocktaking of competences in an enterprise as well as planning of future training, provides opportunities for systematic skill development. 60% of the firms covered by an extensive survey in 2003 declared to carry out systematic stocktaking of in-house skills (Nordhaug et al., 2004). However, a number of case studies indicate that the abovementioned training agreements are infrequently utilised as a tool in competence building projects financed through the national LLL reform (SNF and Fafo, forthcoming). Negotiations around the ongoing LLL reform have revealed that the employers' association is unwilling to negotiate schemes for funding LLL that surpasses training needs defined by the employers (Ure and Teige, 2003). Another unsolved question is how far employers are willing to modify the 'steering right' of the production process by allowing for co-determination of what groups of employees that need training.

The Norwegian reform includes efforts to set up a system for recognition of informal and non-formal competences on an equal footing with formal competences. This principle was pushed forward by many stakeholders in the field of adult education and can be found in an embryonic form in previous White Papers in this field (Tøsse, 1996). The aim is to appraise skills developed outside an institutional school context, thus giving access to formal education. In some cases prior learning is validated to the extent that the study period can be shortened. The main purpose is, however, to assess and recognise such competences with a view to strengthening the job prospects of learners with limited formal competences. In other words, this is an attempt to increase the employability of learners by validating prior experience, included social skills people acquire as citizens. The EU has embarked on a similar attempt to validate informal and non-formal competences. The upcoming pillars for the

EU validation process seem to follow up experiences in the Nordic countries (especially Norway) by systematizing experiences in formal education, the labour market and also the civil sector, including NGOs (EC, 2002; VOX, 2002).

As part of the Norwegian reform, the 'civil sector' (i.a. associations belonging to the 'movement of popular enlightenment' and NGOs in general) has been subject to a systematic attempt to validate competences gained in a multiple of arenas. Exactly this multitude has, according to an evaluation report (VOX, 2002, pp.96ff; Ministry of Education and Research, 2003), retarded a coherent approach to validation of competences and experiences from voluntary work and liberal education. Although the validation projects launched in this sector are few and thematically scattered, there are reasons to conclude that associations involved are not very enthusiastic towards the projects and that their members fear the unnecessary paperwork entailing from a systematic documentation and validation of competences. This attitude has partly to do with the non-institutional origin of (some of) these organisations, and is also linked to the fact that certain activities of adult education associations by nature may not fit into a competence passport.

The citizenship dimension is also supported by what can be called a movement of popular ('folk') education, existing both in Spain and in the Nordic countries. In Spain the movement reached its summit during the political and ideological climate of the 1970s. The basic idea was to democratise education and training and to establish new relations between teachers and learners. The movement was based on ideas of Paolo Freire and Ivan Illich, and it was often organised around groups of neighbours with a low education level. Recently, this movement has become weaker but it is still present in poor suburbs around the main cities of Spain and it is particularly involved in training of immigrants (Escuela Popular; see Centro de Educación de Personas Adultas, 2003). In addition, there are 231 'popular universities' collaborating with NGOs and non-profit associations. They try to mediate between the public administration and citizens (OECD 2002). While the federation for popular universities is linked to local authorities, the umbrella organisation for NGOs is somewhat more distant from public authorities. However, they all depend heavily on public subsidies. Like the public education system, they increasingly try to improve the training offer by means of better training of trainers, systematic introduction of ICT-based learning tools and various measures to control the quality of the training offered.

Study associations are one central element in Nordic popular (or liberal) education. During the first years of the 20th century the Swedish and

Norwegian study associations were born. They particularly recruited from the labour movement, the temperance movement and from 'free churches' striving for independence from the State religion. This tradition thus had its origin in parts of the civil society organising education and training independently from the State, the dominating culture and circles of power (Larsson, 2001).

During the first half of the 1970's adult education was considered in Sweden as key element with regard to the equality in living conditions, in the sense that adult education 'permitted to reach out to socially underprivileged groups' (Rubenson, 2001, p.221). Subsequent to budgetary reforms at the end of the 1970's and onwards, the position of adult education and of popular education foundered. A similar trend in public spending on adult education can be found in Norway (Tøsse, 1996, p.41). Already four years after a Norwegian law on adult learning was adopted in 1976, and which injected more public subsidies for liberal adult education, the impetus faded away. Throughout the 1980's the budget became increasingly directed towards labour market training, in particular when the unemployment rate rose sharply from the mid-1980's (Tøsse, 1996, p.4). This parallel between labour market developments and priorities in adult education is quite similar to the situation in Spain, where the unemployment rate reached a peak of 24% in 1994. Spanish training schemes for the unemployed have been extensively used by university graduates in search for their first job. There is therefore widespread concern that the dominance of a certain age group (25-35) with tertiary education could endanger the objective of LLL for everybody (Fundación Tripartita, 2003, pp.150ff).

This last observation confirms the hypothesis outlined at the beginning of this section: in Spain as well as in Norway (and some other Nordic countries) there are similarities in the way labour market developments structure the employability dimension of LLL. Equally, the citizenship dimension of LLL is in both countries materialised in various measures aimed for low skilled learners (illiterates, immigrants) and linked to certain aspects of 'popular education' (popular schools and universities, folk high schools). Eventually, LLL apart from the training in enterprises, predominantly depends on the public purse and even training arrangements set up as an alternative to the public education can only survive with financial support from public budgets in Norway and Spain. There are scarce financial resources to underpin central LLL measures. In Spain money is channelled to other recipients than those expected. In Norway, disagreement on how to finance LLL measures has retarded the introduction of exploratory projects for financing training at the level of the firm until the last stage of the Competence reform. However, the transformation of education and training systems into a LLL mode is a highly complex and ambitious task entailing needs for raising various funds, depending on the national setting (Ure and Gavigan, 2000).

A shifting focus from 'citizenship' to 'employability' in policy-making on lifelong learning?

The national LLL discourses have been supported by the so-called 'Delors White Paper' (EC, 1993) and later by the debate initiated by the Memorandum on LLL from the European Commission. Also, the European Employment Strategy (EC, 1999) contains specific targets for lifelong learning on which the Member states are asked to report in their annual employment reports to the European Commission.

Much importance has been attached to the 1993 White Paper, on which the then President of the European Commission, Jacques Delors, had a strong say. What was started by the 1990's was an attempt to actively use training policies as a levy in combating a long-term rise in EU unemployment. Certainly, it is no surprise that an average unemployment rate, which in 1994 reached a record of 11.1%, renewed the attention on the link between training and employment. Subsequent to this White Paper, the European Commission tried to encourage the Member states to redefine labour market policies from a passive route (paying subsistence expenses for the unemployed) to an active route, i.a. implying (re)training to meet structural changes in the labour market and in the economy as a whole (Ducatel et al., 2000). The fact that some Member states already had embarked on a route for active labour market policy (EC, 2002, p.86) and not the least that many of them looked to future Member states (such as Sweden and her neighbour countries applying active labour market policies as a part of the nebulous notion of a 'Scandinavian welfare state model'), indicates that there was an interaction between national and transnational driving forces behind the emergence of a LLL policy centred on employability. The European Employment Strategy (EES) is building on this interaction, above all by means of the 'open method of policy co-ordination', which means that the European Commission provides comparative analyses of the performance of the Member states and suggests policy amendments. The Member states have no legal obligation to fulfil these suggestions but they report (annually) to the EC on their performance in various fields, inter alia LLL.

In the EU Joint Employment Report of 2001 there is a summary of Member states' positions on developing lifelong learning strategies. The national performance is assessed along the following dimensions[2] :

Comprehensiveness of strategies
Compulsory education
Formal adult education/training
Workplace/other non-formal/recognised prior learning
Focus on disadvantaged groups
Overall investment/funding schemes
Coherence of strategy
System development (policy needs, planning, targets, implementation, monitoring)
Partnership working (social partners, public authorities, learning providers, civil society)
Cross-cutting aspects (advice/guidance services, education/training/mobility)

The EU joint report reveals that national evaluation reports focus heavily on *policy development* (p. 3). This means that policy reforms in the field of lifelong learning have been carried out across all institutional levels (p.5) but our impression is that there are fewer indications of streamlining policy reforms into a coherent LLL strategy.

As to the next last point on this list (partnership working) few countries report on efforts by the social partners to conclude agreements on training. There are even fewer 'examples of initiatives involving broader-based partnerships extending beyond the social partners to include regional authorities, education and training providers, enterprises, individuals and representatives of civil society' (p.7).

One ensuing question is whether the shaping of a LLL policy throughout the 1990's in the shadow of long queues of unemployed Europeans has entailed a redefinition of the citizenship dimension of learning. Some commentators have pointed to an expansion of continuing vocational education and often a decline of liberal adult education (Raggat et al., 1996). Equally, a shift from popular education to encyclopaedic education and another shift from vocational to encyclopaedic education are reported in Finland (Heikkinen and Laiho, 2000, p.260). It should however be taken into account that Heikkinen and Laiho apply a broader definition of vocational education than Raggat and his colleagues by including 'participation in the world of work' and the constitution of 'people's occupational identities'. This is done with a view to overcoming a dichotomy between education and work with an ensuing dichotomy between general and vocational knowledge (Heikkinen and Laiho, 2000, p.259).

Other analysts of the European Commission's education and training policy in the late 1990's use the term 'vocationalisation'. Field (1998, p.200) writes for example that:

> 'Yet this interest in creativity and an active orientation towards learning is not set in the context of a critical and reflexive citizenship but of the vocationialising of the educational agenda—a process which is found across the member states and in nations such as Australia, New Zealand and the USA....'

There can be little doubt that education and training are presently more geared towards sustaining the employment chances of learners. Raggat et al. (1996) report that this phenomenon can be identified in Britain as well as in other European countries. Rubenson (2001) confirms this trend in an article on adult education in Sweden between 1967 and 2001. Bjerkaker (2001) reports on a similar shift in Norway.

The reasons behind this shift can be valuable enough, and have sometimes allowed more young adults (included 'dropouts') to enter the labour market, but in Britain there has been a massive decline in participation of older people. Raggat et al. (1996, p.3) maintain that:

> 'The concentration on adult learners as part of economic policy therefore raises serious questions about whether the distribution of opportunities for adult learners is equitable. If most opportunities are determined by occupational relevance it limits them to those who are, or could be economically active. Age and gender become important influences affecting access to learning'.

The authors warn that this might have unwanted side effects given that we today approach an ageing population. Moreover, many old people who have received the least initial education, have been infrequent users of opportunities available in later life.

They report from Britain that non-vocational education has been intentionally reconstructed as 'leisure', which provides a justification for removing local authority funding and subjecting it to charges'. This has also been an issue of controversy in Norway (Tøsse, 1996) and in Sweden on which Larsson (2001, p.243) comments in relation to the 'generalisation of study circles'. He claims that study circles are presently used to deliver any type of learning content. In other words, demand/supply mechanisms are becoming decisive in the field of adult education. In addition, the providers and the end-users care less about the democratic and participative values behind learning activities. In Finland popular education is increasingly transformed to 'promotion of leisure activities and individual self-expression' (Heikkinen and Laiho, 2000, p.262).

A preliminary conclusion is that policy-making in LLL both at national and at EU level attaches a strong but not exclusive emphasis on employability. As demonstrated above, (popular) or folk education has had a say in the definition of a citizenship dimension on learning, both in northern and southern Europe. The two dimensions of LLL exist simultaneously although they reflect different perspectives on social participation in learning. Taking our cue from Heikkinen and Laiho (2000, p.259) we will suggest that within the employability dimension social participation is inter alia understood in terms of a promotion of inclusion of vulnerable social groups. On the other hand, a citizenship dimension on LLL related to popular (or folk) education, implies that the citizens are actively learning something close to their own experiences but having implications for a larger community of learners.

What is in it for a European learning citizen?

The policy-making evoked above forms part of the discourse on LLL at national and at European level. In addition, impulses from national labour markets influence many European measures developed in the frame of LLL policies decided by the European Union. Very few European LLL practices exist as such; they have their origin at a national level, or in some bilateral or transnational projects of experimental nature (cf. innovative projects launched by EU programmes in the field of education and training). In this section we will discuss implications for a European citizen in terms of learning conditions emanating from these practices and initiatives. Referring to our discussion on the national origins of European practices in LLL, does for example the local environment of the learner offer a useful framework?

As we saw in the preceding section, a citizenship perspective on LLL is included in the 'Memorandum on lifelong learning' of the European Commission (EC, 2000) but there are few citizenship initiatives among the national follow-up measures. One of six messages in the LLL memorandum published by the European Commission (EC, 2000) was to bring education and training closer to the local level. In a communication published one year after the Memorandum, the Commission formulated the ambition to make a European area of lifelong learning a reality (EC, 2001). Inspired from, inter alia, the experiences in England and Wales with 1500 Learndirect Centres[3], efforts to bring LLL closer to the individual learner are highlighted in this follow-up document. Alongside characteristics of 'learning organisations', local learning centres are heralded:

> '..(Learning) centres should be located wherever potential learners are on a daily basis ... Services for, about and in support of learning should be offered on a 'one-

stop-shop' basis ... Centres should be resourced and staffed by multi-skilled
practitioners from public, private and voluntary/communitary partner organisations.
(EC, 2001, p.15).

Moreover, this vision has been subject to a pilot initiative called 'Regional
networks for lifelong learning', in which one thematic aspect is lifelong
learning in regions. Among 17 networks approved, one based in Spain
addresses 'local school and active life pacts in educating cities'. The coordinator is the 'International Association of Educating Cities'[4]. This
perspective seems to date back to a charter on European LLL cities adopted
in 1998. The network of learning cities of which one can be found in Kent, has
set up a 'checklist' ranging from technology to strategies for the family
(Longworth, 1999, p.205).

As a contribution to the European Commission Memorandum on lifelong
learning, six civil society associations prepared jointly a network response
(platform). Among these six are the European Association for the Education of
Adults and the 'Solidar Platform' of European Social NGO's. The platform
boils down to reactions to the recommendations outlined in the Memorandum
of which the last reads 'Bringing learning closer to the home'. Indeed, this
recommendation has the strongest affinity to a citizenship perspective and the
six associations propose the following actions aiming to implement it:

- connect people in the home with local learning providers
- encourage learning partnerships in the local community
- encourage learning in the workplace

In line with our earlier discussion, lifelong learning for citizenship is thus
situated in relation to the work place and to local communities. This approach
appears as a relevant manner for an 'umbrella' association to mediate between
a transnational body representing national associations that again defend
interests of local groups.

Obviously, a citizenship perspective on LLL should not simply be present in
the making of extensive policy documents. How have civil society associations
and NGO's alike been involved in the implementation of the Memorandum on
LLL? An answer to this question can partly be found in a progress report on the
follow-up to the European Council resolution of 2002 (EC, 2003). In this report
there are many references to partnerships' between 'multiple stakeholders' but
the real contribution from stakeholders labelled 'civil society' is not detailed.

Certainly, there is a long way of mediation from individual learners at a
local level up to European associations building a 'platform' with a view to
influence a memorandum from the European Commission. At the end of the
road, we encounter the learning citizen, who also can be identified in study

circles as reported from the Nordic countries or as a participant in a local training initiative for immigrants to Spain.

A question arises on how this mediation can be increased. Does the European lifelong learner act locally and think globally? There are few signs of this today but perhaps the mushrooming of NGO's in Europe and a tighter network of associations for learners, which can increase the representation and mediation between these, can define a clearer citizen perspective on LLL.

The hesitant meditation of citizenship perspectives is linked to the slow penetration of LLL in the national systems. This is again related to the absence of strong social actors that can bring forward the citizen perspective on LLL. NGO's can play a role as we saw in Norway and Spain but their role is presently rather weak. To be more specific, NGO's favouring a 'social responsible economy' (cf. in Spain) take active part in lifelong learning activities. During its 7th European congress the following education and training objective was formulated:

> 'Stimulate the discussion on the future model of the (European) Union and on governance in all European countries, particularly by using the method of 'popular participative teaching' in order to develop the social dialogue'. [5]

At the moment this is a bold ambition but our discussion has shown that there are some past experiences supporting this view. The feasibility of the citizenship dimension of learning can further be analysed in relation to some trends towards individualisation of learning.

Citizenship and individualisation of learning

We have seen that the employability dimension of LLL is gaining ground in Spain, Norway and in other Nordic countries. To what extent does a deepening of the citizenship dimension of LLL depend on widespread practices of collective learning? The perspective outlined in a policy document from a Swedish action programme on LLL can provoke some thoughts on this question. Here it is claimed that LLL, and in particular life-wide learning:

> '...implies a shift in responsibility for education and learning from the public to the private and social spheres. Education monopolies are being dismantled and replaced by a diversity of learning environments. Subsystems should be designed in relation to each other. The direction and responsibility of the formal education system should be assessed in relation to the learning taking place in other environments' (National Agency for Education, 2000. p.9).

The flourishing of learning environments can be seen from different angles. It can offer more learning opportunities for the informed learner, above all those learners who are able to skilfully navigate on educational web sites in the so-called global Internet village. On the other hand, the citation from the Swedish policy document points towards a certain individualisation of LLL. What are the consequences if LLL is being delegated to various learning environments? It may be that education monopolies are being 'dismantled' but how should the quality control of learning contents be set up in the future?

There is a widespread hostility towards national (state) education systems, also among associations belonging to the movement of popular education. Equally, the power exercised by the teaching profession is coming under pressure. Without assessing pros and cons in this debate, there are reasons to stress that individual learners who might be 'liberated' from the state and teachers' monopolies, indeed are faced with even stronger control efforts in the educational market, for example from editors in electronic publishing, educational software houses and e-learning companies.

This point can also be elucidated from another perspective. When learning becomes ubiquitous it is increasingly detached from institutions and buildings and is starting to look like other services that can be consumed. Edwards (1997) points out that learning opportunities by themselves create new market genres, such as *info-tainment* and *edu-tainment*. He maintains that learning opportunities become part of the consumer society, e.g. when students are referred to as 'customers'.

On the other hand, it has been pointed out that the contemporary individualisation of LLL is not by definition undermining the citizenship dimension of learning (Tøsse, 2001). Today, emancipation and the self-realisation of the learners are at the forefront. They can manage learning tools by means of 'ubiquitous learning' always at their disposal, e.g. mobile telephones and palm devices. Also, there seems to be a certain rebirth of the belief in the counter-weight exercised by the 'civil society'. In this context, the role of non-governmental organisations is being discussed (Siisiäinen, 2000). Furthermore, in our discussion of national experiences with LLL for citizenship we referred to a certain influence from associations linked to the 'non-market economy', in French known as the 'économie sociale' or 'economía social' in Spain.

One crucial development line for LLL in Europe is how learning arrangements set up to spur employability will be shaped in the future. To what extent can such training also reflect a citizenship dimension? On this point Heikkinen and Laiho (2000) are rather pessimistic. They observe a certain dismantling of the educational system as such, and not only of the 'educational monopolies':

> 'The responsibility of educators and teachers for educational interventions is disappearing, when lifelong learning is delegated to the various 'learning environments' of everyday life.' (p.262)

While implicitly referring to the widely heralded Finnish 'best practice' of economic and societal reconstruction after export markets in the former Soviet Union foundered, they warn that the learning needs of potential employees are being defined by 'working life' represented by 'leading employers and professional organisations':

'The promotion of national industries as a component of the construction of an occupationally structured, coherent nation state is replaced by providing optimal infrastructure for industrial clusters, which occasionally operate in a certain national socio-political and educational environment' (Heikkinen and Laiho, 2000, p.262).

These observations support our previous discussion in at least two respects: firstly, they illustrate that training practices at a firm level are highly dependent on what labour market segments they belong to. In Spain and in the Norway we referred inter alia to systematic differences in training investments between branches and sectors. Secondly, they question the possibility of creating systemic elements that can sustain the variety of learning initiatives said to have a lifelong and life-wide perspective. If present education systems are being 'dismantled' because of an individualisation of learning and of a redefinition of education towards consumption of educational services, then some (new) mechanisms for equal access to learning resources should be put into place.

Conclusions

It is not controversial to assume that national education and training systems exist, be they somewhat fragmented as in Spain or more coherent as in Norway. Education and training systems remain predominantly national and the discourse on LLL has at its best directed these systems into a lifelong learning track. It is hard to depict any national LLL system as such. It can neither be found in Spain where the general system is being systematised, nor in Norway where various LLL schemes are developed and intentionally put together into a single framework. The Norwegian LLL reform contains systematic plans for involving all sectors, including the civil society, but this takes time and it still has to put into place financial schemes underpinning those plans. The Spanish education and training system is more dispersed and decentralised, so the central government is trying to streamline it. Although decentralisation does not exclude the emergence of a LLL system, it is difficult to find enough signs of distinct LLL elements of systematic nature that could constitute any Spanish 'LLL system'. The national origin of measures and initiatives for LLL at European Union level is often so unclear that it would be futile to determine any line of cause/effect. In general, various EU financial and political tools (such as the European education and training programmes as well as the European Employment Strategy) are used to implement LLL initiatives.

It may be concluded from Nordic (especially Norwegian) experiences that an employability perspective on LLL has been important in validating informal and non-formal competence, so that knowledge acquired at the workplace and outside a person's working life can be linked to job opportunities. Validation projects have not only been carried out in relation to formal education and the labour market but also for the voluntary sector (civil society). Supported by national experiences, the EU has embarked on a systematic attempt to validate informal and non-formal competences on an equal footing with formal competences. A prevailing citizenship dimension of LLL would have depended on strong social movements at an arm's length from state and private interests. These being weak in the countries scrutinised in this article, the employability dimension of LLL is mainly influenced by business cycles and the unemployment rate. This situation fosters individual learning rather than collective learning practices.

Departing from the distinction between popular, encyclopaedic and vocational education (Heikkinen and Laiho 2000) and their definition of these educational forms, it appears that the 'encyclopaedic education' has been gaining ground also within vocational educational. In particular, the 'folk education' is loosing significance in the Nordic countries and in Spain.

Our discussion confirms the theoretical challenge to integrate the analysis of—on the one hand—dominant learning models in education and training systems and—on the other hand—individual and collective learning at a firm level. The latter depends on the interaction between the work organisation of firms and characteristics of the labour market. In-company training has traditionally been subsumed into the realm of continuing vocational training, which forms part of the national repertoire of LLL. The reasons for sectorial and branch-specific variations in access to training for employees are related to how learning intertwines with transformation of work organisations. This points towards research on LLL, which detects possible consequences for the learning employee of national and European LLL measures at a firm level.

What are the major effects of a prevailing employability dimension in LLL for the European learner? If the ultimate aim for a European citizen is to have a job, LLL measures launched at European and national level seem to have spurred the employability of workers. Less is achieved when it comes to developing other learning contexts, as well as in linking the work place to non-labour environments.

We have identified a few driving forces towards more individual learning, to the extent that there might be question of 'individualisation' of learning. Individual learners mastering ICT are being empowered and they can acquire certain learning autonomy. The weakening of popular ('folk') education has led to fewer arenas for the sharing of learning experiences and perhaps to less collective learning.

The collective dimension of learning could be further developed at a European level. This can partly be done by continued involvement of the social partners in the implementation of LLL policies. Equal importance could be attached to a systematic inclusion of experiences from the third sector (cf. the regained interest in NGO's and pilot projects in Norway), including social actors belonging to the 'économie sociale' (cf. experiences from Spain). There seems to be some convergence between ongoing work to improve the performance of education and training systems and of popular (or folk) education. National ministries as well as NGO's tend to improve their offer by means of better training of trainers, systematic introduction of ICT-based learning tools and various measures to control the quality of the training offered.

There are few signs that a revitalisation of popular ('folk') education building on the specific political and ideological climate of the 1970s, can spur the collective dimension of learning. The learning model 'folk education' has been anchored in ideas about active citizenship but not always in civic values emanating from the work sphere. Perhaps 'vocational education' surpassing the employability dimension could enrich 'folk education'. This may be one major challenge for lifelong learning that only can be faced by combined national and European efforts. In addition, we should bear in mind that learning is a global affair surpassing European frontiers, not only for doing affairs.

Notes

1. I am grateful to associate professor Rune Sakslind at the Institute of Sociology, University of Bergen, for providing helpful comments on an earlier version of this article. It builds upon a joint paper presented at a Eurone&t workshop held in June 2003: Ure, O.B. and Teige, B.K: 'The role of social partners in lifelong learning reforms for employability. Observations from Norway, the United Kingdom and Spain'. In that paper UK and Norway was covered by my colleague Berit Teige.

2. Joint Employment Report for 2001, Annex 1 to COM (2002) 629 final.

3. cf.: http://www.learndirect.co.uk/.

4. Information note on the R3L initiative, Brussels 7 April 2003.

5. Declaration from a conference in Gävle, Sweden 7-9 June 2001. Cf. http://www.econosoc.org/publications/index.htm.

References

Agenda Utredning & Utvikling AS (2003) 'Evaluering av realkompetanseprosjektet', Final report to the Norwegian Ministry of Education and Research.' Oslo: Agenda Utredning & Utvikling AS.

Ashton, D., Sung, J. & Turbin, J. (2000) 'Towards a framework for the comparative analysis of national systems of skill formation.' *International Journal of Training and* Development, Vol.4(1), pp.8-25.

Field, J. (1998) *European Dimensions: Education, Training and the European Union.* London: Jessica Kingsley Publishers Ltd. (Higher Education Policy Series 39).

Bjerkaker, S. (2001) 'Voksnes learning: Voksenopplæring i lys av pedagogikk, politikk og forvaltning' Oslo: Universitetsforlaget. Bjørnavold, J. (2000) 'Making learning visible: identification, assessment and recognition of non-formal learning in Europe.' Luxembourg: CEDEFOP/European Commission.

Bonal, X. (2001) 'Expansion of new vocationalism and realities of labour market: view from the Spanish periphery.' *Journal of Education and Work*, Vol. 14(2), pp.177-187.

Centro de Educación de Personas Adultas (2003) 'La propuesta de la educación popular.' Escuela Popular La Prospe de Madrid, Centro de Educación de Personas Adultas Parque Alcosa de Sevilla. Atrapasueños editorial.Ducatel, K. et al. (2000) The Information Society in Europe—Work and Life in the Age of Globalization. Lanham: Rowman & Littlefield.

Edwards, R. (1997) *Changing Places? Flexibility, Lifelong Learning and a Learning Society.* London: Routledge.

European Commission (2003) 'Implementing lifelong learning strategies in Europe. Progress report.' Brussels: European Commission/CEDEFOP (17.12.2003).

European Commission (1993) *White paper on Growth, Competitiveness, and Employment: The Challenges and Ways Forward into the 21st Century.* Brussel, 5 December.

European Commission (1999) *The European Employment Strategy. Investing in People.* Luxembourg Office for official publications of the EC.

European Commission (2000) Working paper, SEC (2000) 1832.

European Commission (2002) 'Employment in Europe 2002: Recent trends and prospects.' http://europa.eu.int/comm/employment_social/news/2002/sep/employment_in_europe2002.pdf

European Commission (2002) 'The social situation in the European Union 2002', DG Employmenten.pdf" http://europa.eu.int/comm/employment_social/social_situation/docs/SSR2002_ en.pdf

European Commission, Directorate-General of Education and Culture (2003)'Continuing training in enterprises in Europe: results of the second European Continuing vocational training Survey in enterprises'.

http://europa.eu.int/comm/education/programmes/leonardo/new/leonardo2/cvts/cvts_en.pdf

European Commission (2004) Final proposal to the European Commission from working group on 'Common European principles for validation of non-formal and informal learning'. Unpublished note, Brussels 3 March 2004.

Fratczak-Rudnicka, B. & Torney-Purta, J. (2001) 'Competencies for civic and political life in democracy'. Study was carried out by the Swiss Federal Statistical Office under the auspices of the OECD. http://www.portal-stat.admin.ch/deseco/news.htm

Fundación tripartita para la Formación en Empleo (2003) 'Consolidación y desarrollo de la Formación Continua en España.' www.fundacióntripartita.org

Heikkinen, A. & Laiho, K. (2000) 'Social participation as a challenge to lifelong learning in Europe.' In S. Tøsse (ed.) 'Reforms and Policy—Adult Education Research in Nordic CountriesTrondheim, Tapir Academic Press.

ILO (2003) *Report IV (1)*. *International Labour Conference 91st Session 2003*.Geneva: ILO.

Korsgaard, O. (2002) 'A European demos? The Nordic adult education tradition faces a challenge.' Comparative Education, Vol. 38(1), pp7-17.

Larsson, S. (2001) 'Les cercles d'études et la démocratie en Suède.' In L. Tanguy 'La formation permanente entre travail et citoyenneté.' *Education Permanente*, n° 149/2001-4. Luisant, France : Editions Alterna.

Laso Ayuoso, R. & Estrada, B. (n.d.) 'Contextualising the Spanish learning agenda: historical legacies, contemporary policies.' CEISI, unpublished working papers from Work package 1 and 2 of the FP5 project 'Learnpartner' (Learning in partnership: Responding to the restructuring of the European Steel and Metal Sector').

Longworth, N. (1999) 'Making lifelong learning work: learning cities for a learning century.' London: Kogan Page.

Martínez Lucio, M. & Stuart, M. (2003) 'Training and development in Spain: the politics of modernisation.' *International Journal of Training and Development*, Vol.7, pp.67-77.

Michelsen, S. & Høst, H. (2002) 'Some remarks on Norwegian VET policies and Lifelong Learning.' In K. Harney et al (eds) 'Lifelong Learning: One Focus, Different Systems. p. 87-97: Peter Lang.

Ministry of Education and Research (2003) *Læringsbarometeret*. http://www.kompetanseberetningen.no/no_pages/docs/total-laeringsbarometer.pdf

National Agency for Education (2000) 'Lifelong learning and life-wide learning.' Stockhold: Liber Distribution.

Nordhaug, O. et al. (2004) 'Kompeanse i norske bedrifter: Verdiskaping, drivkrefter og behov.',Søkelys på arbeidsmarkedet 1/2004, ISF, Oslo 2004.

OECD (2002) *Thematic Review on Adult Learning. Spain*. Background Report. Paris: OECD.

Raggat, P. et al. (1996) *The Learning Society. Challenges and Trends*. London: Routledge.

Rubenson, K. (2001) 'L'éducation des adultes en Suède de 1967 à 2001.' In L. Tanguy (ed.) 'La formation permanente entre travail et citoyenneté.' *Education Permanente*, n° 149/2001-4. Luisant, France: Editions Alterna.

Sakslind, R. (ed.)(1998) 'Danning og yrkesdanning. Utdanningssystem og nasjonale moderniseringsprosjekter'. KULTs skriftserie nr. 103, 1998. Norges forskningsråd.

Siisiäinen, M. (2000) 'Social capital, power and the third sector.' In M. Siisiäinen, P. Kinnunen & E. Hietanen (eds) *The Third Sector in Finland*. Helsinki: Finnish Federation for Social Welfare and Health.

Skule, S., Stuart, M. & Nyen, T. (2002) 'International briefing 12: Training and development in Norway.' *International Journal of Training and Development*, Vol. 6(4), pp.263-276.

SNF & Fafo (forthcoming) 'Evaluering av Kompetanseutviklingsprogrammet. Underveisrapport 2005'. Institute for Research in Economics and Business Administration and Fafo, Institute for Labour and Social Research. To be published September 2005.

Tøsse, S. (1996) *Fra lov - til Reform*. Trondheim: Tapir Forlag.

Ure, O.B. & Gavigan, J.P. (2000) 'Lifelong learning: Beyond education and training.' IPTS report 46.

Ure, O.B. & Teige, B.K. (2003) 'The role of social partners in lifelong learning reforms for employability. Observations from Norway, the United Kingdom and Spain'. Research paper to the FP5 project Eurone&t.

VOX (2002) 'Dokumentasjon og verdsetting av realkompetanse. Realkompetanseprosjektet 1999-2002.' http://www.vox.no/archive/realN.pdf

CHAPTER TEN

Making Citizens:
From Belonging to Learning

TERRI SEDDON AND SUZANNE MELLOR

'Right now we wish to create a Europe of citizens,
a kind of hybrid reality which is federal when it comes to
the economy, national when it comes to security
and more and more regional when it comes to reality.
History is grey and muddy, but I think in the long run it will
create a feeling that somewhere Europe exists.'

(Moisi, 2004, p. 8)

Introduction

The European Union has committed itself to the strategic goal of positioning Europe as the 'the most competitive and dynamic knowledge-based economy in the world, capable of sustainable economic growth with more and better jobs and greater social cohesion' (European Council, 2000). Articulating the goal in this way acknowledges that the primary economic objective goes hand in hand with social and civic objectives aimed at establishing a tolerant Europe that is socially inclusive and supports active citizenship. This rhetoric frames up the kind of idea that French foreign policy analyst, Dominique Moisi, expresses in the quote above. In today's globalising world, European integration entails a double agenda: the construction of 'Europe' as a legitimate and powerful collective agency in world affairs, and the formation of new kinds of citizens. We would argue that in order for the double agenda to be effected, these new citizens will need to be able to straddle the imperatives of the knowledge economy and societal security, able to draw the best from national traditions and supra-national developments, while exercising and actively protecting democratic values.

Our aim in this chapter is to interrogate this double agenda that we see as centred on reworking citizenship, through the idea of the 'learning citizen'. We approach this topic by reflecting on a country that has been generally successful in integrating European communities into a multicultural and pluralist democracy of the kind envisaged in an integrated Europe. Specifically, we consider the successes and challenges that have confronted Australia as it worked to modernise its democratic politics. In adopting this approach we are not suggesting that Australia offers any simple lessons for Europe or that Australian democracy is the best model for European integration. Indeed, we recognise that Australia offers a relatively simple small-scale case of political integration, compared to Europe with its ambition of bringing 25, possibly more, nations with diverse cultures and sub-cultures into a coherent governance structure. However, a small case-study is sometimes helpful in crystalling issues and strategy, and it is with this orientation that we draw from Australian research and our own professional experience, to see what can be learned from the Australian case that might shed light on the 'European learning citizen'.

We begin by outlining what we understand by citizenship and how it is under pressure from broad social and economic changes in many countries of the world—Australia as much as Europe. We argue that current conceptions of citizenship are unhelpfully bifurcated in the legacies of social democratic centralism and the ambitions of market liberalism. In the main body of the paper we use this conceptualisation of citizenship to consider citizenship and citizen formation in Australia. Firstly, we make a case for considering Australia as a productive illustration when investigating European integration and citizen re-formation, insofar as it provides evidence of the ways that Australia, a largely European country, has successfully integrated diverse European communities into a functioning pluralist democratic polity.

Secondly, we outline the factors that have facilitated the formation of Australia as a collective agency based in a pluralist democracy. We then consider citizen formation within this democratic framework, highlighting its successes and the limits of its success. The usefulness of the case-study holds true, despite one important difference: in Australia citizen formation and learning has always had to work with a dominant model (Anglo-Saxon, Westminster, system, an agreed theoretical relationship of citizens to the rule of law, and so on). Whilst the argument can be put that having this dominant model has simplified the task, it can equally be argued that having a range of models facilitates the discussion of options and a societal evaluation of goals.

Having outlined the Australian situation as a case, we return to the question of European integration and ask what does it mean to create 'European learning citizens'.

Understanding contemporary citizenship

Our analysis is informed by an understanding of citizenship which affirms what citizens *do* as the primary concern in citizen formation. Authentic citizenship is the 'power to act' in a certain capacity, in particular contexts, in ways which can enhance the individual and society. Underpinning this power to act as citizens is the civic knowledge that it is both lawful and appproporiate for citizens to act in these particular ways. It encompasses the possession of a civic competence which is born of civic learning in the broadest sense. Additionally, the power to act will only be taken up by those with civic competence who are dispositionally-inclined to do so, and this disposition to engage as a citizen is also born of civic learning and experience in the broadest sense.

Discussion of definitions and conceptualisations of citizenship has been actively undertaken by many theoreticians and practitioners, from a range of fields but most especially in education, since the 1990s. (Ichilov, 1990; Gilbert, 1996; Hannam, 1999; Prior, 1999). The contested nature of any definition attests to the importance of unpacking the meanings different writers might have when they use the terms. Prior's six dimensions of citizenship have the advantage of providing us with a synthesised coverage of the concept.

Whilst there are differences of opinion about the relative importance of each of Prior's dimensions, (and he argues all are required for the confident and full engagement of citizens within the polity), their inter-relatedness and the contested nature of each of them is sufficient for us to argue their individual and collective importance. This synthesized conceptualisation has proven its usefulness in the field, in the analysis of citizens views on citizenship learning in Pacific Islands (Mellor and Prior, 2004). The Prior conceptualisation informs the discussion that follows.

Citizenship focuses our attention, firstly, on the way the power to act is critical to the formation of a collective agency, a state, which can legitimately act on behalf of the people and for the public good. The collective agency exercises this authority because its actions rest upon citizen action, involving equal participation within rule-governed decision-making processes. The legitimacy of states, and the democratic politics which sustain them, are undercut when people's opinions about what should be done by or within the collective agency are excluded. Secondly, citizenship encourages us to confront questions critical to our lifeworld: Who am I? What can I do? What

FIGURE 1: Prior's six dimensions of citizenship

Dimension 1: Civic knowledge:
(understandings about political organizations, decision making processes, institutions, legal requirements)

Dimension 2: A sense of personal identity:
(a feeling of self-worth, belonging efficacy, resilience)

Dimension 3: A sense of community:
(locating oneself within a community(s), some perhaps imagined communities).

Dimension 4: Adoption of a code of civil behaviours:
(civil and ethical behaviour, concern for the welfare of others)

Dimension 5: An informed and empathetic response to social issues:
(environmental issues, social justice, equality and equity).

Dimension 6: A skilled disposition to take social action:
(community service, active participation in community affairs)

may I hope for? In this respect, citizenship is a domain of political and social activity centred in interactive rather than cerebral experience. Davidson (1997) crystallises these two dimensions of citizenship, operating within a political context:

> 'A citizen is always defined primarily by what that person *does* rather than what they *get*, and the definition identifies particular activities among the myriads which make up our lives. But the *context* of these activities is political: they presume a political context or world as constituted by these activities and as constituting them. This constituted world of the *state* decides what sort of acts identify who is a citzen. Finally, the territorial dimension of an area within which they are enacted decides who *belongs* to a particular body of citizens—who has the right to participate in the acts of citizenship themselves. The rules of inclusion and exclusion are explained by the history that political world tells about itself. This gives it its self-identity as it reflects upon itself. Ultimately, what is important is not the truism that there is always a community prior to the context and the acts of citizenry within it, but how that community defines itself and what it thinks is 'good' (Davidson, 1997, p.3; emphasis included).

Citizenship depends partly on the discursive construction of political community, its rules of inclusion and exclusion, and its conceptions of the good society. It also depends upon the way this self-identity as individual and as part of a political community is consolidated in practical activities, like processes of decision-making, voting, organising, and educating, that to a greater or lesser extent realises that political community's hopes and aspirations.

Citizenship also requires citizens to realise that they have a capacity to act in ways that can make a difference for the 'I' or the 'Other', the individuals, the groups or communities or society to which she or he belongs (Mellor, 1995). A sense of citizenship is personal because how you utilise it in your life is determined not by the law, but by you. This utilisation is affected by your knowledge of how your citizenship rights and skills can be applied to achieve your values and goals. Citizens who are not taught to develop civic competency and how to exercise their civic and citizenship rights have significantly less civic efficacy than those who have been taught. Citizens are implicated in legislators decisions, even if unwittingly. For if legislators can change lives, it is because the citizenry has allowed it or has participated in it.

Learning to be and act as a citizen is therefore critical to citizen formation, the exercise of citizenship within democratic politics, and the sustainability of the political community as it develops over time and changing circumstances. Such activity which sustains a democratic politics is the primary justification for citizenship education. Such education can range from formal curricula in civics and citizenship education through to everyday community participation where people learn to live together and make decisions about their futures. It is neglected at some cost as many have pointed out (Orwell, 1964; Saul, 1997; Kennedy, 2000).

These basic principles of citizenship within a democratic polity are under pressure today. Broad social and economic changes are problematising the character of citizens' 'belonging' to a prior political community that has long defined the basis for citizenship. In the Greek city-states, 2000 years ago, belonging and consequent civic roles were defined by blood ties to particular families. In modern nation-states, belonging has been defined in terms of an 'imagined community', (Anderson, 1991) based on myths about the nation, its origins and its peoples. These myths obscured the actual historical processes by which particular families or ethnic groups came to dominate others and to consolidate their hegemony through nation-building processes which forged the institutions of state and civil society. The legitimacy of these myths rested upon the broad acceptance of a national narrative that ostensibly 'explained' national history and culture.

Today, these older forms of belonging are being weakened. Globalism accentuates flows of commodities, finance, images, ideas and people. It shifts our everyday lived horizons and brings us face-to-face with others, who are like us but different, as a consequence of migration, people displacement and movements of labour. Governments have responded to such changes by shifting away from older commitments to centralised planning through social democratic statism and, instead, affirmed market regulation, individualism and choice. Such market liberalism asserts the ubiquity of the market and the importance of unfettered innovation and individual benefit over collective identities. It emphasises the sense of being individual, disconnected from older social ties and able to pursue ones own particular dreams and aspirations. In this globalised framing, the idea of equality that made good political sense in the context of collectivity is downplayed in favour of political outcomes that affirm individual benefit, valorising human capital, lifelong adaptability, personal agility, freedom to choose and consume, and flexibility as worker. These trends shift the locus of responsibility and risk away from the system and social level to individuals. As individuals are pressed to self-manage as responsible actors and risk-takers, they may become more reflexive, encouraging changing attitudes to authority and identity—what Giddens (1994) terms 'de-traditionalisation.' Yet self-management and responsibilisation can also encourage re-traditionalisation through disengagement, political quiessence fuelled by fear or uncertainty, and quests to find strong leaders who can provide some sense of direction in multi-directional and uncertain times. Through these processes the hold of tradition is both loosened and strengthened in everyday life as established national narratives are challenged by the acknowledgment of cultural diversity and by the sub-cultural narratives articulated by Indigenous Peoples and other minorities.

These contemporary trends shift the basis of citizenship away from belonging but in paradoxical ways. They drive reflexivity about belonging which allows individuals to hold open the question of belonging and their identity, to varying degrees, by playing with multiple identifications (Bhabha, 2004). Rapid change accelerates the extent to which people come together in cross-cultural communication. They must deal with difference in their everyday lives, rubbing up against one another to find ways of coming to agreements as a basis for action. These trends undercut established patterns of collective agency and the delegation of politics to centralised agencies. Instead the politics come home to our everyday life contexts where it is possible to see the importance of recognition as well as redistribution, and their contribution to realising both individual and collective benefits. More and more, individuals are called upon to make judgments which can inform political practices and ethical choices in localised contexts. More and more, these judgments are informed by reflexive assessments of multiple identifications. More and more, such action is framed by the formation of citizens whose hybridity challenges dominant national narratives.

Such paradoxical developments allow us to acknowledge different ways of being an 'active citizen' (e.g. Evans, 1995; Kenny, 2004) in contexts where people mobility, global horizons, cultural difference and reflexive engagement are increasingly common (Yeatman, 1994). As Figure 2 suggests, the active citizen of social democratic statism has been imagined as the 'social activist' , the do-er of public good within collectivist decision-making processes that are aimed at generating collective or universalistic benefits. The active citizen of market liberalism has been presented in recent policy as the innovative entreprenur and 'can-do' achiever who cuts through inertia to generate results and individual or particularistic benefits. This way of being a citizen has been framed by the dominant market narrative, combined with a particular, reductionist, conception of learning, to create a narrow kind of citizenship that doesn't question market liberalism and, more importantly, doesn't know how, or that citizens have the right, to challenge the dominant discourse.

Beyond these romantic images of the 'activist' or 'entrepreneur' as hero, there are more familiar ways of being a citizen that build on learning *and* belonging. Such citizenship serves individualised interests by building individuals' identities and capacities for action and, through these processes of individual capacity-building, contributes to social and community development where practices are developed as shared property of the collective— the group, occupation, nation, even humankind (Connell, 1995).

As Figure 2 suggests, as belonging and centralised governance is weakened as a consequence of changing times, and as the limits of market liberalism are revealed in a selfish society, ways of being a citizen as inter-related capacity-building and community (capability)-development come into view.

FIGURE 2: Beyond activist and entrepreneur

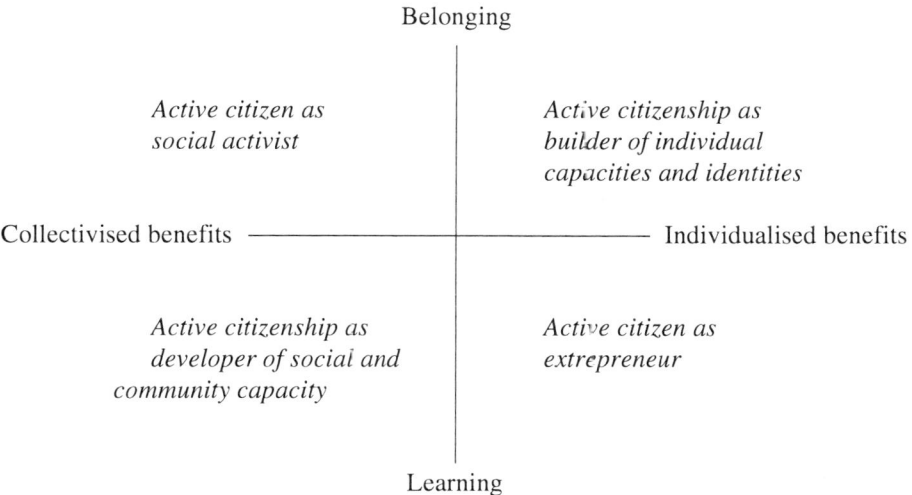

Belonging

Active citizen as social activist

Active citizenship as builder of individual capacities and identities

Collectivised benefits ——————————————— Individualised benefits

Active citizenship as developer of social and community capacity

Active citizen as extrepreneur

Learning

Such re-thinking about citizenship confronts us with some key questions: How to manage belonging and learning in the formation of citizens who both have, and exercise, the 'power to act' within pluralist democratic politics? How to anchor hybrid citizens in local, national and supra-national social spaces and relationships, but in ways that enhance reflexive judgments as a basis for their political practices and ethical choices? How to form citizens whose judgments, based on multiple identifications, allow them to act in contextually-specific ways as activists, entrepreneurs, capacity-builders *and* community-developers? How to organise citizen formation so that democratic politics is not only enacted but also protected in the years to come?

The next section of the chapter considers the way these models of citizenship and trends in democratic politics have played out in the specific practical context of Australia. We begin by considering Australia's success in developing an integrative democratic politics but also note the preconditions and limits of those civic achievements.

Citizenship in Australia

Achievements and challenges

Australia's key achievement has been to construct a successful multicultural and pluralist democracy along lines similar to that envisaged in the project of an integrated Europe.

One phase of integration occurred in 1901, when the six English speaking colonies that then had territoriality over the Australian landmass federated, forming the Commonwealth of Australia. While this process of political integration parallels the formation of Europe in creating an overarching political entity and collective agency, there are significant differences. It occurred in a very different socio-political context to that which now exists a century later, and the scale and complexity of contemporary European integration makes Australia's political integration seem simple by comparison. Each federating colony was an administrative unit governing largely immigrant local populations on behalf of the British Crown and through British institutions, and the rules of civic and political engagement were nineteenth century in their framing, not particularly suited to dealing with many of the civic issues now presenting.

A more significant integration was required during the two decades after the second world war with the acceptance of a greatly-diversified immigrant population into Australia. During the post-war period large numbers of non-English speaking European migrants were admitted to Australia and, initially, as far as possible, were assimilated into the prevailing Anglo-Celtic culture. However by the 1970s, a third stage of integration policy was required when increasing migrant diversity, coupled with the democratic politics of ethnic communities, pressed Australia away from its policy of assimilation and encouraged bipartisan support for multiculturalism.

As Table 1 shows, Australia remains a largely European country, drawing its population predominantly from Europe and its diasporas. Australia is home to the largest concentrations of Estonians and Maltese outside of Estonia and Malta. The city of Melbourne has the second-largest Greek population in the world. Australia is a place where Europeans from many different nationalities live together pretty much in harmony. Multiple identities are maintained, as a matter of course, and are experienced in inter-cultural marriages and schooling by nearly everyone.

TABLE 1: Demographic composition of Australia, 2001 Census

Country	Population	Percentage of total population
Australia	13629481	77.0
Other Australasia and Oceania	454984	2.6
UK & Ireland	1086479	6.1
Europe & USSR	1037798	5.9
Middle East & North Africa	213652	1.2
Asia	970428	5.5
Americas	159859	0.9
Africa	140559	0.8
TOTAL	17693240	

Source: *Australian Bureau of Statistics, Cat. no. 3105.0.65.001 Australian Historical Population Statistics Table 86. Population, sex, country of birth (a), states and territories. 2001 census (usual residence)*

The commitment that individuals who are resident in Australia express towards the country is also high. The 2001 Australian census found that the rate of citizenship take up by residents born overseas was 75.1 percent, although this rate varied by country (e.g. Greeks 98%, Japanese 23%) and by category of migrant expressing the intention to apply (humanitarian 98%, employer sponsored 65%) (Ferguson and Gardiner, 2004, pp.166-7).

In the 2001 Australian Electoral Survey (AES), Bean (2004) found that 86% of the sample (N=2010) believed that Australian citizenship was preferable to that of any other country. Having Australian citizenship was judged to be 'most important' by 56% of the AES sample and 'fairly important' by a further 33%. Having citizenship was judged to be fourth most important out of 7 items, following 'feeling Australian' (64% = 'very important); 'speaking English' (62%); and respecting Australia's political institutions and laws (61%). Only 32 percent of the AES sample felt that being born in Australia was 'very important'. Older people were more positive about Australian citizenship than younger people. Rural people were more positive about being Australian citizens than city-dwellers (Rural strongly agreeing = 74%; Inner metropolitan strongly agreeing = 63%). Interestingly, more significant variations in attitudes to citizenship were evident by birthplace. The Australian-born expressed the strongest support for being a citizen of Australia rather than of another country (75%). They were followed, in order, by Eastern Europeans (65%), Northern Europeans (59%), Southern Europeans (52%), British Isles (44%) and Asia (36%) (Bean, 2004).

The purpose of providing such data is to demonstrate the range of distinctive reactions to these key determinants of identity. It is not possible here to unpack the reasons for the response variations except to point out that many factors influence such decisions. These include the reasons people immigrated, the inter-country arrangements that exist, as well as the acceptance and success they experience in their new place. Assimilation does not always result in high levels of acceptance and the pluralism inherent in the policy of multiculturalism, with its concommitant encouragement of multiple identities, appears to have facilitated high levels of a sense of 'belonging' amongst first and second generation immigrants in Australia. Being born here was not the key determinant of being an Australian, having Australian citizenship was.

In 1994, this positive assessment of Australian citizenship was affirmed in a report, titled *Whereas the People* (Civics Expert Group, 1994), commissioned by then Prime Minister Paul Keating. This inquiry was charged with investigating the state of civics and citizenship education in Australia in the context of a wider public debate about whether or not Australia should become a Republic with its own head of state [since currently, the Australia's head of state is the Queen of England]. In *Whereas the People* the Civics Expert Group (CEG) endorsed Australia's success:

'As we approach the Centenary of the Commonwealth, Australians are able to look back on a remarkably successful record of democratic self-government. The public institutions created in the closing years of the last [18th] century have proved flexible and resilient. The outcomes of the democratic process enjoy popular acceptance.

In contrast to most other countries, we have seldom experienced a challenge to the legitimacy of our civic order or resorted to violence. The political process has operated peacefully. The rule of law abides. There is a high level of tolerance and acceptance. At the same time there is evidence that Australian citizenship is in need of restatement, and that more could be done to promote informed and active citizenship. The past fifty years, in particular, have brought profound changes in the ways that Australians organise their affairs.

Our society has become more diverse: large-scale immigration, changed economic and international relations, the claims of indigenous peoples, the removal of discrimination against women and changes in family structures have all yielded a different, more complex society. We have become a nation of people from many cultural backgrounds, speaking many languages, and practising many religions' (CEG, 1994b, pp. 3-4).

But the authors cautioned that this more complex society has 'great implications for citizenship'. Participating in democracy in Australia, they argued, entailed only modest levels of active citizen engagement and the citizens had a poor knowledge of civics. This 'civic deficit' was in tension with the way Australia had accommodated difference and Australians had valued diversity as 'a national strength' (p. 4). The appreciation of diversity, the authors argue, had not been accompanied by better and new understandings of citizenship, full recognition of the importance of public institutions, or a rich grasp of decision-making processes through which differences are addressed and resolved. And this tension presented dangers to the Australian democracy:

'When the lack of knowledge of how governmental institutions work and an uncertainty of what the civic ethos means is coupled with mistrust of politics, a danger arises. Our system of government relies for its efficacy and legitimacy on an informed citizenry; without active, knowledgeable citizens the forms of democratic representation remain empty; without vigilant, informed citizens there is no check on potential tyranny…our democratic values require that every citizen has equal opportunity to participate in the exercise of these rights and responsibilities. Without civic education that democratic ideal is not maintained' (CEG, 1994a, pp.15-16).

Overall, these data and indicators paint a positive picture of Australian citizenship learning. Australia has been doing something right to create a functional polity out of such cultural and political diversity. There are limits to this success, however, particularly relating to the 'democratic deficit'. But, by and large, Australians have tackled and made a good show of constructing a collective capacity for action, while addressing cultural difference and plurality. In the next section we further consider what has facilitated this effective multicultural and pluralist collective agency. We then move on to consider the challenges presented by the democratic deficit.

Australian ways of belonging

Australia's formation as a successful pluralist democracy has been shaped by the way belonging has been managed through its history of colonisation and migration, the pattern of inclusion and exclusion that this history established, and also by the character of institution building and institutional reform which has created contexts that promote citizens belonging.

Exclusion has been structured around two principles. The first is premised on the view that the British settled an empty land when they put up their flag in Sydney Cove in 1788. This view was formalised in the legal principle of *Terra Nullius* which rendered any pre-existing rights of Indigenous Australians invisible within legal frameworks. Indigenous traditions and patterns of governance and decision-making were obscured and marginalised in the formation of Australia and its patterns of citizenship. The 1990 Wik judgement in the Australian High Court, which overturned the principle of *Terra Nullius* and affirmed the existence of Indigenous land rights, has led to some legal and socio-attitudinal change, as commitments to reconcilation between Indigenous and non-indigenous Australians have gained greater public affirmation . Only in the last decade has the imported Australian democracy been required to enter into any compact with its Indigenous population, unlike in New Zealand where the indigenous Maoris retained a political presence through the negotiated 1840 Treaty of Waitangi.

The second principle of exclusion was based on policies which defined who could be admitted to Australia—a migrant nation with approximately 98 percent of its population being of immigrant stock. Until the second world war much of this migration was from Britain and Ireland, and therefore compatible with the myths of 'national family'that supported national belonging although such belonging was also inclusive of age-old contestations between these groups Since then, demand for labour, pressures to increase the internal market and humanitarian principles have dictated principles of admission that were more generous to non-Anglo-Celtic migrants, initially non-English speaking Europeans, and later people coming from Africa and particularly Asia. By the late 1960s, prior commitments to the White Australia policy were being overturned in support of migrants who were not only non-English speaking but also coloured, and to celebrate cultural diversity. There has been bipartisan support for multiculturalism ever since, although as Davidson (2004) notes, this history established 'pariah groups' which persist ideologically and are mobilised from time to time for political advantage. This principle of exclusion has always had as its defining focus the underlying fear of a relatively empty land being swamped by groups alien to the dominant values, behaviours and goals, though opinion and policy has changed over time as to which groups and practices fall within the acceptable. (Indeed over the last several decades there has not always been broad social consensus on what are the dominant goals of the society.)

Once a migrant was inside the country, a broadly inclusive ethos prevailed. In part this ethos was shaped by the importation of relatively homogeneous British institutions and their formation within the context of a hegemonic Anglo-Celtic culture, but the explicit class and ethnic divisions evident in Britain were not embraced to the same degree. Through the late 19th and early 20th century, a distinctive 'workingman's welfare state' (Castles, 1988) was constructed which allowed practical and progressive realisation of inclusivity and the idea of a 'fair go' for all. Welfare provision was structured around entitlements for targeted categories of recipients (eg. the employed, aged, infirm and unemployed) that 'were universal in principal and selective in practice' (Roe, 1998, p.75). The categories of recipients were all equally entitled to take up their benefits and encouraged to collectively pursue grievances or seek redress for mistreatment. The centrepiece of this welfare state was the concept of the basic wage for all workers. This provision, introduced as part of the so-called 'Harvester Judgement' in 1907, was a wage sufficient to support a male breadwinner, his wife and three children in modest comfort. Institutionalising this basic wage through a system of industrial awards (to protect working families), complemented by tariff protection (to protect businesses from international competition) and the White Australia policy (limiting the import of cheap labour), provided security in terms of basic standards of living for the working population and their dependents. This pattern of social protection was supplemented by specific welfare payments, such as the age pension and child endowment, to support particular categories of individuals who fell beyond the structure of work-related welfare.

These patterns of institution-building were reformed as migration diversified, in part by extending the categories of people eligible for support (e.g. introducing the category NESB or Non-English Speaking Background). Post-1945 assimilation policies had, by the 1970s, given way to multiculturalism that acknowledged and valued cultural difference. Requirements for becoming an Australian citizen have also softened over time. Currently, migrants and refugees can take out Australian citizenship after 2, out of a total of 5, years as permanent residents. They must also be able to understand the nature of their citizenship application and speak basic English, unless they are over 50 or have a physical or intellectual impairment. Since 1987 migrants have not had to renounce citizenship in their country of origin, if that country allowed dual citizenship. This means that dual citizenship is a reality for many Australians. It has complemented the formation of dual identity Australians who identify as Chinese-Australians or Greek-Australians. Some even retain pension arrangements with their countries of origin, especially in relation to support of older family members in family-reunion migration, depending on between-country arrangements.

Such institutional measures constructed Australia as a social space where belonging was associated with a distinctive regime of inclusion and exclusion. Like other countries it was restrictive in terms of entry but inclusive for those admitted. This belonging was not a visible matter or a caste but was a private concern, a compact between the individual and the state. There was no institutionalisation of second-class citizens because migrants were mostly able to access welfare support whether or not they took out citizenship. Yet the nature of these institutional arrangements were relatively blind to women, positioning them, along with children, as dependents on male bread winners. And it excluded the majority of Indigenous Australians (those who were not landholders). Until the 1970s these Indigenous 'non-citizens' were managed as a dependent population of state wards through a system of state or church administered reserves and many did not gain the right to vote in Commonwealth elections until the 1967.

Apart from these restrictions, Australia offered opportunities for people from different cultures to rub up against one another and learn to live together with tolerance. Public schools, for instance, are required to take all enrolments within their zone, irrespective of background or origins. As a result public schools commonly enrol students from many different cultural backgrounds but the kids get on, even when there is a history of cross-cultural conflict in the countries of origin (eg. beween Turks and Greeks). During the break-up of the old Yugoslavia, for instance Australian schools in all state jurisdictions adopted pro-active policies of explicitly addressing inter-racial/ethnic conflicts that could have spilt over into full-blown re-enactments in classrooms and school grounds of ancient but painfully-immediate versions of the new wars. Teachers in some schools reported that during some days of heightened war conflict they did little else but deal with the values and identity confusion, and the consequent anger, fear and distress of their Croatian and Slav students. Australian schools for over 50 years now have actively contributed to a positive tolerance (indeed a celebration) by all of difference, and have implemented government and community policies to provide support for those whose language or cultural skills were such as to potentially marginalise them, or negatively impact upon their capacity to learn. A study of Year 11 students in Victoria (aproximately 16 year olds) showed that the tolerance they practise is firmly-grounded in a known reality.

A study of female student, in explaining her tolerant behaviours at a co-educational public school where over 50 percent of the students came from 40 different non-English speaking (NESB) language backgrounds said: 'Look Miss, there are just too many different races here to be stupid enough to pick on someone for their race... it'd be my turn next' (Mellor, 1998). One criticism of private schools in Australia is that by their narrower social cohort they restrict the options their students have of living and learning together in ways that support tolerant diversity.

Yet despite constructing belonging in ways that support successful pluralist democracy in Australia, the processes of citizen formation have not provided people with a strong understanding of civics or their responsibilities as citizens, or encouraged them to participate as active citizens in democratic governance. In the next section we consider responses to this 'democratic deficit' and the way it relates to the wider trend to affirm lifelong learning.

Australian approaches to civics learning and citizenship making

A civics education which foregrounded antecedent British history and institutions was part of the formal school curriculum until world war 2. In the 1970s, civics and citizenship education were rolled up into more diffuse social studies teaching. This curriculum shift coincided with significant migrant diversification in Australia. Before the war, it made sense to teach kids in schools about their civic responsibilities in terms of Britain and the British Crown. Once the myth of Australia as an Anglo-Celtic country (or British branch office) was confronted by growing numbers of migrants from countries other than Britain, the rationale for developing a strong sense of belonging to Britain was challenged. The rationale was further weakened as Australia's primary political alignment shifted from Britain to the US and trade diversified towards Europe and, more recently, Asia. Curriculum shifted so students learned more about current Australia and less about its antecedents. History was popular but in schools it was not generally linked to questioning the present. Again, acceptance of the status quo was the preferred norm, and passivism was normative behaviour. A consequent cynicism about the lack of impact the citizenry could have on decision-makers became a recogniseable Australian trait, and the laconic lack of enagagement was both caused and followed by alienation from the political process. Students in the IEA Civics study reserved their deepest lack of trust for political parties and the national government (Mellor et al., 2001, Table 6.14. p94).

Multiculturalism pressed these developments further, celebrating the many cultures that made up Australia. But such curriculum trends further problematise the idea of belonging—to what do people belong? They also undercut the old rationale for civics and citizenship education as supplementary to learning from the processes of living together. The questions proliferate: If civics and citizenship education is no longer supplementing belonging, what should be learned and taught? What is the 'good society' to which Australia aspires? Can schools and other established institutions of education and training move beyond a supplementary role in supporting citizen formation? What would this more substantial role for education and training entail?

In *Whereas the People,* the Civics Expert Group highlighted the challenges presented by these broad social changes and their implications for citizenship in a country where understandings and practices of active citizenship were relatively weak. They recommended an ambitious strategy to address Australia's 'democratic deficit' by supporting civics and citizenship education in and beyond established institutions of education and training. This strategy advocated revision of the school curriculum, introduction of civics and citizenship education in vocational and further education provision (in Technical and Further Education (TAFE) Institutions and community providers) and in higher education. They also recommended ways of supporting adults as they learned about citizenship through participation in voluntary associations. But these recommendations were soon overtaken by the prevailing politics that accompanied economic reform

The critique of Australian civics and citizenship education articulated in *Whereas the People* (CEG 1994b,a) was carried forward through the 1990s in ways that informed education and training policy and, particularly, professional practice. Yet this concern with the social and civic outcomes of Australian education and training was increasingly marginalised by dominant economic policy discourses focused on increasing Australia's international competitiveness through workforce development. The release of *Whereas the People* in 1994 at the virtual death knell of the Commonwealth Labor government under Paul Keating contributed to this sidelining. In 1996 the change of Commonwealth government brought the Liberal-National coalition, under John Howard, to office.

For education practitioners this marginalisation was experienced as a denial of their educational commitments to preparing students to take up their adult roles as citizens in a democracy (Ryan, 2003) and through patronising judgments that they were still 'locked in the 1970s'. For policy-makers there seems to have been an uneasy but erratic recognition that people needed some understanding of democracy—a policy trajectory that indicates continuing contestation and debate about the place of civics and citizenship education within policy processes.

The recommendations of *Whereas the People* for civics and citizenship education in education and training beyond the schools sector, in TAFE Institutes and universities, and in the community, simply disappeared. Instead, adult education was pressed by government policies to meet vocational outcomes, and to respond to commercial imperatives, given teeth by sharp reductions in public funding (to be made up by commercial income) and the construction of the education and training market which gave private providers access to public funding.

Within school education the legacy of *Whereas the People* was more contested. *Discovering Democracy* (2004), a curriculum resources package for schools initiated in response to those recommendations, was supported by the Coalition Commonwealth government. In 1999, the State and Commonwealth Ministers of Education agreed upon a statement of National Goals for Australian Schools (DEST, 1999) which endorsed civic outcomes, including developing student's capacity for active citizenship, although this commitment, particularly to active citizenship, was not clearly realised in subsequent government policy.

As a part of the *Discovering Democracy* program, the Commonwealth Department of Education, Training and Youth Affairs funded Australia's involvement in the International Association for the Evaluation of Educational Achievement (IEA) Civic Education Study. Australia's reluctant participation in the first phase suggests some hesitancy on the part of government and, ultimately, Australia's involvement was justified on educational grounds. In Phase 1, researchers from 24 countries wrote case studies of the provision civic education in their countries. The observations were used to validate the international suite of items testing students' civic knowledge and a survey of their civic engagement. These were implemented in Phase 2, with a sample of 90,000 14 year old students in 28 countries. The Australian sample of 3331 students was tested in 1999 and returned a student participation rate of 92 percent. A teacher questionnaire and a school questionnaire were also developed and administered at each school site, completed by 3 teachers and the principal (Mellor et al., 2001). The results of this study provided a picture of 14 year-olds' civic knowledge and civic engagement in Australia and also relative to the international sample made up of students from 28 countries, including Australia.

This survey of the cognitive and affective learnings of 14 year-olds found that relative to other countries, the sample of Australian 14-year olds was average relative to the international mean on the total civic knowledge scale and below average on the civic engagement scales. The civic knowledge of Australian students varied enormously, with two percent of them having a 65 percent probability of answering every question correctly, while 10 percent had the same probability of not being able to answer any of the civic knowledge questions correctly. The sample of Australian 14 year olds performed better than their international peers on average on the interpretative skills. This probably reflects Australian students' greater experience with a style of open pedagogy rather than greater civic achievement. In terms of attitudes to civic engagement, Australian students' scores were below the international mean in relation to responses to items on conventional citizenship, social movement citizenship and expected participation in political activities. They were also, though less significantly, below the international mean on items relating to confidence in participation in school.

As (Mellor et al., 2001) report, the data indicates a number of contra-dictions. Australian students express their commitment to traditional democratic values but few see themselves engaging with the political system that guarantees those values. They are positive about participating in their own schools (despite reporting limited opportunities for such participation), not averse to participating in community groups, and saw 'good citizens' participating in social movement politics. Yet they are reluctant to engage with conventional political processes.

Mellor et al. (2001) propose two explanations that may account for these findings. First, they suggest that Australian students pick up their general knowledge of democracy and their sense of natural justice and equity from the prevailing social and political culture but have only a weak to moderate understanding of the formal political system and its democratic values. The authors counter-point this imbalance between a theoretical understanding and emotional commitment as a 'democracy of the mind', as opposed to a 'democracy of the heart'. (p.14).

Secondly, Mellor et al. (2001, p.15) suggest that Australian students are positive about participation in contexts in which they perceive that they have some capacity for effect but are alienated from the broader political arena which seems too remote for them to ever successfully participate in it. Students therefore look to participate outside of formal democratic structures, participating on their own terms in community activities and social movements. Such participation is seen as the responsibility of the individual citizen but, Mellor et al. (2001, p.15) question the sufficiency of such a position in protecting democratic values and the political structures that sustain them now and in the future.

The manifest shortfall in student understandings about democracy, and the consequent impact on the future strength of Australian democracy informed the conclusions to the Australian report *Citizenship and Democracy* which stated:

> 'The preparation of future citizens cannot afford to be left to chance. Directions need to be set at all levels of education to indicate this is one of the priorities for the future.' (p137)

The report concludes with a call for more comprehensive implementation of formal civic education in schools (to teach the processes, rules, and so on) and greater opportunities for students to engage in meaningful decision-making in schools (with a view to students developing greater citizenship competence, and an increased inclination or disposition to enagage.) It reflects that this will require professional development for teachers and a consideration of a broad range of pedagogies.

Following the IEA Study and the ten years of the *Discovering Democracy* programme, national sample assessment will be conducted in 2004 and at three year intervals thereafter. The assessment will be conducted at Years 6 (end of primary school) and 10 (end of compulsory schooling). The assessment domain makes explicit the critical distinction between civics and citizenship learning outcomes (see Figure 3) The significance of the multiple roles this assessment domain will have for the learning citizen should not be under-estimated. In the absence of formal curricula in most educational jurisdications in Australia it will inevitably help frame schools' curriculum delivery and teachers' pedagogic practices.

FIGURE 3: Key performance measures for national assessment

KPM 1: Civics: Knowledge& Understanding of Civic Institutions & Processes
Knowledge of key concepts and understandings relating to civic institutions and processes in Australian democracy, government, law, national identity, diversity, cohesion and social justice.

KPM 2: Citizenship: Dispositions & Skills for Participation
Understandings related to the attitudes, values, dispositions, beliefs and actions that underpin active democratic citizenship.

These developments in school education hold open a place for civics and citizenship education, and for questionning the processes of citizen formation in Australia. It means that the critical legacy of *Whereas the People* is sustained, albeit in constrained ways, and that its case—that Australia's democratic deficit threatens our democracy because lack of knowledge and engagement means that there is no check on potential tyranny—still waits to be addressed.

Reframing education and training as Lifelong Learning

Through the 1980s, Australian public policy 'changed its mind' (Pusey, 1992) about the kind of nation-building that supported belonging as the principle for citizenship. Australian governments shifted away from the kind of broad social democratic principles that had been embodied in the workingman's welfare state for much of the 20th century. Instead they pressed towards economic rationalism in government, affirming market regulation, implementing corporate managerialism across the public sector, and asserting the significance of learning through life for all Australians.

Early on, such economic reform was accompanied by new and cosmopolitan national narratives which built on and illustrated Australia's multicultural and democratic achievements. This narrative emphasised Australia's success in dealing with difference, its readiness to reach out to Indigenous Australians and South East Asia, and to step beyond the historic ties to Britian and the British Crown as an independent Republic. It framed a sense of Australian identity which was proud to be multicultural and open to the world. But political opinion baulked at this.

In 1996, the Liberal-Country Party Coalition government, led by John Howard, was returned to office and quickly set aside Labor's agenda of cultural and democratic reform. Instead there was a reassertion of old narrative themes—the importance of old alliances especially with the US, support for the monarchy and a calculated undermining of the referendum on the Republic, retreat from Asia in terms of foreign policy, and also from reconciliation with Indigenous Australians. These themes provided the basis for rolling back public policy developments on many fronts by reasserting the principle of belonging to the dominant culture and its rhetoric of 'them' and 'us'. 'Them' included 'dole bludgers' and 'welfare cheats', justifying punitive welfare reforms; Aborigines and Torres Strait Islanders who couldn't manage their affairs, justifying 'practical reconciliation' and disestablishing agencies that have supported Indigenous governance; 'career women' who want jobs as well as babies, justifying childcare provision that encourages women to stay at home. The list has grown the longer Howard's Coalition government has been in office, and until recent times many Australians appear to not have had the concepts or the langauge to decry these exclusionary policies. As with all policies built upon fear, the population's better nature and a more open appreciation of the feasibility of a negotiated position or the possibility of greater inclusiveness in policy has been undermined. Refugees have suffered from this exclusion the most and, of course, they are the very same source of population growth that Australia has traditionally feared but, in recent decades, accommodated with no trouble.

While the recommendations of *Whereas the People* were largely lost in this change of government and shift in political rhetoric, economic reform had never-the-less fuelled learning in powerful ways. As Pusey (2003) suggests, the effects of economic reform and the implementation of market regulation pressed people everywhere to learn more and more—for work in a rapidly changing labour market, for being good parents or careful investors for their retirement, for making informed choices about schools, telephone and utility companies, shopping, lifestyle, health and wellbeing, even politicians.

Market reform insists that we learn, all the time, about everything, exhaustively and exhaustingly all through our lives. But it also insists on learning that is utilitarian in character and oriented to enhance productivity, narrowly conceived. It is learning framed largely by the market rather than by by citizenship.

Government policy has channelled these imperatives for learning in three main directions.

First, it has become almost universally accepted that learning is important in today's Australia because it helps individuals to live with rapid social and economic change. This commitment to learning is widely accepted in the community, acknowledged as good management practice in many workplaces, and is endorsed virtually as bipartisan policy. However, this support for learning does not always translate into support for education and training. The endorsement of learning has been accompanied by de-institutionalising and de-regulatory commitments that are actively diversifying the social spaces within which learning is acknowledged, actively supported and, commonly, credentialled (Seddon and Clemans, 2003).

Second, the shift away from centralist social democratic government towards decentralised governance has meant that individuals are often more involved in decision-making at localised levels and are required to make decisions about a wider range of issues, compared to the past. These new practices of government based on policy steering rather than service delivery, and often operationalised through social partnerships, create contexts where participation in pluralist decision-making is essential. In partnerships many agencies are required to work together to realise particular ends and, commonly, to access government or other funding to support initiatives. Successful partnership working depends upon individuals finding ways of working with difference to reach productive agreements and courses of action despite value pluralism. It also requires participants to work with accountability regimes that depend upon evidence-based evaluation and strategic planning. While rarely named, the notion of citizenship is valorised with these developments. Individuals cannot depend upon governments providing goods and services in the old way but must, themselves, be active in negotiating and organising such provision amongst diverse partners (Seddon and Billett, 2004).

Finally, the affirmation of learning has been channelled in particular ways through the restructuring of education and training. In the late 1980s, the then Labor Commonwealth government committed itself to making Australia a 'Clever Country'. The intention was to up-skill the workforce to make Australia internationally competitive by increasing access to education and training and by actively encouraging participation in learning by people of all ages. This agenda was maintained by the Coalition government, after 1996, albeit with somewhat different rhetoric and a stronger emphasis on market regulation, choice and priveate educational investment (Axford and Seddon, 2004).

This policy agenda was strongly focused on learning for work. It entailed the re-regulation of education and training based on market principles and corporate managerialism but it also encouraged interest in different modes of learning (eg. via ICT) and places for learning (eg. in workplaces, community settings, as well as established institutions like schools). Yet this learning was framed within an accountability framework which, particularly beyond the years of compulsory schooling, privileged vocational learning and employment outcomes at the expense of other kinds of learning, including citizenship.

These policy trends drove increased participation in education and training. From 1982 to 1992, Year 12 school retention increased from 36 percent to 77 percent, due to the collapse of the fulltime youth labour market and the development of innovative education and training initiatives. Between 1985-86 and 1997-98, tertiary education participation increased by 85 percent (from 282,359 to 521,783 equivalent fulltime students). Enrolments of 15-64 year olds in vocational education and training institutions increased from 8.4 percent to13.2 percent between 1991 and 2000 (Watson et al., 2003, p.155). Yet while participation increased, the question of what learning would support new forms of citizenship appropriate to a multicultural and pluralist democracy in a rapidly globalising world was refocused within school education.

These three policy trajectories cut across each other. On the one hand, the reinvention of government, and the implementation of policy steering and market reform, drive lifelong learning as a lived response to change in people's everyday work-lives. Workplaces and community settings are increasingly acknowledged as learning-places as well as work-places, alongside established education and training institutions. And decentralised decision-making and partnership-working that accompany new governance arrangements, whole-of-government initiatives and other government steering, encourage participation in pluralist decision-making and implicitly provide both a rationale for, and endorsement of, active citizenship.

On the other hand, while education institutions, workplaces and communities are increasingly acknowledged as learning contexts, they are largely judged within the frames of economic rationalist discourse, a discourse that attends to economic and business outcomes but is largely blind to social and civic outcomes. In these contexts too, the assertion of managerial prerogative can create a kind of despotic order in which people are not acknowledged as participant citizens but are constrained, and sometimes coerced, to fall in line.

In this paradoxical context that both affirms and undermines democratic politics, people live contradictions through both harmonsied compliance and through active political practices and ethical choices which realise individual and collective benefits. There is evidence of innovative learning and action that takes up opportunities to participate in pluralist decision-making in ways that serve the public good by supporting individuals and collectives, and their rights and representation within the public sphere (e.g. Seddon, 2000, 2001). These initiatives demonstrate active citizenship writ small. They gain a point of purchase at sub-national and organisation levels but, from this base, reach out into wider issues relating to economic, political, social and symbolic citizenship (but not necessarily to formal political participation). Through these activities some Australians are finding ways of sustaining themselves as individuals and as collectives, learning about citizenship and developing citizen skills in their homes, workplaces, and lifeworlds (MaRhea and Seddon, 2004). In small ways they are re-affirming the importance of citizenship and democratic politics, and they are acting as active citizens—as critical activists, capacity-builders and community developers, and entrepreneurs as the context permits.

Forming the learning citizen

The formation of learning citizens is a contradictory development driven by the weakening of citizen belonging and the intensification of learning. These conditions, generated in the context of social, economic and political changes that accompany globalism and intensified competition, initially enabled multicultural citizenship in Australia. But the learning that underpinned the formation of multicultural citizens was framed in political terms as a process of generalising a multicultural national narrative and building political commitment and a sense of political agency to a many cultured community. Education and training supported these processes of citizen formation.

Today, the trends towards weakened belonging and intensified learning are further advanced than in the 1970s. More significantly, the kind of learning that is endorsed as being in the national interest has been reframed. In an act of political will, Australian governments since the late 1980s have asserted an economic framing of social and political life. As Beilharz (1994, p.144) notes, 'A certain kind of politics thus ruled because it was authorised to do so by a certain kind of economics; a certain kind of economics was claimed inevitable by the politics which authorised it.' Consequently, learning has been framed economically and this has no place for the question of citizen formation and democratic processes. While commitments to learning framed politically persist, they exist as a marginalised and sometimes subversive discourse alongside the mainstream economic view of learning. While education and training continues to support identity formation that is sympathetic to multiculturalism, this work is increasingly squeezed to the early years of compulsory schooling by the pervasive economism of human capital discourse operationalised through the entire curriculum. The priority is with individual benefit and preparation for economic adult roles—whether via university or vocational training. This preoccupation with learning for work that pervades the post-primary years of schooling and post-school education and training renders identity formation sympathetic to multiculturalism into an issue of human resource development. Its about supporting learners to develop capacities so that they can work in teams, demonstrate social competence and deal with difference particularly at work.

The idea of a 'learning citizen' problematises this paradoxical process of identity formation that acknowledges democracy but as a passive precondition for the market and enhanced international competition. Juxtaposing 'learning' and 'citizen' challenges the current learning agenda that endorses learning for the world of work and for individuals' economic roles but downplays the importance of supporting their learning as they move through changing political roles and shifting political circumstances. By naming 'citizen' this formulation problematises the political outcome that is realised through the contemporary learning agenda, and the education and training policies and practice on which it builds. The idea of the 'learning citizen' questions what kind of citizen is being formed through the contemporary learning agenda.

Turned into a focus for discussion, the idea of the 'learning citizen' can go beyond passively problematising the current learning agenda and provide a context within which the tensions between lifelong 'learning' and 'citizen' can be made explicit and explored. It is an opportunity to re-open the question of how to form the citizens who will be fundamental to the successful operation and protection of Australia's future democracy. In debating this issue, it will be necessary to acknowledge the marginalisation of political education in contemporary education and training, and the limits of education in the 1970s which, perhaps, under-emphasised work-related learning and adults' economic roles. This discussion invites us to explore the different ways of being an active citizen in a globalising world and the contexts in which being an activisit, an entrepreneur, a builder of individual identity and capacity to act, ora developer of social and community capacities serves our democratic politics best. The idea of the 'learning citizen' creates the discursive conditions for an explicit dialogue about the creative tensions between learning and citizenship and puts the place and necessity of economic and political, and social and personal, learning firmly on the contemporary education and training agenda.

There are signs that this dialogue about the purposes of education and its contribution in the national interest is developing. It is evident, for example, in the way practitioners in education and training continue to rub against the grain of education and training policy. Teachers continue to support student learning in ways that help to develop students' sense of social justice, their ability to work together as well as their understanding of the world of work. The IEA Study reported that in 1999 over 90 percent of the practitioner respondees believed that 'teaching civic education at school makes a difference to students' political and civic development' and that it 'matters a great deal for our country' (Table7.13, p.118). This is a widely acknowledged pedagogical imperative that seems to come with teaching as a job, rather than being an ideological position which is held voluntaristically and can be overturned by the appllication of approriate incentives and disincentives. Yet goodwill alone will not be sufficient for Australian teachers in schools, TAFE Institutes and universities to find ways of supporting students to develop appropriate civic knowledge and civic competence. Targeted pre-service training and professional development will be required because, as the IEA study found, less than a third of teachers of 'civic-related' subjects had formal qualifications in civics (Table 7.8, p.110).

The dialogue is also evident in the unwillingness of education policy makers to entirely disregared civics and citizenship education, at least in the schools sector. This has driven the specification of active citizenship as a National Goal, maintained a modest curriculum and professional development agenda via *Discovering Democracy*, and led (unexpectedly) to nationally endorsed learning outcomes in civics and citizenship—a step that gives some teeth to the motherhood idea that we must prepare young people for their civic roles. Yet this wobbly current commitment defines school education as the site where the democratic deficit will be fixed up and absolves other education and training, and other learning sites, from responsibility. While individuals are expected to learn throughout life to support their participation in the workforce, is it enough for governments to just 'front-end-load' education for citizenship through schools? Using national assessment as a driver for educational change is a blunt policy approach. However it may be that the reporting of civic and citizenship achievement outcomes will facilitate the foregrounding of school curriculum audits and increased civics and citizenship education provision in schools. Strong reporting may also drive recommendations for civics and citizenship education in higher education, via teacher education programs. It may even be sufficient to inform, skill and engage young citizens, whose decision-making and active citizenship actions as adults in the future will protect Australian democracy.

Dialogue is also visible in the post-schools sector as education and training institutions struggle to find ways through the policy imperatives driving commercialisation and privatisation that also enable them to realise their established responsibilities to the public good. This work of negotiating government policies in ways that permit institutional survival alongside service to communities keeps alive the commitment to do the public good. It provides a moral and ethical anchorpoint for staff who are subject to persistent change and challenge to their identities. This anchorpoint gives them a basis for identification against which judgements about ethical practices in the 'delivery of goods and services' can be made and from which stronger arguments about the necessity of social and civic, as well as economic, outcomes can be articulated. Rooting practice in moral and political choices also allows staff to recognise the limits of corporate managerialism and to problematise the soft (and sometimes hard) despotism that is the reality of unfettered of managerial prerogative.

Further dialogue is proliferating in the complex joined-up government initiatives aimed at regional development and building community capacity. These initiatives bring education and training providers into networks of cross-portfolio service providers, employers, community agencies and local governments. Participation in these social partnerships demands cross-agency working to address intractable social and economic problems. Such participation brings participants and learners face to face with difference. It encourages the kind of reflexive questioning and fluidity of thinking and acting that sustains learning and a commitment to ethical practices that are fundamental to democratic politics (but which run against the grain of official education and training discourses with their emphasis on promoting closure around particular identities: the national citizen, the A-student, the competent trainee or the skilled and employable worker). Active participation of this kind shows that shared decision-making within rules, guided by democratic politics, is critical in realising the kind of economic outcomes (e.g. employment outcomes for young people) demanded by government resource and accountability regimes. Multi-agency work requires pluralist governance. It needs individuals who have the capacity to act as citizens and the dispositions to participate in decision-making and community building. The lack of individual citizen capacity is as much a stumbling block in these social partnerships as one-eyed government agendas which can only see and value economic outcomes.

The challenge for Australia is to re-call the importance of political learning that leads to social and civic outcomes, as well as economic learning and outcomes. Yet this dialogue must be advanced while Australia basks in a publicly-affirmed self-identity as a successful multicultural nation. We detect a broad fear that the one-eyed government learning agenda focused on economic and human resource development may blind Australia to the fragility of its multiculturalism and the limitations of multiculturalism as a sufficient goal for democratic politics. For, as has been demonstrated in recent social tensions in Australia, living together in tolerant ways provides no protection for our democratic processes.

Challenges for the European learning citizen

Today, globalism and intensified international competition is undercutting the structural and cultural preconditions for citizenship based on the principle of belonging on a world-wide scale. Looking at the experience of Australia—a country recognised for its success in building a multicultural and pluralist democracy—offers some insights into processes of multicultural citizen formation and the contradictions that accompany the idea of a 'learning citizen'.

It seems that multiculturalism and pluralist democracy are enhanced when migrants are admitted to citizenship without stigma. Australia has been more or less selective in terms of admission but, once inside the country, migrants have been able to take up full citizen entitlements. There has been no institutionalised second-class citizens, except our own Indigenous Australians. Meeting people's material needs has helped to forge a sense of being Australian and valuing that identity, although arguably it has encouraged a concern with what the state gives its citizens rather than what citizens do. Reciprocity has more often been a hallmark of Australian citizen engagement in social than in political processes. The implication of these structural and cultural conditions has been to create spaces where people can learn to live together.

Yet these structural and cultural conditions have not created institutional frameworks that extend active citizen engagement and knowledgeable participation in democratic politics. Structural and cultural changes are driving widespread commitments to learning but this is oriented largely to lifelong economic roles and responsibilities that are understood in utilitarian ways, oriented to a narrow conception of productivity, rather than to lifelong long political duties and entitlements. Such learning does little to address the democratic deficit identified in *Whereas the People* and, arguably, has accompanied an erosion of democratic politics in Australia over the last decade. Yet, in a contradictory way, the social, economic and political trajectories that are driving rapid change are also increasing lived confrontation with different cultures, involvement in localised pluralist decision-making and, perhaps, growing grass-roots awareness of the fragility of Australia's democratic achievements and their need for protection. In this contradictory context, the idea of a 'learning citizen' does more than name contemporary practices of citizenship but problematises the processes of citizen formation and the complacent assumption that economically framed learning is sufficient to realise Australia's economic interests and guarantee its status as a democracy.

There are four main conclusions from this Australian case study which we believe can speak back to Europe as it goes about constructing the European Learning Citizen.

As the Australian case suggests, the formation of European citizens depends upon establishing structural and cultural conditions that support inclusion of all those within the framework of Europe. Being a part of a collective agency that supports its members and of which they can feel proud encourages identification with Europe as a supra-national collective agency. Inclusion presents challenges, of course, because the capacity of Europe to integrate all citizens without stigma is already compromised by the conditions attached to membership and by the funding implications of European enlargement. It means that there are different challenges to be faced here, although some Australian strategies (e.g. dual citizenship, transferable pension rights) may offer fruitful leads.

The formation of European citizens will involve negotiation of the diverse traditions and practices of citizenship in different member states with a view to developing distinctive ways of being European citizens. The diversity of democracies within Europe and their different practices and processes are significant resources for this process but only if there can be open dialogue and decision-making about these various models and their implications for processes of citizen formation. The current preoccupation about Europe becoming 'the most competitive and dynamic knowledge-based economy in the world' is a concern in this regard because it suggests policy priorities are oriented towards international competition at the expense of social development rooted in, and building productively on, the culture and traditions of member states. If the Australian case is anything to go by, such policy priorities will drive the TINA principle (There Is No Alternative) in ways that are likely to make open dialogue, pluralist decision-making and distinctive patterns of European cultural development very difficult.

The idea of a 'learning citizen' is paradoxical but also a potentially generative way of approaching the question of European citizen formation. It builds upon the contemporary preoccupations with learning but anchors them in the idea of a citizen with particular identities, dispositions and powers to act within the political sphere. Currently, 'learning' is framed within globalised economic and human resource development policy discourses. It is oriented to human capital formation that emphasises individual benefit and individual preparation for adult economic roles. Approaching the question of citizen formation through the motif of the 'learning citizen' is a way of keeping debates about education and training policies and practices open to, and explicit about, the importance of social and civic outcomes, as well as economic outcomes. There are, of course, no guarantees that this discursive framing will be sufficient to arrest the economising of education and training in Europe, along the lines taken in Australia. However, the diversity of member states and the palpable dangers of not getting European citizen formation right are likely to encourage serious political engagement on this question, although this debate is also vulnerable to the priority of becoming the 'United States of Europe', head to head with the United States of America.

Finally, the kinds of citizen formation that are required in our globalising times is a question that Europe is particularly well placed to address. This is partly because Europe has committed itself to an integrating regional agenda that must grapple with questions of cultural difference, economic inequalities and variable visibilities in terms of symbolic representations. The sheer complexity of Europe, with its different political histories and democratic traditions, and the risks associated with failure, will make it obvious that social and civic outcomes are critically important alongside economic outcomes in education and training. It is hard to imagine Europe endorsing the kind of lifelong learning agenda that has been implemented in Australia. The way Europe will debate these questions about the purposes of education and training in a world where the global and local inflect each other, and where citizens must be prepared as actors within multicultural democracies, will generate resources not only for Europe but also for the rest of the world. For it is important to remember that such resources which can inform policies that support global-local democratic ('post-national') politics, and the learning processes that form citizens who understand and enact their entitlements and duties within the framework of democratic decision-making, are critical not just to the project of European integration but to democratic politics on a global scale.

References

Anderson, B. (1991) *Imagined Communities: Reflections on the Origin and Spread of Nationalism.* London: Verso.

Australian Bureau of Statistics (2004) 'Australian Historical Population Statistics.' http://www.abs.gov.au/ [Accessed 7/6/04].

Axford, B. & Seddon, T. (2005) 'The idea of a learning society: An Australian perspective.' In M.Kuhn & R. Sultana (eds) *The Learning Society in Europe and Beyond.* Frankfurt: Peter Lang. (in press)

Bean, C. (2004) 'Voting and citizenship.' In G. Patmore & G. Junwirth (eds) *The Vocal Citizen.* Melbourne, Australia: Arena.

Beilharz, P. (1994) *Transforming Labor: Labor tradition and the Labor decade in Australia.* Cambridge: Cambridge University Press.

Bhabha, H. (2004) 'Vernacular cosmopolitanism.' Paper presented at the State Library, Melbourne, 11 May 2004.

Castles, F. (1988) *Australian Public Policy and Economic Vulnerability.* Sydney: Allen and Unwin.

Civics Expert Group (1994a) *Whereas the People.* Canberra: Australian Government Publishing Service, http://www.rpdc.tas.gov.au/soer/source/220/index.php [Accessed 7/6/04]

Civics Expert Group (1994b) *Whereas the People: Executive Summary.* Canberra: AGPS.

Connell, R.W. (1995) 'Education as transformative work.' In M.Ginsburg (ed.) *The Politics of Educators Work and Lives.* New York: Garland.

Davidson, A. (1997) *From Subject to Citizen: Australian Citizenship in the Twentieth Century.* Cambridge: Cambridge University Press.

Davidson, A. (2004) 'Citizens and pariahs: Australia faces globalisation.' In G. Patmore & G. Junwirth (eds) *The Vocal Citizen.* Melbourne, Australia: Arena.

DEST (1999) *The Adelaide Declaration: The National Goals for Australian Schools.* http://www.dest.gov.au/schools/adelaide/adelaide.htm [accessed: 7/5/04]

Discovering Democracy (2004) Canberra: Department of Education, Science and Training, http://www.curriculum.edu.au/democracy/ [accessed 7/6/04].

European Council (2000) *Presidency Conclusions, Lisbon European Counci,, 23 and 24 march 2000.* http://ue.eu.int/ueDocs/cms_Data/docs/pressData/en/ec/00100-r1.en0.htm [accessed, 4/6/04].

Evans, K. (1995) 'Competence and citizenship: Towards a complementary model (for times of critical social change).' *British Journal for Education and Work,* Autumn.

Ferguson, L. & Gardiner, W. (2004) 'Fostering Australian citizenship in a changing world'. In G. Patmore & G. Junwirth (eds) *The Vocal Citizen.* Melbourne, Australia: Arena.

Ichilov, D. (1990) *Political Socialization, Citizenship Education and Democracy.* New York: Teachers College Press.

Giddens, A. (1994) *Beyond Left and Right: the Future of Radical Politics.* Cambridge: Polity Press.

Gilbert, R. (ed.) (1996) *Studying Society and Environment.* Melbourne: Jacaranda.

Hannam, D. (1999) 'Schools for democracy: from rhetoric to reality.' *Connect* No. 118, August, Melbourne [contact: r.holdsworth@edfac.unimelb.edu.au].

Kennedy, K. (2000) 'Building civic capacity for a new century: Engaging young people in civic institutions and civic society.' *Asia Pacific Education Review,* Vol.1(1), pp.23-29.

Kenny, S. (2004) 'Non-Government Organisations and contesting active citizenship.' In G. Patmore & G. Junwirth (eds) *The Vocal Citizen.* Melbourne, Australia: Arena.

MaRhea, Z. & Seddon, T. (2004) Negotiating nation: globalisation and knowing.' In E. Zambeta & D. Coulby (eds) *Globalisation and Nationalism, the 2004 World Yearbook.* London: Kogan Page.

Mellor, S. (1995) 'What can history contribute to the development of a citizenship curriculum?' Paper presented at the ACE Civics and Citizenship Education Conference, Melbourne, 16 November 1995.

Mellor, S. (1998) ''What's the Point?' Political Attitudes of Victorian Year 11 Student.' *Australian Council for Educational Research Research Monograph 53,* Melbourne, Australia, ACER Press.

Mellor, S. (2004) 'Solving some civics and citizenship education conundrums.' InSite Newsletter 9. http://www.curriculum.edu.au/democracy/newsletter/current/dd_news.htm

Mellor, S.; Kennedy, K., & Greenwood, L., (2002) *Citizenship and Democracy: Students' Knowledge and Beliefs: Australian Fourteen Year Olds & The IEA Civic Education Study.* Melbourne, Australia: ACER Press.

Mellor, S. & Prior, W. (2004) 'Promoting social tolerance and cohesion in the Solomon Islands and Vanuatu.' In W.O. Lee, D.L. Grossman, K.J. Kennedy & G.P. Fairbrother (eds) *Citizenship Education in Asia and the Pacific: Concepts and Issues*. Comparative Education Research Centre, University of Hong Kong, Kluwer Academic Publishers.

Moisi, D. (2004), quoted in P. Fray, 'Expanding the state of the union.' *The Age*, 1 May 2004, p.8.

Orwell, G. (1964) *Animal Farm: A Fairy Story*. London: Longman.

Prior, W. (1999) 'What it means to be a 'Good Citizen' in Australia: perceptions of teachers, students, and parents.' *Theory and Research in Social Education,* Vol. 27(2), pp.215-247.

Pusey, M. (1992) *Economic Rationalism in Canberra: The Nation-Building State Changes its Mind*. Cambridge, Cambridge University Press.

Pusey, M. (2003) *The Experience of Middle Australia: The Dark Side of Economic Reform*. Cambridge: Cambridge University Press.

Roe, J. (1998) 'The Australian way.' In P. Smyth & B. Cass (eds) *Contesting the Australian Way: States, Markets and Civil Society*. Melbourne: Cambridge University Press.

Ryan, C. (2003) 'Social responsibility and economic rationalism: Consonance and dissonance in Victorian schools.' Unpublished EdD thesis, Monash University, Melbourne, Australia.

Saul, J.R. (1997) *The Unconscious Civilization*. Maryborough, Victoria: Penguin Books

Seddon, T. (2000) 'Capacity-building: Beyond state and market.' *Pedagogy, Culture and Society*, Vol 7, pp. 35-53.

Seddon, T. (2001) 'Exploring capacity-building: From functionalist to political analysis.' *Australia and New Zealand Journal of Vocational Education Research*, Vol.9(2), pp. 61-86.

Seddon, T. & Clemans, A. (2003) 'Understanding new learning spaces.' Paper presented at the European Education Research Conference, Hamburg, September 2003.

Seddon, T. & Billett, S. (2004) *Social Partnerships In Vocational Education and Training: Building Community Capacity*. Adelaide: National Council for Vocational Education Research. http://www.ncver.edu.au/publications/1466.html [Accessed 4/6/04]

Watson, I.; Buchanan, J.; Campbell, I. & Briggs, C. (2003) *Fragmented Futures: New challenges in Working Life*. Sydney: The Federation Press.

Wiseman, J. (2004) 'Broadening and deepening democracy: learning from recent experiments in citizen and community engagement'. In G. Patmore & G. Junwirth (eds) *The Vocal Citizen*. Melbourne, Australia: Arena.

Yeatman, A. (1994) *Postmodern Revisionings of the Political*. New York: Routledge.

CHAPTER ELEVEN

Models of Lifelong Learning and the Knowledge Economy/Society in Europe: What Regional Patterns are Emerging?

ANDY GREEN

Introduction

Lifelong Learning has become the key leitmotif of education policy at the turn of the new Millennium (EC, 2000; OECD, 1996; UNESCO, 1996). As a new and near-universal meta-discourse of policy, it seeks to address the secular trends which in all countries place heavy new demands on education, including those of demographic ageing, increasing cultural pluralism and social diversity and, not least, of the rise of the knowledge-based economy (Green, 2003; OECD, 1996). Within Europe, it has been charged with a major role in achieving the Lisbon Summit goals of making Europe 'the most competitive and dynamic knowledge-based economy in the world capable of sustainable economic growth with more and better jobs and greater social cohesion.' In other words, lifelong learning is seen as crucial for the realization of the so-called knowledge society. However, there are many different visions and models of lifelong learning, just as there are many different visions of the knowledge economy/society.

The union of *les pays* in Europe is also a union of *les regions,* each of which have common and distinctive historical trajectories, cultures, political systems and economies. A long and distinguished tradition of comparative historical and social science has sought to map these European regions in terms of their economies (Braudel, 1992; Leonardi, 1995; Maurice and Sellier, 1986; Piore and Sabel, 1984), welfare regimes (Esping-Andersen, 1990), geo-political systems (Mackinder, 1969; Rokkan, 1968, 1970) and citizenship concepts

(Brubaker, 1992; Kohn, 1982). In this chapter we seek to identify whether there are distinctive models of lifelong learning within the western European states and whether these follow regional patterns.[1]

A quantitative approach to this question would ideally identify and measure the key characteristics for each of the countries and test statistically whether these correlated with given geographical regions. It is not easy to do this, however, due to the small number of country and regional units involved. The analysis here, therefore, is conducted through a qualitative comparative logical approach with statistics used, in the main, merely for descriptive purposes. The approach in the first instance is to identify the key systemic characteristics that vary across countries and regions and to ascertain whether there are sets of characteristics which are common to countries in certain regions and different from those in countries in other regions. We do this along four dimensions. The first of these concerns the visions and objectives of lifelong learning in different countries; the second, the institutional architecture of the formal education systems; the third, the typical characteristics of curriculum and assessment; and the fourth, the modes of regulation of the systems as a whole. We then consider the educational outcomes of the lifelong learning systems on various measures for which we have data and how these may relate to some of the major aggregate measures of social and economic characteristics of states.

The final section will provide a preliminary comparative socio-historical explanation of some of the major regional differences as we have found them. The procedure is inevitably broad brush: we are not only looking at systems as whole, i.e. from 'cradle to the grave,' even where in many cases these are very diverse and seem to lack the internal coherence associated with the notion of 'system'; we are also seeking to identify ideal typical features which may be of use in generating hypotheses for future cross-national and cross-regional comparative work.

Visions of lifelong learning

Lifelong learning implies the distribution of learning opportunities throughout the lifetime; the Knowledge Society implies that these opportunities should be available to all and occur in all areas of society, from the school and college, to the home, the community and the workplace (Green, 2000). These notions have become fashionable for good reasons. Rapid changes in technology and work organization mean that more people will be required to have high levels of skill and to undertake re-training continuously throughout their working lives. Increased leisure time for adults, won through shorter working hours or enforced through unemployment, allows new opportunities for formal and informal learning and creates demand for education at different phases of the life cycle. Longer life expectancy and the ageing of populations, mean that more active retirees are seeking stimulation through new forms of learning. These greater demands for learning opportunities cannot be met entirely by the existing institutions for formal learning, nor need they be. Information technology makes possible a variety of new modes and sites for learning (OECD, 1996).

So much is common in the new rhetoric shared by policy-makers across the developed world. However, beyond this there is little agreement. Visions of lifelong learning and the knowledge economy/society differ markedly in both ends and means. In some versions the main objective is individual development and improved quality of life; in others it is the promotion of social equality and social cohesion; most commonly, perhaps, it is enhanced productivity and national economic competitiveness. There is equal divergence in the policy maps for achieving the economy/knowledge society. Some stress the role of the market and the responsibility of the individual; some advocate multiple stake-holding and social partnership; others, although increasingly rarely, advocate the central role of the state in orchestrating and managing the learning society. The outcomes of these different models would, of course, be highly divergent—as varied, in fact, as are the current systems of education and training across the developed countries.

General policy documents and commentaries on lifelong learning and the learning society rarely fall into neat and distinctive categories. More often they display, overtly or covertly, different emphases which might, when implemented as specific policies in particular contexts, yield substantially different results. It is easy enough to identify, say, the OECD's *Lifelong Learning for All* (1996) as a text which gives substantial emphasis to economic competitiveness and the role of markets in lifelong learning provision. Equally, one could cite from the contemporaneous UNESCO report, *Learning—the Treasure Within* (UNESCO 1996), as one which gives pride of place to considerations of life quality, social cohesion and equity and which sees lifelong learning as above all a matter of public responsibility. However, clearly both pay tribute to the multiple goals and means normally associated with the rhetoric of lifelong learning. For the purposes of analysis, however, it is useful to construct some ideal-typical models, even if they do not correspond precisely to any particular policy position. These models, differentiated according to their core organizational principles, represent positions along a continuum.

At one extreme there is the market-led model which conceives of the learning society as a grass-roots, demand-led efflorescence of new opportunities, networks and partnerships, facilitated by new technologies and driven by the market. In this model the individual takes primary responsibility for his or her own learning and governments limit their roles largely to advocacy and 'steering'. Organizations recognize their interest in developing learning environments, and invest in them to a degree which is commensurate with the benefits they deliver for them. At the other extreme is the state-led model which gives the key role to the state as the organizer and principal funder of lifelong learning. This model rejects the market approach as leading to under-investment and inequality. Instead of leaving the market to make the key decisions about how much should be invested in what, it accords public authorities with key roles in planning and regulation in the interests of the overall public good. In between there is another possible model, based on social partnership, which recognizes the importance of individual responsibility and also advocates multiple agency, diverse stake-holding and maximal use of new learning technologies. However, it differs from the first in placing greater stress on the limitations of the market and the importance of regulation (Green, 2003).

Looking across the different states of Europe now, one would be hard put to assign countries or regions to any of these different models on the basis of their lifelong learning vision statements, since most of these now share the common *patina* of international education speak on lifelong learning goals. There are clearly some countries, such as the UK, which would appear to place the main emphasis on achieving economic competitiveness and which accentuate the role of the market in achieving this. There are others, such as the Nordic states, which tend to emphasize the role of lifelong learning in generating social cohesion, and where the state would appear to be still seen as the main actor. However, official policy documents will usually combine reference to a variety of means and objectives and can be hard to differentiate in terms of their rhetorics. We have therefore not sought here to do a reading of the various policy statements across Europe. The meta-visions referred to above can serve as a lode star for our further analysis but the most important road map will be actual policies, structures and processes, rather than policy visions. The next section therefore deals with these.

Institutional structures

The state plays the major role in the provision of formal education through compulsory schooling and higher education all across western Europe. In most countries, there are, in addition, a number of private fee-charging primary and secondary schools. These are usually subsidized by the state and are required to follow national curricula and other standards regulations, but they exist in the main to provide specialist forms of schooling based on religion or philosophical principles, as with the Steiner and Waldorf schools. There are some exceptional countries in this regard. Denmark and Germany, for instance, have only a very few of these quasi-public schools, whilst in the Netherlands they make up the majority. In England, on the other hand, where the private sector is no more numerically dominant than the average, the private schools are fully independent, having neither direct state subsidies nor requirements to follow the national curriculum. These differences can be important, and most certainly are in the case of the exceptionally elitist, so-called 'public schools' in England. However, private schooling does not form the predominant part of lifelong learning systems anywhere and this analysis consequently focuses on the public sector provision. The most obvious differences between countries in institutional structures lie in the state sectors and these can be examined phase by phase, starting with the secondary schools, since less variation is to be found in primary schools.

Public sector primary education is provided in all western European states in comprehensive institutions which recruit on a neighbourhood basis. They vary according to whether they are secular or denominationally organised and differ in curricula aims and pedagogic methods, but the basic institutional structure is fairly invariant. Lower secondary education, however, shows some marked structural differences across countries. In the majority of EU states now lower secondary schools are organised on a comprehensive, largely non-selective basis. School choice operates for these schools in some countries, most notably in the UK and the Netherlands, but also in more limited ways in France and Sweden and elsewhere, which means that school may be operating a degree of covert selection in admissions, but these comprehensive schools are still largely non-selective and recruit mostly on a neighbourhood basis (OECD, 1994).

These types of schools vary according to how far they track their students internally. Most countries operate some form of setting in the core subjects, such as Maths and the national language, and some countries, notably in the Mediterranean region, have grade repeating, so that children progress at different speeds up through the grade system. However, there are a number of countries, including all the Nordic states, which have largely abolished all forms of internal selection. These are also the countries, uniquely in Europe, which have all through primary and lower secondary schools, so that children stay with the same class and often the same form teachers throughout their compulsory education. These differences are significant as we shall argue below. The major differences in Europe, however, are between these largely comprehensive systems and those which remain selective on the basis of ability.

Only a few states have retained selective lower and upper secondary schooling in the state sector. These include Austria, Belgium, Germany, Northern Ireland, Luxembourg, the Netherlands (predominantly) and German-speaking Switzerland—all countries geographically proximate to Germany and subject to its historical influence except the one outlier: the province of Northern Ireland in the UK. In the German model, which its neighbouring states follow closely, children are tracked at the end of the primary level into different types of school—the academic *Gymnasium*, the vocationally-oriented academic *Realschule* and the general, less academic, *Hauptschule*. Only a small proportion go to comprehensive *Gesamtschule* which by law can only exist alongside the other forms of selective school. Constitutionally, parents in Germany have the right to choose the kind of school their children go to, but after the orientation phase children are reassigned to schools at other levels if there performance is not at the standard of the chosen school, so this system is *de facto* selective by ability (Green, Wolf and Leney, 1999; Weiss, 1993).

This regional differentiation in lower secondary institutional structures is reproduced to some extent in the patterns for upper secondary provision. Broadly speaking we can identify three main types of upper secondary organisation (OECD, 1986). The most common type within western Europe now involves a predominance of school- or college-based provision in differentiated, dedicated public institutions, some of which specialize in academic education and others in vocational provision. France and the Mediterranean states mostly follow this pattern, as do most Nordic states and the UK, although the UK is more mixed than most having retained 11-18 secondary schools along side dedicated upper secondary schools and colleges. Countries vary in the degree to which their upper secondary institutions articulate with one another. Some have general or polytechnical vocational schools (like Denmark, England and Scotland) and some have mainly monotechnic vocational schools, as in France and other Mediterranean states. In France, for instance, the upper secondary sector includes the general *lycée*, the *lycée technique* and sectorally differentiated *lycées professionnels*, as well as some *lycées polyvalents* and an apprentice training route (Wolf and Rapiau, 1993). However, there is a degree of integration between the curricula in the programmes in the different institutions ensured by the common structure of *baccalauréat* exams.

The second type of upper secondary organisation is represented by the comprehensive high school system. This was originally developed in the USA, but has only one examplar in Europe—the Swedish *Gymnsieskola* which incorporates the academic general programmes and the vocational programmes within one institution, albeit that this may be multi-sited (Boucher, 1982).

The major distinction within western European states however, is between these school-based systems and those which are predominantly apprenticeship-based. Several countries, particularly in northern Europe, have retained a residual apprentice sector, but there are only a handful where the sector recruits the majority of the post-compulsory population who then receive a combination of employment-based learning and vocational school tuition, as in the German Dual System (CEDEFOP, 1995; Green, Wolf and Leney, 1999). These countries (and regions in countries) include: Austria, Germany, German-speaking Switzerland and Denmark (although here the apprenticeship is a hybrid system which includes trainees receiving work-experience but who are college-based in the *Erhvervs Faglige Grunduddannelser* system). It is notable that several of the countries that have retained this distinctive form of apprentice training as the main mode of transition from school to work are also the countries which have retained selective lower secondary schooling.

The institutional structures of higher education in western European countries vary in a number of ways (Teichler, 1993; Teichler and Sadlak, 2000). One of these concerns the staging and length of undergraduate degrees. England and Wales, for instance have three year bachelor degrees as the predominant undergraduate level, followed by one or two year Masters degrees, and doctorates for a minority of students. Many other countries in Europe have longer undergraduate course with the Masters as the main qualification level, although there may be other staging posts along the way (Green, Wolf and Leney, 1999). This difference between countries may, however, erode as countries adapt through the Bologna process to the Anglo-Saxon model. The major differences in institutional structures are between those countries which have more or less unified higher education systems (i.e. with one type of university institution), such as Italy, Sweden and the UK since 1992, and those countries which have binary structures of general, long-cycle universities and short-cycle polytechnics with more specialist vocational degrees. The German and Austrian *Fachhochschulen* represent a common model of the latter, but similar kinds of binary system exist in Belgium, Greece, Ireland, the Netherlands, Portugal, Spain. Some countries have even greater institutional diversity, including Denmark and France. In the latter there are general long-cycle universities, *Instituts Universitaires de Technologie* (IUTs) offering two year courses (Teichler, 1993) as well as the élite *Grandes Écoles* and other small *Écoles Specialisés*. Specialist research institutes, such as the *Collège de France* and the INRS also exist here (Green, Wolf and Leney, 1999, p.211, Figure 5.2). There is little obvious regional patterning in these country variations for higher education, although the German-speaking speaking states are again notable for having a common model.

Non-university adult education and training tends to be very diverse in every country and rarely can be said to constitute of system as such. Most countries have some level of public provision for leisure and interest-oriented general adult education, as well as special vocational programmes for skills upgrading or re-training for those facing redundancy or already unemployed. In most countries the majority of adult training takes place in the workplace, as far as we can tell from surveys such as the EU's Continuing Vocational Training Survey (CVTS—see European Commission, 2002). There are distinctive arrangements in certain areas, such as the long Grundvig-inspired tradition of state-subsidized *Folkschuler* in Denmark and its equivalents in other Scandinavian states. These residential institutions for adults, which seek to provide general education for enlightenment and social solidarity, are fairly specific to the Scandinavian countries, although trade union organised residential schools can be found in the UK and other countries. Together with the other state-funded adult education and training institutions in these countries they represent a high level publicly provided and largely free adult education and training, probably not equalled in other regions (OCED, 2000, 2003 unpublished) and may be said to represent a distinctive regional characteristic. Another distinctive phenomenon is extensive legal entitlement to adult training (including paid training leave etc) which exists in France, Italy, Spain and elsewhere (Green, Hodgson and Sakamoto, 2000). The institutional basis of provision here varies, although social-partner or state-based training levies often form a common financial underpinning.

Curriculum and assessment

Historians and comparative educationalists use a variety of typologies to differentiate between the broad cultural traditions in the major regions of Europe, stereo-typically represented as universalism in France and southern Europe, cultural particularism in Germany and the German-speaking states, communitarian solidarism in Scandinavia and liberal individualism in the UK and Ireland (Green, 1990; Lauglo, 1990; McLean, 1990). A common Greco-Roman legacy and the impact of the French Enlightenment and Revolution are seen as constitutive of the typically state-centred and integrative notion of citizenship and nationality in France and some of the states influenced by it (Brubaker, 1992). This in turn is seen to antecede the strongly assimilationist notion of culture and the encyclopaedic/rationalist knowledge traditions which are visible in education (McLean, 1990). In Germany, and to some extent in other German-speaking countries, different histories have led to ethno-cultural rather than primarily political notions of citizenship and nationhood which have been associated with more particularistic cultural traditions and more differentionist tendencies within education (Brubaker, 1992; McLean, 1990). Liberalism in England and its influence across the British Isles, is, on the other hand, associated with philosophical empiricism and traditions of knowledge specialisation and individualised, child-centred pedagogy (Green, 1990; McLean, 1990).

Curriculum and assessment systems are far too specific and culturally particular to be assigned simple classifications across Europe. However, the broad regional differences in knowledge traditions are manifest in some of the more obvious curriculum and assessment variations across Europe. In terms of the curriculum, France and the Mediterranean states (excluding Malta) do generally maintain an encyclopaedic approach through to the end of upper secondary schooling. This is apparent in the range of subjects followed by students right through to matriculation, which typically includes, at the upper end, not only one or more specialist subjects but also core studies in Maths, the national language and civics, all of which must be passed to gained a matriculation certificate. This embodies a commitment to imparting what the French call *culture générale* which is seen there and elsewhere as a crucial part of general citizenship formation (Green, 1998). Significantly, the requirement is extended to those studying vocational courses which often include general subjects as up to fifty per cent of the curriculum.

At the other end of the spectrum are the English-speaking and German speaking countries where upper secondary education is typically far more specialised. In the German speaking countries the academic *Abitur* exam allows students to choose two major subjects, but a core curriculum is also required, as it is in the programmes leading to vocational certification. In England, the specialisation is taken further with currently no requirements for students taking a core taught curriculum in either general academic (AS and A2s), the general vocational (AVCE) or the vocational programmes (National Vocational Qualifications). This unusual degree of specialisation will change if new proposals are adopted for an English baccalaureate type system at the upper secondary level (Green and Evans, 2005), but to date it has been a long-standing feature of the system. Specialisation on degree programmes is also more pronounced in England than in most other countries in Western Europe.

Qualification systems vary in their details substantially from country to country, but there is a sense in which they can be ranged along an axis which corresponds to the universalistic/integrative—particularistic/differentiated axis in knowledge traditions and curricula. At one end of the continuum one would have integrated national qualification systems. Here most programmes at given level would lead to a common, overarching (albeit usually sub-divided) qualification and would share certain common requirements such as reaching a given standard in Maths and other core subjects. At the other end of the scale one would have a more laissez-faire situation where there were diverse qualifications at each level with no integrating components or common titles to diplomas. On these criteria France (with the *Baccalauréat*) and Spain (with the *bachillerato*) would be at the more integrative end of the spectrum and England, Malta, Northern Ireland and the German-speaking countries at the more differentiated and particularistic end. Sweden, although less so the other Nordics, would probably also come at the more universalistic and integrative end since all matriculating upper secondary students gain a certificate which entitles university entry (although not to any subject since the *numerous clausus* often applies in popular subjects).

Regulation and governance

Regulation and governance has probably been the area where there has been the most intensive policy reform activity worldwide in education over the past twenty years and Europe has been affected by this also. Lifelong Learning involves both formal and informal learning, and clearly not all areas of the latter are as intensely regulated as the former, but nor are they totally exempt. Although it is difficult to talk of a single system of regulation for lifelong learning in any country, since different sectors are typically regulated in different ways, it is not inappropriate to consider the characteristics of systems in a summative way.

Generally, the recent tendency across Europe has been for Governments to seek to increase the efficiency and responsiveness of formal educational provision by devolving more power and decision-making for its operational parts from central government to lower levels. Lower level authorities, including provider institutions themselves, may be given more autonomy over educational processes and more control of budget allocation so that they can determine the most efficient means to meet demand and to realise government objectives. This form of 'steering by goals,' now widely endorsed by many governments, is generally considered to represent a net decentralisation of power, but it generally also involves increased central government regulation of qualifications, standards and performance monitoring. Another widespread tendency has been to try to improve the performance of educational providers through generating more competition, either by shifting some provision into the private sector or by introducing quasi-market relations in to the public sector. The two tendencies are often connected but by no means identical. We can envisage differences in modes of regulation along two axes. One represents the level at which state authority is exercised in the public sector. The other represents the overall relation between the public and private or state and civil society (Green, 2000). The general tendency, therefore, can be see as a shift along the one axis from central to local and institutional control, and along the other, from state to market. However, despite the secular trend, countries are still very differently positioned along these two axes in terms of how the different parts of their lifelong learning systems are regulated.

In the school and higher education sectors in western Europe there has been relatively little movement along the state-civil society axis overall, in the sense that not much of the provision has actually been privatised. However, there has been a marked tendency in some countries to introduce competition and market forces into the public sector through such measures as school choice and diversification and, in higher education, performance-based funding for research. Increased testing of students and evaluation of institutions can also been seen as part of this trend in as much as results are published to provide information for markets to function. In terms of changes along the other axis, power has been devolved from the centre to the level of the elected regional authority (regionalisation), to the regional arm of the central state (deconcentration), to the local or municipal authority (localisation) or to the institutions themselves. In most cases each level maintains some powers but the balance of power between levels has shifted (Green, Wolf and Leney, 1999). So much for the general direction of change. In comparative terms, however, there are still marked differences between countries according to where they lie along each axis, and these differences tend to be regionally patterned.

France and the southern European states remain the most centralised and the least affected by marketization at the school level. France, Italy and Spain have each introduced a measure of devolution to the regions. In all cases this has been through a combination of regionalisation and deconcentration so that regional powers are shared between regional authorities and regional branches of the central ministry. Greece, Luxembourg and Portugal remain highly centralised. The Mediterranean states still mostly employ and pay teachers as civil servants, in France, Italy and Greece, for instance, still posting them to their schools through central procedures. This places severe limitations on degree of institutional autonomy since institutions neither hire, evaluate, nor fire the teachers and since teacher pay, which forms the major part of education budgets, cannot therefore be devolved to the level of the school. School competition policies are also limited in most of these states. Institutional diversification has generally not proceeded far within the compulsory education systems since the emphasis is still on standardisation and uniformity. School choice has been introduced in some areas but only in a limited way in most cases. In France for instance, where there is a right in many regions for parents to express a preference for a particular lower secondary college within their catchment area, this preference is not always granted since parental rights have to be balanced against the responsibility of the local authorities to ensure that overall provision and general public interest is not damaged by the exercise of choice, as for instance if a parental desires to exit a school would make that school unviable or less effective (OECD, 1994).

German-speaking countries, and others proximate to them, show the same limitations as the Mediterranean states in terms of market mechanisms and but tend to follow a regional model rather than the more centralised, statist model prevalent in southern Europe. Germany has a federal system which gives the *Lander* legal powers over schools. Austria and German speaking Switzerland are also partly federalised, although to a lesser extent than Germany. Belgium has adopted a complex system of devolving regulatory powers to its different language communities. The Nordic states, with the exception of Denmark, used to have rather centralised systems, but they have now generally moved towards a more localised model of control. In some cases, and particularly in Sweden, there has been an effort to introduce a measure of school choice and diversification, at least in the large urban areas, but the vast majority of children across the Nordic countries still attend their local comprehensive school (OECD, 1994). The all-through system of primary/lower secondary schooling common to all Nordic countries removes the issue of secondary school choice for most parents since children simply continue in their existing school when they reach secondary age (Green and Wiborg, 2004).

The UK (particularly England) and the Netherlands are the two states that have gone furthest in introducing market principles into the school systems, having both introduced a wide degree of school specialisation and choice. England represents the largest contrast to the other regions of Europe in this case because here it is the schools themselves which hire, fire and pay the teachers and which therefore spend the vast majority of the education budget— currently over eighty five per cent. School autonomy in operational matters in England is such that school heads often now regard themselves chief executives of mini-enterprises. In both England and the Netherlands institutional autonomy and quasi-marketization of schooling are seen as part and parcel of the same movement. However, this does not mean that they can be regarded as falling unproblematically in the institutional autonomy/quasi-marketised quadrant in Figure 1 below because as schools have gained greater operational autonomy they have also been subject to ever increasing central bureaucratic control in terms of quality control and performance evaluation. With the introduction of a national curriculum for the first time in 1988 in England, and with increasing government intervention in standards through testing regimes and reforms in the qualification systems, governments have greatly increased control over the main drivers of the system, so that the shift has been both towards institutional and central control.

Adult training systems are regulated rather differently from school systems in all countries, not least because the majority of adult training is employment-based and therefore largely employer-controlled in most cases. However, adult skills training is subject to state interventions and the forms and degree of interventions do differ quite markedly between states. Whereas one can still apply the same axis as regards level of control for those parts within the public sector, the state/civil society continuum needs to be considered in a more nuanced way here. The two extremes—entirely state systems and entirely private systems—do not in fact exist in any state. The differences tend to be in the middle range of the continuum between countries (like England) which have what one might a 'voluntary partnership' or network model of provision, countries, like most of those in the southern Europe, which have a kind of state-coordinated social partnership model, and those in the German-speaking and Nordic regions which have what one might call 'formalised' social partnership systems.

In the formalised social partnership model most adult training is provided by employers (although in the Nordic countries there are also very substantial state-funded training programmes for the unemployed). Provision is coordinated and regulated by elaborate systems of corporatist intermediation by the social partners—the employer representatives and the employee representatives—in conjunction with their educational partners. The systems are formalised through national regulations and national social partner bodies coordinated under the aegis of the state (like the BIBB in Germany which sets the detailed standards for apprenticeship occupation). The degree of formal regulation varies from country to country, but for the most part these systems rely on cooperation through agreements reached by the social partners in the different sectors. Sectoral labour market agreements may cover qualification requirements and pay for different occupations, which impact on the supply and demand of training (as in most of the countries in the region); they may involve rights to paid training leave or for training prior to redundancy (as in Sweden); and in some countries, like Denmark, they involve sectoral levies on employers for training. In most cases employer representatives and employee representatives have the major say in bodies which set standards for qualifications and training in the different occupations (Green, Hodgson and Sakamoto, 2000). France and the Mediterranean states often have similar sector agreements as the above which will provide the framework for adult training. However, social partnership in these states is generally less developed, particularly outside of France, since the employer and employee organisations are less encompassing and less organised. In the absence of such effective social partnership arrangements one therefore often finds greater involvement by the state with formalised legal requirements on firms to train and rights for employees for training (e.g. the entitlement to paid training leave in France and Italy). The training levies on firms for training in France and Spain, for instance, are enshrined in national law, and substantially controlled by the state, particularly in Spain.

England stands in marked contrast to both of the models above. Social partnership in labour market matters is very weak and government intervention in work-based training minimal. Few sectors have agreements on qualifications and pay for occupations or training rights for individual employees (Brown, Green and Lauder, 2001). There are no statutory rights for adults to receive training at work and training levies only operate in two sectors. Employers have been forcefully opposed to such regulation in the past and trade union powers were so weakened by legislation in the Thatcher years that they play little role such bodies as there are, such as the standard setting bodies, which play a role in regulating training. Employment training in the UK generally is largely on a voluntaristic basis which leaves employers to make their own business decisions in relation to training. However, governments have been keen in recent years to encourage employer initiatives in this area and have done this by facilitating networks in different sectors and by institutions voluntary partnership bodies such as the local lifelong learning partnerships. It is also likely in the future that the local Learning and Skills Councils, the state bodies which fund post-compulsory education, and the state organised Regional Development Associations, will play an increasing role in coordinating actions between the social partners on training (DFES, 2003). Hence it is right to term this model a voluntary partnership or network model rather than a purely voluntaristic market model.

Modes of regulation in lifelong learning systems do vary considerably according to region. The Mediterranean states (plus Luxembourg) tend to be the most centralised and to adopt state coordinated models of social partner control in adult training. The Nordic countries and the countries in the German-speaking areas tend to locate control more at the federal or local areas and to adopt formalised systems of social partnership control in adult training. The UK and the Netherlands are the most decentralised in terms of the levels of institutional control (although centralised as regards standards setting) and, in the English case, adopt a voluntarist or network model of partnership in adult training (Brown, Green and Lauder, 2001).

The levels of spending on education and the sources from which it derives are also to some extent regionally patterned, at least as regards the Nordic and Mediterranean states. As Figure 2 below shows, total spending on education as a proportion of GDP tends to be high in the Nordic states, middling in the

FIGURE 1: *Models of Regulation*

State	State-led SP	Formalised SP	Voluntary Partnership	Market
State..Civil Society				
Centralized	LUXEMBOURG GREECE PORTUGAL FRANCE	AUSTRIA		
Regionalized	ITALY SPAIN	GERMANY BELGIUM		
Localized	SWEDEN NORWAY	FINLAND DENMARK		
Institutionalized			NETHERLANDS	UK

German speaking states and low to middle in the Mediterranean and English-speaking states. The proportion of total spending coming from private sources is low in Nordic and Mediterranean states but there is little regional patterning for the English-speaking and German-speaking states. The fact that the Nordic and Mediterranean states have high proportions of total educational expenditure coming from public sources accords with their relatively state-centric, non-marketized modes of regulation.

Learning outcomes: How far do data on outcomes in education show regional patterns of variation?

Enrolment in upper secondary education and training is high in most developed countries now, at least for the first year or two after graduation from lower secondary education, so there is not much variation in total participation rates for 16 years olds. However, we can find more variation in the distribution of enrolment between types of programme and in the rates of graduation from upper secondary. Using OECD data (OECD, 2001) for the distribution of upper secondary enrolments by types of programme in 1999, we find substantial differences between countries where most of the participation is in general academic type programmes and others where it is mainly in vocational programmes.

FIGURE 2: Spending on Education 1999

	Total spending as % of GDP	% from private sources
Denmark	7.2	5.0
Korea	7.0	43.0
Norway	6.9	2.0
Iceland	6.9	–
Sweden	6.8	3.0
USA	6.4	25.0
Austria	6.4	6.0
Canada	6.2	19.0
France	6.2	8.0
Switzerland	5.9	9.0
Portugal	5.7	1.0
Germany	5.5	22.0
Australia	5.5	25.0
Spain	5.3	17.0
Belgium (Fl)	4.7	–
Italy	5.0	5.0
UK	4.9	9.0
Japan	4.7	25.0
Ireland	4.7	10.0
Netherlands	4.6	7.0

From: OECD, *Education at a Glance*, 2001, p. 24, Summary of Indicators.

In terms of regional clusterings, Germany and proximate states follow a distinctive pattern of vocational predominance in upper secondary programmes, with Austria, Belgium, Switzerland, Germany and the Netherlands having only between 22 and 35 percent of total enrollees in general programmes. The Nordic states also form a cluster in the middle of the rank ordering with Denmark, Finland, Norway, Sweden and Iceland having between 46 and 67 per cent in general programmes. The two Asian states, Japan and Korea, have a relatively high proportion of upper secondary enrollees in general programmes. The other regional/cultural groupings do not show any clear pattern because only two English-speaking countries are in the table and since the Mediterranean states are quite disparate on this measure.

Graduation rates from upper secondary level education (figure four) show some degree of clustering for some regions but not others. The Asian States, Japan and Korea, both have high rates of graduation. The Nordic states, including Denmark, Finland, Iceland and Sweden, fall in the upper middle

FIGURE 3: *Enrolment in General upper Secondary Programmes as Proportion of Total Enrolments in Public and Private Upper Secondary Programmes, 1999*

Canada	91.8
Ireland	70.4
Portugal	75.0
Greece	74.2
Japan	73.6
Spain	68.8
Iceland	67.2
Korea	62.1
Sweden	49.9
Finland	46.8
Denmark	46.7
Norway	46.4
France	42.4
Luxembourg	36.3
Germany	35.4
Italy	35.3
Sweden	36.4
Switzerland	34.6
Belgium	34.3
Netherlands	33.4
UK	33.3
Austria	22.1

Source: OECD (2001) *Education at a Glance* p. 145, Table C2.1

range of the rankings. For states in the German region, Germany and the Netherlands have high rates of graduation, while Belgium and Switzerland are average and Luxembourg is low. The Mediterranean states, excepting France, are all in the lower half of the rankings.

Participation in adult continuing education and training shows stronger regional patterns. According to data from the *International Adult Literacy Survey* (IALS), the Nordic states have the highest rates of participation, Denmark, Finland, Sweden, and Norway being in the top four positions in the country rankings out of 17 states. The English speaking countries fall in the middle of the rankings, while the Mediterranean and German areas are not well enough represented to draw any conclusions. The average Nordic participation rate is about 14 percentage points higher (53 versus 39) than that of a group of English Speaking countries including Australia, New Zealand, the United states and the UK. (see Rubenson, unpublished).

FIGURE 4: Upper Secondary Graduates Rates 1999: Ratio of Upper Secondary Graduates in Public and Private Institutions to Total Population at Typical Age of Graduation

Japan	95
Germany	92
Netherlands	92
Korea	91
Denmark	90
Finland	89
Ireland	86
France	85
Belgium (FL)	83
Switz	83
Iceland	82
US	78
Sweden	74
Italy	73
Spain	73
Greece	67
Luxembourg	60

Source: OECD, 2001, p. 146, Table C2.2

In terms of achievement levels, IALS also shows that there are very clear regional patterns, at least with regard to the Nordic and English-Speaking countries which belong to the only regional/cultural groupings well enough represented to make a judgement. The average scores for Nordic countries, as shown in figure five, are amongst the highest of all the 22 countries on all the measures of literacy and numeracy. For prose literacy Denmark, Finland, Norway and Sweden had average scores in country rank position 1, 2, 3 and 8 respectively. For document literacy their averages were the highest (Sweden - 1; Norway -2; Denmark - 3; Finland - 4) for all countries. Their averages were also amongst the highest in numeracy (Sweden – 1; Denmark – 2; Norway – 4; Finland – 7).

By contrast the English-speaking countries, with the exception of Canada, all had averages in the bottom half of the country rankings on all measures. For prose literacy rank positions were: New Zealand - 7; Australia - 9; US - 10; UK - 13 and Ireland - 14. For document literacy the ranking were: Australia - 11; New Zealand - 14; US - 15; UK - 16 and Ireland - 17. For numeracy (the quantitative literacy scale) the rankings were: Australia - 12; US - 13; New Zealand - 15; UK - 17; and Ireland - 18 Germany and the Netherlands had

FIGURE 5: *Proportion of 16-65 Year Olds Participating in Adult Education and Training during the Previous Year 1994 – 1998*

Country	Total Participation Rate*	Mean Number Hours per Adult**
Finland	56.8	121.2
Denmark	55.7	122.2
Sweden	52.5	–
Norway	47.9	114.9
New Zealand	47.5	135.0
UK	43.9	93.9
Switzerland	39.7	58.6
US	39.7	67.4
Canada	37.7	115.1
Netherlands	37.4	90.6
Slovenia	31.9	67.3
Czech Rep	25.5	42.7
Ireland	24.3	115.1
Belgium (FL)	21.2	27.4
Hungary	19.3	36.1
Chile	18.9	49.2
Portugal	14.2	–
Poland	13.9	20.8

Source: *OECD, 2000, p. 153, Table 3.11.*

* Full-time students aged 16-24 and people who obtained less than 6 hours of training are excluded. ** Mean number of hours per adult = Mean number of hours per participant x participation rate/ 100

average scores on all measures in the middle of the top half of rankings. Switzerland's average scores are in the middle on all.

Equality of outcomes

Differences between regions in degrees of dispersal of literacy scores are also very marked in the IALS survey. In terms of the range between the 5th and the 95th percentiles of scores, across the three measures, the Nordic countries all fall into a group which OECD classify as having 'consistently small' dispersal in scores. Canada, the UK and the US fall into the group classified as having 'consistently large' dispersal, although Australia and New Zealand have 'consistently moderate or varying' degrees of dispersal. Countries in the German region, however, do not fit a regional pattern. Germany and the Netherlands are classified as 'consistently small', but Switzerland and Belgium are classified as 'moderate or varying' (OECD, 2000, p. 14).

High levels of inequality in outcomes in the English-speaking states compared with low levels in the Nordic states are also reflected in the measures for socio-economic gradients which show the impact of parental education on individual outcomes. The OECD group countries according to the steepness of the gradient for document literacy scores of the population aged 16-25. Australia, Canada, Ireland, New Zealand, UK and US all have gradients of a similar steepness with an average gap of 30 percentage points in the scores of an average young person whose parents had eight years of schooling and someone whose parents had twelve years of schooling (OECD, 2000, p. 30). By contrast the four Nordic countries all have a much shallower gradient. The OECD gloss that: 'The striking degree of homogeneity in these results [for the Nordics] points to the existence of a degree of commonality in Nordic approaches to education and society.' (p. 32).

Similar regional clustering on country education inequality measures can be found in the data from the *Programme for International Student Assessment* (PISA). PISA tested 15 year olds in reading and mathematical and scientific literacy in 28 OECD and 4 non-OECD countries in 2000 (OECD, 2001b). Taking a basic standard deviation measure of skills dispersal (averaging the standard deviations for the three tests conducted in reading, mathematical and scientific literacy), we find that the most unequal of the 22 advanced states in the sample are (in descending order) Belgium, Germany, New Zealand, the US and Switzerland (with the UK coming soon after). The most equal (in descending order) are Korea, Finland, Japan, Canada and Ireland.

The alternative measure of inequality, based on the strength of social inheritance (in terms of parental wealth, occupation, education, and cultural capital combined) in educational outcomes, suggests a similar country patterning. The advanced states where social inheritance appears to have the greatest impact are: Germany, Switzerland, UK, USA, Belgium, France, Australia and New Zealand. The countries where the effect is least are: Korea, Japan, Italy, Spain, Sweden, Canada, the Netherlands, Greece, Finland and Norway (OECD, 2001, Table 8.1). The country groupings are similar again. East Asian and Nordic states tend to predominate amongst the more education equal countries. Anglo-Saxon countries and countries in the region proximate to Germany tend to be most unequal.

Breaking down the social inheritance syndrome into the separate effects of parental wealth and occupation, also repeats the pattern. Parental wealth has the highest impact on USA, Luxembourg, New Zealand, Portugal and Germany, and the lowest effect in the Netherlands, Japan, Finland, Italy, and Norway. Parental occupational status has the strongest effect in Germany, Switzerland,

Luxembourg, Portugal, the UK and Belgium, and the lowest in Korea, Finland, Canada and Italy. The only change to the pattern here is that Portugal has found itself in the more unequal group of countries.

The patterns above suggest regional affinities in terms of levels of educational equality. The Nordic countries form one rather well delineated group. The English-speaking countries, excepting Southern Ireland and Canada, form another. The third group include some German-speaking countries and multi-lingual countries which are geographically close to Germany and may be expected to share certain influences, although the Netherlands is not in this group. Clearly each group of countries have a number of socio-political characteristics in common which may in part explain the commonalities in levels of educational equality. However, it would be hard not to conclude that education system characteristics were not also regionally patterned, and that these may also play a part.

What can we conclude from this analysis of intra-regional commonalities and inter-regional differences in lifelong learning? There would seem to be strong evidence of regional types in some case but less so in others. The German-speaking states, the Nordics states and the English-speaking states all fall into fairly distinctive regional patterns on most indicators of structure, curriculum and outcomes. The southern European states have some commonalities but are generally considerably more diverse as a group.

The southern European states tend have more centralised education systems with small private sectors, low private spending on education and relatively little use of market mechanisms in their forms of regulation. Most of them have comprehensive lower secondary systems with some tracking and grade repeating, school-based and differentiated upper secondary systems and binary type structures in higher education. Their curriculum traditions are generally encyclopaedic rather than specialised and differentiated. Their outcomes are rather varied both in terms of average levels of attainment and dispersal of skills.

The English-speaking states, excepting Canada, have been quick to introduce decentralising and diversifying measures and have gone furthest towards creating quasi market structures in education. Their lower secondary systems are nominally comprehensive (except in Northern Ireland), but generally involve substantial elements of selection and tracking and with school choice and school diversity policies are becoming increasing differentiated. Their upper secondary systems have weak apprentice sectors and multiply differentiated school-based provision. Their curriculum and assessment systems demonstrate high degrees of specialisation and differentiation. In terms of outcomes they have quite varied levels of participation and achievement, although most of them fair rather poorly on the adult literacy measures. However, they have in common high levels of inequality on all the measures used here.

The German-speaking states, and others close to them, also show some distinctive patterns. In their modes of regulation they are still relatively state-centred and non-market oriented, although often decentralised to the level of the provincial state, and they rely heavily on formalised systems of social partnership in their vocational training systems. They are the only states to maintain selective systems of lower secondary education and they have predominantly apprentice-based systems of upper secondary education and training. In curriculum terms they have a marked tendency towards specialisation deriving from a culturally particularistic knowledge tradition. Outcomes in these countries are somewhat more varied than structures and traditions as far as we can see from the available data. Participation in upper secondary education is high, and unusually concentrated in the vocational lines, although participation in higher education is not high relative to other western European states. High levels of inequality are a marked characteristics in the data for 15 year olds, but this may be mitigated later by the effects of the rather universalistic apprentice education which follows this. Germany, for instance, is one of the most unequal countries in terms of its scores for 15 year olds in PISA but one of the most equal in terms of its adult literacy scores in IALS.

The Nordic region would appear to be the most homogeneous on most of the measures. All the Nordic countries share an emphasis on public educational provision administered locally and have rather low levels of private schooling and marketization in education. Compulsory schooling in all Nordic the states is organised in a unique system of all through primary/lower secondary comprehensive schools with little tracking of students and no grade repeating. Upper secondary and higher education tend to be in differentiated (although not in Sweden) with the vocational training sector largely integrated into the school system. Curricula are encyclopaedic through compulsory schooling and become more differentiated thereafter, but there remains a strong core of general education in all post-compulsory programmes in all countries. In terms of outcomes, the Nordic states stand out for their high levels of publicly-subsidized participation in adult learning and for their high average standards of achievement and relatively low levels of inequality both amongst 15 year olds and adults.

Models of the knowledge economy/society

How do these different regional patterns of lifelong learning relate to what we know of the different models of the knowledge economy/knowledge society and how far are they determinants of them? A full analysis would go beyond the parameters of this chapter but a few of the more outstanding relationships can be considered.

The literature on the knowledge economy/society frequently distinguishes between 'high skills' economies, 'low skills' economies and economies that have combinations of high skills and low skills sectors (Albert, 1993; Ashton and Green, 1996; Brown, Green and Lauder, 2001; Crouch, Finegold and Sato, 1999; Hutton, 1995). High skills economies which compete successfully in the global markets are characterised by high productivity levels across many sectors of the economy which in turn depend on high levels of skills dispersed throughout the economy. By contrast high skills/low skills economies may achieve international competitiveness from high productivity in certain sectors, and cost competitiveness in others, but do not have high levels of labour productivity across a wide range of sectors. Their skills profiles tend to be highly polarised, with high skills in some sectors and low levels of skill in others, and their wage structures consequently demonstrate considerable inequality. The UK and the US are often taken to be examples of the more polarised types of high skills economy, whereas Germany, Japan and certain other northern European countries are often seen as more uniformly high skills. The latter types of knowledge economy typically also tend to demonstrate greater equality of incomes and some of the social attributes that may go with more equal resource distribution, such universalistic and generous welfare systems (Esping-Andersen, 1990) and high levels of social trust (Fukuyama, 1996). These high skills economies are sometimes referred to as 'high skills societies' or 'knowledge societies' (Brown, Green and Lauder, 2001).

On the basis of our analysis of regional characteristics of lifelong learning systems, we might expect the Nordic countries, with their high levels of participation and achievement and relative equality of outcomes, to approximate best to the model of Knowledge Society. On the other hand, the English-speaking countries, which are characterised by high level of inequality in skills outcomes, might be expected to fit better the model of the polarized or mixed high skills economies. Furthermore, if a wide dispersion and relative equality of skills and income is important for certain social outcomes, as many would argue it is (Green, Preston and Sabates, 2002; Hutton, 1995), then we would expect the Nordic societies to show more of the social characteristics of a cohesive knowledge society than the English-speaking countries. Such data as we have would suggest that this is indeed the case and that the different lifelong learning systems are implicated in this.

The OECD analysis of the IALS data shows that there is a significant correlation between average literacy levels and the main measure of economic competitiveness: GDP per capita (OECD, 2000, p.80). There is also a strong cross-national correlation between aggregates for literacy levels and the proportion of workers in high skilled jobs, taken to include legislators, senior officials and managers, professional and associate professionals. The Nordic countries not only have high GDP per capita relative to the average for the OECD and Europe (see also Figure 8). They are also amongst the top 6 of 18 countries in the proportion of workers in high skilled jobs. The English-speaking countries, with the exception of the USA and Canada, generally have lower GDP per capita and a lower proportion of workers in high skilled jobs. On the OECD indicator used here, they are ranked in the lower half: the UK (8th), the USA (9th), New Zealand (12th), Australia (13th) and Ireland (14th). The definition of high skilled jobs here clearly contains a bias towards service sectors in the economies since it does not include technicians. This may explain the lower position of Germany, which competes economically mainly on its high skills, high productivity manufacturing industries, rather than on service sectors, and which relies heavily on high skilled technicians which do not fall within the high skills classification here (Streeck, 1989).

In terms of the social outcomes associated with the knowledge society we can also see clear regional patterns which would appear to link different types of lifelong learning regime with different levels of social cohesion. Research

FIGURE 6: Proportion of Workers 19-65 in High Skilled Jobs, 1994-1998

Sweden	55.7
Netherlands	51.7
Finland	46.6
Switzerland	44.7
Norway	44.3
Denmark	41.7
Czech Republic	40.5
Canada	39.4
UK	36.9
USD	35.8
Hungary	35.3
Germany	34.4
New Zealand	33.9
Austria	33.9
Ireland	31.5
Slovenia	29.4
Poland	28.7
Portugal	25.6
Chile	16.5

FIGURE 7: Relationship between Social Cohesion and Education Inequality

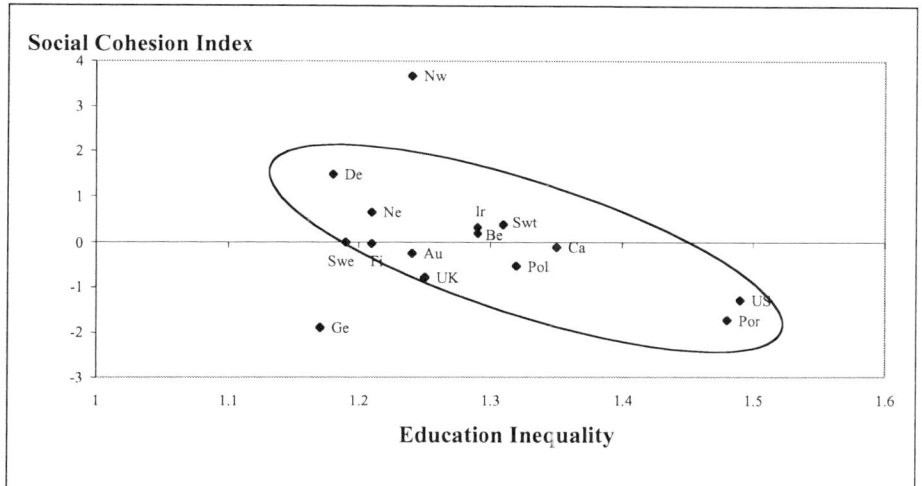

conducted by the Wider Benefits of Learning Centre at the Institute of Education in London (Green, Preston and Sabates, 2002), analyses the relation between educational equality and social cohesion using IALS data on adult literacy scores across countries to estimate skills distributions and Interpol and World Values Survey data on aggregate levels of trust, civic cooperation and violent crime for a combined indicator of social cohesion.

As Figure 7 shows there is a strong correlation cross-nationally between skills distribution and social cohesion (excluding Norway and Germany, a negative and significant correlation of -0.765 exists between social cohesion and education inequality).

The Nordic countries have low levels of educational inequality and high levels of social cohesion on this combined measure. English-Speaking countries in the sample, such as Canada, the UK and the US, tend to have rather higher levels of inequality and lower levels of social cohesion. It is clearly not possible from these correlations to determine which way causation runs, but there would seem to a relation of some sort between educational inequality and social cohesion.

Debating the relative merits of different models of the knowledge economy/society

The relative merits of the so called Anglo-Saxon model, with its typically polarised labour markets, and the knowledge society model, with its more even distribution of skills, have been hotly debated in the literature on political economy in Europe (see Lloyd and Payne, 2004, for an overview). Typically the two are presented as binary opposites which represent the major alternatives for competitive economies in the globalized world. Hutton (1995) contrasts the 'shareholder' model of Anglo-Saxon capitalism with the 'stakeholder' model said to be represented by Germany, Japan and some other northern European states. Dore, more recently (2000), contrasts the 'stockmarket capitalism' of the USA and other Anglo-Saxon economies with what he calls the 'welfare capitalism' of Germany and Japan. In both cases similar theoretical models are being applied.

Shareholder economies are said to give primacy to market mechanisms and to the overriding rights of investors; stakeholder economies balance the rights of shareholders and other stakeholders in the enterprise, and they moderate the effects of the markets through regulation and interest group intermediation between concerted social partner bodies. In the shareholder model innovation and competitiveness are achieved through flexible labour markets, low levels of regulation, high rates of employment, long working hours and lower rates of social expenditure. These promote high productivity and rapid growth but come at the price of poorer public services, greater inequality and low levels of social cohesion. In the stakeholder or social model, social expenditure is higher and there is more regulation of labour and other markets, which tends to enhance public services and promote equality and social cohesion. However regulation, high social costs, and lower employment rates may lower overall productivity and growth. The stakeholder model is often identified with the core social market economies of Europe, and is sometimes seen as the contributing the distinctive nature of social Europe.

In line the with the rather binary models provided by some of the political economists, policy makers often come to see the relationship between these two models of economic competitiveness as being characterised by a series of 'trade-offs' where mutually incompatible benefits have to be weighed against each other—job creation and low unemployment against income equality and job quality; long work hours and high incomes against leisure time and quality of life; innovation and economic dynamism against regulation of standards and the environment. A high national income in terms of GDP per capita, so it is argued, depends on high labour productivity, long working hours and high rates of employment. High rates of employment may be achieved, on the US model, through flexible labour markets but these reduce job protection and work quality for the employed and tend to increase wage inequality. Longer working hours can raise average incomes but reduce leisure time, creating the paradox of the high skilled elites in the USA, described by Robert Reich, who have a surplus of disposable income but no time to enjoy it (Reich, 2000). Low levels of regulation may increase opportunities for innovation and stimulate economic dynamism but they may also lower product and service standards and pose a threat to the environment. So-called 'third way' politics, as practised in the UK, seek to square the circle through combining flexible labour markets with policies for 'social inclusion' where equity is equated with opportunities labour market participation. But, as critics point out, 'social inclusion' in economic terms does not necessarily increase equality where it fails to address low pay. Economic competitiveness, on this way of thinking, would still seem to be at odds with social cohesion.

Research into recent trends in western economies, however, suggests that the various binary models which pit economic competitiveness against social cohesion need to be re-thought and that there are possible models of the knowledge society which combine both.

The Nordic countries clearly present the best example of this. As Figure 8 shows the Nordic countries generally have high levels of GDP per capita and rank relatively well on World Economic Forum measures of business competitiveness and innovative capacity. Norway, Denmark and Iceland are ranked respectively as 1st, 3rd and 4th on GDP per capita in 2002 amongst the more affluent of the world's economies (with only Sweden lagging somewhat behind at 19th place) and Denmark and Iceland rank third and fourth place on business competitiveness. The Nordics also generally rank highly on internet use and relatively highly on innovative capacity. On most economic measures the Nordic countries are amongst the most competitive in the world. They are also, as we have seen already, amongst the most income equal and most socially cohesive countries in the world. How are these dual benefits achieved and what role does education play?

Recent research by de Mooij and Tang (2003) provides part of the answer. In their detailed analysis of the varying components of productivity across major economies, the two authors confirm that there is, to some extent, a trade off between competitiveness and social cohesion in the effects of different labour market policies. Countries, like the US and the UK, which boost their overall productivity through high rates of employment, do tend to have higher rates of income inequality. At the same time, several countries with lower rates of inequality, such as Belgium, France and the Netherlands, also have rather lower employment rates which bring down their overall productivity, despite in the French case having very high levels of labour productivity per hour. This is conventionally explained in terms of the effects of different labour market mechanisms. Flexible labour markets tend to allow higher job growth and increase the rate of employment whilst labour market regulation, which may reduce job growth, can promote income equality.

FIGURE 8: *Economic Competitiveness Measures*

Country	GDP per Capita in 2002		Business[1] Competitiveness (Rank)	Innovative capacity[2] Rank	Internet use[3]	
	(Rank)		Rank	Rank	(Rank)	
Norway	36 047	(1)	22	22	5 048	(8)
United States	35 158	(2)	2	1	5 375	(5)
Denmark	29 975	(3)	4	8	4 651	(11)
Iceland	29614	(4)	14	18	6 076	(1)
Canada	28 699	(5)	12	12	4 838	(10)
Austria	28 61	(6)	17	16	4 093	(17)
Switzerland	28359	(7)	7	9	3 261	(24)
Australia	27 756	(8)	11	15	4 237	(14)
Ireland	27 642	(9)	21	19	2 709	(29)
Netherlands	27 275	(10)	9	11	5 304	(6)
Belgium	26 695	(11)	15	17	3 286	(23)
Germany	26 324	(12)	5	5	4 237	(15)
Hong Kong	26 235	(13)	19	25	4 309	(13)
France	26 151	(14)	10	10	3 138	(25)
Finland	25 859	(15)	1	2	5 089	(7)
United Kingdom	25 672	(16)	6	3	4 061	(18)
Japan	25 650	(17)	13	4	4 485	(12)
Italy	25 570	(18)	24	21	2 709	(28)
Sweden	25 315	(19)	3	7	5 730	(2)
Taiwan	23 420	(20)	16	13	3 825	(20)
Singapore	23 393	(21)	8	6	5 396	(4)
Spain	20 697	(22)	25	24	1 931	(33)
New Zealand	20 455	(23)	18	23	4 834	(9)
Israel	19 382	(24)	20	14	3 014	(27)
Greece	18 184	(25)	39	32	1 547	(37)
Portugal	17 808	(26)	36	33	3 554	(22)
Slovenia	17 748	(27)	30	29	4 008	(19)
Malta	17 344	(28)	42			
Korea	16 465	(29)	23			

1. Business competitiveness Index from Global Competitiveness Report, p. 39.
2. US Utility Patents for Invention granted per million population from Global Competitiveness Report p. 93.
3. Ranking based on internet users per 10 000 inhabitants, 2002 in ibid p. 444.

However, as de Mooij and Tang show, some labour market regulatory mechanisms appear to escape this trade off. They find that benefit duration, union density and employment protection do have a statistically significant large and negative effects on participation, whilst at the same time increasing income equality. This fits with the classic trade-off argument. However, some labour market policies and institutions seem to escape this trade-off. Strong trade unions, as measured by union coverage, may tend to increase unemployment at the same time as reducing inequality, but centralised unions, conducting concerted cross-sectoral bargaining, tend to reduce unemployment and promote pay equality. Also active labour market policies, including amongst other things, assistance with job search and training for the unemployed, boost employment rates and lower unemployment rates at the same time as mitigating income inequality. Centralised trade union bargaining and active labour market policies have, of course, been notable features of many of the Nordic countries which achieve both high productivity, high rates of employment and also low levels of income inequality.

The evidence also suggests that lifelong learning regimes play a part. The Nordic countries have high aggregate levels of attainment and skills both amongst the young people (in PISA surveys) and amongst adults (in IALS) and show more equal distributions of skills than countries in other regions. We have suggested above how the unique institutional structures of lifelong learning in these countries may contribute to this. The wide distribution of skills achieved in these countries no doubt plays its part in the levels of labour productivity achieved across different sectors of their economies which forms an important component of the overall productivity outcomes. At the same time, widespread uptake of adult learning and particularly the training provided for the unemployed and those about to be made redundant through active labour market policies, promotes the higher employment rates which also contribute to overall productivity. Relative equality of incomes is no doubt due partly to labour market institutions, including minimum wage law and mechanisms for concerted and centralised pay bargaining. Nevertheless, given the exceptionally strong correlations in cross-country studies between skills equality and income equality (Green, Preston and Sabates, 2002; Nickel and Layard, 1998) it seems likely that education also plays a substantial role. Educational equality may well also be promoting social cohesion both indirectly through its contribution to income equality which supports cohesion and, directly, through its promotion of solidaristic values which underpin social and institutional trust (Green, Preston and Sabates, 2002). Nordic countries are noted for the emphasis placed in the curriculum in compulsory schools and in the folk high schools on the development of collective identity and community spirit. These values undergird the universalistic welfare systems that also play a major role in establishing social cohesion.

Nordic states are not, of course, paragons in all aspects of social cohesion. Eurostat surveys, for instance, have shown that levels of tolerance for cultural and religious diversity are relatively weak in the Nordic states relative to other areas of western Europe, and particularly southern Europe, although, to be fair, these attitudes correlate highly across countries with actual levels of immigration. Danish respondents, for instance, show high levels of tolerance for lifestyle diversity, but rather low tolerance for people of other nationalities, religions of cultures (See Preston, Green and Malmberg, 2003). This raises further questions about how far the notable levels of trust and social cohesion in the Nordic states depend on relatively high ethnic and cultural homogeneity which has historically characterised these countries. Nevertheless, on most of the measures employed here, the Nordic states do appear to constitute a region in Europe which achieves a remarkable marriage of economic competitiveness and social cohesion. Given the singularity of the regional characteristics identified with the Nordic states here, a case should perhaps be made for greater differentiation in the models of the knowledge economy/society that are employed in the literature.

As the earlier discussion stressed, many of the comparative political economy models work on a basic dualism between two kinds of high skills economy. On the basis of the findings here we would do better to distinguish between three major types of high competition economies in western societies. The Anglo-Saxon market economies remain distinctive, characterised by polarised high skills/low skills labour markets that trade off economic competitiveness against social cohesion. Germany other core states of northern Europe (to use de Mooij and Tang's terminology) have more equal distribution of skills and greater equality of incomes but achieve high levels of social cohesion at the price of lower overall productivity, since employment rates have tended to remain low as well as working hours. The Nordic states represent a third type, which needs to be distinguished from that of the 'core' states, on the grounds of the higher overall levels of per capita income, achieved in part through higher employment rates, and also because of the substantially better outcomes in terms of income equality and the measures of social cohesion. These states would appear to be closer to combining the twin EU Lisbon goals of economic competitiveness and social cohesion than other states in Europe through somehow avoiding the trade-offs often taken to be inherent in these two aspirations. It is argued here that education and training play an important part in this.

Conclusions

Has *Homo Sapiens Europæus* then arrived in the form of the Nordic Society? We might wisely judge any such conclusion to be a little foolhardy. In the first place, in today's economically globalised world, with all its massive economic and political convulsions and its inbuilt centrifugal social forces, any forms of apparent equilibrium between economic competitiveness and social cohesion may seem highly precarious. For the Nordic states this often shows up in the obvious fault lines around the costs of social spending and the tensions around immigration and diversity, the two of which linked in the mistaken logic of the of the centre and far right political (what about the public cost savings from immigrant rejuvenation of the otherwise ageing populations?). In the second place, and somewhat ironically, the Nordic model retains a rather ambiguous relationship with Europe of the European Union, to say the least. Scandinavians are not at all sure that the EU will guarantee the survival of their social welfare societies, so much so that Denmark and Sweden continue to hedge over joining the Euro and Norway remains out of the Union altogether. So not exactly *Homo Sapiens Europæus Copulatus*. Nevertheless, if we are to take the Lisbon declaration seriously, and if social cohesion is to be more than a gestural appendage to economic competitiveness in the credo of the EU, then we must give the distinctive achievement of the Nordic model its due. It comes closer to the vision of a 'competitive and dynamic knowledge-based economy …with more and better jobs and greater social cohesion' than any other region. The Nordic model of lifelong learning would seem to play an important role in this.

The provisional analyses of the data conducted here do suggest that there are some distinctive regional patters in lifelong learning in Europe, particularly if we extend the meaning of regional to include countries which are not geographically proximate but which have historico-cultural affinities. System characteristics clearly do not all cluster on such regional lines and there is still considerable diversity in the systems within each region, and particularly so in the region described here as the Mediterranean states. The commonalities are sufficient for us to talk in general terms about a Nordic regional model of lifelong learning and we can also ascertain some general and distinctive characteristics in what might be termed the German model. The English-speaking countries are, of course, neither geographically proximate nor mostly within Europe but they do also seem to manifest distinctive common characteristics, and are recognized to so do by policy-makers in Europe and elsewhere. In all cases we may assume, although we have not analyzed it here, that these regional/cultural commonalities derive from longstanding historical affinities in cultures, political systems and socio-economic structures.

What seems equally clear is that these different models of lifelong learning do correspond in significant ways with the different models of the knowledge economy/knowledge society that have been identified in the literature. The model of the knowledge society combining high levels of economic competitiveness with relative equality and high levels of social cohesion is most closely approximated by the Nordic states and it would seem that the forms of lifelong learning in these states make a considerable contribution towards this. On the other hand, there are other countries which achieve high levels of economic competitiveness based on rather more polarized distributions of skills and incomes which would seem to achieve only lower levels of social cohesion. These are best referred to as knowledge economies rather than knowledge societies and are typically represented by UK in Europe and, globally, by the USA. We may also distinguish a third model in the core areas of Europe, most often associated with Germany and the social market economy, which lies somewhere between the two in terms of economic competitiveness and social cohesion. It should not pass unnoticed that the three models of the knowledge economy/society in northern Europe equate closely in geographical terms with Esping-Anderson's *Three Worlds of Welfare Capitalism* (1990) characterised politically by social democracy in Scandinavia, Christian democracy in core Europe and liberalism in the Anglo-Saxon world. Economic, welfare and lifelong learning models thus converge on the same regional groupings.

In many ways these three models still represent the alternative futures for Europe. How European states choose to organise their lifelong learning systems will in no small part determine which of these models of the knowledge economy/society come to characterise the Europe of the future.

Note

1. We have not sought to classify the new member states, although this would be a valuable exercise, because their systems are in many cases still emergent and would therefore constitute as much trickier task. Where OECD data is used countries other than those in western Europe are included in the analysis but the main emphasis here is on western Europe.

References

Albert, M (1993) *Capitalism against Capitalism.* London: Whurr Publishers.

Ashton, D. & Green, F. (1996) *Education, Training and the Global Economy.* Elgar: London.

Braudel, F. (1992) *Civilization and Capitalism, 15th-18th Century. Vol. 1.* Berkeley: University of California Press.

Boucher, L. (1982) *Tradition and Change in Swedish Education.* Oxford: Pergamon Press.

Brown, P.; Green, A. & Lauder, H. (2001) *High Skills: Globalization, Competitiveness and Skills Formation.* Oxford: Oxford University Press.

Brubaker, R. (1992) *Citizenship and Nationhood in France and Germany.* Cambridge, Mass: Harvard University Press.

CEDEFOP (1995) *Vocational Education and Training in the Federal Republic of Germany.* Berlin: CEDEFOP.

Crouch, C.; Finegold, D. & Sato, M. (1999) *Are skills the Answer? The Political Economy of Skill Creation in Advanced Industrial Countries.* Oxford: Oxford University Press.

Department for Education and Skills (DFES) (2003) *Skills Strategy White Paper: 21st Century Skills: Realising Our Potential.* London: DFES.

Dore, R. (2000) *Stock Market Capitalism: Welfare Capitalism, Japan and Germany Versus the Anglo-Saxons.* Oxford: Oxford University Press.

Esping-Andersen, G. (1990) *The Three Worlds of Welfare Capitalism.* Polity: Cambridge.

European Commission (EC) (1999) *Continuing Training in Enterprises: Facts and Figures. European Training Youth.* Brussels: EC.

European Commission (2002) *Continuing Vocational Training Survey 2.* Luxembourg: Office for Official Publications of the European Communities.

European Commission (2000) *A Memorandum on Lifelong Learning* at website: http://europa.eu.int/comm/education/life/memoen.pfd

Fukuyama, F. (1996) *Trust: The Social Virtues and the Creation of Prosperity.* London: Penguin.

Green, A. (1990) *Education and State Formation.* London: Macmillan.

Green, A. (1998) 'Core Skills, key skills and general culture: in search of the common foundation in vocational education.' *Evaluation and Research in Education,* Vol. 12(1), pp 23-44.

Green, A. (2000) 'Lifelong learning and the learning society: different European models of organization.' In A. Hodgson (ed.) *Policies, Politics and the Future of Lifelong Learning.* London: Kogan Page.

Green, A. (2003) 'The many faces of lifelong learning: recent education policy trends in Europe.' Journal of Education Policy, Vol.17(6), pp.611-626.

Green, A. & Evans, K. (2005) 'Youth transitions and the 14-19 'Occupational Route in England.' (forthcoming)

Green, A.; Hodgson, A. & Sakamoto, A. (2000) 'Financing vocational education and training.' In P. Descry & M. Tessaring (eds) *Training in Europe. Second Report on Vocational Training Research in Europe 2000*: Volume 1, Cedefop Reference series. Luxembourg: Office for Official Publications of the European Communities.

Green, A. Preston, J. & Sabates, R. (2002) *Education, Equality and Social Cohesion: A Distributional Approach*. Working Paper NO. 7 Wider Benefits of Learning Centre. London: Institute of Education.

Green, A.; Wolf, A. & Leney, T. (1999) *Convergences and Divergences in European Education and Training Systems*. London: Bedford Way Papers, Institute of Education.

Green, A. & Wiborg, S. (2004) 'Comprehensive Schooling and Educational Inequality: An International Perspective.' In M.Benn and C. Chitty (eds) *A Tribute to Caroline Benn: Education and Democracy*. London: Continuum.

Hutton, W. (1995) *The State We're In*. Kent: Mackays of Chatham.

Kohn, H. (1982) *The Idea of Nationalism*. Malabar: Krieger.

Lauglo, J. (1990) 'Factors behind decentralisation in education systems: a comparative perspective with special reference to Norway.' *Compare*, Vol. 20(1), pp.21-29.

Leonardi, R. (1995) *Convergence, Cohesion and Integration in the European Union*. London: Macmillan.

Lloyd, C. & Payne, J (2004) *'IdleFancy' or 'Concrete Will?' Defining and Realising a High Skills Vision for the UK*, SKOPE Research Paper No. 47. Warwick: SKOPE, University of Warwick.

Mackinder, H. (1969) *The Scope and Methods of Geography and the Geographical Pivot of History*. London: Royal Geographical Society.

Maurice, M. & Sellier, F. (1986) *The Social Foundations of Industrial Power*. Cambridge, Mass: MIT Press.

McLean, M (1990) *Britain and a Single Market Europe: Prospects for a Common School Curriculum*. London: Kogan Page.

de Mooij, R. & Tang, P (2003) *Four Futures of Europe*. The Hague: Centraal Planbureau.

Nickell, S. & Layard, R. (1998) *Institutions and Economic Performance*. LSE Discussion Paper. London: LSE.

OECD (1986) *Education and Training Beyond Basic Schooling*. Paris: OECD.

OECD (1994) *School: A Matter of Choice*. Paris: OECD.

OECD (1996) *Lifelong Learning for All*. Paris: OECD

OECD (2000) *Literacy in the Information Age*. Paris: OECD.

OECD (2001) *Education at a Glance*. Paris: OECD.

OECD (2001b) *Knowledge and Skills for Life: First Results from PISA 2000*. Paris: OECD.

OECD (2003) *Beyond the Rhetoric: Adult Learning Practices and Policies*. Paris: OECD.

Piore, M. & Sabel, C. (1984) *The Second Industrial Divide*. New York: Basic Books.

Preston, J.; Green, A. & Malmberg, L. (2003) *Macro-social Benefits of Education and Training: A Review of International Evidence and Comparative Literature*, WBL Research Report No. 9. London: Institute of Education.

Rokkan, S. (1968) *Comparative Research Across Cultures and Nations*. Paris.

Rokkan, S. (1970) *Citizens, Elections, Parties : Approaches To The Comparative Study Of The Processes Of Development*. New York: McKay.

Rubenson, K. (2002 unpublished) *The Nordic Model of Adult Education*. Vancouver: Centre for Higher Education Research, University of British Columbia.

Streeck, W. (1989) 'Skills and the limits of neo-liberalism: the enterprise of the future as a place of learning.' *Work, Employment and Society*, Vol. 3(1), pp.89-104.

Teichler, U. (1993) 'Structures of higher education systems in Europe.' In C. Gellert (ed.) *Higher Education in Europe*. London: Jessica Kingsley.

Teichler, U. & Sadlak, J. (eds) (2000) *Higher Education Research: Its Relation to Policy and Practice*. Oxford: Pergamon Press.

UNESCO (1996) *Learning—The Treasure Within*. Report of the International Commission on Education for the 21st Century. Paris: UNESCO.

Weiss, M. (1993) 'New guiding principles in educational policy: the case of Germany.' *Journal of Education Policy*, Vol. 8(4), pp. 307-320.

Wolf, A. & Rapiau, M.T. (1993) 'The academic achievement of craft apprentices in France and England: contrasting systems and common dilemmas.' *Comparative Education*, Vol. 29(1), pp.29-43.

CHAPTER TWELVE

Manufacturing the 'European' in Education and Training

ANJA HEIKKINEN

Bringing back anthropology in education

It is commonplace to analyse education from the perspective of its responsiveness to the changing economy and industries. This chapter demands for recognition of the ethical, emotional, religious and military imperatives underlying the current integrated educational and business/economical discourse. In order to justify this, the anthropological base of education needs to be made visible. In this context, to put it shortly, anthropology is conceived as the study on how humanness is geographically and historically constituted between nature and culture (Siikala, 2002; Göller, 2000; Wimmer, 2004). Education as theory and practice relates normatively and politically to anthropology: it intervenes in the growth of human beings and promotes projects of certain economical and social orders among humankind. At the same time it allows the emergence of certain nature-culture collectives with characteristic approaches of humans towards nature (Latour, 2004). The recognition of anthropology as the base of education implies that beside social sciences and humanities, natural sciences and technology should be consulted in educational reflections. These demands may seem extensive, but so is the project of contemporary market capitalism, which is evolving into global knowledge-based economies (KBE) and into global divisions of labour, industries and employment.

This chapter discusses the anthropological commitments in the interconnected economical and educational agendas of the construction of a EU-Europe-society with a European population. The ´European dimension´, expected to be found in the shared, inherited intellectual, economical, political and educational values, is commonly sought from inside the EU-Europe. It should enable the coming about of the Knowledge-Based Economy/Society, the Area of Higher Education and Research and the world-quality referenced education and training system. The next section questions why the construction of the ´non-European´ inside and outside EU-Europe remains silenced in this discourse. The populations in the member states are expected to develop a European identity, but outsiders are welcome only if they contribute to the competitiveness of companies in the EU-Europe. While educational concerns are always raised from a certain historical and geo-political context, the following section discusses the historical struggles of manufacturing the 'European' from the location of Finland. The fourth section depicts the anthropological nature of the integrated economical and educational policy, through reading of exemplary national and EU documents. In the emerging global order, the competencies of the nation-states are delegated to the global industrial clusters and markets. The struggle for economic dominance requires Europeans as human resources, designed and managed by a new nobility: the fifth section asks for planetary historico-political deconstruction of the coded wars of hegemonic practices and discourses about education and work.

The 'stretchy' wars about the economic domination of planet earth

A typical notion about the deepening integration process in Europe since the 1940s is that, if nothing else, it has been beneficial for maintaining peace in Europe. The notion as such is questionable, since there have been warlike developments in Europe (e.g. the prolonged dictatorships in Portugal, Spain and Greece, violence in Ireland, in the Balkans and in Eastern Europe) and most member states have engaged in military actions outside Europe, especially through NATO. The military aspects of European integration, and their relation to economy and industries, and to divisions of work and education, may not be recognised without historicising the concepts of war and militarism. Although during the 20th century demonstrations and upheavals against racial and economical oppression became moderated through ideologies of peace, Foucault asks for the identification of the transforming programmes of totalitarian governance. '(S)ociety, the law and the State are (not) like armistices that put an end to wars, or that they are the products of definitive victories. Law is not pacification, for beneath the law, war continues to rage in all the mechanisms of power, even in the most regular... the war is that is going on beneath the peace: peace itself is a coded war... There is no such thing as a neutral subject. We are all inevitably someone's adversary' (Foucault, 2004, p.51). According to Foucault, history as discourse and action is continuation of war—struggle on exercise of ontological, epistemological and moral power—despite the parallel development of philosophical and juridical discourses about universal progress towards rationalism, social pacification and justice. Bruno Latour (2004) has extended the notion of war to cover the history of planet earth under the hegemonic politics of human species and with the intra-species struggles on its domination. On the other hand, Touraine (2000) has argued for the reciprocal becoming of the subject and society. Thus, the shaping of the borders of 'EU-Europe' takes place in parallel to the shaping of the borders of the 'European' subject.

The struggle on ownership, control and exploitation of natural resources by humans has always gone hand in hand with military, political, ideological and educational supremacy. The colonisation of the planet earth by the superior nation-state-societies in Europe gained its peak by the beginning of the World War I, when about 85 % of its surface was controlled by Britain, Portugal, Spain, the Netherlands, Belgium, Germany and Russia (the role of the latter is often disregarded). The task of legitimisation of economical and political oppression and annihilation has also always belonged to the hegemonic intelligentsia. Anthropological argumentation has been fundamental for justifying the binary opposition between the superior us, and the inferior, exotic and dangerous other (Said, 1987).

Despite the seemingly successful implementation of the contemporary neo-liberalist regime, the comprehensive imperative to manufacture the European population challenges existing management and governance patterns in the member states of the EU. It is a question of how to legitimise the contradictions between recognising the 'us' as European citizens and the 'us' as human resources for companies operating in EU-Europe. The analyses of totalitarianism by Labarthe and Nancy (2002) are relevant for anthropological reflections on how this is done in the context of contemporary politics and economy. They describe totalitarianism as a struggle for a universal ideology, which would unify the world and its population. Totalitarian governance is exercised through aesthetic politics, which is simultaneously figuring and constructing a mythical reality. This takes place in prophecies, which show what and who belong to the future and what and who are going to fade away. In totalitarianism the making of the universal community relates to the configuration and construction of ideal humanness. The construction of a harmonious totality requires internal and external war against non-humans. Through shared war the charismatic totalitarian leaders—and the intelligentsia providing them ideological instruments and legitimisation—mobilise masses, which are composed by atomic individuals (Labarthe, 2002, p.58; Nevanlinna, 2002, p.108). Labarthe and Nancy, however, do not recognise the dramatically increased importance of education for legitimising the revised forms of totalitarian governance. Yet the demand of ideal humans to identify with the totality and its ideological leaders (like the ICT and media industry) as its representation instead of occupation, class or any other non-totalitarian collective, has become more comprehensive than ever.

The taint of Finnishness: wars on recognition

In the manufacturing of the 'European', certain metaphors and cultural categories function as containers, which enable the mobilisation of mentalities developed during the making of the nation-states. The 'European' of the early 20th century referred to the nationalist idea of territorial rights and obligations, to the ownership of natural resources and industries, of a specific sphere of intellect and ideology and to the shared values among distinctive populations, especially in the former British colonies (Hage, 2003; Heikkinen, 2003). The contemporary counter-movements have largely been marginalised in the collective narratives of nation building. While the roots of 'Europeanness' are commonly featured in Greek philosophy, scientific knowledge and Christianity (e.g. Boyd and King, 1977; Bowen, 1972; Arendt, 1992), the period of World War II and post-war reconstruction was crucial for the identification of populations in the nation-state societies of Europe (Giddens, 1998; Habermas, 1998; Alasuutari, 1996). However, the meaning of the period may have been different depending on the situation and traditions of different countries before and during the war.

Do Finns have a history?

Finland is commonly considered as an example of a peripheral, suppressed and backward country in Europe, which was saved through joining the EU during the breakthrough of global market capitalism. From the location Finland, such a view reminds about the long-lasted dilemma about the recognition of Finnishness. In anthropological discourse, people's feelings of belonging are commonly related to their conceptions of humanness as characterising 'us', opposed to the non-humanness, barbarity—queer language, religion, habits—and brutality of 'them/the other' (Silverman, 1999; Hage, 2003). However, belonging is seldom analysed from the perspective of the inferior, colonised or dominated others. This has been characteristic for the history of Finns as a section of Finno-Ugrian people of the north (Apo, 2002; Hakkinen, 2002; Ilomäki, 2002). Military, political, economical or cultural wars generally trigger the identification of 'us' against 'they/the others'. Also the constitution of Finnishness inwards and outwards was related to the repeated wars, which endangered the survival of Finns as a population inhabiting a transforming and diverse borderland.

The religious, political and economical positioning of people living in Finland in relation to the superpowers of Europe gained momentum during the Catholic and Orthodox crusades from Sweden and Russia since the 12th century. Through force and by adjusting indigenous beliefs and ways of life under new world-views, new habits and social structures were implemented during the 14th century. From this time onwards, the role of people inhabiting Finland was to pay taxes, to serve as a gun fodder, as a frontier settlement, and as a buffer zone in the competition on power, land and political supremacy between Sweden and Russia. While the land had no strategic natural resources, the people were left to fend for themselves. 'Finnishness' was silently forming among the people, developing such traits as 'self-supportiveness' and a cautious and passive resistance towards invaders. After the Napoleonic wars and separation from Sweden-Finland since 1809, the intelligentsia of the Autonomous Grand Duchy of Finland in the Russian Empire started the debate about whether Finland and Finns do exist at all. The crucial issue was whether Finns in fact had any history, without which no group or nation could argue for holding an identity During the 19th century, the dominant cultural projects promoting Finland were based on enabling the interconnected creation of a political, economical and cultural nation-state-society (Heikkinen, 1995; Heikkinen et al., 1999; Alapuro et al., 1989).

A philosopher and statesman Johan W. Snellman (1806-1881) crystallized the shared elements of the Finnish nation-building projects. According to him, the nation is the self-reflective consciousness of people who are becoming aware of their existence and conditions for their existence, among all the other people of humankind. Language was fundamental in the reflective process: it embodied the historically transforming experience of the people. 'Only the existence of many nations can save humankind from falling down... If only one language, one civilisation or culture would dominate the whole globe, would not then the disappearance of this civilisation or culture also be common for the whole humankind?' (Snellman, 1845). For Snellman, the category 'sivistys' (Bildung/cultivation) meant a process of becoming of individual and collective (national) reflective consciousness and its practical actualisation in societal institutions and everyday life. The process of 'sivistys' was entirely dependent on the reciprocal making of 'kansa' (people/Volk) and 'sivistyneistö' (the cultivated/*die Gebildete*). According to Snellman, 'the Finnish people will never achieve anything through force, but only through the power of their 'sivistys'' (ibid.).

In the making of the Finnish nation-state, all forms of education served the promotion of political and occupational citizenship, participation in the nation-state society, in national industries and in work. (Heikkinen et al., 1999, Siltala, 2000). People's internalised fear for existence and recognition could be translated into an imperative about becoming fit for the nation. One of its crucial elements, which is still very up-to-date in the harmonisation of alcohol taxes in the EU, is a myth about the inherited backwardness of Finnish drinking habits.

> 'After the elites became more Finnish during the first half of the 20th century, the belief in the 'Finnish boozer mentality' was transformed into a sort of self-directed racism in which one's own ethnic group or at least a significant part of it was defined as uncivilized and pathological. The roots of this phenomenon can be sought from the traumatic political events of 1905-1918—civil war about the ownership of the 'nation-sate-society' between the 'landowners and economical and intellectual elites' and the rural workers and small farmers and the industrial workers—as well as from the nearly century-long (the 19th century—AH) struggle against rural poverty and cultural backwardness' (Apo, 2002, p.197).

In a manner similar to that experienced by indigenous people in so many other parts of the world, Finns were 'racialised and inferiorised as intrinsically unable to access the 'civilised state'' (Hage, 2003, p.113) in the struggle about the competence and power to design the future of the nation-state.

From pagans, through mongoloids, towards respectable Europeans

The domestication of the independent Finnish nation-state during the 1910s-1930s took place between rising racist ideologies on both sides of its borders. Swedish and continental researchers, for instance, considered Finns and Lapps to belong to the inferior Asian race (Kemiläinen, 1994). Finnish artists and scientists, on the other hand, were enthusiastic about 'opening the windows' to, and identifying with Europe, especially with Germany (Glimell, 1997; Kettunen, 1994). Even the participation in the beauty contests with other Western countries was motivated by the mission to show that the Finns were no representatives of the 'mongoloid race'. On the other hand, the big wood processing and metal industries looked to the US and Sweden for models in the organisation of the management and production processes. National consensus was sought from internal racism towards the communists and from external racism towards the Soviet Union. White Finnishness was promoted through extensive land reforms and one-sided labour contracts, which created new strata of loyal small farmers and decent (craft-like) workers. The *untainted Finnishness,* required for becoming recognised by the West, moderated its high and low versions into the middle. The negotiation between projects of Small Farmers, Industrial and Welfare Finland led to recognition of all work—also female-dominated—as occupational, and to the promotion of industries through the development of branch-specific vocational education (Heikkinen et al., 1999).

For Finland, involvement in the World War II was about maintaining its independence, but at the cost of collaboration with fascist Germany. The defence, however, required consensus between diverse political and mentality projects (Heikkinen, 2001a; Kettunen, 2001). The settlement of homecoming soldiers and half a million refugees from the lost Karelia as well as the war-payments to the Soviet Union depended on the compromise between the different projects of Finland. During the 1960s social democrats came to power and implemented a political and economical programme fusing Industrial and Welfare Finland. This led to forced modernisation and devastation of traditional ways of life and inhabitancy, to the collapse of small farming and to the migration of people to Southern cities and as guest labourers to Sweden. The external, though economically beneficial, enemy remained the Soviet Union, but alongside communism, the *outdated indigenous industries*, skills and competences became major internal enemies for the industrial and educational reformers of the 1970s (Heikkinen, 1999). Since the middle of the 9th century, the Finnish national economy had been dominated by the capital-intensive export industry. The rapid collapse of speculative economy and the fall of Soviet trade, together with global economic recession in the 1990s, increased its importance enormously. The educational reform plans from the 1980s transformed into rationalisation programmes, introducing accountability and market-principles into the institutes and the teaching profession. Occupationally oriented education and its governance became defined as a part of an educational cluster serving productive clusters, controlled by experts from industry and technology.

The new constellation was characterised coarsely by the leading export industry: 'The Finnish basic (export) industry demands the state and other public authorities to change their attitudes towards enterprises and to transform into guardians of the interests of Finnish enterprises by supporting and marketing them. The director of the Finnish Union of Energy (Pentti Sierilä, TELI) characterises this transformation in a very straightforward manner: 'The state should abandon its tzarist, caring and guiding traditions and develop into a marketing company (for enterprises)' (*Helsingin Sanomat*, 30 June 1995).

The re-orientation of Finnish political and industrial elites from responsiveness to the people towards anticipation of expectations of the EU elites started well before officially joining as a Member State in 1995. The policies, which were constrained by the imagined, virtual EU, led to redefinition of the internal and external enemies (Kantola, 2002). The *tainted Finnishness* required healing and curing from the sick dependency on universal public welfare, from the devastating sameness hindering innovation, entrepreneurship and self-determination of the population. The new homeland in the making was only embracing the ones shown fit to belong to the winners of globalisation. The hegemonic ideals imposed from new industrial and occupational order to education were well represented in an advertisement for staff recruitment by the telecommunication company Nokia:

> 'Are you ready for a challenge? Are you looking for an opportunity and willing to take on responsibility? At Nokia, WE can give you both. Opportunity in Nokia knows no boundaries, it reaches all parts of the world. Wherever there is a mobile phone network, or being planned, WE are there... To succeed in OUR world, you have to be able to make independent decisions, but you must also be able to work as a part of a team. You must see an opportunity behind every problem... You must keep on learning... As we stand on the threshold of a new millennium, WE are looking for people who want to be the first and the fastest in developing new technologies. If you like the way WE think... One of these jobs could open a world of opportunity for you.' (*Helsingin Sanomat*, 13th September, 1998)

The eagerness of Finnish policy makers to comply with trans-national powers and the readiness of the people to let it happen indicate the longevity of personal and collective mentality structures of Finnishness (Hakamies, 2002, p.230; Kemiläinen, 1994). The feelings of inferiority and shame integrate with the defence of 'us' by cautious adjustment to the 'other', the superior and the successful. The cumulated incapacity of the Finns to respect themselves and each other has repeatedly led to disregard of their indigenous forms of life, their skills, competences, industries and education.

Education in the making of the European subject

Population of Learning Europeans

The educational policy of the EU does not explicitly address the people of Europe. In the construction of the new geographical and cultural territory of the EU-Europe, nation-state-societies are substituted by member states, which through their selected representatives replace the people in negotiation and decision-making concerning their future. The turn towards comprehensive EU policy focussing on learning and knowledge instead of education and training, started in the mid-1990s, is documented, for instance, in the White paper on teaching and learning in the knowledge-based society (European Commission, 1995). Learning was explicitly subsumed to the economic, technological and social making of the EU-Europe. Although it confirmed that the competent actors of the EU-Europe were the member states, not its people or citizens, the member states were expected to achieve the EU policy goals through European people, citizens and employees.

During the 1990s, the role of member states in the implementation of the EU policies took place through national education reforms. Thus, in Finland, vocational educators were no longer considered as proponents of their occupation, but didactic-managerial experts, who required academic qualification. Vocational institutes transformed into partners of educational service networks at regional, national and trans-national level (Helakorpi et al., 1995). An advocate of Europeanisation in the board of education characterised the future educational policies in 1996: 'Teaching is old-fashioned and... doesn't meet the needs (of future, industry, clients—AH)... This is a consequence of the vocational education system, which is formed by history and diverse cultures of action... When WE don't have the courage (to change) WE are digging earth under OUR feet, because WE will soon be out, outdated, old-fashioned. WE should run this engine in a completely different manner and not remain prisoners of any traditional thinking... It will not be beneficial in the future. This relates to the issue of culture... For example, in this training for vocational exams (accreditation of vocational qualifications - AH), WE are too old-fashioned. WE should much more provide opportunities... WE should have markets.' (Heikkinen et al., 1999, p. 158).

The EU programmes implementing the 1990s educational policies, promoted the generation of 'good practice' derived from carefully selected countries, fields of industry and types of organisations. In the EU-supported projects researchers identified with the assumptions, values and interpretations about 'Europeanness', as suggested in the programmes. Although most researchers were not economists, they adopted vocabulary from the worlds of business and economics (Lundvall et al., 1999). The binary oppositions between learning and education, and between employment and occupations as collectively controlled forms of learning and work, made the core of the EU-project discourse. The 'traditional', institutionalised, reproductive, externally controlled, rigid education and training 'has not had the long-term desired effects for industry.' The 'new' informal, company specific, company and employee controlled, flexible and applicable learning 'enables permanent innovative learning for the organisation' (Heikkinen, 2001b).

Innovative learning was universal and international, as long as it referred to the sort of knowledge creation wanted by companies in the global markets. The politically neutral and universal progressiveness of informal learning was guaranteed by the use of information and communication technology (ICT). Informal learning was non-institutionalised, non-bureaucratic, tacit and experiential, both self-directed and controlled by individuals, teams and organisations. It was motivated by individual and organisational competitiveness, not by non-organisational or collective values. Individuals and organisations were considered equal in their struggle for survival in the global markets. However, competitiveness required motivation from inside the current 'community of practice' (Wenger, 1999). This should respond to people's expectations on safety, threatened by the imperatives for individualistic innovativeness and competitiveness. The economist discourse of learning remained silent about unions, whose origin had been in securing and defending the weaker in the national and trans-national labour markets (see Kettunen, 2001). Organisational partnerships and direct encounters made non-organisational mobilisation superfluous, when the old oppositions and inequalities were considered to have disappeared. While life-long learning was evaluated and legitimised according to its innovativeness, its management required the world to transform into learning organisations. As a laboratory for learning, the world would become manageable by applying appropriate theories of learning (Latour, 2004; Lehtonen, 2000).

Human resources for the Knowledge-Based Economy

The policies of lifelong learning have smoothly progressed to the policies of business/economic management of learning (European Commission, 2000; 2001). Although the knowledge-based society should build on learning for active citizenship and social coherence, these are equalled with employability, mobility and ICT competency of individuals, critical in the labour markets. As the European Commission notes, 'Labour shortages and competence gaps risk limiting the capacity of the European Union for further growth, at any point in the economic cycle... Lifelong learning, therefore, has a key role to play in developing a coordinated strategy for employment and particularly for promoting a skilled, trained and adaptable workforce. This means removing the barriers that prevent people from entering the labour market and limit progression within it. Tackling inequality and social exclusion is part of this' (European Commission, 2001, p.5).

Meanwhile, the commitment to sociological and psychological constructivism in education has provided appropriate theories and models of learning for the making of the learning Europe. The capacity to 'learn' has become the basis for the participation of individuals, organisations and member states in the competitive and progressive EU-society. Instead of educational qualities, only success and competitiveness count as proper outcomes of learning. Education is transformed into a business of co-ordination, standardisation and management of competence building and innovation strategies. '(T)he assessment and forecasting of competence needs across European labour markets... will be relevant to the national and sub-national levels. Similarly, partnership working will inevitably include cooperation between actors at national and European level; European funds will have an impact on adequate resourcing at all levels; and the evaluation of national strategies will continue to take place in the context of the European Employment Strategy' (European Commission, 2001, p.9).

The strategy of transforming education into the comprehensive management of learning and innovation is visible in different educational sectors. In these vocabularies the population of EU-Europe is characterised as human resources. 'The transition towards a knowledge-based economy capable of sustainable economic growth with more and better jobs and greater social cohesion brings new challenges to the development of human resources' (European Commission, 2002, p.1). Employability, the capacity to work and learning merge in the new guidelines for the employment policies, where 'the promotion of the development of human capital and of lifelong learning goes in the same direction' (European Commission, 2003). The vocabularies in the Finnish education reforms overlap with the EU-policy. The challenge of becoming 'European' is featured through threatening and seductive visions of the future. 'In the EU, Finland has become part of the European domestic markets, where labour force, services, capital and products move without obstacles. This sets Finnish education system in front of a huge challenge: WE have to produce such labour force, which can compete equally with the other citizens in EU/EEA area in the same labour market' (Act 2003, p.10). The internal enemies of competitiveness are the un-skilled, poor learners; the external enemies are well educated, highly skilled outside the EU. While many European countries already recruit such a work force, Finland has to compete by providing high competences.

The transformation of education into the management of learning does not make superfluous the professional care for learners. In its diverse forms it becomes an essential part of consultative practice, therapeutic 'soft pedagogy', which supports the rhetoric of 'soft capitalism'. 'In de-politicised context, notions of 'safe space'... 'creating new identities'... take on a distinctly introspective tone. They appear to provide a source of comfort and personal engagement in situations that are impersonal, oppressive or alienating... therapeutic pedagogy offers well-meaning reassurances of inclusion divorced from a political and ideological context and therefore without moral commitment' (Eccleston, 2004, p.126; Heikkinen, 2004). Since basic skills like literacy, numeracy and ICT are the foundation for further learning, 'groups most alienated from learning... may require tailored measures' (European Commission, 2001, p. 10). While lifelong learning means adaptation to the changing competence needs of industry and employers, learning facilitators like teachers, trainers, adult educators and guidance workers are needed to assist people to learn in non-formal and informal environments. In order to make the learners participate in learning and up-skilling themselves and the labour markets engage in competence forecasting, the internalisation of the learner subjectivity must be systematically surveyed through evaluations and feedback from guidance and consultations. The creation of a culture of learning in the EU requires that the value of learning in formal, non-formal and informal settings be assessed by comprehensive European standards. All forms of learning should be identified, assessed, and made visible and valued according to the needs and occupational standards set by employers (Colardyn and Bjornavold, 2004). Standardised certificates and qualification systems would concretise European citizenship: Europeans are valued 'according to their accessibility as labour force for companies in Europe' (European Commission, 2003).

When access to cheap labour and natural resources or endless expansion of markets is no more possible, EU-Europe relies on its innovativeness, its ability to create brands and its internal effectiveness. In the context of endogenous growth, competitiveness of individuals, nations and trans-national clusters require fusion of education with business/economy (Pöysti, 2005). Economical power and wealth are no more gained through traditional wars or colonisation. It is exercised by a strategic combination of economical, ideological and military actions, and by internalised war and colonisation of the global subject. For the new Europeans, life long concern for recognition by the markets requires continuous struggle against the weak, failing self, and against the frightening other selves. In the reproduction of a vicious circle from people's existential vulnerability, through fear and hate to destruction, education has more markets than ever.

FIGURE 1: Education as the manufacturing of subjects for the global market economy

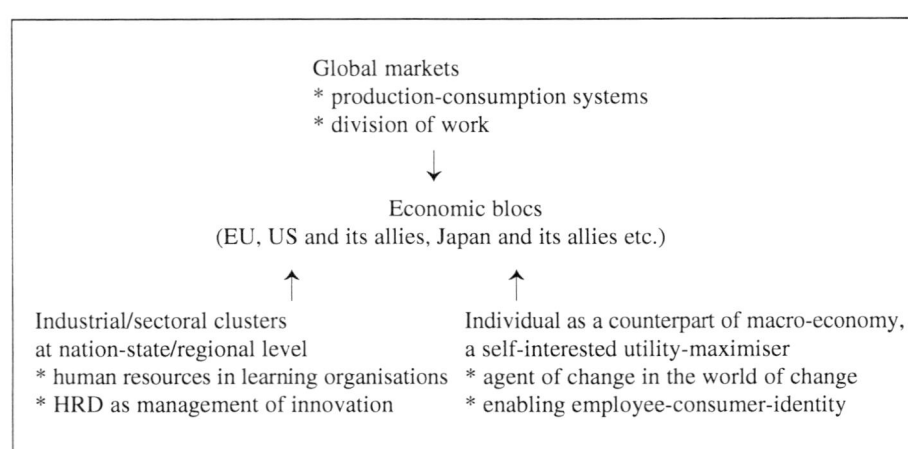

The Deconstruction of the Coded War

The prophecies constructed in the EU and member state policy documents suggest criteria for identification of internal enemies. Similar to the making of the nation-state-societies, the making of the 'EU-society' requires that its inhabitants become a population (Foucault, 2004). The merging of the societal and the economical in the concept of the EU-society is glued together by the discourse of learning. The competitive European knowledge-based economy-society is made up of innovative learning organisations, of flexibly usable labour-force, of life long learning, and of self-directed and entrepreneurial employees. Learning relies on the 'culture of learning': habits, attitudes, meanings adopted in the company-organisation, which are crucial for its success in the markets. In the culture of learning all other terrains of culture are subsumed under the organisation. As Axmaccher noticed in Germany in the late 1980s, the increase of company-oriented education and human resource development was an indicator of the transformation of *Beruf* into organisation as a profane religion. By substituting other collective references of identity, organisation constituted a new totalitarian entity, which demanded entire engagement from its members (Axmaccher, 1990).

The further the EU-society discourse develops, the more explicitly it refers to its population as human resources, which are worthy of cost-effective investment, able to profitable work-performance, and fit for appropriate consumption (e.g. European Commission, 2000, 2003). Their innovation capacity is a target of surveillance through expanding quality assurance and of manipulation through co-ordinated management of learning. The ideal Europeans are talented, enterprising, engaged and competitive, self-directed and reflective, flexible and mobile, programmable and self-assessing: in short, they are superior learners (Miller, 2002; Heikkinen, 2003).

The prophecies do not question why and with which social consequences people become problems for—and excluded from—the EU-society. The ideal learners have no bodies, sex, age, families or relatives, no social or ethnic characteristics. The major concern in learning is 'organisational inclusion', people's commitment to organisational mission, sharing of knowledge and knowledge-creating activity. In "the so-called openness of our liberal democratic societies today... it is no longer a question of up or down, but in or out; those who are not in want desperately to be so; otherwise they find themselves in a social emptiness' (Silverman, 1999, p.144; also Putnam, 2000). The low achievers, unproductive, poor and needy, the incompetent, disengaged and dissident, the rigid and non-collaborative are trans-national excess-population. They represent wasted investment and failure in the development of European human resources. On the surface, the ideal of a lifelong learning employee may seem de-gendered and to provide new opportunities for middle-class women to compete in the markets. On a closer look, it seems to promote a new gender order at work. It integrates the feminine ideal of a flexible and engaged employee working for the organisation-family with the masculine ideal of a self-directed, strategic and competitive knowledge creator. The losers are men and women, who are not able or willing to strategically develop gendered attributes in constructing their identity (Heikkinen et al., 2002; Dybbroe et al., 2003).

The contemporary socio-economical and cultural epoch is commonly characterised as the erosion of nation-states and as the complementary triumph of post-modern individualism and fragmented identity-politics (Silverman, 1999; Urry, 2000; Brown and Lauder, 2000; Bauman, 2002). However, the reading of EU-documents suggests that nation-states remain crucial for the implementation and legitimisation of the prophecy of Europeanness. While nation-state societies develop into trans-national (multicultural) societal entities, the previous criteria for collectivist and totalitarian identity-politics must be changed. 'The global/transcendental capitalism needs the state, but does not need the nation. National and sub-national… governments all over the world are transformed from being primarily the managers of a national society to being the managers of the aesthetics of investment space… how are we to make ourselves attractive enough to entice this transcendental capital hovering above us to land in our nation?' (Hage, 2003, p.19). If in the past Europeanisation meant colonisation of the globe by the superior Whites, in the contemporary EU-Europe it refers to developing the superior, highest performing human resources, which attract the trans-national capital to stay.

The prophecy of universal European values ignores the internal historical diversity of economy, industry and education in Europe. Recent debates about inclusion of Christianity as a fundamental value into the new EU constitution show the importance of religious values in the making of Europe. Even a minor comparative exercise reminds us of different meanings of categories like state, power, citizenship and education (Hyvärinen et al., 2003). Thus, for instance, in countries with a strong Catholic and Orthodox tradition (southern and eastern Europe, France and parts of Germany), family, state and church have a different moral power related to people's participation and belonging in different spheres of life. The church has remained a crucial provider of religious values and morality, the family or kinship as the main institution for their realisation. The nation state as the third moral power has become adjusted to religion and family. The central European versions of Protestantism represent industry-oriented concepts of participation and belonging. Religious values do not remain elevated abstractions or charity: they materialise in economy and enterprise as indicators for virtuous and industrious life. While family and enterprise integrate, family values and morals are exercised in the bourgeois community (civil society/Bürgergesellschaft). The state has come to represent a third, objective power, which negotiates industrial with family values. In Nordic countries, popular religious movements negotiated the Lutheran Protestantism with indigenous values and morals. This led to simplicity and practicality in religious ethics, but also preached modesty in diligence and devoutness. In the nation-building process, familial, communal and religious values were channelled to the nation-state society. E.g. according to the Finnish constitution, the state gained its power from the people and exercised it for the people (PL, 1919). Thus the Nordic welfare state should represent a metacollective moral agency, responsible to the people on the materialisation of their will. In the myth of Europeanness, the celebration of cultural diversities remains rhetorical. By ignoring the underlying variety of values and morals in Europe, it prescribes homogeneity of European action and communication space beyond traditions and cultures.

The participation of people in the stipulated action and communication space tuned by European values remains, however, conditioned by their linguistic, rational—also ICT-based—communication competence. While linguistic communication dominates other forms of human encounters, the equality of potential Europeans depends fundamentally on that. Unification requires certain linguistic and cultural patterns to become hegemonic or transformation of the diversity into communicative pidgin. Europeanness hides its relation to the wider project of globalisation, where the borders of capitalist society are shaped parallel to the shaping of the global subject (Touraine, 2000).

Personification and belonging intermingle in the 'homelikeness' of language (Pylkkö, 1998). Language is not just communication (reflecting the outer world) or expression that a subject exercises with other subjects. Neither is it a conceptual tool, functioning as a servant of rational humans in a rational world. Language has an a-conceptual essence, which underlies its meaning and which provides the possibility to participate in other people's experiences. Even if some hegemonic language would not substitute the native, its 'homelikeness' may become lost. 'A Finn can no more talk about her/his Finnishness just like that, because during these days she/he has to use concepts, but the concepts cannot come close to that, which precedes the concepts. Therefore Finnishness often reveals itself only in anxiety, in fear and alienness, in an inconceivable experience, that the concept of a person and a thing, through which the Westerns structure their experience, is foreign to the Finn. The mind of the Finn is inhabited by an alien subject, which occupies the space of the mind. Therefore, the Finnish language is withdrawing in front of its weight and brutality. The only thing left is a nihilism, which is no more any ism, but only an experience of being left without an essence; because the part of the language, which could still provide us with such an essence, has been carved off. At the same time, the language left is no more than a grotesque of an Indo-European language, a kind of pidgin' (Pylkkö, 1998, p.45).

The deconstruction of the myth of EU-Europe requires going beyond the text to identification of its advocates and designers. EU policies are an outcome of negotiations between the 'Eurobusnocracy'—EU officers, EU-oriented national bureaucrats, selected groups of (scientific) experts and representatives 'stakeholders'. The consensual rhetoric neatly puts together concepts and arguments with culturally diverse and intrinsically contradictory connotations. This may be seen as a revision of cosmopolitan ideologies in Europe from Plato to Rousseau, Kant, Humboldt, J. S. Mill, Hegel and in Finland to J. W. Snellman. The educational ideals allowed elitist humanism, which legitimised the rise of certain individuals into designers of other people's lives. According to Humboldt, the object 'towards which every human being must ceaselessly direct his efforts, and on which especially those who design to influence their fellow-men must ever keep their eyes, is the individuality of power and development' (von Humboldt, 1987, p.24). The superior humans embody individual vigour and manifold diversity, which combine in their originality. Foucault, on the other hand, shows how the military subordination of Gauls by the Romans led to the creation of a new civilian, administrative and juridical nobility, which organised the new imperial state. The emergence of the 'Eurobusnocracy' can be compared with the new nobility, which was allowed by their 'acute, sophisticated, and masterly understanding of Roman right, and knowledge of the Roman language' (Foucault, 2004, p.145).

In the prophecies of KBE and KS, their inhabitants possess unforeseen individual freedom and communality through their ICT-extensions. However, the ICT-competent mutants are as much extensions of the ICT, which conditions and controls their minds and interactions. 'Our way of extermination of ourselves in uninterrupted on-line communication', 'organisational and ICT totalitarianism' are not prescribed by socio-technical laws, but have their human designers (Silverman, 1999; Nancy and Labarthe, 2002). Consideration of ICT-humanness in the perspective of planetary society and subject challenges the progressivism of White technology. As representatives of 'the other', company and customers cannot provide people an ethical sense of meaning and belonging. Organisational religiosity, authoritarian and enterprising selfhood does not compensate the lack of personal freedom and collective solidarity. The policies of exclusion cause inability to meet the standards of Whiteness both inside and outside Europe. In his rereading of the age of Enlightenment, Foucault shows 'how 'minor' knowledges were disqualified in order to promote the centralisation, normalisation, and disciplinarization of dominant knowledges, rather than the progress of reason' (Foucault, 2004, p.288). Discourse within the historical dimension looks beneath the form of institutions and legislatures, and tries to 'revive the forgotten past of real struggles, concealed defeats and victories, and the blood that has dried on the codes.' The discourse that deciphers war's permanent presence within society is essentially a historico-political discourse, a discourse in which truth functions as a weapon to be used for a partisan victory, a discourse that is darkly critical and at the same time intensely mythical' (ibid., p.270).

The 'job of making the EU-Europe is not yet done', but global capital is already altering its course. While the rhetoric of more and better jobs in Europe is challenged by the transfer of the capital and production outside (the core) of Europe, planetary polylogues on the making of Europeanness and non-Europeanness seem increasingly relevant at local, national and trans-national levels. The deconstruction of 'bunkered communal mentalities' triggered by global capitalism requires collaborative memorising of their history, in the asymmetries of home and alien. 'A reflexive critical attitude towards sub-national communal formations can play an important role in combating the dominant paranoia (paranoid nationalism—AH)' (Hage, 2003, p.119). The deconstruction of the repeated coded wars calls researchers and educationists to mobilise discussion on planetary recognition of indigenous forms of life, on fair division of work, on participation in negotiating aims and rules of the collective reproduction of the means of livelihood (cf. Narotzsky, 1997).

References

Act on University Degrees (2003) *Proposal for Act and Decree of University Degrees.* Helsinki: OPM. [in Finnish]

Alapuro, R., Stenius, H. & Liikanen, I. (eds) (1989) *People in Movement.* Helsinki: SKS. [in Finnish]

Alasuutari, P. (1996) *The Second Republic.* Jyväskylä: Vastapaino. [in Finnish]

Apo, S. (2002) 'Alcohol and cultural emotions.' In A/.L. Siikala (ed.) *Myth and Mentality.* Tampere: Tammerprint.

Archer, M. (1996) *Culture and Agency: The Place of Culture in Social Theory.* Cambridge: Cambridge University Press.

Arendt, H. (1992) *Vita Activa oder vom tätigen Leben.* München: Piper.

Axmaccher, D. (1990) *Religion, Berufsaskese und Mitarbeiterentwicklung.* In *Zeitschrift für Berufs- und Wirtschaftspädagogik* 2/1990.

Baumann, Z. (2002) *Flexible Modernity.* Tampere: Vastapaino. [in Finnish]

Bowen, J. (1972) *A History of Western Education.* London: Palgrave Macmillan.

Boyd, W. & King, E. (1977) *The History of Western Education.* London: A&C Black. [first published 1921]

Brown, P. & Lauder, H. (2000) *Capitalism and Social Progress.* London: Palgrave.

Colardyn, D. & Bjornavold, J. (2004) 'Validation of formal, non-formal and informal learning: policy and practice in EU Member States.' In *European Journal of Education*. Vol 39, 1/2004., pp. 69-89.

Committee Report 14/1997. *The Joy of Learning: The National Strategy for Life Long Learning.* Helsinki. [in Finnish]

Dybbroe, B. & Ollagnier, E. (eds)(2003) *Challenging Gender in Life Long Learning: European Perspectives.* Roskilde: Roskilde University Press.

European Commission (1995) *White Paper: Teaching and Learning. Towards the Learning Society.* Brussels: European Commission.

European Commission (2000) *Memorandum on Life Long Learning.* Brussels: European Commission.

European Commission (2001) *Making a European Area of Lifelong Learning a Reality.* Brussels: European Commission.

European Commission (2002) Declaration of the European Ministers of Vocational Education and Training, and the European Commission, convened in Copenhagen on 29 and 30 November 2002, on enhanced European cooperation in vocational education and training. Brussels.

European Commission (2003) 'Communication from the commission: *Education & Training 2010. The success of the Lisbon strategy hinges on urgent reforms.*' 11.11.2003. Brussels.

Foucault, M. (2004) *Society must be Defended.* London: Penguin Books.

Giddens, A. (1998) *The Third Way.* Malden: Macmillan.

Glimell, B. (1997) *Den Produktiva Kroppen. En Studie om Arbetsvetenskap som Idé, Praktik och Politik.* Stockholm: Brutus Wästlings.

Göller, T. (2000) *Kulturverstehen. Grundprobleme einer epistemologischen Theorie der Kulturalität und kulturellen Erkenntnis.* Würzburg: Königshausen und Neumann.

Habermas, J. (1998) *Die postnationale Konstellation.* Frankfurt am Main: Suhrkamp.

Hage, G. (2003) *Against Paranoid Nationalism.* Annandale: Plutopress Australia.

Hakamies, P. (2002) 'Proverbs and mentality.' In A.-L. Siikala (ed.) *Myth and Mentality.* Tampere: Tammerprint.

Heikkinen, A. (2003) 'Vocational education as a co-constitutor of Europe as a project.' In E. Figueira et al. (eds) *Culture, Values and Meanings in European Vocational Education and Training.* Lisbon: Inofor.

Heikkinen, A., Korkiakangas, M., Kuusisto, L., Nuotio, P. & Tiilikkala, L. (1999) *From Promotion of Industry towards Quality Control of Education Services.* Tampere: University of Tampere Press. [in Finnish]

Heikkinen, A. & Henriksson, L. (2002) 'Manufacturing the life long learning employee for organisations.' In K. Harney, A. Heikkinen, S. Rahn & M. Schemman (eds) *Life long Learning—One Concept, Different Systems.* Franfurt am Main: Peter Lang.

Heikkinen, A. (2001a) 'Transforming centres and peripheries in vocational education—the case of Finland.' In X. Bonal, A. Heikkinen, C. Mayer, M. Singh & T. Takala 'Centres and Peripheries in Vocational Education.' Special issue of *Journal of Education and Work*, Vol. 2, pp.227-250.

Heikkinen, A. (2001b) The Europe of Learning Organisations. In final report of 5th framework project Forum for European Research on Vocational Education and Training. University of Bremen: ITB & Brussels: EU.

Heikkinen, A. (2004) 'Evaluation as 'management by projects'-policies.' *European Educational Researcher*, Vol.2, pp.6-18.

Helakorpi, S. & Suonperä, M. (1995) 'Towards networking learning environments—highway to Europe.' *Kasvatus*, Vol. 5, pp.475-484. [in Finnish]

Von Humboldt, W. (1987). *Ideen zu einem Versuch, die Grenzen der Wirksamkeit des Staats zu Bestimmen.* Stuttgart: Reclam. [first published 1792]

Hyvärinen, M. &Kurunmäki, J., Palonen, K., Pulkkinen, T., Stenius, H. (2003) *Concepts in Movement*. Tampere: Vastapaino. [in Finnish]

Kantola, A. (2002) *Market Discipline and the Managerial Power*. Tampere: Loki-kirjat.[in Finnish]

Kemiläinen, A. (1994) *Finns, Odd people of the North. Race-theories and National Identity*. Helsinki: SHS. [in Finnish]

KeSu (2003) *Education and Research 2003-2008. Development Plan*. Helsinki: OPM. [in Finnish]

Kettunen, P. (1994) *Protection, Performance and the Subject*. Helsinki: SHS. [in Finnish]

Kettunen, P. (2001) *The Order of Work*. Tampere: Vastapaino. [in Finnish]

Lacoue-Labarthe, P. & Nancy, J.-L. (2002) *The Nazi Myth*. Tampere: Vastapaino.[in Finnish]

Latour, B. 2004. *The Politics of Nature. How to bring Sciences into Democracy?* Cambridge & London: Harvard University Press.

Lundvall, B.-Å. & Borras, S. (1999) *The Globalising Learning Economy: Implications for Innovation Policy*. Luxembourg: Office for Official Publications of European Community.

Miller, D. (2002) 'The unintended political economy'. In P. du Gay & M. Pryke (eds) *Cultural Economy*. London: Sage.

Narotzsky, S. (1997) *New Directions in Economic Anthropology*. London-Chicago: Pluto Press.

PL 731/1999 *The Finnish Constitution*. Revised version from the Act of 1919. [in Finnish]

Pylkkö, P. (1998) 'The Finnish language is withdrawing and letting us in peace from each other.' *Niin & Näin* 1/1998, pp. 44-49. [in Finnish]

Pöysti, T. (2005) 'Effectiveness and efficiency as aims of adult education politics.' *Aikuiskasvatus* 1/2005. [in Finnish]

Said, E. 1987 (1978) *Orientalism*. London: Penguin Books.

Siikala, A.-L. (ed.) (2002) *Myth and Mentality*. Tampere: Tammerprint.

Siltala, J. (2000) *Sons of the White Mother*. Juva: WSOY. [in Finnish]

Silverman, M. (1999) *Facing Postmodernity*. London: Routledge.

Touraine, A. 2000. Can We Live Together? London: Polity Press.

Urry, J. (2000) *Sociology Beyond Societies*. London: Routledge.

Wenger, E. (1999) *Communities of Practice. Learning, Meaning and Identity*. Cambridge: Cambridge University Press.

Wimmer, F.M. (2004) *Interkulturelle Philosophie*. Wien: WUV.

CHAPTER THIRTEEN

The European Dimension in Teacher Training in France: Squaring the Circle?

DOMINIQUE ULMA

Introduction

How can the European dimension in education be promoted in France? The French teacher training system is original in Europe in that the students are all postgraduates, and cannot enter a teacher training college (*Institut Universitaire de Formation des Maitres – IUFM*) unless they have a Bachelor's degree. Therefore, they are not really students, but trainees (*stagiaires*), and are being paid during their probation year, which is also their initial training year. It is assumed that academic studies have been completed in the University before they entered *IUFM*, so the teacher training colleges have mostly a vocational mission. This teacher training system is modelled on what is known as the 'consecutive model', and is specific to France as well as to Ireland and the UK's PGCE (Postgraduate Certificate in Education), while most of the other European countries have a so called 'concurrent' teacher training system, where vocational skills and academics are taught in the same institution for 3 to 5 years after the end of secondary school (Vaniscotte, 1996).

Although they are not like the other students, *IUFM* student teachers are considered eligible for the Erasmus mobility programme by the European Commission (Education and Culture), just as the other students. But in spite of the official agenda of the European Higher Education Area announced in the Sorbonne in May 1998 and officially launched in Bologna in June 1999 (also known as the Bologna Process), very few *IUFM* student teachers enjoy an Erasmus mobility experience to study abroad, and on a larger scale, very few have the opportunity to study another educational system, even for short periods, either abroad or at home.

This paradox needs to be explained, and the purpose of this paper is to show why teacher training in France is so self-centred. Focused on primary education, and based upon official data, inquiries and interviews, the results will be followed by proposals to develop a European awareness in teacher training in France.

Education and the construction of European citizenship

Why is it important to promote a European awareness in Education? Some reasons are related to European integration and globalisation, but there are reasons internal to a specific country as well. Today's education has to take intercultural pedagogy into account: any school group is a melting pot, and it is highly important for student teachers to learn how to live together in the classroom, in the neighbourhood, in the country, and in the continent. Also intercultural education is linked with the feeling of one's identity and experience. Florence Legendre's inquiry (2002) shows that young primary school teachers who have an ethnocentric conception of identity usually have not had an experience of cultural diversity. Therefore, it is not possible to develop an intercultural training only on a theoretical basis: it is necessary to experience otherness, to 'incorporate' it, as Bourdieu would say, this being the condition for information to become knowledge.

The experience of otherness and cultural diversity concerns every child, and the aims of group cohesion within the classroom meet the aims of wider social cohesion in the European context. The European experience can be the mainspring for a cultural education free from folklore and guilty conscience, because the Europe of citizens can be built to last through the understanding and acceptance of others. But to reach this goal, teachers have to be trained, and, if we accept the principle of 'isomorphism'[1] when trying to design effective teacher training programmes, then as trainers we have to ensure that trainees personally experience otherness and cultural diversity to be able to promote intercultural and European awareness in the classroom.

As far as academic contents are concerned, the European dimension in teacher training for primary education in France is limited to specific topics in few subjects: history (the main steps in European construction), geography (European countries and landscapes), and how European institutions work. Training for modern languages teaching would be an excellent way to open pupils to cultural aspects, but it deals mostly with linguistic and didactic aspects, while in other fields of study European matters are seldom mentioned, and only in small doses, if at all.

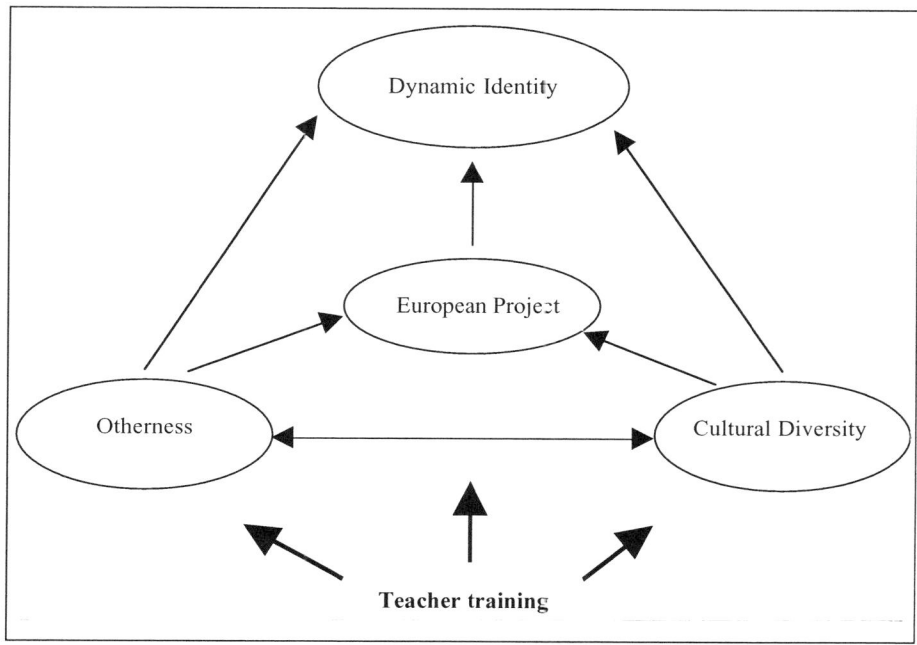

Very few initial teacher training institutions in France offer introductory modules in comparative education, and even fewer offer modules about European education systems. As far as numbers are concerned, student mobility is still marginal and mostly for short periods of time (less than four weeks). An inquiry, ordered in Spring 2003 by the French Socrates-Leonardo Agency, surveyed 18 out of the 31 *IUFMs*: a picture full of contrasts emerged from the survey, showing significant disparity between the institutions. This situation is not specific to France, and in 2000, only 2.3% European students spent part of their studies in another European country, in spite of the many incentives from the EU.

Why is European dimension so poorly taken into account in primary school teacher initial training in France, when at the same time the EU is so active in attempting to bring about the European Higher Education Area, a commitment towards which was made in Bologna and again in Lisbon?

It is possible to assume the following reasons. First, future teachers, like the rest of the population, are very poorly informed about Europe. Second, the European dimension is not sufficiently taken into account in initial and in-service training. Third, institutional barriers often discourage any initiative to promote the European dimension, or make it impossible to do so due to the specificity of French teacher training. This training allows for only one year, with strict assessment procedures that cannot be assigned to partner institutions.

Beyond these considerations there is a widespread lack of awareness of the European stakes in education, nor of the new missions assigned to the school system by the European integration process and globalisation, and most of all, lack of awareness of the high stakes for the education for European citizenship.

These assumptions have been checked and confirmed by several means. First, a survey of how each *IUFM* is involved in promoting the European dimension in initial teacher training sets the context. Second a questionnaire given to students and lecturers in one *IUFM* in Autumn 2000, while France had the presidency of the EU, shows very low levels of awareness of European aspects. And third an inquiry, confirmed by interviews, among French and other European Erasmus students, establishes the reasons why they had applied for Erasmus mobility, and what this experience has brought them. Matching up the data, it is possible to demonstrate what are the barriers and the levers to a better integration of the European dimension in teacher training.

The involvement of teacher training institutions in developing a European dimension

In February 2001, an appraisal of all the *IUFMs* pointed out a growing involvement of these institutions in the international field, but also showed that only second-year student teachers can experience mobility, because the time and energy of first-year students are taken up by the preparation for the competitive exam that allows them to become trainees in the second year. Socrates figures confirm it: in 1992-93, student Erasmus mobilities in the education sector (code 05) were only 2%, and in spite of a significant rise, they represent only 3.4% of the total in 1999-2000.

The main problem is related to the duration of Erasmus mobilities. Since initial training is limited to one full academic year for all the student teachers, the 12-week minimum for participation in an Erasmus mobility programme seems far too long, and very few *IUFMs* will allow their students to go abroad for such a long period of time. On the other hand 12 weeks is too short a period to allow young teachers to be deeply transformed personally and professionally.

Furthermore, the initial training for primary school teachers is based on the principle of block-release, which provides for nine weeks of teaching practice, divided into three blocks (usually 2+3+4 or 3+3+3), during which time student teachers have full responsibility for a class, while tenured teachers get in-service training. Thus, as long as students are needed to teach, and as long as teaching practice represents one third of the assessment process, it is very difficult to find 12 weeks without teaching practice, much less the same 12 weeks that would suit the host institution as well. Even if the home institution agrees to send student teachers for a 12-week period which includes a teaching practice block (meaning the students will 'miss' out on it), it will also have to agree to consider any kind of school experience provided by the host institution as an equivalent, and to delegate assessment of the work done to the host institution.

To the detriment of the students, most *IUFM* lecturers are not ready to accept this situation, even after more than 15 years of working with Erasmus programmes. Indeed, even before they apply for mobility, rumours reach student teachers warning them that Erasmus students tend to experience academic difficulties or may even fail to graduate. This kind of rumour-mongering creates an environment which is not conducive to participation in mobility programmes, with students who are otherwise keen to go abroad giving up under the pressure. 'Rumours' are indeed backed up by the figures: there is a slightly higher failure rate among Erasmus student teachers when compared to the average rate. This is due to increased requirements from lecturers, who are more demanding on these students. It is also due to the fact that mobility sometimes reveals some weakness that would not have appeared until later, had these students not taken part in a mobility programme. And of course, in spite of a strict selection process, some Erasmus students have actually more difficulties than others, but no more than student teachers who stay home.

Furthermore, spending three months abroad cuts off the Erasmus students from their classmates, and when they are away during the first semester, they cannot integrate into their student cohort because the others have built up a common history and the Erasmus student has become a stranger. It is easier for the students who are abroad during the second semester, during which most of the teaching practice takes place, since the student teachers are in any case scattered and more involved in an individualised process. But for all of them, there is often a problem of official recognition of what they have studied during their stay abroad: Can they share what they have learned with their colleagues? How will it be taken into account in the final assessment and graduation process? Indeed, will it be taken into account at all? Will there be anything left of this experience after they have left *IUFM*?

Thus, while the value of the Erasmus experience is clear, the way teacher training is organised in France creates difficulties and obstacles that militate against effective outcomes. In reality, the duration of initial training, concentrated as it is in an eight-month course, leads some lecturers (and students) to consider that a three-month stay abroad compromises the quality of training, with the result that teacher trainees have to take responsibility for classrooms when they are insufficiently trained.

These are reasons why mobility programmes must be seriously prepared for, very well monitored, as well as enhanced and disseminated. Only teacher training institutions with a high interest in international development invest sufficient commitment in managing the mobility experience, and among the 31 *IUFMs* in France, 18 only have an Erasmus university charter, and fewer than 15 are ready for it, having learnt a great deal about it through their involvement over several years. When the remaining *IUFMs* have participated in mobility programmes, they have preferred those programmes that require a greater number of their trainees to be away from their home institution for a shorter period of time. A perusal of the relevant statistics given by the Socrates-Leonardo da Vinci French National Agency (2004) shows us that the number of Erasmus students is very low compared to the total number of students in teacher training: for instance, the *IUFM* in Versailles, the biggest one in France, and the one which has the highest number of partners (i.e. 28 partner institutions in 18 countries), manages to send only 2.58% of its students to the Erasmus programme. The increase shown in Table 1 below is the sign of a dynamic policy, but the results are still marginal, even though far higher than the national figures.

TABLE 1: Mobility in Europe of the students from the IUFM in Versailles

Academic year	Student Mobility	Country	Number of Institutions	% students / total number of students	Total number of students
1999-2000	21	5	7	1,48	1423
2000-2001	40	14	17	2,12	1887
2001-2002	51	14	18	2,32	2192
2002-2003	60	17	22	2,58	2322

Source: IUFM in Versailles, International Office, 2003

As a comparison, in 2002-2003 in France, there were only 280 Erasmus students in teacher education altogether, that is 0,33% of the 25.000 to 30.000 French trainees (source: Socrates-Leonardo da Vinci French National Agency, 2004)

In the *IUFMs* where short mobility periods are organised, the figures are not higher, and in spite of the large variety of subjects and topics of these modules, students usually have to give up one or two weeks of their winter holidays so that they do not 'miss' too many lectures in their home institution. Indeed, any time spent away from *IUFM* is considered by most lecturers (and by a significant number of students) as 'lost time', implying that there is nothing to learn from a different educational system and culture. It is very difficult to convince people that such an experience is profitable, and that Erasmus students, who keep in touch with their home institution all the time, do not lose anything, but grow richer.

Moreover, mobile student teachers, either with the Erasmus programme or on shorter mobility modules, are asked to report their experiences in a written essay. This means they are required to do more work than their colleagues. I maintain it is unfair to suspect that those who opt to go abroad are doing this merely to have a good time.

However, opening one's mind to the European dimension does not inevitably mean mobility, and several *IUFMs* offer 'at home' modules, centered on comparative education, lectures on European educational systems, and thematic European weeks and events. Yet, these programmes are, just like the mobility schemes, completely optional, except in one *IUFM* (Bretagne), where a one week presentation of European educational systems is compulsory for all second-year student teachers (including students preparing to teach in secondary schools). Only two *IUFMs* offer the possibility of mentoring Erasmus students (incoming European students and/or outgoing French students) during their mobility periods. This indirect experience and the privileged relations the students build with their partners can provide what I would like to call the 'stepping aside' stance that will allow them to have a fresh look at their own educational system. This is due to the fact that everyone, and especially teachers, have been bred and trained in the idea that their educational system is the best, which means that it is necessary to look aside and to compare in order to see it as it is, with its specificities, its oddities, and its flaws. Mobility and partnership experience is a powerful lever to modify one's outlook on one's educational system and cultural customs—to develop cultural awareness and intercultural skills.

Student and lecturer views on the European dimension in education

Although the effects of partnership and mobility have been surveyed (Regnault, 1999; Teichler & Jahr, 2001; Murphy-Lejeune, 2000, 2003; Masson, 2002; Foerster & Simon, 2003; Ulma, 2003) and several studies have pointed out that the experience of mobility is quite enriching (e.g. in opening up towards others, and in developing tolerance, cultural awareness, self-confidence, social skills and of course professional skills), Europe is still a minor concern in teacher training colleges in France. To understand why the situation is as it is, I have carried out an inquiry among students and lecturers in my own institution.

My questionnaire was based upon an empirical statement: although various, interesting and accessible information exist about Europe, the main actors and future actors in education have no interest in it and do not wish to be informed. Such a lack of information and motivation means that very few primary school teachers and classes are and will be involved in European projects, or will develop the European dimension in their everyday teaching practices.

The period chosen for the inquiry was France's turn to hold presidency of the EU during the second semester of 2000. At that time, the media were active in informing the citizens about the EU and the coming of the Euro. So, if European awareness was low during an official communication campaign, it could be considered to be a reliable sign of a lack of both students' and lecturers' concern about Europe during the rest of the time when the EU features less centrally in the media.

The questionnaire had 18 questions altogether, of which 10 were about the interviewees' knowledge about Europe and its presence in primary school curriculum and syllabus, 4 were about their representations and European awareness, and the last 4 were about their opinions and any suggestions they could think of to insert a European dimension into school curricula and practices.

The results for the knowledge questions show that the lecturers are just slightly better informed than the students, except of course for history and geography teachers, who are in any case teaching about Europe. Most of all, the lecturers' knowledge about Europe is extremely diverse, but when they could add an opinion, a lot of them criticised the way the EU is run. This implies they are better informed and more concerned than the students, as they have their own opinion. Indeed, their sources of information are more diversified and reliable than the students', but their involvement in Europe in general, and Europe at school in particular, is weak. Some of them are strongly Eurosceptic, much more so than the students, who tend to be indifferent.

The lack of concern among lecturers is confirmed by the small number of questionnaires collected: most of them are not interested in European matters, and even fewer have understood the stakes of integrating a European dimension in primary schooling. Another confirmation comes from the lecturers' attitude towards Erasmus students, either French outgoing students or European incoming students. Usually, incoming Erasmus students report that the lecturers were kind to them, but paid no specific attention to their attendance, and acted normally, just as if there was nothing different. Only a limited number of lecturers really adapt their teaching practices to foreign students, for instance by giving them special instructions for group work, asking them to make a presentation of their educational system or the way a specific subject is taught in their home countries, and even more seldom, use the presence of foreign students to modify their teaching methods (but when they do, they are unanimously convinced of the improvement and ask for Erasmus students to visit their classes again). Moreover, they rarely use a foreign language to communicate with them, even when the students' command of French is poor. Needless to say, without the help of open-minded, dynamic and willing lecturers, the development of the European dimension becomes difficult, and all the more so since students are themselves hesitant.

The students polled by the survey do not seem confident in their knowledge of Europe, and become even less so as the questions become more specific. They are not only short of information and knowledge, but confuse many things, mixing up the EU with the Council of Europe, for instance. Vague knowledge combined with a lack of interest in current affairs, limited experience of European contacts (e.g. travel in the Schengen area), and beginner's limited professional skills contribute to a decidedly unconcerned vision of Europe among future teachers.

This is confirmed by the answers to the questions about their concept of Europe. What emerges most clearly from the answers is that Europe is understood by most of the students in terms of its geographic and economic aspects, and that peace, citizenship, and culture, or the concept of Europe as an ideal and a project, are seldom mentioned. Therefore, it is logical that most of them do not know whether they feel European, or say they do not, even though they grant that it might be important to feel European. But, to give an optimistic point of view, when asked what they would like to feel more European about, the students say they want a Europe that would be more humane, closer to its citizens, more democratic, more social, and less submitted to liberal economy and globalisation. Thus, the situation is not desperate, all the more so as research (Masson, 1996) has proved that children of primary schooling age are keen on subscribing to the European project: children as young as 8 are able to mention the symbols of the EU, the concepts of democracy and freedom, while more subtle concepts like community and the principles of Europe appear a few years later. Young children also have notions, even vague ones, about how the EU works, and about how important the European integration process has been to guarantee peace since the end of the Second World War. Pupils' concern and motivation for Europe is an excellent basis to develop this dimension in schools.

But their future teachers, who readily admit the importance of a European awareness in education, currently seem to have no idea of how this can be achieved, though they do feel that the teaching of modern languages and comparative education might have an important part in educating tomorrow's

European citizens. On this specific point they are much more open to Europe than their lecturers. Official statistics from the French Ministry of Education (2001) confirm that young teachers' second aim for education is to develop citizenship.

TABLE 2: *The two main aims of primary schooling according to primary school teachers, depending on their experience (in %) (maximum two answers)*

	Beginners	Senior teachers
Teaching pupils to read, write and count	60	59
Educating future citizens	**38**	**26**
Training pupils to acquire work methods	20	19
Training children to social life	12	11
Developing children's autonomy	20	29
Giving appeal to learning and knowledge	48	52

Source: French Ministry of Education (2001)

However, the concrete ways to develop citizenship through European awareness are not well articulated, and students usually consider Europe an extra subject, whereas it is already part of the curriculum. Nevertheless, the teaching subjects reported to be related to Europe are, logically, history and geography, social education and languages. Arts are also mentioned (linked with cultural concerns), but math and French are rarely suggested, while some inappropriate suggestions in a primary school context appear, like economy, law and politics.

What emerges is the strong attachment to teaching subjects, while the European dimension seems to belong to cross-curricular topics and skills. A cross-disciplinary approach would allow more coherence and significance to the European idea. The principle of partnership and mobility is mentioned under the suggestions for school correspondence, exchanges and travels, by only about 12% of the polled students (and not at all by the lecturers).

The global results of this inquiry show that students' involvement in Europe is generally more important than that of lecturers, and that they usually have a better understanding of the importance of Europe for the schools, in spite of their general lack of information (and curiosity?), leading to many cases of confusion and approximation.

However, the situation appears quite encouraging: young teachers seem ready for integrating a European dimension in their practices, but as beginners have very few ideas about the means to manage it. They seem ready for whatever the institution has to offer them to become more strongly convinced. Their aims are to open children to otherness, and they acknowledge that exchanges and partnerships are powerful methods. According to the principle of isomorphism in education, experiencing exchanges and partnerships should be the best way to achieve this objective, and students who have experienced mobility should have a distinctive point of view, and should be ready to open their teaching to the European dimension, for instance by organising exchanges or partnerships for their pupils.

The benefits of a European experience for future primary school teachers

International exchanges entail drastic changes, and it is useful to know how to make suggestions for teacher training. For some specialists in this field, taking part in an Erasmus mobility programme when in College comes too late. To analyse the changes the European experience brings to students, I have carried out an inquiry and interviews among Erasmus students, both outgoing French students and incoming European ones.

The first part of the inquiry was submitted to incoming Erasmus students just as they were about to leave France, and to outgoing student teachers just when they had come back to France. A second part was submitted approximately three months later, so as to have student reactions both on the spot and deeper impressions after a while back in their home institutions.

The first point is that male students rarely apply for a mobility programme. Of course, primary education is predominantly female, but the proportion of males in the Erasmus programme is about 8% lower than the proportion of males in the whole of primary education. Other research (Masson, 2002; Dehalu, 2003) has given the same results. It should be pointed out that during selection interviews, male students seldom have a professional project to motivate their application, while female applicants are more often self-assured and determined.

The key motivation driving students' decisions to take part in a mobility programme is to discover another educational system, another country, another culture, and to learn about how modern languages are taught. Applicants, however, seldom make a clear distinction between their personal motives and their professional aims. This is understandable as they are selected during the first year of *IUFM*, while they are preparing for the competitive exam to enter probation, and have only a slight idea of what teaching entails. In other words, their professional identity has not yet emerged. For instance, it is exceptional to interview students who have figured out that studying abroad might help them develop an objective and reflexive outlook on the French system and on their own teaching methods.

Pierre Dehalu (2003) has shown that the most achieving students will not take any risk and will usually not apply for a mobility period. Those who do opt for a mobility programme tend to be well-balanced, outgoing individuals who feel the need to live a new experience and want a positive challenge for themselves, their relatives and the institution. Female students are more ready for such an experience than their male counterparts.

European incoming students are usually younger than their French student teacher counterparts, and they often add the goal of self-development to their list of motivating factors: most of them still live with their parents and their stay in France will be their first long-term experience of an independent life.

Before they go, Erasmus students have developed an idea of the host country, and portray it in specific ways—portrayals that are usually based on folklore or holiday experiences.[2] It is of course very different to study and live in a country for a minimum of three months. But it is yet another instance of what Bourdieu refers to as 'reproduction', because the selection process will tend to favour flexible students who have already travelled and stayed abroad. It would indeed be taking too much of a responsibility to send for a period of at least three months fragile students who could risk failure. So the most skilled ones will reinforce their abilities, experience, and ultimately their 'social capital'.

In spite of their determination and resourcefulness, their excitement and happiness, most applicants grow anxious as the date of departure gets nearer, and even more so when they travel alone. But motivation and great expectations are a good antidote, and after a short period of adaptation, their lives get organised in the host countries, and most of their problems are overcome.

What all the Erasmus students, the French and the other Europeans, mention as the best experience in their mobility period are the relations they have built with other Erasmus students from all over Europe, and sometimes from other continents. They even add that they have more contacts with other Erasmus students than with local students or lecturers. The French movie *L'Auberge Espagnole* by Cédric Klapish gave an image of this experience, somewhat caricatured, but based on facts, of how Europeans can meet and get to know each other.

The contribution of European mobility can be analysed in several respects: social, personal and professional. Social skills like open-mindedness, a more acute sensitivity to otherness, tolerance, cultural enrichment, wider cultural awareness and self-confidence or patience are often mentioned by Erasmus students a few weeks after they have come home. Similar progress has been assessed by all similar studies (Alred, 2000; Murphy-Lejeune, 2000, 2003;

Dehalu, 2003). Elizabeth Murphy-Lejeune shows how their 'mobility capital' is modified by such an experience, how their motivation, the difficulties of arrival and integration in a new social environment, in one word, 'culture shock' combined with day-by-day familiarization with a new area, bring them to elaborate new ways of thinking space and belonging to places. They also get more independence and courage.

On specific personal and cultural skills, such as command of language and better knowledge of the host country culture, all the students assert they have been enriched by the experience, and usually have improved both their level of English and their level of the language spoken in the country, even when it is a brand new acquisition for them (like Hungarian, Finnish or Polish). Such abilities help them to better respect cultures in general, and to consider their own culture as one among others. In other words, they gain in intercultural awareness.

Language command also enhances professional skills, and for primary school teachers who now have to teach a modern language, linguistic mastery, oral fluency, a good command of vocabulary and vernacular phrases will be necessary, as well as good knowledge of the corresponding culture.

On the professional side, staying abroad can promote an epistemological breakthrough, and can modify one's relation to learning. As they go about building a professional identity as teachers, these students have the opportunity to encounter different pedagogical organisations, and different teaching methods. Even when, paradoxically enough, they cannot speak the language used in the classroom, they learn by being very active in observation and they can draw lessons from what they see (better understanding, more acute analysis). This experience is really important from the cognitive point of view.

Moreover, mobile students discover that Europe is already one in terms of pedagogical theories: Freinet, Montessori, Piaget, Comenius are references in most educational systems. The conception of childhood and of learning processes is sustained by the same theories and is reliant on a common history in Europe, and on the fact that the scientific community has long been international. This helps young future teachers assimilate concepts and appropriate teaching models and principles.

Some students even understand that they are not only being trained to become French teachers, but European teachers as well. This is confirmed by the increasing number of ex-Erasmus students who, once they graduate, try to build their careers abroad.

The impact in terms of professional identity is major: pupils considered as individuals, dynamic conceptions of team work and teaching, but also the promotion of humanistic values in the classroom, such as mutual understanding, respect, tolerance, peace.

However, and this is certainly the most important point, their view on their own educational system is deeply changed by a detached look developed by 'stepping aside'. Moving physically brings displacement in points of view, because students then have a multi-perpectival approach to education, children, learning, and teaching. Their knowledge of educational matters becomes multidimensional. Mobility is the tool to achieve that aim, with comparison as a main means. Students put their own system and teaching methods into perspective, in a mirror effect. Foerster & Simon (2003) have reached similar conclusions: the students they polled have a reflexive look on the French educational system, have greater open-mindedness, a better sense of anticipation and organisation, and often a better aptitude for partnership and networking. They also have better understood the implications of underachievement and the question of children with special needs, thanks to the intercultural dimension. Indeed, being themselves in the situation of non-native speakers during their stay abroad, they have greater empathy for non-native French-speaking pupils, and listen better to their special needs—once again, therefore, an indication of the effectiveness of isomorphism in teacher training.

This is the most powerful effect on a teacher's professional identity, and nothing better than the direct experience of mobility can bring that about. This is why it is now necessary to promote at least partnership, and preferably mobility in teacher training, if we want to achieve a knowledge-based society where education has an important part to play in the construction of the European learning citizen.

Developing a European dimension in teacher training institutions

In this chapter I have made a case for partnership and cooperation to become a regular feature of teacher training institutions, with the wholehearted support of lecturers, students, and administrative staff. The international dimension would therefore become a normal part of one's educational and professional experience, rather than an exceptional initiative taken up by a few. It is necessary to point out that the European dimension is added value to teacher training and to school practice. But to make it acceptable, it is also necessary to show that it is not a new and extra subject: on the contrary, Europe is a state of mind, a way of 'thinking European', and several means must be promoted for it to become a normal dimension in teacher training.

First, it is necessary to increase the number of those who benefit from mobility programmes. This does not necessarily mean a very lengthy stay abroad: short mobility stints of three or four weeks, when carefully prepared and organised, can bring a lot to the students. Such a module has to become official in terms of academic recognition, whereas it is currently optional and limited to the happy few. Short mobility programmes can focus on teaching practice and/or on comparative education (about educational systems, but also about specific subjects, such as reading literacy, scientific education, or early-age schooling).

Of course, participation in longer mobility programmes such as Erasmus should be encouraged and supported as well. French teacher training institutions are now required to hasten the conversion of their curricula and syllabuses to the ECTS.[3] Today, the figures for participation in Erasmus are far from the initial ambitions set out for the programme: the latter only involves 1% of European students (all fields included). The initial targets in Bologna and Lisbon were 10% by 2010.[4]

For the *IUFMs* in France, a lot of work has to be done to convince lecturers and decision-makers, because, as I have shown, students are keen to apply for mobility, but often give up because of insufficient recognition and prestige given to this formative experience. Technical barriers have to be lowered too, to allow student teachers to have the Erasmus mobility taken into account in the graduation process: on this too, the ECTS can be helpful.

Better management of the mobilities is also necessary in terms of information for applications, selection of applicants, mobility preparation (including linguistic aspects), and mobility support, assessment and promotion. This means an efficient coordination team in each College. Yet nothing is possible without a decisive European policy for the whole institution: without this, the Erasmus experience remains a marginal aspect of the student teacher's initial training.

It is obvious that only a limited, even though increasing, number of students will enjoy an Erasmus or short-time mobility period. So, to involve more, if not all, students, the following aspects must become compulsory in teacher training: comparative education, information on European educational systems, initiation to partnership and exchange experiences[5], induction into project-based pedagogy, intercultural education, and education to 'otherness'. Modules can be organised and can involve local lecturers as well as staff from partner institutions during teaching staff mobilities and research exchanges. European incoming students must be better integrated in projects run by French student teachers, with mentorship being one among many effective ways to create closer contacts.

The notion of individual professional careers has to be developed to insist on quality and added value, with the help, for instance, of a 'portfolio' system. A professional and personal portfolio would include a cognitive dimension, a pragmatic dimension and a communication dimension, but would focus on professional skills to be developed before taking part in partnerships or mobilities, and would assess students' progress. To be really significant and efficient, it would be useful to follow each student teacher after graduation, with the contribution of inspectors and advisors.

Teaching and non-teaching staff must both be involved in developing a European dimension in teacher training and in primary schooling. Just as it is valid for students, isomorphism is a good lever to convince lecturers and decision-makers of the importance of partnership, and direct experience is better than a thousand words. Cooperation and exchanges can be developed in European research teams, because the essential educational questions are the same in every country. Once again, the Erasmus programme affords many opportunities—and funding—to develop such projects. But for those who do not take part in exchange programmes, comparative education modules should be offered as in-service training. Just as for students, partnership and mobility should become a regular feature of staff development: the exchange of views and of practices encourages the 'stepping aside' process referred to earlier, leading to a critical reflexivity that puts national conceptions into perspective, and to a redefinition of value systems thanks to objectivization and dialogue—what Morin (199) calls 'dialogisme'.

Teacher training institutions in France (and in Europe) should strive to train young teachers *to* mobility, but it is obvious that students can also be trained *through* mobility and partnership. The development of a more objective outlook on their regular experience—that is, in making the familiar appear strange—helps them gain or strengthen comprehension skills, mutual understanding skills and cooperation. It not only helps develop their openness to others and a deeper understanding of the European dimension, but also reinforces a reflexive understanding of their own systems and of the practice of teaching. The inter-national dimension certainly has an impact on the intra-national dimension: the development of a reflexive stance—referred to in French as *décentration*, a technical term coming from optics which connotes the cognitive ability to have a reflexive view on one's practices or ways of thinking—opens up the education area in such a way as to have a significant influence on living together in Europe as well as on living together in the classroom.

Notes

1. The *isomorphism* theory in education is based on the fact that individuals usually reproduce the methods they were taught when at school. So, teachers will use the very methods they want their pupils to develop. For instance, in teacher training, lecturers who want their students to develop active and child-centred teaching methods will themselves use these methods in their own teaching, so that the students experience them directly. In other words, the isomorphism theory is 'do what I do', and not 'do what I say but do not do myself'.

2. Their representations are not always positive: for instance, European students often say they are attracted by France, but not by the French.

3. The European Credit Transfer System ensures transparent equivalence between European Higher education institutions. One full academic year is worth 60 ECTS, with 180 ECTS leading to a Bachelor's degree, and 300 to a Masters.

4. Recent figures (March 2004) are encouraging in that they show that Erasmus student mobility increased by 7% in 2002-2003. The figures for the ten new Member-States are even higher (20%).

5. Technical help to launch partnership projects should be more widely accessible.

References

Alix, C. & Kodron, C. (2002) *Coopérer, se comprendre, se rencontrer.* Paris-Francfort: OFAJ-DIPF.

Alred, G. (2000) 'L'année à l'étranger: une mise en question de l'identité.' *Recherche et Formation pour les professions de l'éducation,* No.33, pp.27-44.

Bell, G.H. (1991) *Developing a European Dimension in Primary Schools.* London: David Fulton Publishers.

Bell, G.H. (1995) *Educating European Citizens. Citizenship values and the European Dimension.* London: David Fulton Publishers.

Buszello, H. & et Misztal, M. (1999) *The Idea of Europe – Europe as an Idea. A Reader on the Question: What is Europe?* Kraków: Wydawnictwo Naukowe WSP.

Dehalu, P. (2003) 'L'apport des programmes de mobilité internationale à la formation initiale des maitres en Communauté française de Belgique.' *Le courrier de l'ADECE* n° 17 (June). Strasbourg: ADECE.

Étienne, R. & Groux, D. (eds)(2002) *Échanges éducatifs internationaux: Difficultés et réussites.* Paris: L'Harmattan, Coll. Éducation comparée.

Foerster, C. & Simon, D.L. (2003) 'Un parcours professionnel innovant pour l'Europe: de la formation à la pratique en classe.' *Études de Linguistique Appliquée,* No. 129 (January-March).

Gœthe-Institut / The British Council / ENS-CRÉDIF (1994) 'La dimension européenne dans la formation des professeurs de langues: nouvelles directions.' *Triangle* 12. Paris: Didier Érudition. 143 p.

Groux, D. (ed.)(2002) *Pour une éducation à l'altérité.* Paris: L'Harmattan, Coll. Éducation comparée.

Groux, D., Perez, S., Porcher, L. *et al.*(eds)(2002) *Dictionnaire d'éducation comparée.* Paris: L'Harmattan, Coll. Éducation comparée.

Groux, D. & Porcher, L. (1997) *L'Éducation comparée.* Paris: Nathan, Coll. Les Repères pédagogiques.

Groux, D. & Tutiaux-Guillon, N. (eds)(2000) *Les échanges internationaux et la comparaison en éducation. Pratiques et enjeux.* Paris: L'Harmattan, Coll. Éducation comparée.

Janssen, B. (ed.)(1993) *La dimension européenne pour enseignants — Rapport de la deuxième Conférence sur la dimension européenne dans l'enseignement et dans l'éducation.* Bonn: ZEB Europa Union Verlag, Europäische Bildung 14.

Kastoryano, R. (ed.)(1998) *Quelle identité pour l'Europe ? Le multiculturalisme à l'épreuve.* Paris: Presses de Sciences Po.

Mailhos, M.-F. (2000) 'Les stages d'éducation comparée : outils de formation et de transformation.' In D. Groux & N. Tutiaux-Guillon (eds) *Les échanges internationaux et la comparaison en éducation. Pratiques et enjeux.* Paris: L'Harmattan, Coll. Éducation comparée.

Masson, M. (1996) *Comment enseigner l'Europe de l'école au lycée?* Paris: Armand Colin, Coll. Formation des enseignants.

Masson, P. (2001) *Formation des enseignants et dimension européenne. Le cas du Nord-Pas-de-Calais.* PhD in Education Sciences. Lille 3 University.

Masson, P. (2002) 'La formation des enseignants à l'international : un état des lieux.' In D. Groux (ed.) *Pour une éducation à l'altérité.* Paris: L'Harmattan, Coll. Éducation comparée.

Morin, E. (1990) *Penser l'Europe.* Paris: Gallimard, Coll. Folio actuel n° 20.

Murphy-Lejeune, E. (2000) 'Mobilité internationale et adaptation culturelle: les étudiants voyageurs européens.' *Recherche et Formation pour les professions de l'éducation*, No. 33, pp.11-26.

Murphy-Lejeune, E. (2003) *L'étudiant européen voyageur—Un nouvel étranger.* Paris: Didier, Coll. Essais.

Persec, S. & Mailhos, M.-F. (1995) 'De la reconnaissance à l'intégration: la problématique des IUFM.' *Revue internationale d'éducation*, No. 6 (June), pp. 91-103.

Regnault, É. (1999) 'De la fécondité de la mobilité étudiante.' *Les Cahiers Pédagogiques,* No. 378 (November). Survey *Apprendre des autres. L'éducation comparée*, pp.25-26.

Teichler, U. & Jahr, V. (2001) 'Mobility during the course of study and after graduation.' *European Journal of Education*, Vol. 36(4), pp. 443-458.

Ulma, D. (1997) 'L'Europe à l'école: pour une éducation citoyenne.' *Études de Linguistique Appliquée*, No. 106, pp.187-200.

Ulma, D. (2003) *Ouvrir l'école primaire française à la dimension européenne: enjeux et perspectives.* PhD in Education Sciences. Paris 10-Nanterre University.

Vaniscotte, F. (ed.) (1995) 'Les enseignants et l'Europe.' *Recherche et Formation*, No. 18 (April). Paris: INRP.

Vaniscotte, F. (1996) *Les écoles de l'Europe.* I.N.R.P.-I.U.F.M. de Toulouse, Coll. Horizons pour la formation.

Contributors

Odd Bjørn Ure has a master's degree in public administration and organizational theory from the University of Bergen, Norway. His professional career started in the field of international co-operation in research and technology. Later, he concentrated on technology transfer by means of vocational training, before he became a detached national expert in the European Commission. He followed up this experience particularly at the level of higher education. Afterwards Mr. Ure worked at the Institute for Prospective Technological Studies in Seville as a visiting scientist. He is presently senior researcher at Fafo, Institute for Labour and Social Research in Oslo. His main task has been evaluations of a Norwegian reform for lifelong learning. Mr. Ure is member of an expert group set up by the European Commission, DG Education and Culture, to give advice on the dissemination and exploitation of results from programmes run by the Commission service in question. E-mail: Odd.Bjorn.Ure@fafo.no

Roger Dale is professor of Education at the University of Auckland, New Zealand, and Senior Research Fellow in the Graduate School of Education, University of Bristol, England. He has published widely in the area of the political sociology of education and in recent years has focused especially on the relationships between globalisation of education, establishing, with Susan Robertson, the journal *Globalisation, Societies and Education* in 2003. His current research looks at the construction of a European Education Space. E-mail: R.Dale@bristol.ac.uk

John Field is a Professor in the School of Education, University of Stirling, where he directs the Division of Academic Innovation and Continuing Education. He has taught at universities in Britain and Ireland, following a career in vocational education and training. Current research interests include the social and economic contexts of adult learning, with particular interest in the relations between learning, identity, work and social relationships. He has also written widely on the policy and historical aspects of lifelong learning. His books include *Lifelong Learning and the New Educational Order* (Trentham, 2000) and *Social Capital and Lifelong Learning* (Policy Press, 2005). He is presently co-directing a large scale study of learning, agency and identity, sponsored by the Economic and Social Research Council. E-mail: john.field@stir.ac.uk

Andy Green is currently professor of comparative education at the London University Institute of Education, University of London and co-director of the Department for International Development project on *Globalisation, Education and Development*. He has published widely on a range of education issues, with major works translated into Chinese, German, Japanese and Spanish. His published books include: *High Skills: Globalization, Competitiveness and Skills Formation*, Oxford University Press, 2001 (with Phil Brown and Hugh Lauder); *Where are the Resources for Lifelong Learning?*, OECD, 2000 (with A. Hodgson and G. Williams); *Convergences and Divergences in European Education and Training Systems*, IOE, 1999 (with Alison Wolf and Tom Leney); *Further Education and Lifelong Learning: Realigning the Sector for the 21ˢᵗ Century*, IOE, 1999 (edited with Norman Lucas); *Education, Globalization and the Nation State*, Macmillan, 1997 and *Education and State Formation: The Rise of Education Systems in England, France and the USA*, Macmillan, 1990. E-mail: andy.green@ioe.ac.uk

Ian Greenwood is lecturer in Industrial Relations and Human Resource Management in the Labour Studies Division of Leeds University Business School, University of Leeds, UK. His current research interests include developments in workplace learning; social partnership and its impact on collective bargaining; the socio-economic impact of restructuring in the steel industry. He is currently concluding research for a EU Framework 5 project investigating the role that lifelong learning can play as a response to the processes of restructuring of the European steel and metal sector. Contact details: Leeds University Business School, University of Leeds, UK. E-mail: ig@lubs.leeds.ac.uk

Anja Heikkinen is currently a professor of adult education in University of Jyväskylä, and this year a professor of life long learning and education at Tampere University, Finland. Over and above an academic career, she has extensive experience as a teacher of philosophy, math and sciences in upper secondary schools and in vocational and vocational institutes, as well as in educational administration at local and national levels. Her research has focused on intra- and inter-national relations in the world of work and learning, especially from the gender point of view. E-mail: hoanhe@edu.jyu.fi

Ewart Keep has a BA in modern history and politics (London University) and a PhD in industrial relations (Warwick University). Between first degree and doctorate, he worked for the Confederation of British Industry's Education, Training and Technology Directorate. Since 1985 he has been employed at the University of Warwick, firstly in the Industrial Relations Research Unit (IRRU), and, since 1998, as deputy-director of the ESRC centre on Skills, Knowledge and Organisational Performance (SKOPE). He has acted an advisor to the National Skills Task Force, the Cabinet Office, the DTI, the DfES, and the Scottish Parliament, and has published extensively on UK vocational education and training policy, work-based learning for the young, the links between skills and competitive strategy, and the learning society and learning organisation. Contact details: ESRC Centre for Skills, Knowledge and Organisational Performance, University of Warwick, England CV4 7AL. E-mail: skopeek@wbs.ac.uk

Michael Kuhn is policy analyst and director of the Forum for European Regional Research at the University of Bremen. His background is educational theory, philosophy and political science. He worked in numerous international research projects mainly under Programmes of the European Union, and has coordinated 6 socio-economic research projects under European social research Programmes. Recent publications include: *The European* (published by Peter Lang forthcoming); *Building the European Research Area, Socio-Economic Research in Practice*, (co-edited with Svend Otto Remoe, published by Peter Lang in 2005); *Towards a Knowledge Based Economy?—Knowledge and Learning in European Educational Research* (co-edited with Massimo Tomassini, Robert Jan Simons, published by Peter Lang forthcoming); *The Learning Society in Europe and Abroad,* (co-edited with Ronald Sultana, published by Peter Lang forthcoming). E-mail: mkuhn@uni-bremen.de

Gabriele Laske is an industrial psychologist with a background in project management, organisational design, problem solving, curriculum development, and intercultural communication. She also has a great deal of experience in managing European Community projects and programmes. After many years of working as Senior Researcher at the Institute for Technology and Education (ITB) at the University of Bremen, she is now Manager and Senior Researcher with ICCR—Intercultural Comparison and Research—an independent research and consulting company. E-mail: gabriele@world12.net

António M. Magalhães is Associate Professor of Education at the Faculty of Psychology and Education of the University of Oporto. He is also researcher of the Research Centre on Higher

Education Policy (CIPES) of the Foundation of Portuguese Universities. Recent publications, co-authored with Stephen R. Stoer include: *Theories of Social Exclusion* (published by Peter Lang in 2003); 'Performance, Citizenship and the Knowledge Society: a new mandate for European education policy', *Globalisation, Societies and Education*, Vol.1(1), pp.41-66 (2003) and 'Education, Knowledge and the Network Society', *Globalisation, Societies and Education*, Vol.2(3), pp.319-335 (2004). E-mail: antmag@netcabo.pt

Suzanne Mellor is a Senior Research Fellow at the Australian Council for Educational Research. She has a 20 year background as a practitioner in schools and in universities training teachers, writing for a range of student and teacher markets. She managed state final school level examinations, coordinating curriculum writing for accrediting bodies, devising and providing a wide range of professional development activities for teachers of History and English. Since 1989 at ACER she has been involved in a wide range of local, national and international research. She has undertaken case-study and survey research, and has written reports for contracting authorities which elaborate and synthesise the opinions and concerns of practitioners and other stakeholders identified in the research. She is editor of the Australian Education Review. She has undertaken substantial work in Citizenship Education over the last decade. She has written review papers, published widely and presented at national and international conferences, especially in regard to issues associated with appropriate pedagogy and political attitudes and values. She conducts professional development for all jurisdictions. As the Australian Manager for Phase Two of the IEA Civics Education Study, she was the main author of the national report: *Citizenship and Democracy: Students' Knowledge and Beliefs: Australian Fourteen Year Olds* and the IEA Civic Education Study, released in March 2002. In 2003-4 she has been the ACER Project Manager for the Australian National Civics and Citizenship Assessment Project, contributing to and managing all aspects of the work. She will write the national report in 2005. E-mail: Mellor@acer.edu.au

Mark Murphy is Lecturer in Education at the University of Stirling, Scotland. His main areas of interest include university adult education, educational sociology, critical theory and education, political economy of post-compulsory education and international adult education. He has numerous publications in the fields of adult and higher education, and his work has involved him in educational debates in Ireland, Scotland and the United States. E-mail: mark.murphy@stir.ac.uk

Palle Rasmussen is Professor of Education and Learning Studies, and Head of the Department of Education and Learning at Aalborg University, Denmark. His theoretical and empirical research focuses include lifelong learning, learning and competence in work organisations, educational policy, professional education and sociological theory. Recent publications include 'Education for everyone: secondary education and social inclusion in Denmark,' *Journal of Education Policy*, 2002, Vol. 17, No. 6 and *Educational Policy and the Global Social Order* (Aalborg University: Centre for the Interdisciplinary Study of Learning 2003). E-mail: palleras@learning.aau.dk

Susan Robertson is a Reader in the Sociology of Education at the University of Bristol. She took her PhD in Sociology/Policy at the University of Calgary in 1990. She has researched and taught in universities in Australia, Canada, New Zealand, and since 1994, in the United Kingdom. She is currently the coordinator for the recently created Centre for Studies of Globalisation, Education and Societies, the Coordinator of the EU thematic network Globalisation and Europeanisation Network in Education (GENIE) and co-editor of *Globalisation, Societies and Education*. Her own research interests are around understanding globalisation, the nature of states, education policy and the changing nature of teachers' labour. She has written on these areas in journals such as *British Sociology of Education, Comparative Education Review, Discourse*, and *International Studies in the Sociology of Education*. She is currently co-director for a major ESRC project on ICT and the Knowledge Economy. E-mail: s.l.robertson@bristol.ac.uk

Terri Seddon is Professor of Education at Monash University and Director of the Centre for Work and Learning Studies. She has longstanding interests in social and historical analysis of education and educational change. She is currently researching the changing politics of education and training which accompanies cross-sectoral blurring of boundaries and marketised education and training reform. Her research has focused on post-compulsory education and, over the last ten years, adult and vocational education and training. She has published four books: *Reshaping Australian Education: Beyond Nostalgia* (with Lawrence Angus, 2000); *Pay, Professionalism and Politics: Reforming Teachers? Reforming Education?* (1996); *Context and Beyond: Reframing the Theory and Practice of Education* (1993); and *A Curriculum for the Senior Secondary Years in Australia* (with Christine Deer, 1992). E-mail: Terri.Seddon@ Education.monash.edu.au

Mark Stuart is Head of the Industrial and Labour Studies Division at Leeds University Business School, University of Leeds. He holds a PhD from the University of Leeds. He has published numerous scholarly articles, book chapters and research reports and is the co-editor of *Partnership and Modernisation in Employment Relations* (with Miguel Martinez Lucio) and *Trade Unions and Training: Issues and International perspectives* (with Richard Cooney). He is an Associate of the ESRC Centre for Skills, Knowledge and Organisational Performance (SKOPE). Contact details: Leeds University Business School, University of Leeds, UK. E-mail: m.stuart@ukonline.co.uk

Stephen R. Stoer is Professor of Education at the Faculty of Psychology and education of the University of Oporto. He is also researcher of the Centre for Research and Intervention in Education (CIIE) of the same faculty. Recent publications, co-authored with António M. Magalhães include: *Theories of Social Exclusion* (published by Peter Lang in 2003); 'Performance, Citizenship and the Knowledge Society: a new mandate for European education policy', *Globalisation, Societies and Education*, Vol.1(1), pp.41-66 (2003) and 'Education, Knowledge and the Network Society', *Globalisation, Societies and Education*, Vol.2(3), pp. 319-335 (2004). E-mail: stevestoer@netcabo.pt

Ronald G. Sultana is professor of comparative education and educational sociology at the University of Malta, where he directs the Euro-Mediterranean Centre for Educational Research. His main research interests are in the link between education and the world of work, Vocational Education and Training, and the formation of teachers. His present work focuses on lifelong approaches to career guidance in both the education sector and in public employment services across Europe, and has most recently published *Guidance Policies in the Knowledge Society: Trends, Challenges and Responses across Europe* (Cedefop, 2004). He is the founding editor of the *Mediterranean Journal of Educational Studies*, and his comparative research work has led to the publication of over 80 refereed papers, and 3 authored and 12 edited volumes. E-mail: ronald.sultana@um.edu.mt

Dominique Ulma is a lecturer at the *Institut Universitaire de Formation des Maîtres* in Versailles. Since 1990 she has been in charge of initial and in-service training for Primary school teachers. She also has nine years of experience as a coordinator for International Relations, and has completed a Ph.D. in Comparative Education on the question of the promotion of a European dimension in French Primary schools, which is the field of her current research. E-mail: dominique.ulma@versailles.iufm.fr